Yankee 6-27-94

Mozart and his Circle

A Biographical Dictionary

Mozart and His Circle

A Biographical Dictionary

Peter Clive

Yale University Press
New Haven and London

First published 1993 in the United Kingdom
by J.M. Dent, The Orion Publishing Group.

Published 1993 in the United States of America
by Yale University Press.

Typeset by Deltatype Limited, Ellesmere Port, Cheshire
and printed in Great Britain by
Butler & Tanner Ltd, Frome and London.

Library of Congress catalog card number: 93–60860
International standard book number: 0–300–05900–0

10 9 8 7 6 5 4 3 2 1

for Megan

Contents

Illustrations

Acknowledgments

Acknowledgment is due to the following for their permission to reproduce illustrations:

Bayerische Staatsgemäldesammlungen, Munich, 21; Bayerisches Nationalmuseum, Munich, 11; British Library, London, 7; from the collections of the Theatre Museum. By courtesy of the Board of the Trustees of the Victoria & Albert Museum, 27; Gemäldegalerie Alte Meister – Staatliche Kunstsammlungen, Dresden, 18; Gesellschaft der Musikfreunde, Vienna, 15; Historisches Museum der Stadt Wien, 13, 14; Hunterian Art Gallery, University of Glasgow, 4; Internationale Stiftung Mozarteum, Salzburg, 2, 3, 5, 22; Kunsthistorisches Museum, Vienna, 10; Österreichische Nationalbibliothek, Vienna, 12, 19; Reiss-Museum der Stadt Mannheim, Graphische Sammlungen, 17; Royal College of Music, London, 16; Staatliches Museum Schwerin, 9; Staatsbibliothek zu Berlin – Preussischer Kulturbesitz, Musikabteilung, 20, 23, 24, 26.

Preface

This book provides information on some 280 persons with whom Mozart came into personal or professional contact – sovereigns, court officials, patrons, theatre managers, publishers, musicians, singers, actors, writers, librettists, piano makers, pupils, physicians, friends, and members of his family. There are also articles on a few early biographers, among them Constanze Mozart's second husband, Georg Nikolaus Nissen, and on the sculptors of the well-known Mozart statues at Salzburg and in Vienna, Schwanthaler and Tilgner. In addition, information is given about the two masonic lodges ('Zur Wohltätigkeit', 'Zur neugekrönten Hoffnung') to which Mozart belonged. Finally, since the dictionary lists almost all the singers and actors who appeared at the first performances of Mozart's operas, some notes are provided, in a separate section, on those stage works, with particulars of the dates, places and casts of the premières and certain other relevant data.

While the articles present concise biographical information about the individuals concerned – unless, like Beethoven or Joseph Haydn or Goethe, they are exceptionally well known – the emphasis is always on the person's contacts with Mozart. Accordingly, a prominent place is given throughout to quotations from the Mozarts' correspondence (all translations are my own).

Sources

The principal sources used are cited in abbreviated form at the end of each article. Full details of these publications will be found in the Bibliography. This is, of course, a select bibliography; many other items were consulted in the preparation of this book. It may be thought surprising that mention is only very rarely made, among the sources, of O. E. Deutsch's *Mozart: Die Dokumente seines Lebens* (cited as *Mozart: Dokumente*) and the edition of the Mozarts' correspondence by Deutsch and W. A. Bauer (cited as *Mozart: Briefe*). The reason is that these two works would merit mention in respect of almost every article. Both have proved invaluable aids: the first for its wealth of data on Mozart's life and the generous quotations from contemporary documents and publications; the second not only for the carefully established text of the letters (from which I have translated numerous passages), but also for the excellent notes by J. H. Eibl. The reader may therefore assume as a matter of course that these two works have been consulted with great profit in nearly every instance, and that an important part of the information presented here is contained in them, although, in most cases, I have confirmed or supplemented it from other sources. The reader may, furthermore, conclude that where no sources are cited at the end of an article, the information will have been drawn almost exclusively from one or both of these books.

Titles

Ranks of nobility have been rendered by the most closely corresponding titles in English (thus, 'Graf' by 'Count'). Functional or honorific titles have been translated as literally as possible (for instance, 'Hofrat' as 'court councillor').

Preface

Asterisks

The first mention in the Chronicle and in an article of a person, lodge or opera featured in a separate dictionary entry is marked by an asterisk. The sole exception is Leopold Mozart, whose name occurs very frequently throughout the book.

I wish to thank Callista Kelly, Doris Cole and their colleagues in the Interlibrary Loans Section at Carleton University, Ottawa, for their invaluable assistance; the librarians of the Internationale Stiftung Mozarteum, of the Institut für Musikwissenschaft of the University of Salzburg and of the University of Toronto Music Library for their help; Liselotte Homering, Head of the Theatre Department at the Reiss Museum, Mannheim, and Dr Gerhard Croll, for providing certain information; Peter Zohar for reading the original typescript and sharing the proof-reading; and, above all, Peter Branscombe for his most interesting comments and excellent advice, of which I have, gratefully, taken full account. I have also greatly appreciated the very competent and patient guidance I have received from Julia Kellerman, of Dent's, and the outstanding work done by the copy-editor, Ingrid Grimes.

1993   *Peter Clive*

A Chronicle of Mozart's Life

1756
27 Jan Mozart is born at eight o'clock in the evening, in the family's flat in Johann Lorenz Hagenauer*'s house [later No. 9 Getreidegasse] in Salzburg.
28 Jan At Salzburg Cathedral, Mozart is baptized Johannes Chrysost[omus] Wolfgangus Theophilus. Godfather: Johann Gottlieb Pergmayr*.

1762
12 Jan Wolfgang and Nannerl* travel with their father to Munich. There the children perform before the Elector Maximilian III Joseph.
18 Sep First journey to Vienna, where the Mozarts arrive on 6 Oct. They are received by Emperor Francis I and Empress Maria Theresa* at Schönbrunn on 13 Oct. Thereafter the children perform repeatedly at court, and in various aristocratic houses.

1763
5 Jan The family arrives home.
9 Jun They undertake a very successful journey to England, with stops (and concerts) at Munich, Augsburg, Schwetzingen, Frankfurt am Main, Koblenz, Brussels (5 Oct–15 Nov), and Paris (18 Nov 1763–10 Apr 1764).

1764
1 Jan They are received at Versailles. During their stay in Paris Wolfgang publishes his first compositions.
23 Apr They reach London where they are received by King George III on 27 Apr. Over the next fifteen months the children give many concerts, and Wolfgang meets Johann Christian Bach* and Giovanni Manzuoli*, and brilliantly passes a musical test conducted by Daines Barrington*.

1765
24 Jul The Mozarts leave London. At The Hague (10 Sep 1765–late Jan 1766) both children are taken seriously ill.

1766
May The family returns to Paris for two months (10 May–9 Jul 1766), and, following

a lengthy stay in Switzerland (20 Aug–19 Oct) and a briefer one at Donaueschingen, reaches Munich on 8 Nov and arrives back in Salzburg on 29 Nov.

1767
12 Mar The first part of *Die Schuldigkeit des ersten Gebots**, with music by Mozart, is performed in Salzburg.
13 May Widl*'s tragedy *Clementia Croesi* is performed in Salzburg; the interlude *Apollo et Hyacinthus** has been set to music by Mozart.
11 Sep Second journey to Vienna, interrupted by a period (23 Oct 1767–10 Jan 1768) spent in Bohemia, in a vain attempt to escape a smallpox epidemic raging in Vienna: both children catch the disease and are treated for it at Olmütz [Olomouc]. After some days at Brünn [Brno], where Wolfgang and Nannerl play at a concert, the Mozarts return to Vienna.

1768
19 Jan They are received at court. Wolfgang, encouraged by Emperor Joseph II*, works on an *opera buffa, La finta semplice**, but all Leopold's efforts to secure a performance end in failure, for which he blames above all the theatre impresario Affligio*. However, *Bastien und Bastienne** may have been staged at Dr Mesmer*'s house during the autumn.

1769
5 Jan The family arrives back in Salzburg.
Spring Performance of *La finta semplice* at Salzburg?
13 Dec Mozart and his father travel to Italy, with the moral and financial support of Archbishop Schrattenbach*, who names Wolfgang third (unpaid) court Konzertmeister and makes a contribution to their expenses.

1770
During this trip Mozart gives numerous concerts and meets many influential persons. The itinerary includes Verona (where his portrait is painted by Saverio dalla Rosa for Pietro Lugiati*), Milan (where he benefits from Count Firmian*'s patronage), Bologna

I

(where his musical skills are tested by Padre Martini*), Florence (where he meets the English violinist Thomas Linley* and is received by Archduke Leopold, the future Emperor Leopold II*), Rome, and Naples (where he stays from 14 May to 25 Jun). The northward journey passes once again through Rome (where Pope Clement XIV confers on Mozart the Order of the Golden Spur) and Bologna (where, on 10 Oct, he is admitted to the Accademia Filarmonica). In Milan, which he reaches on 18 Oct, he supervises rehearsals for *Mitridate*, of which he conducts the première on 26 Dec.

1771
4 Feb After leaving Milan, Mozart and his father spend a month in Venice, and eventually return to Salzburg on 28 Mar.
13 Aug Mozart's second journey to Italy with his father. They arrive in Milan on 21 Aug. By the end of that month Mozart has begun the composition of *Ascanio in Alba**, which will be given for the first time on 17 Oct, in celebration of Archduke Ferdinand*'s marriage to Maria Beatrice Ricciarda d'Este. The Archduke is inclined to engage Mozart at his Milanese court, but is discouraged by Maria Theresa. Mozart and his father return to Salzburg on 15 Dec.

1772
Spring Mozart dedicates *Il sogno di Scipione** – originally composed in homage of Archbishop Schrattenbach who had, however, died on 16 Dec 1771 – to the newly elected Archbishop Count Colloredo*.
21 Aug Mozart is confirmed in his (hitherto unpaid) post of Konzertmeister and granted an annual salary of 150 gulden.
24 Oct Third journey to Italy. On 4 Nov Mozart and his father arrive in Milan, where the première of *Lucio Silla** takes place on 26 Dec.

1773
17 Jan At the Theatine Church, in Milan, Venanzio Rauzzini* sings the motet *Exsultate, jubilate* K165 which Mozart has written for him. Leopold's efforts to procure for Wolfgang an appointment at Archduke Leopold's court at Florence meet with no success.
13 Mar They return home.
14 Jul Mozart travels to Vienna with his father. They pay several visits to Dr Mesmer. On 5 Aug they have an audience with Maria

Theresa, who receives them 'very graciously', but their hopes of an engagement in Vienna remain unfulfilled, and they return on ?27 Sep.
Autumn The Mozarts move to the 'Tanzmeisterhaus' on Hannibal-Platz in Salzburg (*see* RAAB).

1774
4 Apr Gebler*'s play *Thamos, König von Ägypten* is performed in Vienna, with Mozart's music.
6 Dec Mozart and his father travel to Munich.

1775
Jan Nannerl joins them in time for the première of *La finta giardiniera** on 13 Jan. On 12 Feb Leopold conducts a mass composed by Wolfgang in the court chapel. While in Munich, Wolfgang engages in an informal piano contest with Ignaz von Beecke* at Franz Joseph Albert*'s inn.
7 Mar Leopold, Wolfgang and Nannerl return to Salzburg.
23 Apr *Il re pastore** is performed in Salzburg in honour of the visiting Archduke Maximilian*.

1776
21 Jul Performance of the 'Haffner'* Serenade K250/248b.

1777
Aug Although the archbishop has refused Leopold Mozart's earlier request for leave for himself and Wolfgang, the latter presents a fresh petition. In response, Colloredo decrees that 'father and son have permission to seek their fortunes elsewhere'. Alarmed by this threat of dismissal, Leopold requests to be kept on in the archbishop's service; the request is granted.
23 Sep Mozart sets out from Salzburg with his mother, hoping to find a permanent appointment in Munich or Mannheim. In Munich (24 Sep–11 Oct) he has interviews with the Supervisor of Entertainments, Count Seeau*, and is received by the elector. In Augsburg from 11 to 26 Oct, he meets the celebrated piano maker Johann Andreas Stein* and enjoys the company of his amusing cousin Maria Anna Thekla Mozart* (after his departure he corresponds with her).
30 Oct Mozart and his mother arrive in Mannheim, where he becomes friendly with

the musicians Christian Cannabich* and Johann Baptist Wendling*, hears the famous tenor Anton Raaff*, meets Fridolin Weber* and falls in love with his daughter Aloisia*.

1778
14 Mar Disappointed in his hopes of obtaining employment in Germany, Mozart finally moves on to Paris which he and his mother reach on 23 Mar. There he meets Legros*, the director of the Concert Spiri-tuel, renews acquaintance with Raaff, makes plans (which do not progress very far) for new operas, and contributes music to Noverre*'s ballet *Les petits riens* κAnh.10/299*b*, which is performed at the Opéra on 11 Jun. Mozart's ('Paris') Symphony κ297/300*a* is well received at the Concert Spirituel on 18 Jun (and repeated on 15 Aug). His mother dies on 3 July, and he then lodges with Madame d'Epinay and Baron Grimm* (with whom his relations soon become strained). His prospects in Paris appear increasingly unpromising, and he leaves on 26 Sep, travelling via Strasbourg, Mann-heim, and Munich (where the Webers now reside and where Aloisia rejects his love).

1779
In mid-Jan he returns to Salzburg. There he is appointed court and cathedral organist, in succession to Adlgasser*, at an annual salary of 450 gulden.

1780
Sep–Oct The Mozarts become friendly with Emanuel Schikaneder*, whose the-atrical company is performing in Salzburg.
5 Nov Mozart travels to Munich to pre-pare for the première of *Idomeneo*, which takes place on 29 Jan 1781.

1781
While still in Munich, Mozart is instructed to join Archbishop Colloredo in Vienna; he arrives there on 16 Mar. The following weeks mark the major turning-point in his life. Irked by the archbishop's autocratic manner and outraged at being treated like a mere servant, he obtains his dismissal, which is confirmed on 8 Jun by a kick from Count Karl Joseph Arco*. By then Mozart is lodg-ing with Caecilia Weber*, Fridolin Weber's widow (the Webers moved to Vienna in the autumn of 1779 when Aloisia was engaged at the court theatre). Mozart now falls in love with Constanze Weber*, Aloisia's younger

sister (Aloisia herself has been married to Joseph Lange* since Oct 1780). His father urges him to find other lodgings; he does so during the summer.
Dec He informs his father of his desire to marry Constanze; he has, in fact, been put under some pressure by Constanze's guardian Johann von Thorwart* to marry her. On 24 Dec Mozart engages in a piano contest with Muzio Clementi* at court.

1782
Mozart leads a busy and enjoyable life, composing, giving concerts, teaching pupils, developing useful contacts with various prominent persons. However, he is still searching (unsuccessfully) for an appoint-ment which would guarantee him financial security.
Spring He becomes a regular participant in Baron van Swieten*'s Sunday concerts.
16 Jul Première of *Die Entführung aus dem Serail*.
4 Aug Mozart marries Constanze at St Stephen's Cathedral, Vienna. The wedding feast is provided by Baroness Waldstätten*.

1783
15 Feb Mozart asks Baroness Waldstätten for money to pay a debt. This is the earliest known indication of Mozart's serious finan-cial problems.
Mar He performs a number of his compo-sitions at the Burgtheater, Vienna, on 11, 23 and 30 Mar. The emperor attends the last two concerts.
17 Jun Birth of Raimund Leopold Mozart*.
late Jul–late Nov Mozart visits Salzburg with Constanze. This is the last time that he and Nannerl meet. On 26 Oct his (incom-plete) Mass in C minor κ427/417*a* is per-formed at St Peter's Abbey, with Constanze taking one of the soprano parts. At Linz, on the return journey, he composes a new symphony (κ425), which receives its first performance there on 4 Nov. During his and Constanze's absence from Vienna, their son Raimund Leopold, whom they have left with a foster mother, has died (19 Aug).

1784
9 Feb Mozart begins to keep a catalogue of his compositions. The first entry is the Piano Concerto in E flat κ449, written for his pupil Barbara von Ployer*.
Feb–Mar Between 26 February and 31

3

March Mozart gives fourteen concerts at Prince Galitsin*'s and Count Johann Baptist Esterházy*'s, as well as three subscription concerts in a private hall at Johann Trattner*'s house (where he and Constanze have their lodgings at the time). The list of subscribers contains 176 names.

29 Apr At the Kärntnertor-Theater, in the presence of Joseph II, Mozart plays the Violin Sonata K454 with Regina Strinasacchi*, for whom it was written.

13 Jun Giovanni Paisiello* attends a private concert, at which Mozart plays the Sonata for two pianos K448/375a with Barbara von Ployer.

21 Sep Birth of Carl Thomas Mozart*.

14 Dec Mozart is admitted to the 'Zur Wohltätigkeit'* Masonic Lodge.

1785

11 Feb Leopold Mozart arrives in Vienna to visit his son and daughter-in-law. That same day Wolfgang gives the first of five subscription concerts at the 'Mehlgrube'. He plays at several other concerts during Feb and Mar.

12 Feb Mozart and his father take part in a performance, at the Mozarts', of the quartets K458, 464 and 465. Joseph Haydn* is present and compliments Leopold on his son's genius. (The three quartets, together with three others, are later dedicated to Haydn.)

13 Mar Performance of the cantata *Davidde penitente* K469 at the Burgtheater; it is repeated on 15 Mar.

6 Apr Leopold Mozart is admitted to the 'Zur Wohltätigkeit' Lodge.

24 Apr The cantata *Die Maurerfreude* K471 is performed in honour of Ignaz von Born*.

25 Apr Leopold leaves Vienna. He will not see Wolfgang again.

17 Nov Mozart's *Maurerische Trauermusik* K477/479a is performed at the 'Zur gekrönten Hoffnung' Lodge.

23 Dec Mozart plays his new Concerto in E flat K482 at the Burgtheater, between the first and second parts of Carl Ditters von Dittersdorf's oratorio *Esther*.

1786

7 Feb First performance of *Der Schauspieldirektor**, at Schönbrunn Palace.

13 Mar Mozart conducts a concert performance of *Idomeneo* (in a revised version) at Prince Auersperg's. This is the first time that the opera has been heard in Vienna.

7 Apr Mozart plays the Concerto in C minor K491 at what will be his last grand concert at the Burgtheater.

1 May First performance of *Le nozze di Figaro** at the Burgtheater.

18 Oct Birth of Johann Thomas Leopold Mozart*.

Nov Mozart, who is planning a visit to England, asks his father if he will take his two children (Carl Thomas and Johann Thomas Leopold) while he himself and Constanze are away. Leopold's curt refusal casts a new shadow on relations between father and son which have been rather cool since 1781.

15 Nov Death of Johann Thomas Leopold Mozart.

1787

8 Jan Mozart and Constanze set out for Prague, where performances of *Le nozze di Figaro* by Bondini*'s company are causing a sensation. They stay with Count Thun-Hohenstein*. Mozart conducts a performance of *Figaro* on 22 Jan. He receives a commission from Bondini to compose an opera for the next season. The Mozarts leave Prague around 8 Feb and reach Vienna some four days later.

7 Apr Beethoven* arrives in Vienna to study with Mozart, but has to return to Bonn soon afterwards because of his mother's illness. It is not known whether he met Mozart.

28 May Death of Leopold Mozart in Salzburg.

1 Oct–?16 Nov Mozart and Constanze travel to Prague for the première of *Don Giovanni** on 29 Oct.

7 Dec Mozart's hopes of an official appointment in Vienna are finally realized as he is named court *Kammermusicus* [chamber musician] at an annual salary of 800 gulden.

27 Dec Birth of Theresia Constanzia Adelheid Friederike Maria Anna Mozart*.

1788

7 May First Viennese performance of *Don Giovanni*.

Summer Composition of Mozart's last three symphonies K543, 550 and 551. His daughter Theresia Constanzia Adelheid Friederike Maria Anna dies on 29 Jun. His financial problems increase and he requests loans from his friend Michael Puchberg*, who will come to his aid repeatedly during the following years.

?Nov At Jahn's Rooms in Vienna Mozart conducts a performance of his re-orchestrated version of Handel*'s *Acis and Galatea* K566.

1789
6 Mar At Count Johann Baptist Ester-házy's, Mozart conducts a performance of his re-orchestrated version of Handel's *Messiah* K572.
8 Apr–4 Jun Journey to Berlin, via Prague, Dresden and Leipzig, mostly in the company of Prince Karl Lichnowsky*. At Dresden, on 14 Apr, Mozart plays the Concerto in D major K537 at court before the Elector Frederick Augustus III of Saxony and his consort. In Leipzig, on 12 May, he performs two concertos and a fantasia at a concert at the Gewandhaus. He arrives in Berlin on 19 May and, that evening, attends a performance of *Die Entführung aus dem Serail* at the National Theatre. On 23 May he is present at a concert given by his former pupil Johann Nepomuk Hummel*, and on 26 May he plays before King Frederick William II* at the royal palace. He leaves Berlin on 28 May and, after stopping at Prague, returns to Vienna on 4 Jun.
29 Aug New production of *Le nozze di Figaro* at the Burgtheater.
16 Nov Birth of Anna Maria Mozart*, who dies the same day.
22 Dec First performance of the Clarinet Quintet K581 at a concert of the Ton-künstler-Societät at the Burgtheater, with the participation of Anton Stadler*, for whom it was written.

1790
26 Jan Première of *Così fan tutte** at the Burgtheater.
20 Feb Death of Joseph II. He is succeeded by his brother Leopold, Grand Duke of Tuscany, who arrives in Vienna on 13 Mar.
23 Sep–10 Nov Mozart travels to Frankfurt with his brother-in-law Franz de Paula Hofer* for the coronation of Leopold II (on 9 Oct). They arrive in Frankfurt on 28 Sep. Mozart lodges with the theatre director Johann Böhm*. At a concert on 15 Oct he plays two concertos (K537 and perhaps K459). After leaving Frankfurt on 16 Oct, he gives a concert in the elector's palace at Mainz on 20 Oct, and, following stops at Mannheim and Augsburg, reaches Munich on 29 Oct. There he performs at a concert in

honour of King Ferdinand IV and Queen Maria Karolina of Naples. He returns to Vienna on 10 Nov. From a financial point of view, the trip has been a disappointment.
14 Dec Mozart is present at a farewell dinner for Haydn, who is about to set off for London.

1791
4 Mar Mozart plays his Concerto K595 at a concert given by the clarinettist Joseph Beer* at Jahn's Rooms. This is Mozart's final concert appearance.
9 May Mozart's petition to be appointed (unpaid) assistant to Leopold Hofmann, Kapellmeister at St Stephen's Cathedral, is accepted, on the understanding that he will succeed to the position when it falls vacant.
4 Jun Constanze takes the cure at Baden, where Mozart visits her several times. She returns to Vienna in mid-July.
Jul Mozart is invited by Domenico Guardasoni* to compose an opera (*La clemenza di Tito**) for the coronation of Leopold II as King of Bohemia, in Prague. He also receives, through an intermediary, a commission for a Requiem from an unnamed person (in fact, Count Walsegg-Stuppach*).
26 Jul Birth of Franz Xaver Wolfgang Mozart*.
24 or 25 Aug Mozart travels with Constanze and Franz Xaver Süssmayr* to Prague, for the coronation. On 2 Sep *Don Giovanni* is performed, probably under Mozart's direction, in the presence of Leopold and his consort Maria Luisa*. They also attend the première of *La clemenza di Tito* on 6 Sep. He and Constanze return to Vienna in mid-Sep.
30 Sep Première of *Die Zauberflöte** at the Freihaus-Theater, Vienna.
Oct Constanze again takes the waters at Baden.
18 Nov The masonic cantata K623, the last work recorded in Mozart's catalogue of his own works, is performed at the inauguration of the new temple of the 'Zur neugekrönten Hoffnung'* Lodge.
c.20 Nov Mozart takes to his bed, which he will not leave again. He is treated by his personal physician Dr Thomas Franz Closset*, who consults Dr Mathias von Sallaba*.
4 Dec Preoccupied with the uncompleted Requiem K626, Mozart sings through the score with Benedikt Schack*, Franz Xaver

A Chronicle of Mozart's Life

Gerl*, and his brother-in-law Franz de Paula Hofer. He also gives instructions to Süssmayr on how to finish the work.

5 Dec   Mozart dies (according to his sister-in-law Sophie Haibel*, in her arms) at five minutes before one o'clock in the morning.

His death mask is taken by Count Joseph Deym von Stržitež*.

6 or 7 Dec   In the afternoon, Mozart's body is blessed at St Stephen's Cathedral and then taken for burial to St Marx cemetery.

Dictionary

Persons

Adamberger, Johann Valentin (b. Rohr, near Rottenburg, Bavaria, 22 February 1740, or Munich, 6 July 1743; d. Vienna, 24 August 1804). German tenor; the original Belmonte (*Die Entführung**) and Herr Vogelsang (*Der Schauspieldirektor**).
After studying with Giovanni Valesi*, he sang from 1762 with considerable success in Italy (under the name 'Adamonti'); he also performed in Germany and, between 1777 and 1779, at the King's Theatre, London (where he sang the title roles in Antonio Sacchini's *Creso* and J. C. Bach*'s *La clemenza di Scipione*). In 1780 he was engaged in Vienna, making his début on 21 August as Count Asdrubal in *Die verfolgte Unbekannte*, a German version by Johann Gottlieb Stephanie* of Anfossi*'s *L'incognita perseguitata* (*see* PETROSELLINI). He soon became the leading tenor and the highest paid member of the German opera company; later he transferred to the Italian company. Among his other roles: Don Alonzo in *Der eifersüchtige Liebhaber*, a German version of Grétry's *L'amant jaloux* (12 October 1780); Orest in Gluck*'s *Iphigenie in Tauris*, in German (23 October 1781); Admeto in Gluck's *Alceste* (3 December 1781) and Orfeo in Gluck's *Orfeo ed Euridice* (31 December 1781), both in Italian; Ruggiero in Sacchini's *La contadina in corte* (19 April 1782); and Pirolino in Vincenzo Righini's *L'incontro inaspettato* (27 April 1785). After retiring in 1793, he had a successful career as a singing teacher.
While Adamberger was widely praised for his musicianship and the beauty of his voice, some contemporaries detected a displeasing nasal quality in his higher notes. Charles Burney* was evidently not among his admirers, to judge by his caustic comment that 'with a better voice [he] would have been a good singer'. Mozart, on the other hand, was clearly more than satisfied with Adamberger's vocal ability, for he assured the poet and dramatist Anton Klein in a letter in May 1785 that there could be no better German singers than Cavalieri*, Adamberger, and Teyber*; Germany had reason to be proud of them. And Gebler* wrote of Adamberger: 'He combines great artistry with a marvellous voice. Not a syllable escapes the listener, not even in the most difficult passages.' As for Joseph II*, he called him admiringly 'notre incomparable Adamberger'.
In addition to the roles in *Die Entführung* and *Der Schauspieldirektor*, Mozart wrote for him the aria 'Per pietà, non ricercate' K420 to sing in Anfossi's *Il curioso indiscreto* (in the event, Adamberger did not do so), the recitative and aria *Misero! o sogno . . . Aura, che intorno spiri* K431/425*b*, the aria 'A te, fra tanti affanni' K469 (no. 6 in the cantata *Davidde penitente*), and probably the tenor part in the cantata *Die Maurerfreude* K471 (*see* BORN). In a letter to his father on 23 January 1782, Mozart refers to Adamberger as a 'good friend'. In 1783, Adamberger and his wife, the actress Maria Anna Adamberger*, were among the guests invited to a ball given by Wolfgang and Constanze in their Viennese apartment; and when Leopold Mozart visited Vienna in 1785, he was asked to dinner by the singer. Like Wolfgang, Adamberger was a freemason and member of the 'Zur neugekrönten Hoffnung'* Lodge.
His daughter Antonie Adamberger (1790–1867) was herself a member of the Burgtheater, from 1807 to 1817; she excelled in tragic roles. She also made a name

for herself as an interpreter of Schubert's songs.
(Burney[2], Gebler, *London Stage*, Michtner)

Adamberger, Maria Anna ['Nanni'], *née* Jaquet or Jacquet (b. Nuremberg, 23 October 1752; d. Vienna, 5 November 1804). Actress and singer at the Vienna court theatre from 1768 to 1804; she married Johann Valentin Adamberger* in 1781. At the première of *Der Schauspieldirektor** she took the speaking role of Madame Vogelsang (or Madame Krone?).

Her parents Karl and Theresia Jaquet [Jacquet], both well-known actors, had made their début at the Kärntnertor-Theater in Vienna on 10 April 1760 as Achill and Clitemnestra in a German translation of Racine's *Iphigénie*. Karl, who specialized in playing older men, was a particular favourite with the public.

She herself began appearing in children's roles in 1760, before making her formal début in 1768 as Maria in *Der Kaufmann von London*, a German version of George Lillo's domestic tragedy *The London Merchant* (1731); she went on to become one of Vienna's most popular actresses. In his *Reminiscences* Michael Kelly* called her 'the incomparable and matchless Madame Adamberger'. Her younger sister Katharina (1760–86) also acted at the National Theatre.
(Kelly, Zechmeister)

Adlgasser, Anton Cajetan (b. Inzell, Bavaria, 1 October 1729; d. Salzburg, 21 [?22] December 1777). Organist and composer; a close friend of the Mozart family.

In 1744 Adlgasser was a pupil at the choir school attached to the Salzburg court orchestra. Later he studied the organ and violin, and probably became a pupil of Johann Ernst Eberlin*. In 1750 he was appointed court and cathedral organist, in which posts he was eventually succeeded by Mozart. By 1760 he was also organist at the Dreifaltigkeitskirche [Trinity Church], where his successor would be Michael Haydn*. In 1764 Archbishop Schrattenbach* sent him to Italy for a year to complete his studies.

Adlgasser married three times: in 1752, Maria Josepha Katharina Eberlin (Eberlin's daughter); in 1756, Maria Barbara Schwab; and in 1769, Maria Anna Fesemayr*. Leopold Mozart was a witness at all three weddings, at the last one together with Wolfgang. Adlgasser died shortly after suffering a stroke while playing the organ at a cathedral service (the incident is described in dramatic detail in Leopold's letter of 22 December 1777).

Adlgasser is better known for his sacred than his secular compositions. In 1767 he collaborated with Michael Haydn and the eleven-year-old Mozart in the oratorio *Die Schuldigkeit des ersten Gebots**. Mozart's only known reference to Adlgasser's merit as a composer is to be found in a letter, written in Italian, to Padre Martini* on 4 September 1776, in which he praises both Adlgasser and Michael Haydn as 'bravissimi contrapuntisti'. Since, however, apart from Wolfgang's signature, the letter is entirely in Leopold's hand, it is unclear whose opinion it really expresses.
(Pauly[1])

Affligio [Afflisio, Afflissio; real name: ?Maratti], **Giuseppe** (b. Naples, 16 March 1722; d. Portoferraio, Elba, 23 June 1788). International adventurer, professional gambler (whose fortunes fluctuated wildly), and theatrical impresario.

In his memoirs, Casanova relates meeting Affligio at Pesaro in 1745 (when he called himself 'Don Pepé il Cadetto'), then in Venice, later still in Lyons (where he went by the name of 'Maratti'), and in 1753 in Vienna (where he had become 'Count Affligio'). Casanova describes him as an elegant and handsome man who nonetheless had the 'face of a gallows bird'. For a time Affligio was attached to a Tyrolean regiment in which he had purchased a captain's commission. In 1756 he was obliged to leave Vienna, having been arrested and charged with the attempted seduction of a lady. But he returned later and, on 10 May 1767, signed a ten-year contract, to take effect the following year, as 'sole holder of the entire franchise for spectacles in Vienna', thereby becoming responsible, among other things, for all productions of Italian *opera buffa* and *opera seria*. But he soon found himself beset by serious financial problems, largely due to the expense of maintaining the French theatrical company. It was during this rapidly worsening crisis that he was faced with – and resisted – Leopold Mozart's determined efforts, in the summer of 1768, to secure a performance of the twelve-year-old Wolfgang's opera *La finta semplice**. In 1769 Affligio was forced to seek an associate with whom to share the management of the theatres; he found one first in Baron Bender, then in the composer Gluck*. Finally, however, on 31 May 1770, he was obliged to transfer all his 'licences' to a Hungarian nobleman, Count Kohary, after which he left Vienna for the last time. (Kohary was himself financially ruined by 1773 and replaced by a triumvirate of administrators.) In 1778 Affligio was arrested at Bologna for forging bills of exchange, and the following year he was condemned to life servitude in the galleys. (Affligio, Casanova, Prod'homme)

Albert, Franz Joseph (b. 1728; d. Munich, 7 November 1789). Proprietor of the well-known 'Zum schwarzen Adler' ['Black Eagle'] inn, at No. 19 [later 23] Kaufingerstrasse in Munich. Albert's famous guests included Goethe*, who spent the night of 6–7 September 1786 at the inn, while on his way to Italy.

Albert had bought the house in 1755. In 1759 he married Maria Anna Lechner (1724[?36]–82), who bore him eight children, one of whom, Carl Franz Xaver (1764–1806), ran the inn after his father's death. Albert was said to be 'enthusiastic about all great and beautiful things'. He was particularly fond of music and owned a pianoforte; while Mozart was in Munich for the première of *La finta giardiniera** (December 1774–March 1775), Albert arranged a piano contest between him and Beecke* at the inn.

Mozart did not himself stay there on that occasion, but he did so on his next visit to Munich, with his mother*, in September–October 1777. 'I cannot describe to you how delighted Herr Albert was to see me,' he wrote to his father on 26 September. 'He is a thoroughly honest man and our very good friend.' Albert gave prompt evidence of his friendship when, aware of Mozart's desire to obtain a court appointment (*see* SEEAU), he undertook to find ten benefactors willing to pay one ducat a month each in order to enable Mozart to spend that winter in Munich. On 6 October Mozart's mother informed Leopold that Albert had already obtained the agreement of eight people and was confident of finding others, and that, in addition, he intended to arrange weekly concerts for Mozart's benefit at the inn. In the end, nothing came of the proposal, perhaps because of Leopold's serious reservations. On 18 December he wrote to Wolfgang, who was by then in Mannheim: 'All those efforts to collect ten persons who might make it possible for you to stay on, seemed to me *far too grovelling*.' And on 12 February 1778: 'Would it really have brought you any honour, if the scheme had worked out, to be dependent on ten persons and on their monthly charity?' Leopold was nevertheless highly appreciative of Albert's kindness: 'He is a most honest person,' he had written on 6 October, 'and full of kindness towards his fellow-men, for which . . . I have always greatly admired him.' On 4 October 1777, a week before his departure from Munich, Mozart played his piano concertos K238, 246 and 271 at a concert at the inn.

He stayed there again from 29 October to 6 or 7 November 1790, on his return journey from Frankfurt, but Albert was dead by then. The inn remained in the family's possession until the death, in 1843, of Carl Franz Xaver's son Max Joseph Albert. In 1845 it was acquired by Johann Ernst Maulick and became the 'Hotel Maulick'.

(Valentin²)

Albertarelli, Francesco (fl. late 18th century). Baritone. He made his début in Vienna on 4 April 1788 as Biscroma in Salieri*'s *Axur, re d'Ormus*. On 23 April he sang Don Gavino in Paisiello*'s *La modista raggiratrice*, and on 7 May the title role at the Viennese première of *Don Giovanni**. That same month Mozart composed the arietta 'Un bacio di mano' K541 for him to sing in Anfossi*'s opera *Le gelosie fortunate* on 2 June. He later appeared as the Marchese di Selva Oscura in Weigl*'s *Il pazzo per forza* (14 November 1788) and as Brunetto in the pasticcio *L'ape musicale* (27 February 1789). He left Vienna after the 1789 season. In 1791 and 1792 he sang at concerts in London.

(Michtner, *London Stage*)

Albrechtsberger, Johann Georg (b. Klosterneuburg, near Vienna, 3 February 1736; d. Vienna, 7 March 1809). Austrian organist, composer and teacher. He was educated at Melk Abbey and in Vienna. In c.1755 he was appointed organist at Raab [Györ] in Hungary, and subsequently held a similar post at Melk. In 1772 he was made second court organist in Vienna; on 1 December 1791 he was promoted to first organist, a post he retained until April 1793. After Mozart's death he applied for, and obtained, the position of assistant Kapellmeister at St Stephen's Cathedral, and later succeeded Leopold Hofmann (d. 17 March 1793) as Kapellmeister there.

He composed both church and instrumental music, and was much admired as a master of counterpoint. Joseph Haydn*, writing to Joseph Eybler* from Eszterháza on 22 March 1789, asked him to 'embrace for me those two great men, Mozart and Albrechtsberger'. And Mozart, in a testimonial for Eybler dated 30 May 1790, describes him as 'a worthy pupil of his famous master Albrechtsberger'. Nor was this insincere flattery, for in a letter to Constanze* from Dresden on 16 April 1789 Mozart wrote, with reference to Johann Wilhelm Hässler*: 'He is incapable of executing a fugue properly, and does not possess a sound technique. He is thus far from being another Albrechtsberger.' But the most striking proof of Mozart's high regard for Albrechtsberger is provided by an incident recalled by his sister-in-law Sophie Haibel* in a letter to Constanze and Nissen* on 7 April 1825: on his deathbed Mozart instructed Constanze to keep his death a secret until she had informed Albrechtsberger, because the post at St Stephen's 'was his by right in the eyes of God and the world'.

Among Albrechtberger's many pupils were Beethoven* and Hummel*. Such was his fame that, according to Constanze's letter to Carl Thomas Mozart* of 4 September 1808, her other son, Franz Xaver Wolfgang Mozart*, was offered a well-paid position in Count Baworowski's household near Lemberg [Lvov] 'merely because he had studied with Albrechtsberger'.
(Freeman[1])

Amicis, Anna Lucia de (b. Naples, *c.*1733; d. Naples, 1816). Italian soprano; the first Giunia (*Lucio Silla**). According to Charles Burney*, she studied with the well-known Italian contralto and teacher Vittoria Tesi-Tramontini (1700–75). Starting in comic opera in the mid-1750s, she later became a brilliant and much admired interpreter of *opera seria*. After appearances in Italy, as well as in Paris, Brussels and Dublin, she was engaged in 1762 at the King's Theatre, London, where, Burney recalled, she 'captivated the public in various ways. Her figures and gestures were in the highest degree elegant and graceful; her countenance, though not perfectly beautiful, was extremely well-bred and interesting; and her voice and manner of singing, exquisitely polished and sweet. She had not a motion that did not charm the eye, or a tone but what delighted the ear.' Regarding her performance as Bellarosa in Baldassare Galuppi's *La calamità de' cuori* on 3 February 1763, Burney wrote that its arias seemed to have been 'originally intended for the display of all the enchanting powers of the young Anna de Amicis'. On 19 February she sang Candiope at the première of J. C. Bach*'s *opera seria Orione, ossia Diana vendicata*, and on 7 May the title role at the first performance of his *Zanaida*.

When Mozart made her acquaintance at Mainz in August 1763, she was on her way back to Italy. In 1768 she married the Florentine physician Francesco Buonsollazzi. Mozart met her again in Naples in May 1770 and heard her at the Teatro San Carlo. 'De Amicis sings incomparably,' he wrote to Nannerl* on 29 May. In fact, he hoped that she might be engaged for the opera which he was to compose for Milan (*Mitridate**), but this wish was not realized. She was, however, engaged for *Lucio Silla* and appeared delighted with the music Mozart had written for her. 'De Amicis is our best friend,' Leopold Mozart reported to his wife* from Milan on 26 December 1772, after the final rehearsal. 'She sings and acts like an angel.'

On 9 May 1778 she appeared in the title role at the Italian première of Gluck*'s *Alceste* at Bologna. She pursued her public career in Italy until 1779, after which she sang for several years in private performances in Naples.
(Antolini, Burney[2], Hansell[1], *London Stage*, Terry)

André, Johann Anton (b. Offenbach, 6 October 1775, d. Offenbach, 6 April 1842). Composer and music publisher. He learned to play the piano and violin at an early age and also studied composition. By the time he was twenty, he was working in the music publishing firm founded in 1774 by his father Johann [Jean] André (1741–99).

Shortly after the latter's death, he undertook an extensive business trip, during which he bought a large number of Mozart's manuscripts from Constanze* for 3150 gulden, under a contract signed in Vienna on 8 November 1799. He subsequently published many of these works, in generally excellent editions. In 1805 he published

Anfossi, Pasquale

Mozart's own catalogue of his compositions covering the period from February 1784 to November 1791 (2nd edition, 1828). He also began preparing a catalogue of Mozart's early works. The letters addressed to him by Constanze and Nissen* are of considerable interest, notably those dealing with the authenticity of the Requiem, of which he brought out two editions, in 1827 and 1829. His own compositions include keyboard and chamber music, as well as orchestral works and two operas: *Die Weiber von Weinsberg* (1800) and *Rinaldo und Alcina* (1801). (*See also* ZAIDE.)
(Plath², Wirth¹)

Anfossi, Pasquale (b. Taggia, near San Remo, 5 April 1727; d. Rome, February 1797). Italian operatic composer. Several of his more than seventy operas were produced in Vienna during Mozart's lifetime, among them *Il curioso indiscreto* and *I viaggiatori felici* in 1783, *Il trionfo delle donne* in 1786 (originally produced in Venice as *La forza delle donne* in 1778; a German version, *Die Stärke der Weiber*, had been performed at the Kärntnertor-Theater in 1780), and *Le gelosie fortunate* in 1788. It was the success of Anfossi's *La finta giardiniera*, produced in Rome in December 1773 or January 1774, that prompted Mozart's setting of the same libretto. Anfossi's opera was given at Würzburg in August 1774, and in Vienna on 13 June 1775 (five months after the Munich première of Mozart's opera).

In his Contredanse K607/605a Mozart quoted themes from Anfossi's opera *Il trionfo delle donne*.
(Robinson M.F.¹)

Antretter. Salzburg family friendly with the Mozarts. Johann Ernst Antretter (b. Grabenstätt, Chiemsee, 9 January 1718; d. Salzburg, 15 January 1791) studied law at Salzburg University and subsequently occupied various, increasingly important posts in the archiepiscopal service; he was ennobled in 1756. After the death of his first wife, Maria Katharina Wilhelmseder (1713–48), he married Maria Anna Elisabeth Baumgartner (1730–96) on 21 October 1749. In 1765 they acquired a large residence in the town [later No. 4 Mozart-Platz]; it was sold at auction in 1793. Of their eleven children, only four reached adulthood: Judas Thaddä Simon (b. 1753), Dominik Maria Cajetan (b. 1758), Siegmund Maria Blasius Mathias (b. 1761), and Ernst Sigisbert Valentin (b. 1766). One daughter, Elisabeth Magdalena Katharina Maria Anna (b. 1763), took piano lessons with Nannerl*; she died in 1775, aged twelve. Nannerl may have taught one or other of the boys as well, for there is still mention after 1775 in her diary, and also in the Mozarts' correspondence, of her frequent visits to the Antretters.

In July 1773, while in Vienna, Mozart composed the Serenade K185/167a and the accompanying March K189/167b for Judas Thaddä von Antretter, to mark the end of the scholastic year 1772–3. The music was performed in early August under the direction of Joseph Meissner*. 'We are glad that the Finalmusik was well received,' Leopold Mozart wrote to his wife* from Vienna on 12 August 1773. Judas Thaddä became a theatre prompter. In 1797 or 1798 he published a *Theater-Taschenbuch* in Salzburg. The Divertimento K205/167A was perhaps also composed for the Antretters.
(Croll², Schuler⁶)

Arco, Johann Georg Anton Felix, Count (b. Vienna, 24 April 1705; d. Salzburg, 2

September 1792). Senior official at the Salzburg court: privy councillor (1733), high chamberlain (from 1750), high steward (from 1786). He was twice married: in 1729 to Countess Ernestine Josepha Khuenburg (1705–30), and in 1731 to Countess Maria Josepha Viktoria Hardegg (1710–75). Among his children were Karl Joseph Arco* and Antonia Maria Josepha Felicitas, later Countess Lodron*, who both played an important role in Mozart's life. His grandson Leopold (*see* BULLINGER) is frequently mentioned in the Mozarts' correspondence.

Count Arco himself took a kindly interest in Wolfgang's early career. In 1769, on the eve of the latter's first journey to Italy, he provided Leopold Mozart with a letter of introduction to his cousin Count Francesco Eugenio d'Arco (1707–76), the founder of the family's Mantuan branch, who received the travellers very cordially. And according to Leopold's letter to his wife* and Wolfgang of 29 December 1777, the old Count Arco expressed himself strongly in favour of Wolfgang's being appointed court organist in succession to Adlgasser*; at the same time, he condemned the manner in which Wolfgang had hitherto been treated at Salzburg. (Schuler[9])

Arco, Karl Joseph (Maria Felix), Count (b. Salzburg, 9 March 1743; d. Salzburg, 3 November 1830). Salzburg court official. Son of Count Johann Georg Anton Felix Arco* and of his second wife; brother of Countess Lodron*. In 1779 he entered Archbishop Colloredo*'s service as chamberlain, councillor and master of the kitchens; he also served as prefect of Neuhaus. He retired in 1805. He never married, but fathered an illegitimate daughter, Rosina (b. 1785), whose mother was Maria Cäcilia Gschwendter, the widow of court councillor Johann Anton Chrysostomus Gschwendter (1701–81).

In May and June 1781, in Vienna, Mozart had several important conversations with Arco, whose family had always been well disposed towards the composer (*see* ARCO, JOHANN GEORG ANTON FELIX). Increasingly determined not to return to Salzburg, he tried to hand Arco his request for dismissal on 10 May, the day after his quarrel with Colloredo. By refusing to accept it, and also in the advice he gave at a further interview later that same month, Arco may well have had Mozart's interests in mind. Certainly Arco's warning about the fickleness of the Viennese public (quoted in Mozart's letter to his father of 2 June) was not without justification: 'A man's reputation does not last long here. At first he hears nothing but praise and earns a good deal of money, that is quite true. But for how long? After a few months the Viennese want something new.' In the end Arco lost his temper and, on 8 June, in an incident which has become famous, he confirmed Mozart's dismissal with a kick to his backside. Mozart angrily recounted the incident in a letter to his father the next day. Only reluctantly, because of Leopold's repeated objections, did he refrain from informing Arco of his intention to return the kick, should they ever meet again. (Schuler[9])

Artaria. Austrian art, map and music publishers. In Mainz, in 1765, the cousins Carlo Artaria (1747–1808) and Francesco Artaria (1744–1808) and their uncle Giovanni Casimiro Artaria (1725–97), all originally from Blevio on Lake Como, set up as art dealers. The following year the two younger men moved to Vienna where they established a business which, under their guidance and later, under that of other members of the family (as well as, occasionally, of partners drawn from outside), flourished until well into the twentieth century. (The Mainz branch existed until 1793 when it moved to Mannheim and combined with the firm of Mathias Fontaine to form an art bookshop and publishing business which survived until 1867.)

In Vienna Artaria soon expanded its activities into both geography and music, trading in printed music from 1776 on and producing its first publication, six trios by Paolo Bonaga, in August 1778. In April 1780 Artaria published Joseph Haydn*'s piano sonatas H XVI:20, 35–39, the first of more than three hundred editions it was to issue of his compositions.

Mozart's contacts with the firm began in the summer of 1781. On 25 July he informed his father that he was arranging for Artaria to engrave 'six sonatas'; these were the violin sonatas K296, 376/374d, 377/374e, 378/317d, 379/373a and 380/374f (see AUERNHAMMER) which appeared in late November. (Altogether Artaria issued some fifty editions of Mozart's works during his lifetime, including the first editions of about thirty compositions. Among the latter were the piano sonatas K330/300h, 331/300i and 332/300k in 1784; the 'Haffner' Symphony K385 (see HAFFNER), the six string quartets K387, 421/417b, 428/421b, 458, 464 and 465 (see HAYDN, JOSEPH), and the Piano Sonata K457 (see TRATTNER), all published in 1785; the variations for piano K264/315d and 352/374c, and the variations for piano and violin K359/374a and 360/374b, all in 1786; the 'Kegelstatt' Trio K498 (see JACQUIN) in 1788; the song *Das Veilchen* K476 (see GOETHE) and the String Quintet K515 in 1789; and the String Quintet K516 in 1790. Eventually Artaria was to publish more than eighty first editions of Mozart's works. In addition to its own publications, the firm also took over some of Hoffmeister*'s.

Artaria's publishing venture flourished until the mid-nineteenth century. Its list included such other prominent names as Gluck*, Hummel*, Rossini, Sarti*, and Beethoven*, of whose works it published several first editions, including the piano trios op. 1 in 1795, the piano sonatas op. 2 in 1796, the cello sonatas op. 5 in 1797, the violin sonatas op. 12 in 1798–9, and the 'Hammerklavier' Sonata op. 106 in 1819. The music publishing house was eventually closed down in 1858 by August Artaria (1807–93), a grandson of the co-founder Francesco Artaria, but the firm was still to produce, between 1894 and 1918, the series *Denkmäler der Tonkunst in Österreich*, directed by the musicologist Guido Adler (1855–1941). Artaria finally ceased its publishing activities altogether in 1932, and from 1934 carried on business as art dealers and auctioneers.
(Schmid[1], Weinmann[2,6])

Attwood, Thomas (baptized London, 23 November 1765; d. London, 24 March 1838). English composer and organist. He was a chorister at the Chapel Royal for seven years, and, from 1781, a Page of the Presence to the Prince of Wales [the future George IV], who sent him to study music in Italy. After receiving instruction from Felipe Cinque and Gaetano Latilla in Naples (1783–5), he studied composition with Mozart in Vienna from August 1785 until February 1787. His exercises, together with Mozart's corrections, have survived. Kelly* relates that Mozart told him: 'Attwood is a young man for whom I have a sincere affection and esteem; he conducts himself with great propriety, and I feel much pleasure in telling you, that he partakes more of my style than any scholar I ever had; and I predict, that he will prove a sound musician.' Attwood, who met Leopold Mozart in Salzburg during his return journey to England (*see* STORACE), apparently hoped to arrange a contract for Wolfgang for an opera or a subscription concert in London. However, nothing came of this idea.

He himself had a highly successful career, being appointed organist of St Paul's and composer to the Chapel Royal in 1796, a professor at the newly founded Royal Academy of Music in 1823, Musician-in-Ordinary to George IV in 1825, and organist of the Chapel Royal in 1836. He was also one of the founder members of the Philharmonic Society in 1813, and served as one of its directors for some twelve years. He wrote the music for more than thirty stage productions, starting with the musical romance *The Prisoner* in 1792. Later he turned increasingly to the composition of church and organ music. His style in melody and harmony strongly showed the influence of Mozart, whose symphonies he regularly included in the concerts he conducted.
(Kelly, Temperley)

Auernhammer, Josepha Barbara (b. Vienna, 25 September 1758; d. Vienna, 30 January 1820). Pianist; pupil of Mozart. Daughter of Johann Michael Auernhammer, an economic councillor, and of his wife Elisabeth, *née* von Timmer. Soon after arriving in Vienna in March 1781, Mozart called on the Auernhammers, whom he may already have met on an earlier visit. Within a short time he was giving lessons to Josepha who was an excellent pianist: 'She plays enchantingly,' he informed his father on 27 June, 'except that her Cantabile lacks the truly delicate, singing touch.' Mozart liked Johann Michael Auernhammer ('a decent and obliging fellow'), but cared little for his wife whom he considered 'silly and spiteful', 'the most foolish and ridiculous gossip in the world', and a domineering wife. As for the daughter, he thought her extremely ugly, and, moreover, 'the most aggravating female I know . . . She is not satisfied that I spend two hours a day with her, she wants me to sit there the whole day.' For Josepha had fallen in love with him and, to his annoyance, encouraged rumours of their impending marriage. 'She is nothing but a silly girl in love,' he complained to his father on 22 August 1781.

Mozart nevertheless continued his contacts with the Auernhammers, but reduced the frequency of the lessons. At a concert at their house, on 23 November 1781, he and Josepha performed his Concerto for two pianos K365/316a, as well as 'a sonata for two pianos which I had expressly composed for the occasion [probably K448/375a]'. He moreover dedicated to her the edition of the six sonatas for violin and piano which Artaria* published later that month (K296, 376/374d, 377/374e, 378/317d, 379/373a and 380/374f). The Abbé Maximilian Stadler* recalled in his autobiography having been taken by Mozart to an impromptu performance of these sonatas, on which occasion Josepha played the piano part, while Mozart accompanied, not on the violin but on a second piano: 'I was quite enchanted by the playing of master and pupil, and never in my life have I heard these works performed so perfectly again.' Mozart and Josepha played the Concerto for two pianos again at a concert in the Augarten in Vienna on 26 May 1782. On 26 October of that year Mozart informed his father that he had promised to perform with her at a further concert the following week. By that time, Josepha's father having died on 22 March

1782, Mozart had arranged for her to live at the house of Baroness Waldstätten*, who offered her free board and lodging. In 1785 the Variations on 'Ah, vous dirai-je, Maman' κ265/300*e* were published by Torricella* with a dedication to her.

Josepha continued to perform in public at least until 1813. She also published a series of piano variations, including six variations on Papageno's aria 'Der Vogelfänger bin ich ja' from *Die Zauberflöte**. On 23 May 1786 she married Johann Bessenig (1751–1837), a city official who later became a town councillor. Their daughter Marianne (1788–1849) pursued a career as a singer and teacher in Vienna (where she appeared at the Kärntnertor-Theater from 1809 to 1814, under the name 'Auenheim'), Prague, St Petersburg, and Altenburg. Among her pupils was the brilliant soprano Henriette Sontag (1806–54), who in 1823 created the title role in Weber's *Euryanthe*. In 1810 Marianne married Joseph Franz Vinzenz Czeijka. (Deutsch[6], Haas[1], Schenk)

Bach, Johann Christian (b. Leipzig, 5 September 1735; d. London, 1 January 1782). German composer; the youngest, and in his day by far the most famous, of the sons of Johann Sebastian Bach. After studying with his brother Carl Philipp Emanuel in Berlin and with Padre Martini* at Bologna, and having become a Roman Catholic, he was appointed organist at Milan Cathedral in June 1760. In December of that year his first opera, *Artaserse*, was produced at Turin. It was followed by two operas written for Naples, *Catone in Utica* (1761) and *Alessandro nell' Indie* (1762), both title roles being sung by the celebrated tenor Anton Raaff*. In the summer of 1762 Bach was engaged as composer at the King's Theatre, London, and, except for rare visits to the Continent, he was to spend the rest of his life in England. He became music master to Queen Charlotte, wrote operas, contributed to several pasticcios, and composed for and managed (together with Carl Friedrich Abel [1723–87]) some highly successful subscription concerts. His output was vast: in addition to the numerous dramatic works, he composed some fifty symphonies, thirty-five keyboard concertos and much chamber music, as well as some sacred music (written mostly before his appointment in Milan).

In 1772, at Mannheim – where his operas *Temistocle* (1772) and *Lucio Silla* (1774) were first produced, again with Raaff as the leading male singer – Bach fell in love with the twenty-year-old Elisabeth Augusta ['Gustl'] Wendling*. However, his proposal of marriage was rejected, and, probably in late 1773, he married the Italian soprano Cecilia Grassi (b. Naples, *c*.1740; d. ?Italy, after May 1782).

Mozart felt great affection for Bach, whom he first met during his stay in London in 1764–5. They renewed their acquaintance in Paris in August 1778. 'You can easily imagine his delight and mine at meeting again . . .' Mozart wrote to his father on 27 August: 'I love him with all my heart, as you well know, and hold him in high regard'. He had, indeed, profound admiration for Bach's compositions and was furious when the Abbé Vogler* disparaged them: 'He belittles the greatest masters. Why, he even spoke slightingly of Bach to me,' he wrote to his father on 13 November 1777. Mozart was especially fond of the aria 'Non so d'onde viene', which Bach had originally written for Raaff in *Alessandro nell'Indie* and which Mozart had heard in London in the pasticcio *Ezio*. In 1778, while at Mannheim, Mozart decided to set the same text (by Metastasio*) for Aloisia Weber* (κ294), 'because I know Bach's setting so well and like it so much and because it is always present in my ear' (letter to Leopold Mozart of 28 February). After hearing Raaff sing Bach's aria in Paris, he assured Leopold on 12 June 1778 that it was his 'favourite piece' (*see also* FISCHER). In that same year he also composed a series of vocal cadenzas to operatic arias by Bach (K293*e*). When he heard of Bach's death, he told his father that it was 'a sad day for the world of music' (letter of 10 April 1782).

J. C. Bach's compositions are considered to have had a very significant influence on Mozart's early musical development.

(Terry, Warburton/Derr)

Baglioni, Antonio (fl. 1786–96). Italian tenor and singing teacher; the original Don Ottavio (*Don Giovanni**) and Tito (*La clemenza di Tito**). Da Ponte, in his memoirs, described him as 'a man of perfect taste and profound musical knowledge who had trained the most famous singers in Italy and whom I had myself come to know as a person of the highest merit' (Da Ponte's niece Giulietta Da Ponte had been among his pupils). In addition to performing in Prague, Baglioni appeared in Venice between 1786 and 1794, and in 1790 also in Warsaw. On 11 December 1796, he sang Polidoro in Valentino Fioravanti's *L'astuta in amore, ossia Il furbo malaccorto* in Vienna.

According to S. Hansell, Antonio 'may have been related to Francesco Baglioni' (*see* BAGLIONI, CLEMENTINA); E. Stiefel and E. Zanetti state that he was Francesco's son.

(Da Ponte, Hansell S.[1], Stiefel[1], Zanetti[1])

Baglioni [?Poggi], Clementina (d. after 1783). Italian soprano who would have taken the part of Rosina at the première of *La finta semplice** which Leopold Mozart tried to arrange in Vienna in 1768. After making her name in Italy (especially in Venice), she was engaged in Vienna in 1762 and appeared as Larissa at the première of Hasse*'s *Il trionfo di Clelia* on 27 April 1762. Her other roles in Vienna included Eurilla in Niccolò Piccinni's *Il cavaliere per amore* (1766), Rosina in Florian Leopold Gassmann's *L'amore artigiano* and Venere in his *Amore e Psiche* (1767), as well as parts in operas by Baldassare Galuppi, Paisiello*, and Salieri*. Joseph von Sonnenfels praised her technique and 'silvery' voice. She left Vienna in 1775 or 1776. In 1783 she performed in Graz.

Most scholars (including S. Hansell, R. Meloncelli, E. Stiefel and E. Zanetti) believe that Clementina was the daughter of the tenor Francesco Baglioni, whose other daughters Anna, Costanza, Giovanna, Rosina and Vincenza were also well-known singers (*see also* BAGLIONI, ANTONIO). Some of Francesco's daughters frequently sang in the same performance; thus, in Vienna, Costanza appeared together with Rosina at the première of Salieri's *La locandiera* on 8 June 1773, and Clementina appeared with Rosina in Gennaro Astarita's *I visionari* in September 1774. Hansell states, furthermore, that Clementina was married to Domenico Poggi*.

(Hansell S.[2], Meloncelli[1], Sonnenfels, Stiefel[1], Zanetti[1])

Barisani. Salzburg family of physicians, originally from Padua, friendly with the Mozarts. Silvester Barisani (b. Castelfranco, 1719; d. Salzburg, 25 January 1810) became personal physician to Archbishop Schrattenbach* in 1766. He and his family (he had nine children) are frequently mentioned in the Mozarts' correspondence. His son Sigmund (b. Salzburg, 1 January 1758 or 1761; d. Vienna, 3 September 1787) was a particularly close friend of Wolfgang in Salzburg. In 1786 he was appointed head of a department of the General Hospital in Vienna. He treated Wolfgang on more than one occasion. Another son, Johann Joseph (1756–1826), was Leopold Mozart's doctor during the last years of his life. (*See also* MOZART, MARIA ANNA WALBURGA IGNATIA.)

Barrington, Daines (b. London, 1727; d. London, 14 March 1800). English lawyer; fourth son of John Shute, first Viscount Barrington (1678–1734). His elder brother, William Wildman Shute, the second Viscount (1717–93), served as secretary at war, chancellor of the exchequer, treasurer of the navy, and joint postmaster-general; a younger brother, Samuel Barrington (1729–1800), became an admiral; his youngest brother, Shute Barrington (1734–1826), was successively Bishop of Llandaff, Salisbury, and Durham.

After studies at Oxford, Daines Barrington practised at the Admiralty Court and served as a magistrate. He also published articles on archaeology, history, geography and natural history, and was a fellow of the Royal Society. He gave up his legal career in 1785 to devote himself to his other interests, which included music.

On 28 November 1769, Barrington presented to Dr Mathew Maty, the secretary of the Royal Society, a report on an examination he had made of Mozart's musical talent during his stay in London in 1764–5: 'During this time I was witness of his most extraordinary abilities as a musician, both at some publick concerts, and likewise by having been alone with him for a considerable time at his father's house; I send you the following account, amazing and incredible almost as it may appear.' He then described how Mozart had passed, brilliantly and with the greatest ease, various tests in score-reading, sight-singing, and improvisation: Mozart's 'extempore compositions . . . of which I was a witness, prove his genius and invention to have been most astonishing.' The report was read at the Society's meeting of 15 February 1770 and printed in its *Philosophical Transactions* in 1771. It appeared, in revised form, in Barrington's *Miscellanies* published in 1781.

(Macdonell, *Mozart: Dokumente*)

Bassi, Luigi (b. Pesaro, 4 or 5 September 1766; d. Dresden, 13 September 1825). Italian baritone; the original Don Giovanni (*Don Giovanni**), and Count Almaviva in the first Prague production of *Le nozze di Figaro** in late 1786 (*see* BONDINI). Bassi studied with Pietro Morandi at Senigallia and with Pietro Laschi in Florence. He apparently made an early operatic début in Anfossi**'s *Il curioso indiscreto* at Pesaro in 1779. The following year he sang at Florence, and in 1781 appeared as Don Rapinzio in Anfossi's *Lo sposo per equivoco* in Rome, and as Pasquino in the same composer's *I viaggiatori felici* in Florence and Bologna. In 1784 he joined Bondini's company in Prague and sang with great success in Martín y Soler**'s *Una cosa rara* and in Paisiello**'s *Il barbiere di Siviglia* and *Il re Teodoro in Venezia*. In 1789–90 he performed in Warsaw, and in the latter year also in Paris.

Bassi possessed a splendid stage presence, being equally effective in tragedy and comedy. On the matter of his singing, however, opinions disagreed. While Niemetschek*, writing in the *Allgemeines Europäisches Journal* in Brünn [Brno] in

1794, declared that Bassi lacked the primary requisite for a singer, namely a voice, a critic in the *Gothaer Taschenkalendar* (1793) praised his voice for its melodious quality and described him as the 'ornament' of the company. And a writer in the *Allgemeine Musikalische Zeitung* (*see* BREITKOPF & HÄRTEL) in 1800 noted that even though Bassi's voice had lost its bloom, it still remained flexible, full and pleasant, 'between tenor and bass'.

In 1794 Bassi sang Papageno (*Die Zauberflöte**) in Italian at Leipzig. During the following two years he appeared in operatic performances in Prague, Leipzig, and Warsaw. After leaving Prague in 1806, he spent some time in the service of Prince Lobkowitz in Vienna. In 1815 he was engaged at Dresden, where he was employed both as singer and opera producer.

(*DEUMM*, Landon[2], Raeburn[3], Zapperi[1])

Bedini, Domenico (fl. *c.*1770 – after 1790). Italian male soprano; the first Sesto (or Annio?) in *La clemenza di Tito**. Niemetschek*'s statement, in an article published in the *Allgemeines Europäisches Journal* at Brünn [Brno] in 1794, that the cast contained a 'wrenched castrato' can only refer to Bedini.

In 1770 Bedini sang Idreno in Anfossi*'s *Armida* at Turin, and in 1772 the title role in Alessandro Felice's *Arbace* in Rome. He further appeared as Icilio in Gaetano Andreozzi's *Virginia* in Genoa in 1787, in Perugia in 1788, and in Reggio in 1791. (Angermüller[15], Landon[2], Raeburn[2], Westrup)

Beecke, (Notger) Ignaz (Franz) von (b. Wimpfen am Neckar, 28 October 1733; d. Wallerstein, 2 January 1803). Pianist and composer. After serving in the Seven Years War, he became personal adjutant to Count Kraft Ernst Oettingen-Wallerstein. When the latter assumed control of the countdom of Oettingen-Wallerstein in 1773 (it was raised to a princedom the following year), Beecke was appointed director of court music at Wallerstein. His own compositions include orchestral works, piano pieces, and songs. His Singspiel *Claudine von Bella Villa*, to a text by Goethe*, was first produced at the Burgtheater, Vienna, on 13 June 1780, but received only one further performance there; it fared better at Mainz four years later.

Mozart first met Beecke in Paris in 1766. In the winter of 1774–5, in Munich, they engaged in a piano-playing contest at the *Zum schwarzen Adler* inn kept by Franz Joseph Albert*. In October 1777, while on his way to Paris, Mozart met Beecke again at the prince's country residence at Hohen-Altheim, on which occasion he played to him his piano sonatas K281/189*f* and 284/205*b*. In October 1790, at Frankfurt or Mainz, they performed a concerto together in public. Mozart seems to have had little regard either for Beecke's musicianship or for his intelligence, to judge by his letter to his father of 13 November 1777.
(Eisen, Layer[1], Michtner, Schmid[2])

Beer, (Johann) Joseph (baptized Grünwald, Bohemia, 18 May 1744; d. Berlin, 28 December 1812). Clarinet virtuoso. Having been taught by his father to play the horn and trumpet, he became a trumpeter in the Austrian army at the age of fourteen. Later, in Paris, he taught himself to play the clarinet and was a member of the orchestra of the Duke of Orléans from 1767 to 1777. He also performed regularly at the Concert Spirituel (see LEGROS). Subsequently he toured in Holland, England, and Bohemia, before taking up residence at St Petersburg where, in 1783, he entered the service of Catherine the Great. On 4 March 1791 he gave a concert at Ignaz Jahn's Rooms in Vienna, at which Aloisia Lange* and Mozart also performed, the latter playing his last Piano Concerto K595. This was to be Mozart's final concert appearance. In April 1792 Beer became a member of the Royal Prussian Orchestra; he spent the rest of his life in Potsdam and Berlin. (Pisarowitz[7], Rau, Weston[1,2])

Beethoven, Ludwig van (baptized Bonn, 17 December 1770; d. Vienna, 26 March 1827). German composer. The sixteen-year-old Beethoven was sent to Vienna in April 1787, with the blessing of Archduke Maximilian*, Elector of Cologne, to study with Mozart. (Christian Gottlob Neefe, his first important teacher, had declared in March 1783, in a communication to Karl Friedrich Cramer's *Magazin der Musik* (Hamburg): 'This young genius deserves support to enable him to travel. He will assuredly become another Wolfgang Amadeus Mozart, if he continues as he has begun.') Beethoven arrived in Vienna on 7 April, but remained only a short time, perhaps as briefly as two weeks, before being recalled to Bonn where his mother had fallen ill (she died on 17 July). It is not know whether he met Mozart during his stay. It was not until November 1792 that he once more set out for Vienna, this time with the intention of receiving instruction from Joseph Haydn*. He never went back to Bonn.

Little information exists concerning his contacts with Constanze*. Some communication is likely to have taken place between them on the occasion of the concert performance of *La clemenza di Tito*￼ which she arranged at the Burgtheater in Vienna on 31 March 1795, since it was announced that he would play a concerto by Mozart (probably K466) between the two parts of the opera. As for Constanze's extant correspondence, it contains only one reference to Beethoven, in a letter to Breitkopf & Härtel* on 25 May 1799, in which she mentions having asked him to compose an accompaniment to the humorous quartet 'Caro mio Druck und Schluck' [KAnh.5/571a]. There is, however, no evidence that he ever did so. On the other hand, Beethoven wrote four sets of variations on arias or duets from Mozart's operas: on 'Se vuol ballare' from *Le nozze di Figaro*￼, for piano and violin WoO 40 (composed 1792–3, published 1793); on 'La ci darem la mano' from *Don Giovanni*￼, for two oboes and English horn WoO 28 (?1795, published 1814); on 'Ein Mädchen oder Weibchen' from *Die Zauberflöte*￼, for piano and cello op. 66 (1796, published 1798); and on 'Bei Männern, welche Liebe fühlen', from the same opera and for the same instruments WoO 46 (1801, published 1802). He also wrote the cadenzas WoO 58 to the first and third movements of Mozart's Piano Concerto K466 (?1809).

Benda, Georg (Anton) [Jiří Antonín] (baptized Staré Benátky, 30 June 1722; d. Köstritz, Thuringia, 6 November 1795). Czech composer and violinist. In 1742 he moved to Prussia and joined Frederick the Great's court orchestra, of which his brother Franz [František] Benda (1709–86), a noted violinist, was already a member. In 1750 he was appointed Kapellmeister at the court of Saxe-Gotha, a post he held until 1778.

He composed sacred and instrumental music, but his most significant achieve-

ment was the creation of the 'duodrama', as exemplified by his *Ariadne auf Naxos* (first produced at Gotha, 27 January 1775) and *Medea* (Leipzig, 1 May 1775). This new genre, which was to influence the development of German opera, was defined by Mozart as follows, in a letter to his father on 12 November 1778: 'There is no singing in it, only recitation, to which the music acts like the obbligato accompaniment to a recitative. Sometimes words are spoken while music is being played, and this produces a most marvellous effect.' Mozart explained that he had been 'absolutely delighted' by the two performances of *Medea* which he had heard during his previous stay at Mannheim (October 1777 to March 1778), and he added: '[Benda] has also composed another [duodrama], *Ariadne auf Naxos*. Both are truly excellent. As you know, Benda has always been my favourite among Lutheran Kapellmeisters. I love these two works so much that I carry them about with me.' Mozart was so impressed by Benda's duodramas that he resolved to write one himself (*see* SEMIRAMIS, also ZAIDE).
(Drake, Wirth²)

Benucci, Francesco (b. *c*.1745; d. Florence, 5 April 1824). Italian bass-baritone; the original Figaro (*Le nozze di Figaro**) and Guglielmo (*Così fan tutte**); he furthermore sang Leporello in the first Viennese production of *Don Giovanni**, and Mozart wrote for him the part of Bocconio in *Lo sposo deluso**.

Benucci was enjoying a highly successful career in Italy (he sang in Venice in 1778–9 and in Milan from 1779 to 1782) when he was engaged for the new Italian company in Vienna in 1783. He made his début at the Burgtheater as Blasio in Salieri*'s *La scuola de' gelosi* on 22 April 1783. On 13 August he scored a great success as Bartolo in the Viennese première of Paisiello*'s *Il barbiere di Siviglia*. In this production Rosina was sung by Nancy Storace*, with whom he is said to have had a love affair later on. In November 1783 he returned to Italy to fulfil a contract in Rome, but from late April 1784 until 1795 he sang in Vienna, with only brief interruptions. His other roles there included Titta in Sarti*'s *Fra i due litiganti il terzo gode* (28 May 1783); Taddeo in *Il re Teodoro in Venezia* (23 August 1784) and the Marchese Tulipano in *La contadina di spirito* (6 April 1785), both by Paisiello; Trofonio in Salieri's *La grotta di Trofonio* (12 October 1785); Ferramondo in *Il burbero di buon cuore* (4 January 1786) and Tita in *Una cosa rara* (17 November 1786), both by Martín y Soler*; and the title role in Salieri's *Axur, re d'Ormus* (8 January 1788).

Benucci quickly became the most admired of the Italian singers. Mozart, in a letter to his father on 7 May 1783, described him as 'particularly good'. Zinzendorf* called him a 'very good' and, on other occasions, an 'admirable' performer. Joseph II*, writing to Rosenberg-Orsini* on 29 September 1786, declared that Benucci 'was worth more than two Storaces'.

Benucci was not only an excellent singer; he was also an outstanding actor, much praised for his natural manner and engaging stage presence, qualities which assured his triumph in *buffo* roles. Michael Kelly*, in his *Reminiscences*, described him and Stefano Mandini* as 'the two best comic singers in Europe'. He also recalled that during Benucci's rendering of the aria 'Non più andrai' at the first rehearsal with full orchestra of *Le nozze di Figaro* 'Mozart . . . *sotto voce*, was repeating, Bravo! Bravo! Bennuci [*sic*] . . . and when Bennuci came to the fine passage, "Cherubino, alla victoria, alla gloria militar", which he gave out with Stentorian lungs, the effect was electricity itself'.

Benucci's last great success in Vienna was the creation of the role of Conte Robinson in Domenico Cimarosa's *Il matrimonio segreto* on 7 February 1792, but he evidently retained his hold over his audience to the very end of his stay in Vienna, for Zinzendorf, commenting on a performance of Paisiello's *La frascatana* on 14 December 1794, noted that Benucci had performed 'like an angel'.

In 1789 he sang in London, where he made his English début at the King's Theatre on 9 May as Count Zefiro in Giuseppe Gazzaniga's *La vendemmia*. In this production he and Nancy Storace (who took the part of Agatina) sang the Almaviva–Susanna duet 'Crudel! perchè finora farmi languir così' from *Le nozze di Figaro*. This is believed to be the first time that music from one of Mozart's operas was sung on the London stage. Benucci and Storace also appeared together in Paisiello's *Il barbiere di Siviglia*, in the roles they had taken in Vienna.

In 1795, at the Scala, Milan, Benucci sang in Anfossi*'s *Gli artigiani* (12 August), Sarti's *Fra i due litiganti il terzo gode* (2 September), and Angelo Tarchi's *L'impostura poco dura* (10 October). These are his last recorded operatic performances.

(Kelly, *London Stage*, Michtner, Payer, Raeburn[4], Zapperi[2])

Berchtold zu Sonnenburg, Johann Baptist Franz von (b. 22 October 1736; d. St Gilgen, 26 February 1801). Prefect of St Gilgen; Mozart's brother-in-law. Son of Franz Anton Virgil von Berchtold zu Sonnenburg (1706–69), Prefect of Hüttenstein from 1745, and of his wife Maria Anna Elisabeth, *née* Gschwendtner von Freyenegg (1709–81).

On 10 July 1769 he married Maria Margarete Polis von Moulin (b. 1746; d. 10 November 1779), and on 12 February 1780 Johanna [Jeanette] Maria Mayrhofer von Grünbichl (b. 1757; d. 15 April 1783). From these two unions he brought five children to his marriage to Maria Anna Mozart ['Nannerl']* on 23 August 1784. He appears to have met the Mozarts no later than 1776. On 8 July 1792 he was created a Baron of the Realm by the Elector of Bavaria Karl Theodor*.

(Eibl in *Mozart: Briefe*, Rieger)

Bernasconi, Antonia, *née* Wagerle [?Wagele] (b. ?Stuttgart, *c.*1741; d. ?Vienna, 1803). German soprano; the original Aspasia (*Mitridate**). After the death of her father, a valet in the service of the Duke of Württemberg, her mother married in 1743 the Italian composer Andrea Bernasconi (*c.*1706–84) who later gave Antonia singing lessons. She began her career in 1762 as Aspasia in her stepfather's opera *Temistocle* in Munich where he had been appointed vice-Kapellmeister in 1753 and Kapellmeister in 1755. Engaged in Vienna in *c.*1766, she initially interpreted *buffa* roles such as Sandrina in Antonio Sacchini's *La contadina in corte*, but she achieved her first notable success in the title role of Gluck*'s *Alceste* on 26 December 1767.

It was for her that Mozart wrote the part of Ninetta in *La finta semplice** in 1768 (but she never, of course, appeared in it). Two years later, Leopold Mozart was able to report to his wife* from Milan (letters of 10 and 17 November 1770) that Bernasconi was so delighted with the music which Wolfgang had written for her in *Mitridate* that she had refused a request by 'an unknown composer' (probably the local Kapellmeister Abbate Quirino Gasparini) to substitute some of the latter's arias for Wolfgang's.

In the early 1770s she sang in various opera houses in Italy and, from 1778 to 1780, at the King's Theatre, London. She first appeared there as Dircea in the pasticcio *Demofoonte* on 28 November 1778. Burney* noted that 'she had a neat and elegant manner of singing, though with a voice that was feeble and in decay'. In 1781 she returned to Vienna with a lucrative contract, which she had apparently obtained partly through Gluck's influence. Mozart, in a letter to his father on 29 August 1781, professed himself puzzled by her re-engagement. While acknowledging that she would always 'remain Bernasconi' in the great tragic roles – presumably a tribute to her noble performance of such parts – he felt that she was no longer suited to the lighter genre; as for her singing, 'it is so bad now that no one will compose for her'. Yet on 12 September he indicated that he would be quite willing to have her sing in the German version of *Idomeneo** which he was planning to arrange – but unfortunately she, like other prominent singers, was too busy rehearsing operas by Gluck. Later that year she appeared, in fact, in new productions in Italian of *Alceste* (in which she again took the title part) and *Orfeo ed Euridice* (in which she was Euridice), and she also sang Iphigenie in a new German version of *Iphigénie en Tauride*. She left Vienna in the spring of 1782. Nothing seems to be known about the rest of her life.

(Burney[2], *London Stage*, Meloncelli[2], Michtner, Münster[4], Zechmeister)

Bernhard, Johann Baptist Anton von (1728–96). Physician practising in Vienna. In 1750 he was appointed an instructor at the university of Vienna. From 1768 to 1770 he served as dean of the faculty of medicine and in 1772–3 as rector of the university.

When Wolfgang fell ill in October 1762, during his first visit to Vienna, his father called in Dr Bernhard. Although the latter wrongly diagnosed the malady (erythema nodosum) as 'a kind of scarlet rash', the patient soon recovered. 'Dr Bernhard . . . could not be more attentive,' Leopold wrote to Lorenz Hagenauer on 30 October. The Mozarts showed their appreciation by giving a concert at his house on 5 November. On 23 November Dr Bernhard took them to the opera.

(Schenk, Werner)

Böhm, Johann(es Heinrich) (b. ?Moravia, between 1740 and 1750; buried Aachen, 7 August 1792). Theatre manager, actor and composer. According to Leopold Mozart's letter to Wolfgang of 10 December 1778, he was also reputed to be a good violinist and conductor.

He was engaged as an actor and, from September 1770, as manager at the theatre at Brünn [Brno]. Subsequently he formed his own travelling company which performed at the Kärntnertor-Theater, Vienna, from March or April to June 1776, sharing the theatre with Noverre*'s ballet troupe. When it was decided in December 1777 to establish a German opera company at the Burgtheater, Böhm was appointed to supervise the productions, but he discovered on his arrival in Vienna at Easter 1778 that J. H. F. Müller* had already assumed that function. During the following months, Böhm and his wife Maria Anna [Marianne] (b. Strasbourg, 1750) appeared in several Singspiels at the Burgtheater, beginning on 9 May 1778 with *Röschen und*

Colas (a German version, prepared by Böhm himself, of the French operetta *Rose et Colas* by Michel Jean Sedaine and Pierre Alexandre Monsigny).

By the end of that year Böhm was busy assembling a fresh troupe, with which he visited Salzburg in April–May 1779 and again from September 1779 to March 1780. There Böhm became well acquainted with the Mozarts. (While generally appreciative of the company's performances, Nannerl* noted in her diary on 9 December 1779 that Böhm's own Singspiel *Die verkapte Braut* was 'a very poor operetta'.) In May 1780 he presented *Die verstellte Gärtnerin*, a German version of Mozart's *La finta giardiniera**, at Augsburg. In later years Böhm concentrated his activities increasingly in the Rhineland.

Mozart lodged with the Böhms during his stay at Frankfurt in September–October 1790. Böhm was then directing a company called the 'Kurtrier'sche Schauspielgesellschaft' ['The Elector of Trier's Company of Actors'], which was presenting several dramatic works in Frankfurt, including Karl Martin Plümicke's *Lanassa* (*see* GEBLER) and, on 10 October, *Die Entführung**. (Böhm had opened the new theatre at Koblenz with the latter opera on 23 November 1787.) After Böhm's death his wife directed the troupe. In 1806 their son Johann (b. 1777) took charge of it.

Böhm's company gave performances (in German) of *Le nozze di Figaro** and *Don Giovanni** in Aachen, Cologne and Düsseldorf in 1793 and 1797. In the latter year they also presented *Die Zauberflöte** in those same cities, as well as at Krefeld. (Branscombe[1], Fellmann, Michtner)

Bondini, Caterina (fl. 1780s). Soprano; wife of Pasquale Bondini*. The original Zerlina (*Don Giovanni**). She had previously sung Susanna in the highly successful production of *Le nozze di Figaro** in Prague in December 1786. The *Prager Oberpostamtszeitung* reported in its issue of 19 December 1786 that at the performance given for her benefit on 14 December 'it positively rained German poems, thrown down from the gallery'; one of them began; 'Bondini sings / And the saddest heart is suffused with joy . . .' A famous anecdote concerning *Don Giovanni* relates how, at a rehearsal, Mozart taught his first Zerlina to scream convincingly during her abduction at the end of Act I by suddenly pinching her. William Kuhe states in *My Musical Recollections* (1896) that he was told the story by Wenzel Swoboda, who was playing the double bass in the orchestra on that occasion. It also appears in Nissen*'s biography of Mozart.

According to some sources (*DEUMM*, Kutsch/Riemens), Caterina Bondini's maiden name was 'Saporiti' and she was the sister of Teresa Saporiti*, the first Donna Anna. These two singers were, incidentally, the only two members of the original cast who did not appear in the performance of *Don Giovanni* which was given in Prague, possibly under Mozart's direction, on 2 September 1791, in the presence of Leopold II*.

Pasquale and Caterina Bondini's daughter Marianne (1780–1813) was also a soprano. In 1807 she sang Susanna in the first Italian-language performance of *Le nozze di Figaro* to be given in Paris. She married the bass Luigi Barilli (1767–1824). (*DEUMM*, Kuhe, Kutsch/Riemens)

Bondini, Pasquale (b. ?Bonn, ?1737; d. Bruneck, Tyrol, 30 or 31 October 1789).

Italian bass and impresario; husband of Caterina Bondini*. He sang with Cajetan Molinari's company in Prague in 1762–3, and later with Giuseppe Bustelli's troupe in Prague and Dresden. In 1777 he became director of a new company at Dresden which, from 1781, also performed at Count Thun-Hohenstein*'s palace in the Malá Strana in Prague.

In 1784 Bondini leased the National Theatre in Prague, which had been built by Count Franz Anton Nostitz-Rieneck (1725–94) and had opened on 21 April 1783 with a performance of Lessing's *Emilia Galotti*. There Bondini presented *Le nozze di Figaro** in late 1786. So successful was this production that Mozart was invited to Prague to attend and direct some performances in January 1787. While he was in Prague, he was commissioned by Bondini to write a new work; the result was *Don Giovanni**, which was first given at the National Theatre on 29 October 1787.

At the same time, Bondini had continued to perform with his company in Saxony. He presented *Die Entführung** at Leipzig on 25 September 1783 and at Dresden on 12 January 1785. In 1787 he appointed Domenico Guardasoni* his co-director, and in 1788–9 Guardasoni assumed responsibility for the operatic activities of the company. In the summer of 1789 Bondini set out for Italy, but died during the journey. (Branscombe², Zapperi³)

Bonno, Giuseppe [Bon, Josephus Johannes Baptizta; Bono, Joseph] (b. Vienna, 29 January 1711; d. Vienna, 15 April 1788). Austrian composer of Italian origin. He studied at Naples from 1726 until 1736. In 1739 he was appointed court composer in Vienna, and in 1774 court Kapellmeister, retaining both posts until March 1788. From *c*.1749 until 1761 he was also Kapellmeister of the Prince of Sachsen-Hildburghausen and conducted the regular Friday evening concerts presented during the winter at the Palais Rofrano [later Palais Auersperg] in Vienna. Between 1732 and 1763 he composed some thirty dramatic works, collaborating first with the librettist G. C. Pasquini and, from 1740, with Metastasio*. About a dozen of these were performed at the Burgtheater, and others at Schönbrunn Palace and at Schloss Laxenburg. He was also a successful teacher of composition and singing. From 1774 he served as vice-president, and from 1775 to 1788 as president, of the Wiener Tonkünstler-Societät; he directed its concerts from 1774 to 1781.

Bonno was on friendly terms with the Mozarts. In 1768 he was among the influential persons before whom Leopold Mozart demonstrated Wolfgang's talent for composition, in order to disprove allegations that he was incapable of having written *La finta semplice**. After visiting Bonno again in 1781, Mozart reported to his father on 11 April: 'He is still the same honest and worthy man.' Leopold called on Bonno during his visit to Vienna in 1785. (Angermüller⁴)

Born, Ignaz von (b. Carlsburg or Kapnik, Transylvania, 26 December 1742; d. Vienna, 24 July 1791. Son of Ludwig Born (d. 1748), a captain in the imperial army, and his wife Maria Katharina, *née* Dentis (d. 1751). From 1753 to 1759 he attended a Jesuit school in Vienna and in October 1760 he joined the order as a novice. However, he left it either in 1761 or 1762 and subsequently studied law at Prague University, but he was increasingly attracted to scientific subjects and eventually became a recognized expert in mineralogy and mining. On 5 August 1765 he married Magdalena von Montag, the daughter of a rich Prague merchant. The couple had two daughters, Maria Aloysia Anna ['Mimi'] (b. 1766) and Josepha Theresia Eva (b. 1768).

In 1776 Born was invited to Vienna and entrusted with the task of classifying the natural science collections in the court museums. Later he was appointed a councillor in the Austrian department for the mint and the mines. He was a prominent freemason and served from 1782 to 1785 as Master of the newly founded 'Zur wahren Eintracht' Lodge, to which he attracted many distinguished persons, including Joseph Haydn* who joined in February 1785.

Born's discovery of an important new smelting process led to his being created a Knight of the Realm by Joseph II* on 24 April 1785. The event was celebrated by a festivity held that same day at the 'Zur gekrönten Hoffnung' Lodge, during which a new cantata by Mozart, Die Maurerfreude K471, was sung by Johann Valentin Adamberger*. Both Mozart and his father were present. (The cantata was also performed on the occasion of Mozart's visit to the 'Zur Wahrheit und Einigkeit' Lodge in Prague on 10 September 1791.) When, under Joseph II's decree of 11 December 1785, the existing eight Viennese lodges were reorganizing into only two, Born became Master of the 'Zur Wahrheit' Lodge (see 'ZUR NEUGEKRÖNTEN HOFFNUNG'). Although re-elected the following year, he soon afterwards withdrew from Lodge activities.

In 1784 his article 'Über die Mysterien der Egypter' appeared in the first issue of the periodical Journal für Freymaurer, published by the 'Zur wahren Eintracht' Lodge. This study may have been responsible for important aspects of Die Zauberflöte*. Whether, as rumour had it, Born actually inspired the opera, and to what extent Schikaneder* and Mozart used him as a model for the wise and kindly Sarastro, are intriguing questions which are unlikely ever to be resolved.

In his obituary of Born, Schlichtegroll* wrote in 1793: 'A fairly short life proved nonetheless long enough for him to make his name known throughout all four continents and, though ailing and frequently tormented by appalling pain, to reshape science, destroy the altars of superstition and kindle the light of truth and wisdom and fan it into a brightly burning flame.'
(Angermüller[13], Lindner, Rosenberg, Zellweker)

Braunhofer, Maria Anna (b. Mondsee, 15 January 1748; d. Salzburg, 20 June 1819). Soprano; the original Göttliche Gerechtigkeit (Die Schuldigkeit des ersten Gebots*) and, according to the libretto of La finta semplice*, the first Giacinta. (See also RE PASTORE, II..)

Her father, Franz Joseph Braunhofer, was organist at Mondsee. Together with Maria Magdalena Lipp*, she was sent by Archbishop Schrattenbach*, no later than October 1761, to complete her musical studies in Venice where both girls remained until June 1764. On 8 January 1765 she, like Lipp, was appointed a court singer at Salzburg, at a monthly salary of just over eight gulden, with a free litre of Tyrolean wine a day. They both retained their appointments until 31 December 1803.

Breicha, Anton Daniel. Czech doctor. In December 1786, the great success in Prague of Le nozze di Figaro* (see BONDINI, PASQUALE) led him to compose a poem paying homage to Mozart, the 'German Apollo'. This tribute was first distributed as a pamphlet, a copy of which Mozart received in Vienna shortly before setting out for Prague on 8 January 1787. Later that year the poem was included, with the title *An Mozart bey Gelegenheit der Vorstellung der Oper 'Le nozze di Figaro'*, in the anthology *Blumen, Blümchen und Blätter* published in Prague by Johann Dionis John. A short time before writing this poem, Breicha had appeared as Hamlet in an amateur performance at Count Franz Trauttmansdorff's private theatre in Prague. (*Mozart: Dokumente*)

Breitkopf & Härtel. German firm of music printers and publishers, founded in Leipzig in 1719 by Bernhard Christoph Breitkopf (1695–1777), and later directed first by his son Johann Gottlob Immanuel Breitkopf (1719–94) and then by his grandson Christoph Gottlob Breitkopf (1750–1800).

During the second half of the 18th century the firm grew in size and reputation, employing a staff of over a hundred and publishing works by prominent composers, including Joseph Haydn*, Leopold Mozart, and C. P. E. Bach. On 1 November 1795 Christoph Gottlob Breitkopf entered into a partnership agreement with Gottfried Christoph Härtel (1763–1827). The following year the latter became the sole owner of the firm (which retained, however, the name 'Breitkopf & Härtel'). Härtel published numerous first editions of Beethoven*'s compositions, as well as collected editions of the works of Mozart, Haydn*, Clementi* and other celebrated composers. He also founded a journal, *Allgemeine Musikalische Zeitung*, which appeared until 1848. The firm itself continued to flourish throughout the 19th century; among its most notable achievements were the first complete editions of J. S. Bach (1851–99) and of Beethoven (1862–5). It remained prominent until the Second World War, during which its publishing works were destroyed. After the war, it split into two branches, one at Leipzig in East Germany, the other at Wiesbaden in West Germany.

While Leopold Mozart's contacts with the firm probably date from c.1764, the earliest extant piece of correspondence is his letter to Johann Gottlob Immanuel Breitkopf of 7 February 1772. His efforts in this and other communications to persuade the firm to publish Wolfgang's early compositions proved unsuccessful, but it acted as distributing agent for some of them. No business letter between the firm and Mozart himself has come to light, although Johann Gottlob Immanuel Breitkopf apparently made his acquaintance during a trip to Vienna in 1786. Constanze* herself knew Christoph Gottlob Breitkopf and his wife, having probably met them at Leipzig in November 1795 during her concert tour through Germany.

In 1798 the firm, which had since Mozart's death published a number of his works, suddenly announced the preparation of a 'correct and complete edition' of his 'authentic compositions', without first contacting Constanze. This announcement was precipitated by the declared intention of the Brunswick publisher Johann Peter Spehr to issue a comprehensive edition of Mozart's works at the Easter fair of that year (in fact, he was to publish only six fascicles). Breitkopf & Härtel then wrote to Constanze on 15 May 1798 to explain the circumstances which had prompted their public announcement and to ask for her support. Her rather guarded reply of 26 May led to protracted negotiations. The *Oeuvres complettes de W. A. Mozart* were printed in fifty fascicles between 1798 and 1808, when the project, though still incomplete, was abandoned. Eventually Breitkopf & Härtel were to publish a truly

complete edition. Entitled *Wolfgang Amadeus Mozart's Werke. Kritisch durchgesehene Gesamtausgabe*, it appeared between January 1877 and December 1883 (with addenda to 1910). The groundwork for this latter venture had been laid by two earlier publications by the same firm: *W. A. Mozart* (1856–9, 2nd edition in 1867), a four-volume biography by Otto Jahn (1813–69), an archaeologist, philologist and writer on art and music; and Köchel*'s *Verzeichnis* (1862).
(Plesske, Schmieder[1,2])

Bridi, Giuseppe Antonio (1763–1836). Banker, amateur singer, friend of Mozart. His uncle (or father) Antonio Giacomo Bridi (1721–99) had met Mozart and his father on several occasions during their journeys to Italy, both at Rovereto where he resided and in Milan. According to Leopold's letter to his wife* of 10 November 1770, the uncle/father was 'a good pianist'; at a concert at Count Firmian*'s palace on 4 January 1771 the older Bridi sang a cantata.

It is not known when Giuseppe Antonio Bridi met Mozart in Vienna. He arrived there *c.*1781, as representative of the bank (and firm?) of Bridi, Parisi & Co. Their first documented contact dates from 13 March 1786, on which day Bridi sang the title role in the concert performance of *Idomeneo** which Mozart conducted at Prince Auersperg's. On 4 November 1787 Mozart wrote from Prague to Gottfried von Jacquin*, regarding the performances of his new opera *Don Giovanni**: 'I wish that my good friends, especially Bridi and you, could be here for just one single evening, to share my pleasure.' This letter is the only known evidence of their intimacy. On 3 April 1800 Bridi sang ('most beautifully', Zinzendorf* noted in his diary) in a performance at Prince Lobkowitz's of Casimir Antonio Cartellieri's opera *Angarda, regina di Boemia*. According to Schönfeld, he was the finest amateur tenor in Vienna: 'He sight-reads without the slightest difficulty and has a soft and expressive voice into which, with the most subtle artistry, he knows how to place as much magic as he wishes. In short . . . he draws on his heart and appeals to the heart.'

Before leaving with Nissen* for Copenhagen in 1810, Constanze* made arrangements through Bridi, Parisi & Co., for the shipment of Mozart's piano (*see* WALTER) and of various effects (including 'all my music' and 'all Bach's and Handel*'s fugues') to Carl Thomas Mozart* in Milan. The company was still operating in Vienna in 1818.

Between 1810 and 1835, on land he had purchased in 1806 near Rovereto, Bridi created a memorial to Mozart which consisted essentially of a stone cenotaph and a tablet commemorating his 'best and most beloved friend, prince of musicians'. He furthermore built a monopteron, the cupola of which was decorated with a fresco by the painter Giuseppe Craffonara (1790–1837) depicting the apotheosis of music: Apollo is shown surrounded by the composers Palestrina, Gluck*, Nicolò Jommelli, Handel, Joseph Haydn*, Antonio Sacchini and Mozart, the latter being once again described as 'princeps' in the art of music.
(Dietrich, Schönfeld, Stolzenburg)

Brockmann, Johann Franz Hieronymus (b. Graz, 30 September 1745; d, Vienna, 12 April 1812). Actor and theatre director; the original Eiler (*Der Schauspieldirektor**). After touring with different companies in Austria, Hungary, and Germany, he made his name in Hamburg before being engaged in 1778 at the

Burgtheater, Vienna, of which he remained a member until 1812. At his début on 30 April 1778 he appeared as Essex in Christian Heinrich Schmidt's *Die Gunst der Fürsten*. He developed into a highly versatile actor, excelling in character roles as well as in the great dramatic parts; he was the most celebrated German Hamlet of his generation. Another famous actor, A. W. Iffland, described his performances as 'truth personified'. In 1778 Brockmann was elected to the newly established executive committee of the Burgtheater, each of whose five members served in turn as director for one month. From 1789 until 1792 he was the theatre's sole director.

His wife, the actress Maria Theresia Brockmann, died in 1793. In his will, Brockmann bequeathed his estate to the actress Karoline [Charlotte] Dauer, the divorced wife of Johann Ernst Dauer*, the first Pedrillo (*Die Entführung**). (Förster)

Bründl, Joseph Anton (b. ?Mühldorf am Inn, d. ?Hallein). The original First Priest of Apollo (*Apollo et Hyacinthus**). He was a pupil at the Salzburg Gymnasium in 1763, and in 1770–71 studied ecclesiastical law. From 1774 to 1783 he was employed as a court singer (bass). He subsequently became a choirmaster at Hallein.

Bullinger, Franz Joseph Johann Nepomuk [Abbé] (b. Unterkochen, Württemberg, 29 January 1744; d. Diepoldshofen, near Leutkirch, Württemberg, 9 March 1810). German Jesuit, son of Georg Friedrich Bullinger, a paper manufacturer, and his wife Veronica. He studied at the Jesuit college at Landsberg am Lech (1761–3), at the Jesuit seminary St Michael in Munich (1763–6), and at Ingolstadt University. From 1768 to 1770 he taught at the Jesuit Gymnasium in Munich, subsequently at Freiburg-im-Breisgau. After the Society of Jesus had been abolished by Pope Clement XIV in 1773, he earned his living as a private tutor in aristocratic households. In Salzburg, where he arrived between 1774 and 1776, he taught Count Leopold Ferdinand Arco (1764–1832), who was then living with his grandfather, Count Johann Georg Anton Felix Arco*; his father, Count Leopold Julius Arco (1732–1803), was in the service of the Bishop of Passau.

Bullinger quickly became an intimate friend of the Mozarts, visiting them frequently, joining in their favourite pastime of shooting at (usually comic) targets, and playing cards with Nannerl*. Wolfgang's journey to Paris with his mother* in 1777–8 was partly paid for with money advanced by Bullinger. The correspondence between Wolfgang and his father during this period contains numerous friendly references to Bullinger, who sometimes added an affectionate postscript to Leopold's letters, as on 6 October 1777: 'My very dear Wolfgang. Think of your best friend once every week.' It was to Bullinger that Mozart wrote from Paris on 3 July 1778, the day of his mother's death, with the request that he prepare Leopold gently for the terrible news – a commission which Bullinger carried out with great tact and compassion, as is clear from Leopold's letter to Wolfgang of 13 July and Wolfgang's to Bullinger of 7 August.

Bullinger left Salzburg around 1784. In November 1786 he visited the town again on his way to taking up a new appointment in Munich. There Leopold Mozart met him once more in February 1787. On 29 May 1787 Theobald Marchand*, alarmed by reports of Leopold's illness, wrote to him that Bullinger, who was about to leave for Salzburg, would bring a small bottle of 'spiritus salis dulcificatus Brecheri', a

medicine that had achieved spectacular results. And he added: 'I am so glad that Abbé Bullinger will be spending some time in Salzburg, for you will thus have a friend who will comfort you.' But Leopold, unbeknown to Marchand, was already dead. Later Bullinger was reportedly employed by Count Waldburg-Zeil in Swabia; in 1803 he became parish priest at Diepoldshofen.
(Schmid[4])

Burney, Charles (b. Shrewsbury, 7 April 1726; d. London, 12 April 1814). English composer, organist, musical historian and teacher. He spent most of his life in London, but in 1770 he travelled through France and Italy and in 1772 through Germany and the Low Countries. As a result of these journeys, he published *The Present State of Music in France and Italy* in 1771 and *The Present State of Music in Germany, the Netherlands, and United Provinces* in 1773. He subsequently incorporated the information contained in these books in his *General History of Music* (four volumes, London, 1776–89).

In the first of the aforementioned books Burney described meeting Leopold and Wolfgang at the church of San Giovanni in Monte at Bologna on 30 August 1770: 'I met with M. Mozart and his son, the little German, whose premature and almost supernatural talents so much astonished us in London a few years ago.' In his journal he noted: 'The little man is grown a good deal but still a little man . . . The Pope has knighted the little great wonder.' Burney had a long conversation with Leopold on that occasion. In the second book he quoted an unnamed correspondent – actually Louis de Visme (1720–76), the British minister in Munich – who had recently visited the Mozarts in Salzburg: 'If I may judge of the music which I heard of [Mozart's] composition, in the orchestra, he is one further instance of early fruit being more extraordinary than excellent.'

One of Burney's children was the novelist Fanny Burney (Madame d'Arblay) who, in 1832, published her *Memoirs of Doctor Burney*.
Burney[3,4,5], Oldman[1,2,3])

Bussani, Dorotea [Dorothea], *née* Sardi (b. Vienna, 1763; d. after 1810). Soprano, specializing in *buffa* roles. The original Cherubino (*Le nozze di Figaro**) and Despina (*Così fan tutte**). Daughter of Karl von Sardi who taught at the Vienna military academy; she married the bass Francesco Bussani* on 20 March 1786.

She was a member of the Italian company at the Burgtheater from 1786 to 1793, making her début at the première of *Le nozze di Figaro*. Among her other roles in Vienna were Ghita in Martín y Soler*'s *Una cosa rara* (17 November 1786), Corina in Pietro Alessandro Guglielmi's *L'inganno amoroso* (9 April 1787), Sandrina in Domenico Cimarosa's *I due baroni* (6 September 1789), Belisa in Paisiello*'s *Il re Teodoro in Venezia* (19 April 1790), and Fidalma in Cimarosa's *Il matrimonio segreto* (7 February 1792). While her singing and acting were generally well received, they did not please everybody. Thus Zinzendorf* considered that her performance as Carolina in Salieri*'s *Il talismano* 'fell far below' that of Luisa Laschi* in the same role. And Da Ponte* remarked tartly in his memoirs that an 'Italian woman' (whom scholars have identified as Bussani), though short on talent, had managed by her grimaces and clowning to win the applause of cooks and servants and wigmakers.

Aggrieved at not receiving the critical acclaim which they believed they deserved, she and her husband did not renew their contracts for the 1794 season but, after a farewell concert on 9 March 1794, left for Italy. They returned to Vienna for three months in 1796, but again failed to achieve the desired success. From 1807 to 1809 Dorotea sang in Lisbon, and subsequently at the King's Theatre, London. W. T. Parke recalled in his *Musical Memoirs* (1830) that although she still had 'plenty of voice', her 'person and age were not calculated to fascinate an English audience.' (Da Ponte, Michtner, Parke)

Bussani, Francesco (b. Rome, 1743; d. after 1807). Italian bass; husband of Dorotea Bussani*. He established a solid reputation in Italy in the 1760s and 1770s, and in the early 1770s he also sang in Vienna, where one of his first roles was the Gran Sacerdote in the 1770 revival of Gluck*'s *Alceste*. He was re-engaged in 1783 and remained in Vienna until 1794. During that time he was consistently outstripped in public favour by Francesco Benucci*, who was his superior both in voice and in acting.

Bussani participated in several notable Mozart performances: he sang both Bartolo and Antonio at the première of *Le nozze di Figaro** (on 13 August 1883 he had been Figaro in the Viennese première of Paisiello*'s *Il barbiere di Siviglia*); he appeared as both the Commendatore and Masetto in the first Viennese production of *Don Giovanni**; and he created the role of Don Alfonso at the première of *Così fan tutte**. Mozart furthermore wrote for him the part of Pulcherio in *Lo sposo deluso**. (*See also* CALVESI.) In addition, Bussani was responsible for stage-managing the performances of Mozart's *Der Schauspieldirektor** and Salieri*'s *Prima la musica, poi le parole* at Schönbrunn on 7 February 1786. His other roles in Vienna included Lumaca in Salieri's *La scuola de' gelosi* (22 April 1783), Belfiore in Sarti*'s *Fra i due litiganti il terzo gode* (28 May 1783), Achmet III in Paisiello's *Il re Teodoro in Venezia* (23 August 1784), Mister Dull in the same composer's *Le gare generose* (1 September 1786), Arteneo in Salieri's *Axur, re d'Ormus* (8 January 1788), and Don Alfonso in Pietro Alessandro Guglielmi's *La bella pescatrice* (26 April 1791).

According to Da Ponte*, who portrayed him as an intriguer and counted him among his worst enemies in Vienna, Bussani prevailed on Rosenberg-Orsini* during the rehearsals for *Le nozze di Figaro* to suppress the dance music in Act III, on the grounds that Joseph II* had forbidden the inclusion of ballets in theatrical productions. Da Ponte adds that the emperor himself subsequently authorized the scene, as a dramatically justified part of the opera.

Bussani left Vienna in 1794, returning there for a short period in 1796 (*see* BUSSANI, DOROTEA). He continued to perform at various Italian opera houses; in 1807 he accompanied his wife to Lisbon. (Da Ponte, Michtner, Piscitelli, Zechmeister)

Calvesi, Vincenzo (fl. late 18th century). Italian tenor; the original Ferrando (*Così fan tutte**). After successful appearances at several Italian opera houses, he was engaged in 1785 at the Burgtheater, Vienna, where he was under contract until 1788, and again during the 1789–92 and 1793–4 seasons. Following his début as Sandrino in Paisiello*'s *Il re Teodoro in Venezia* on 20 April 1785, he quickly established himself as the leading lyric tenor of the Italian company and became one of its most highly paid members. He was particularly admired for his mellifluous voice and his excellent technique. His other roles in Vienna included Artemidoro in Salieri*'s *La grotta di Trofonio* (12 October 1785), the Count in Francesco Bianchi's *La villanella rapita* (25 November 1785), Giovanni in Martín y Soler*'s *Una cosa rara* (17 November 1786), Endimione in the same composer's *L'arbore di Diana* (1 October 1787), and the Marchese Celidoro in Pietro Alessandro Guglielmi's *La bella pescatrice* (26 April 1791). For the aforesaid production of *La villanella rapita* Mozart composed the quartet 'Dite almeno in che mancai' K479, for Francesco Bussani*, Calvesi, Celeste Coltellini* and Stefano Mandini*, as well as the trio 'Mandina amabile' K480 for the last three singers.

Calvesi's wife Teresa, a soprano, was likewise engaged at the Burgtheater from 1785 to 1788, and sang there again during the 1799–1803 seasons.
(Michtner)

Campi, Gaetano. Italian bass; the original Publio (*La clemenza di Tito**). He possessed a pleasing voice and a good technique, but was a far less famous singer than his wife, the brilliant Polish soprano Antonia Campi, *née* Miklasiewicz (1773–1822). They were married in Prague in 1791. At a special Mozart concert there on 15 November 1797 they performed arias and, in addition, Gaetano Campi sang in a trio and a quartet, in both of which Constanze* herself participated. In 1801 they accepted engagements in Vienna where Gaetano Campi was well enough received, though not as enthusiastically as his wife. The couple reportedly had seventeen children, including four sets of twins and one of triplets.

Antonia Campi was a celebrated interpreter of Mozart roles, both in Prague (where she sang the Countess in *Le nozze di Figaro** and the Queen of Night in *Die Zauberflöte** in 1793) and later at the Theater an der Wien in Vienna, where she appeared as Konstanze (*Die Entführung**), Donna Anna (*Don Giovanni**), Vitellia (*La clemenza di Tito*), and the Queen of Night. Having made her Viennese début on 13 June 1801 as Kiosa in Franz Teyber's *Alexander* (*see* TEYBER) at the opening of the Theater an der Wien, she remained a member of the company until 1818 when she transferred to the court theatre. She also made highly successful guest appearances in other cities. She died in Munich on 2 October 1822.
(Fétis)

Cannabich, (Johann) Christian (Innocenz Bonaventura) (baptized Mannheim, 28 December 1731; d. Frankfurt am Main, 20 January 1798). German violinist, conductor and composer. Son of the flautist and composer Martin Friedrich Cannabich (b. ?1675; d. after 1759). A pupil of Johann Stamitz, he joined the Mannheim court orchestra at the age of thirteen. Later he continued his studies in Italy. By 1758 he had been promoted to Konzertmeister of the orchestra, and in 1774 he was appointed director of instrumental music. In 1778 he moved with the court to Munich (*see* KARL THEODOR), and in 1788, following the death of Carl Joseph Toeschi, he became sole director of the Munich court orchestra.

In 1759 he married Marie Elisabeth de La Motte, a lady of the bedchamber to the Duchess of Zweibrücken. Their daughter Rosina Cannabich* was a talented pianist. Their son Karl Konrad Cannabich (1771–1806), a violinist, was a member of the Munich orchestra by 1788, was named its Konzertmeister in 1799, and was appointed court director of instrumental music in 1800. He composed a cantata in

Mozart's memory (*Mozarts Gedaechtnis Feyer, seinen Manen gewidmet*) which was performed in Munich in 1797 and subsequently in Prague. In 1798 he married the singer Josephine Woralek, who was engaged at the Munich opera in 1800.

Mozart first met the Cannabichs in the summer of 1763 at Schwetzingen, and in 1766 he renewed his acquaintance with Christian Cannabich in Paris. It was not until 1777, however, that Mozart came to know the family well during his stay in Mannheim. He repeatedly dined at their house, on several occasions together with his mother*, he gave piano lessons to their daughter and performed at concerts arranged by them. He greatly appreciated the friendship shown to him by Cannabich, who supported his efforts to secure an engagement in Mannheim. He also admired Cannabich's skill as a conductor. 'How disciplined this orchestra is, and what authority Cannabich exercises over it! Everything is done in a serious manner,' he wrote to his father on 9 July 1778. 'Cannabich, who is the best conductor I have ever seen, is both loved and feared by his subordinates. He is, moreover, respected by the whole town, as are his soldiers.' Mozart was less enthusiastic about Cannabich's compositions (mainly symphonies and ballets).

Mozart stayed with Elisabeth Cannabich in Mannheim on his return journey from Paris: 'She was almost beside herself with joy at seeing me once more,' he informed his father on 12 November 1778 (Cannabich had by then moved to Munich.) And on 18 December: 'Of all the good friends who frequent her house I am the only one who enjoys her full confidence and who is acquainted with all her domestic and family troubles and affairs, secrets and circumstances.' There are affectionate references to Cannabich in Mozart's letters from Munich in December 1778 and January 1779, and again in those written the following year during the preparations for *Idomeneo**: 'I cannot describe to you what a good friend Cannabich is to me,' he wrote to his father on 24 November 1780. Cannabich was taking an active part in these preparations: 'At the last rehearsal he was wet through with perspiration,' Mozart reported on 19 December 1780. Cannabich probably conducted at the première.

Leopold Mozart subsequently met Cannabich on several occasions, while Wolfgang last saw him in the autumn of 1790 in Munich, on his return journey from Frankfurt.

(Komma[1], Würtz[2], Zenger)

Cannabich [later Schulz], **Rosina** ['Rosa'] **Theresia Petronella** (baptized 18 March 1764; d. ?Breslau [Wrocław], after 1805). Daughter of Christian Cannabich*; pianist; pupil of Mozart. His original assessment of her pianistic skills (in a letter to his father on 14 November 1777) was rather critical: 'She has great aptitude and learns very quickly. The right hand is very good, but the left, unfortunately, is completely ruined.' Before long he was giving her daily piano lessons. Also, in order to ingratiate himself with her father, he wrote a sonata for her (probably K309/248b), of which the Andante was intended to offer a musical portrait of her character. On 6 December he informed his father that she had played the sonata 'quite excellently' the previous day. In the same letter he described her as 'a very pretty, well-behaved girl', adding: 'She is serious-minded, does not say much, but when she speaks, she does so in a charming and friendly manner.' At a concert at the Cannabichs' on 12 February 1778 she played Mozart's Piano Concerto K238,

Caratoli, Francesco

and at a further concert on 12 March she took part, together with Aloisia Weber* and Therese Pierron*, in a performance of the Triple Concerto K242. Writing to his father from Paris on 24 March, Mozart claimed that, thanks to his tuition, Rosa 'can now perform anywhere. For a girl of fourteen and an amateur, she plays quite well.'

The 'Madame Schulz' who performed at concerts in St Petersburg on 13 February and 12 March 1788, 20 October 1790 and 23 January 1793, and was billed as a pupil of Mozart, may well have been the former Rosa Cannabich, whose married name was indeed Schulz. At the concert in 1790 she was to play a concerto by Mozart and one of her own compositions.

(Höft, Komma[1])

Caratoli [Carattoli], **Francesco** (b. Modena, 1704 or 1705; d. Vienna, 22 March 1772). Italian bass-*buffo* who would have taken the part of Don Cassandro at the première of *La finta semplice** which Leopold Mozart tried to arrange in Vienna in 1768. He came to Vienna from Trieste, probably in early 1763. His roles in Vienna included the Governatore di Malmantile in Domenico Fischietti's *Il mercato di Malmantile* (15 May 1763), Asdrubale in Niccolò Piccinni's *La schiava* (20 April 1765), and Nardone in his *Le contadine bizzarre* (1767). His interpretations of the roles of Fabrizio in Florian Leopold Gassmann's *Il viaggiatore ridicolo* (1766) and Bernardo in the same composer's *L'amore artigiano* (1767) were particularly admired by Joseph von Sonnenfels, who nevertheless reproached him for an occasional tendency towards caricature. Burney*, after attending a performance of the pasticcio *La lavandara astuta* in Milan in July 1770, noted that 'Caratoli diverted the people at Milan very much by his action and humour, though local, and what would not please in England'.

In his petition to Joseph II* on 21 September 1768, Leopold Mozart described Caratoli as being particularly impressed by Wolfgang's opera and eager to appear in it.

(Burney[4], Sonnenfels, Zechmeister)

Cavalieri, Catarina [real name: Catharina Magdalena Josepha Cavalier] (b. Vienna, 18 March 1755; d. Vienna, 30 June 1801). Austrian soprano, daughter of Joseph Cavalier, a Viennese musician. The original Konstanze (*Die Entführung**) and the first Mademoiselle Silberklang (*Der Schauspieldirektor**); she furthermore appeared as Donna Elvira in the first Viennese production of *Don Giovanni** (on which occasion Mozart wrote for her the additional scena 'In quali eccessi . . . Mi tradì quell' alma ingrata' K540c) and she sang the Countess in the revival of *Le nozze di Figaro** in August 1789. In addition, Mozart assigned to her the soprano part in the cantata *Davidde penitente* K469, and wrote for her the part of Bettina in *Lo sposo deluso**. She also sang Galatea in the re-orchestrated version of Handel*'s *Acis and Galatea* K566.

Cavalieri was a pupil, protégée and, reputedly, mistress of Antonio Salieri*. She made a very successful start to her operatic career as Sandrina in Anfossi*'s *La finta giardiniera* at the Kärntnertor-Theater on 13 [?19] June 1775. When the Singspiel company established by Joseph II* opened its first season on 17 February 1778 with Ignaz Umlauf*'s *Die Bergknappen*, she appeared in the principal role of Sophie; at the performance on 23 February she was accorded a special ovation. She triumphed in many roles both in the German Singspiel and, when it had been replaced at the Burgtheater in 1783 by Italian opera, once more in the latter repertory. She sang Ernestina in the performance of Salieri's *La scuola de' gelosi* with which the new era opened on 22 April 1783.

Cavalieri was greatly praised for the beauty of her voice and her acting was judged to be constantly improving. There can be no greater tribute to her virtuosity than the music which Mozart composed for what, in a letter to his father on 26 September 1781, he called her 'supple throat' – notably the great arias 'Traurigkeit ward mir zum Lose' and 'Martern aller Arten' in *Die Entführung*, and the brilliant 'Fra l'oscure ombre funeste' in *Davidde penitente* K469. In a letter in 1785, Mozart referred to her as one of the German singers of whom 'Germany could be proud' (*see* ADAMBERGER, JOHANN VALENTIN). By the end of that decade her career was, however, on the decline and she was frequently obliged to cancel performances because of indisposition; she retired in 1793. One of her last meetings with Mozart – if not the last – occurred on 13 October 1791 (*see* SALIERI).
(Angermüller[15], Michtner, Raeburn[5], Weinmann[11,12], Zechmeister)

Ceccarelli, Francesco (b. Foligno, 1752; d. Dresden, 2 September 1814). Italian castrato, engaged at Salzburg in late October 1777. Initially Leopold Mozart expressed some reservations about his voice, which he found overly nasal, but he quickly formed a more favourable opinion. In a letter to Wolfgang on 1 November 1777 he wrote that Ceccarelli possessed a fine technique, and on 22 December 1777 he reported that Ceccarelli had sung quite excellently at a performance of Wolfgang's Mass K275/272b. Soon Ceccarelli became a regular visitor to the Mozart household. On 28 May 1778 Leopold declared that he had never before met such a sincere and good Italian, not to mention a castrato.

Later Mozart wrote the recitative and aria *A questo seno deh vieni . . . Or che il cielo a me ti rende* K374 (*see* GAMERRA) for Ceccarelli to sing at a concert at Archbishop Colloredo*'s Viennese residence on 8 April 1781. In March 1787 he sang Perseus in Michael Haydn*'s opera *Andromeda e Perseo* at Salzburg. He left that city in early 1788 for Mainz where he remained until 1792. On 15 October 1790 he performed at a concert given by Mozart at Frankfurt am Main. In 1795 he was engaged at Dresden, and there he lived for the rest of his life.

Ceccarelli also sang at several Italian theatres: in Perugia (1770), Venice (1775, 1782, 1783, 1795), Naples (1794, 1795), and Padua (1798).
(Iesuè[1], *DEUMM*)

Cigna-Santi, Vittorio Amedeo (b. Turin, 1725 [c.?1730]; d. Turin, 1785 [after ?1795]). Italian librettist whose text Mozart used in *Mitridate**. For thirty years, starting in 1754, he was principal poet at the Teatro Regio in Turin. He wrote ten opera librettos and adapted countless others. Some of his librettos were later used again by other composers than those for whom he had originally written them. The most popular, *Montezuma*, was set by at least six: Gian Francesco de Majo (1765), Joseph Mysliveček* (1771), Baldassare Galuppi (1772), Giovanni Paisiello* (1772), Giacomo Insanguine (1780), and Niccolò Zingarelli (1781). Several librettos were used by two composers, among them *Mitridate* which, prior to Mozart's opera, had been set by Quirino Gasparini and produced at the Teatro Regio, Turin, in 1767. In

Clementi, Muzio

1777 Mozart composed a new setting for Josepha Duschek* of the scene *Ah, lo previdi! . . . Ah, t'invola agl'occhi miei* K272, taken from Cigna-Santi's libretto *Andromeda* which Paisiello had used in 1774.

(Rolandi, Marocco)

Clementi, Muzio (b. Rome, 23 January 1752; d. Evesham, Worcestershire, 10 March 1832). Composer, keyboard virtuoso, teacher (notably of J. B. Cramer, John Field, and Hummel*) and music publisher (he issued the first edition of Beethoven's Fifth Piano Concerto op. 73 and of his Fantasia for piano, chorus and orchestra op. 80). At the age of fourteen, by which time he had already begun his musical studies, Clementi was taken to England by Peter Beckford (a cousin of William Beckford, the author of *Vathek*). Except for some continental tours, he spent the remainder of his life in England, where he had a highly successful career, particularly as pianist and composer (especially of keyboard and chamber music). His fame spread rapidly on the Continent.

On 24 December 1781 Joseph II* arranged a contest between Clementi and Mozart at the Hofburg in Vienna, for the entertainment of the visiting Russian Grand Duchess Maria Feodorovna, wife of Grand Duke Paul [later Tsar Paul I]. The two musicians were asked to improvise and to play some of their own compositions, as well as to sight-read parts of a sonata by Paisiello* from manuscript. Describing the contest to his father, Mozart wrote on 16 January 1782 that Clementi was a proficient enough pianist, particularly impressive when playing passages in thirds, but that he was utterly devoid of taste or feeling: 'a mere *mechanicus*'. And on 7 June 1783 Mozart wrote disparagingly of Clementi's sonatas ('anyone playing or hearing them will realize that they are worthless compositions') and warned Nannerl* not to spoil her touch and technique by trying to perform them at the speeds indicated: 'Clementi is a charlatan, like all Italians. He writes *presto* over a sonata or even *prestissimo* and *alla breve* – and he plays it *allegro* in 4/4 time. I know this for a fact, for I have heard him do so.' And Mozart expressed again the opinion that Clementi possessed not the slightest taste or feeling. In view of this judgment, it is amusing that the pianist Philipp Carl Hoffmann (1769–1842) should have dedicated to Clementi the cadenzas which he composed for six of Mozart's piano concertos and published in 1801. For his part, Clementi later recalled having been greatly moved and delighted by Mozart's performance on the piano: 'Never before had I heard anyone play with such spirit and grace.'

(Platinga, Platinga/Tyson)

Closset, Thomas Franz (1754–1813). Physician practising in Vienna. According to E. Schenk, he hailed from Malmédy. After studying first philosophy and then medicine at Cologne, where he qualified as a doctor in 1782, he became an assistant to the well-known physician and teacher Maximilian Stoll (1742–87) in Vienna. He set up his own practice in 1787 and also took over Stoll's on the latter's death. His patients included the distinguished diplomatist Prince Wenzel Anton Kaunitz (1711–94) and other prominent aristocrats, such as Count Johann Philipp Cobenzl*.

During the last years of Mozart's life, Closset was his and Constanze*'s personal doctor. He attended Mozart during his final illness, on which occasion he also consulted Dr Mathias von Sallaba*. Sophie Haibel* recalled in her letter to Constanze and Nissen* of 7 April 1825 that on Mozart's last evening they had difficulty locating Dr Closset; he was finally found at the theatre, 'but he had to wait until the play was over'; when he arrived, 'he ordered cold compresses to be put on [Mozart's] burning head. These affected him so greatly that he lost consciousness, and he remained unconscious until he died.'

Dr Closset's brother Nicolas (1756–1824) likewise practised medicine in Vienna. (Schenk, Werner)

Cobenzl, Johann Philipp, Count (b. Laibach [Ljubljana], 28 May 1741; d. Vienna, 30 August 1810). Prominent Austrian statesman and diplomat. Son of Count Gundobald Cobenzl (1716–97) and his wife Maria Benigna, *née* Countess Montrichier; cousin of Countess Rumbeke*. He spent his childhood in Laibach and Görtz [Gorizia], continued his education in Vienna and, from 1758 to 1760, studied at the university of Salzburg. In 1760 he moved to Brussels where his uncle, Count Johann Karl Philipp Cobenzl (1712–70) then held the post of minister plenipotentiary for the Austrian Netherlands. In 1763 Johann Philipp began his own career in government service at the Audit Office for the Netherlands in Brussels. By 1772 he was first councillor at the treasury in Vienna, and subsequently he became court vice-chancellor and minister of state. From 1801 until 1805 he served as ambassador to France.

Cobenzl befriended Mozart soon after the latter's arrival in Vienna in March 1781, having probably already met him in Brussels in 1763. Mozart spent most of July 1781 at the count's estate on the Reisenberg [later Cobenzl] near Vienna. (Arneth, Hüffer)

Colloredo, Hieronymus Joseph Franz de Paula, Count (b. Vienna, 31 May 1732; d. Vienna, 20 May 1812). Archbishop of Salzburg, 1772–1803. Member of a distinguished aristocratic family which took its name from the castle built by Wilhelm von Melz in Friuli in 1302. Second son of Count [from 1763 Prince] Rudolf Wenzel Joseph Colloredo-Melz und Wallsee (1706–88), Vice-Chancellor of the Realm in 1737 and again from 1745, and of his wife Maria Gabriele Franziska, *née* Countess Starhemberg (1707–93). Mozart and Nannerl* played before the father on 11 October 1762, on their first visit to Vienna.

The future archbishop was educated at the Theresianum in Vienna, was made a canon at Salzburg Cathedral in 1747, and subsequently studied at the Collegium Germanicum in Rome. He received several ecclesiastical appointments in Austria and Germany, before becoming Prince Bishop of Gurk in 1761. Following the death of Archbishop Schrattenbach*, he was on 14 March 1772, under pressure from the Austrian court (but even so only on the thirteenth ballot), elected Prince Archbishop of Salzburg. It was not a popular choice in Salzburg whose citizens remained cool towards him until the end. He made his official entry into the city on 29 April 1772 (*see also* SOGNO DI SCIPIONE, II.).

Colloredo was, in many respects, a man of the Enlightenment; in his study stood busts of Rousseau and Voltaire. In a pastoral dated 1 September 1782 he condemned excessive decorations in churches and sought to curb the cult of saints. He furthermore modernized the local school system. He enjoyed watching plays, especially comedies, and encouraged the establishment of a permanent theatre in

Salzburg (one was inaugurated in 1775). He was extremely fond of music and frequently played the violin at soirées at his residence. In addition to German, he spoke fluent French and Italian and understood some Czech.

At the same time, he was extremely autocratic and his dictatorial attitude at times provoked the hostility of the cathedral chapter and of civic officials (*see also* WEISER). He was clearly not a man to tolerate opposition or insubordination from his subjects, least of all from persons in his service, and assuredly not from a twenty-five-year-old musician. The decisive conversation with Mozart took place in Vienna on 9 May 1781 and was described by Mozart in a letter to his father later that day: 'He went on and on without drawing breath – I was the most dissolute fellow he knew – no one served him as badly as I did . . . he called me a lout, a rascal, a scoundrel . . . At last my blood began to boil, and I said, "So Your Grace is not satisfied with me?" —— "What, you dare to threaten me, you miserable scoundrel! There is the door, I want to have nothing more to do with such a wretched young pup." —— At last I said, "Nor I with you."' A month later the dismissal was confirmed by a kick from Count Karl Joseph Arco*.

On 12 December 1800, as the French troops drew near Salzburg (they were to enter the city on 15 December), Colloredo fled, never to return. Under the treaty of Lunéville (9 February 1801) Salzburg was given to Grand Duke Ferdinand III of Tuscany (a son of Leopold II*), in compensation for his loss of the latter territory. The see was secularized; Colloredo, who had settled in Vienna, formally resigned as ruler on 11 February 1803, but remained ecclesiastical head of the diocese. Salzburg fell to Austria in 1805, passed to Bavaria in 1809, and was returned to Austria in 1816.

Hieronymus's older brother Franz de Paula Gundacker I, Count Colloredo (1731–1807), became Vice-Chancellor of the Realm and was created a prince on his father's death in 1788.

Hieronymus's uncle Count Carl Colloredo (1718–86) was commander of the Austrian district of the Teutonic Order. During his stay in Vienna in 1781, the archbishop resided at the house belonging to the Order, and it was there that Mozart was assigned a 'charming room' (according to his letter to his father of 17 March) on his arrival from Munich on 16 March. In early May he had to vacate the room at short notice, and it was then that he became a lodger of Caecilia Weber*, his future mother-in-law.

(Martin, Schuler[10])

Coltellini, Celeste [Celestina] (b. Leghorn, [Livorno], 26 November 1760; d. Capodimonte, near Naples, 24 July 1829). Italian soprano; daughter of Marco Coltellini*. Having made a name for herself in Italy (Venice, Naples), she was engaged in Vienna for the 1785–6 season, after Joseph II* had heard her during his journey to Italy in 1783–4. Although his first impressions had not been very favourable, he wrote to Rosenberg-Orsini* on 16 January 1784: 'After observing Coltellini more carefully and attentively, I cannot deny that she is an actress of the first rank, and even though her voice and singing cannot compare with Storace*'s, she is certain to please when one sees her.'

Coltellini enjoyed a very successful début as Vespina in Paisiello*'s *La contadina di spirito* on 6 April 1785. On 25 November of that year she sang Mandina in

Francesco Bianchi's *La villanella rapita*, on which occasion Mozart wrote for her the soprano part in the quartet K479 and the trio K480 (*see* CALVESI). On 7 February 1786 she appeared in Salieri*'s *Prima la musica, poi le parole* at Schönbrunn (*see* SCHAUSPIELDIREKTOR, DER). She was again engaged in Vienna in 1788, this time together with her far less illustrious sister Anna [Annetta]. Subsequently she returned to Naples. Among her greatest successes there was the title role in Paisiello's *Nina, o sia La pazza per amore* (Caserta, 25 June 1789). Her last recorded appearance was as Clarinetta in Guglielmi's *La finta zingara* in 1791. She retired from the stage upon her marriage, in 1792, to Jean-Georges Meuricoffre (1750–1806), a French merchant and banker, whose uncle, Frédéric-Robert Meuricoffre (1740–1816), had founded a banking house in Naples in 1760 which achieved international standing. Mozart had met Jean-Georges Meuricoffre at Lyons in 1766, and again in Naples in 1770.

Celeste Coltellini was also a talented painter.

(Iesuè², Michtner, Müller von Asow, Payer, Zanetti²)

Coltellini, Marco (b. ?Leghorn [Livorno], 13 October 1719; d. St Petersburg, November 1777). Italian librettist whose text Mozart used for *La finta semplice**. He was also, erroneously, believed to have been partly responsible for the libretto of Mozart's *La finta giardiniera**.

Coltellini was at one time an abbot, but later left the church. His first full-length libretto, *Almeria* (based on Congreve's *The Mourning Bride*), was set by Gian Francesco de Majo and produced in 1761 in Leghorn, where Coltellini was then living. By 1763 or 1764 he was in Vienna, where he appears to have held the post of theatre poet. In 1772 he accepted an invitation to the court of Catherine the Great in St Petersburg, where he lived until his death.

Coltellini's most important librettos include *Ifigenia in Tauride*, set by Tommaso Traetta (Vienna, 1763), *Telemaco, o sia L'isola di Circe*, set by Gluck* (Vienna, 1765), *Amore e Psiche*, set by Florian Leopold Gassmann (Vienna, 1767), and *Armida*, set by Salieri* (Vienna, 1771). Joseph Haydn* likewise used a libretto by him for his opera *L'infedeltà delusa* (Eszterháza, 1773). Coltellini was greatly interested in opera reform and, in this connection, was particularly influenced by the famous librettist Raniero de Calzabigi (who collaborated with Gluck in *Orfeo ed Euridice*, *Alceste* and *Paride ed Elena*).

Coltellini had four daughters, of whom two became painters, and the other two, Anna (Annetta) and Celeste*, opera singers.

(Angermüller², Libby, Loreto, Zanetti³)

Consoli, Tommaso (b. *c*.1753; d. after 1808). Italian castrato who sang at the Munich opera from 1773 until 1778. He probably took the part of Ramiro at the première of Mozart's *La finta giardiniera**. In Salzburg, on 22 April 1775, he sang Adone in *Gli orti esperidi* by the Salzburg court composer Domenico Fischietti (?1725–?1810), and on 23 April he created the role of Aminta in Mozart's *Il re pastore**. In 1774 he had sung Elisa in a shortened version of Pietro Alessandro Guglielmi's *Il re pastore* (based on the same text by Metastasio*) in Munich, according to the libretto published there that same year.

In September 1777, in Munich, Mozart once more met Consoli 'who recognized

me at once and was overjoyed to see me' (letter to his father of 26 September 1777). When the new Elector Karl Theodor* terminated Consoli's contract in 1778, he returned to Italy. On 27 May of that year he sang Poro in Luigi Marescalchi's *Alessandro nell'Indie* at the Teatro San Benedetto in Venice, and in January 1779 he appeared at the same theatre in Joseph Schuster's *La Didone abbandonata*. In December 1782, at the Teatro Regio in Turin, he sang at the première of Salvatore Rispoli's *Nitteti* and shortly afterwards he appeared there in the first performance of Martín y Soler*'s *Vologeso*. He is believed to have spent his final years in Rome, where he had been appointed a papal singer at the Sistine Chapel.
(Cruciani)

Constanze: *see* WEBER, CONSTANZE.

Dal Prato, Vincenzo (b. Imola, near Forli, 1756; d. Munich, ?1828). Italian castrato; the first Idamante (*Idomeneo**). He made his début at Fano, in the Marches, in 1772. In 1779 he was invited to sing at a concert in honour of the visiting Russian Grand Duke Paul [later Tsar Paul I] at Stuttgart. He was subsequently offered an engagement at Munich where he sang from 1780 until 1805.

He seems to have enjoyed a certain reputation as a singer and actor, but Mozart, in letters written to his father while rehearsing *Idomeneo*, was extremely scathing about his vocal and acting deficiencies. 'The day before yesterday Dal Prato sang in the concert [presumably at court] – quite disgracefully,' he reported on 22 November 1780. And later in the same letter: 'When the castrato comes, I must sing with him, for he needs to learn his whole part as if he were a child.' On 27 December Mozart complained that Dal Prato and Raaff* (who sang Idomeneo) were 'the most wretched actors who have ever stood on a stage'. And on 30 December he wrote: '[Dal Prato] is quite hopeless. His voice would not be so bad if he did not produce it in his throat and larynx. But he has no intonation whatsoever, no method, no feeling, but sings – like the best of the boys who come to audition for your orchestra choir.'

Da Ponte, Lorenzo [originally: Emanuele Conegliano] (b. Ceneda [Vittorio Veneto], 10 March 1749; d. New York, 17 August 1838). Italian librettist and poet who wrote the text of *Le nozze di Figaro**, *Don Giovanni**, and *Così fan tutte**. Born into a Jewish family, he later assumed the name of the Bishop of Ceneda who baptized him, his widowed father and his two brothers on 29 August 1763. In 1770 he took minor orders, even though, as he later acknowledged and as his romantic adventures were to prove, he was quite unsuited by temperament and character to the religious calling. There followed an eventful period during which he taught literature at the seminary at Treviso (and was dismissed from his post for expressing 'radical' ideas), resided in Venice (and was banned from that city for adultery), lived at Görz [Gorizia] (where he waged a literary war against a local printer and amateur of letters, Giuseppe Coletti), and spent several months in Dresden (where he served a kind of apprenticeship as an operatic poet under his friend Caterino Mazzolà*). He arrived in Vienna – which he had already briefly visited in late 1780, on his way to Dresden – in 1781 or 1782, armed with a letter of introduction from Mazzolà to Salieri*; before long he was appointed poet to the Italian company.

During the following decade he supplied generally excellent librettos to several composers apart from Mozart, notably *Il ricco d'un giorno* (1784), *Axur, re d'Ormus* and *Il talismano* (both 1788), and *Il pastor fido* and *La cifra* (both 1789) to Salieri, and *Il burbero di buon cuore* and *Una cosa rara* (both 1786) and *L'arbore di Diana* (1787) to Martín y Soler*. He also provided the librettos for two amusing pasticcios, *L'ape musicale* (1789) and *L'ape musicale rinnuovata* (1791). In addition, he may have written the text of Mozart's cantata *Davidde penitente* K469. Da Ponte states in his memoirs that he made Mozart's acquaintance at the house of Baron Raimund Wetzlar von Plankenstern*.

The death of Joseph II* on 20 February 1790 deprived him of his principal patron in Vienna, and he soon fell prey to the machinations of his enemies, of whom the most determined, according to his own account, were Salieri, Johann von Thorwart*, Francesco Bussani*, and a secret government agent, Giuseppe Lattanzi. By the spring of 1791 Da Ponte and his temperamental mistress, the singer Adriana Gabrieli*, had been dismissed. They left Vienna for Trieste in June. There, he later stated, he met and married a young Englishwoman, Anna Celestina Ernestina ['Nancy'] Grahl. (There is, in fact, some uncertainty about her Englishness, as there is regarding the actual marriage ceremony.) In 1792 they travelled to London, where his efforts to establish himself as a librettist (*see* MARTÍN Y SOLER), met with varying success, as did several commercial ventures. In August 1804 Nancy and their four children (there would be a fifth later) went to visit her parents and her married brother in the United States; Da Ponte followed in April 1805. They never returned to Europe.

After an unhappy start as a grocer, Da Ponte embarked on a successful teaching career which culminated, in 1825, in his appointment as the first Professor of Italian Literature at Columbia College [later Columbia University] in New York. That same year he helped arrange the first production of *Don Giovanni* in America (by Manuel García's company). He was also responsible for establishing the first opera house in New York; it opened on 18 November 1833, under the joint management of Da Ponte and an Italian acquaintance named Rivafinoli, with Rossini's *La gazza ladra*. By then he was a widower, for Nancy had died in December 1831.

Da Ponte's autobiography *Memorie di Lorenzo da Ponte da Ceneda scritte da esso* appeared in New York between 1823 and 1827, followed by a revised and enlarged edition in 1829–30. It is a highly entertaining account of love and intrigue and drama – occasionally on stage, but mostly in his own life.

(Angermüller[5], Da Ponte, Fitzlyon, Michtner, Scarabello)

Dauer, Johann (?Joseph) Ernst (b. Hildburghausen, 1746; d. Vienna, 12 [?27] September 1812). German tenor and actor; the first Pedrillo (*Die Entführung**). After performing in several German cities from 1768 (Hamburg, Gotha, Frankfurt am Main, Mannheim), he was engaged in 1779 at the Burgtheater, Vienna, where he made his début on 28 November as Alexis in *Der Deserteur*, a German version of Monsigny's *Le déserteur*.

Dauer quickly became a favourite with the Viennese audiences and remained a popular member of the court theatre for over thirty years. He was particularly successful in Singspiels. His early roles included Crugantino in Beecke*'s *Claudine von Villa Bella* (13 June 1780), Steffen in François Joseph Gossec*'s *Der Fassbinder* [*Le tonnelier*] (29 June 1780), a Frenchman in Franz Andreas Holly's *Der*

Davies, Marianne

Sklavenhändler von Smyrna (13 February 1781), the Turkish slave Ali in Franz Mitscha's *Adrast und Isidore* (26 April 1781), and Julian in *Die eingebildeten Philosophen*, based on Paisiello*'s *I filosofi immaginari, ossia I visionari* (22 May 1781). According to the journal *Meine Empfindungen im Theater*, Dauer 'gave a masterly performance' in the latter role. On 16 July 1782, the day preceding the première of *Die Entführung*, he appeared as Karl Denholm (Charles Surface) in *Die Lästerschule*, a German version of Sheridan's *The School for Scandal*. After the re-establishment of Italian opera at the Burgtheater in 1783, he continued to perform in the German repertory at the Kärntnertor-Theater. The well-known actor and playwright Friedrich Ludwig Schröder (1744–1816), a one-time colleague of Dauer's, assessed his skills fairly critically. While regarding Dauer as a useful enough actor and singer in secondary roles, Schröder (as quoted by F. L. W. Meyer) considered that 'his delivery was, like his own character, somewhat restrained and cool, and his movements rather wooden. None of his interpretations showed any particular intelligence.'

Dauer's wife Karoline [Charlotte] was a member of the Burgtheater from 1780 to 1822. The marriage ended in divorce (*see also* BROCKMANN).
(Meyer, Michtner)

Davies, Marianne (b. 1743 or 1744; d. *c.*1818). English musician. She played the harpsichord and flute at London concerts when she was only seven, and in 1762 began to make a reputation for herself as a performer on the armonica. This was a mechanized arrangement, devised by Benjamin Franklin in 1761 (and so called by him), of the musical glasses which had come to be accepted as a serious instrument by the mid-18th century (Gluck* performed a concerto on twenty-six glasses at a concert in London in 1746). Such popularity as the armonica attained in the later 18th century appears to have been due in the first place to Marianne Davies. She gave concerts in London and Ireland and later in various European cities, often appearing together with her sister Cecilia (?1756–1836) who became a well-known soprano. In 1769, while they were staying with Hasse* in Vienna, he wrote for them a cantata, *L'armonica*, for soprano and armonica, to a text by Metastasio* describing the sound made by the instrument; they performed this work before the court at Schönbrunn Palace. Cecilia had great success as an opera singer in Italy and London in the 1770s, but in 1784–5 she was discovered 'unengaged, and poor' in Florence by the Earl of Mount-Edgcumbe (1764–1839), who related in his *Musical Reminiscences* that 'the English there subscribed for a private concert, at which both sisters performed'.

Mozart heard Marianne Davies play the armonica in London in 1764, and it was very likely this experience which first awakened his interest in the instrument. The Mozarts also became friendly with her family. Wolfgang and his father met them all again in Milan in September 1771: 'She, her sister, and her father and mother were overjoyed [to see me],' Leopold reported to his wife* on 21 September. In 1773 Wolfgang heard Mesmer* play on his own armonica and even tried it out himself, prompting Leopold to write to his wife: 'I wish we had one ourselves' (12 August 1773). Mozart was sufficiently taken with the armonica to compose later two pieces for the blind virtuosa Marianne Kirchgässner*.
(Baldwin/Wilson, Hansell S.[3], Mount-Edgcumbe)

Dejean, Ferdinand (baptized Bonn, 9 October 1731; d. Vienna, 23 February 1797). Physician; amateur musician. He served as a surgeon with the Dutch East India Company from 1758 until 1767, being stationed principally at Batavia [Jakarta]. Following his return to Holland, he studied medicine at Leyden University, graduating on 2 July 1773. Three months later he lost his wife Anna Maria (*née* Pack, previously married to Wilhelmus Johannes Buischman or Buschman); they had a son, Georg Ferdinand, who later became an officer in the Württemberg cavalry regiment. It is not clear whether Dejean ever practised medicine in Europe, where he appears to have travelled a good deal. In 1777–8 he was living at Mannheim where he studied the flute with Johann Baptist Wendling*. In February 1778 he accompanied the latter and Friedrich Ramm* on their journey to Paris. Later (in ?1780) he settled in Vienna.

Mozart made Dejean's acquaintance at Mannheim in December 1777, through Wendling. In a letter to his father on 10 December 1777, Mozart described him as 'a man of independent means, a lover of all the sciences, and a great friend and admirer of myself'. Dejean commissioned three flute concertos and several quartets, for the sum of 200 gulden. However, at the time of Dejean's departure for Paris, Mozart had completed only the two quartets K285 and 285*a*, and the two concertos K313/285*c* and 314/285*d*. As a result he was, to his chagrin, paid only ninety-six gulden. Nothing is known of any contacts between Mozart and Dejean in Vienna.
(Lequin)

Demmler, Johann Michael (baptized Hiltenfingen, near Mindelheim, Swabia, 28 September 1748; buried Augsburg, 6 June 1785). German composer, organist and pianist. He studied with Johann Andreas Joseph Giulini (1723–72), Kapellmeister at Augsburg Cathedral, and in 1774 was himself appointed organist there.

Mozart made his acquaintance at Augsburg in October 1777. At a concert on 22 October Demmler joined J. A. Stein* and Mozart in a performance of the Triple Piano Concerto K242. When Mozart played several solo pieces, Demmler expressed his admiration in an unusual manner: '[He] was constantly moved to laughter,' Mozart wrote to his father on 24 October. 'He is a very strange fellow: when something pleases him greatly, he just howls with laughter. In my case, he even started to curse.'

Mozart thought highly of Demmler's musicianship and, in a letter to his father on 18 December 1778, recommended him for the vacant post of cathedral organist at Salzburg: 'He has considerable natural talent . . . All he needs is a good guide in music – and there I know none better than yourself, dearest father.' (Eventually Mozart himself was appointed to the post.) Demmler's compositions include a series of dramatic works (*Der heilige Alexius, Jakob und Benjamin, Ganymed in Vulkans Schmiede*), as well as symphonies and piano concertos.
(Layer²)

Deyerkauf, Franz Seraph (b. Stein, near Krems, 23 June 1750; d. Graz, 18 December 1826). Tradesman, music-lover. It is not known when he moved to Graz where, on 24 November 1778, he married Catharina Weigl, *née* Drasenberger; at the time he was employed as book-keeper in the firm established by her late husband, Caspar Weigl. Later he became a successful merchant in cloth and silk goods.

Deym von Stržitež, Joseph Nepomuk Franz de Paula

In 1791 Mozart appears to have engaged in negotiations with him, through their mutual friend and fellow-mason Michael Puchberg* (who was, moreover, a distant relative of Deyerkauf), for the sale of certain compositions. Nothing is known about the outcome of these discussions.

Deyerkauf was a great admirer of Mozart's music, and a contemporary paid tribute to the 'worthy Deyerkauf in whose house Mozart's works are constantly performed, repeated, and executed to perfection'. Deyerkauf has, moreover, the distinction of having built the first monument in Mozart's memory: a temple containing the latter's bust was erected in the garden of Deyerkauf's house [later No. 35 Schubertstrasse] in Graz on 15 May 1792. (*See also* SCHLICHTEGROLL.)

Deyerkauf's son Franz (b. 1781) became an art and music dealer.
(Hafner[1])

Deym von Stržitež, Joseph Nepomuk Franz de Paula, Count (b. Vojnice, near Strakonice, Bohemia, 2 April 1752; d. Prague, 27 January 1804). He served as an officer in the Austrian army, but was obliged to flee the country following a duel. On his return to Vienna in *c.*1780 he opened an art gallery under the name 'Müller', which he had assumed while abroad. There he made and exhibited wax portraits and plaster copies of classical works of art, such as the Laocoon group; he also showed a variety of mechanical instruments. On 23 or 24 March 1791, at another location in Vienna, he opened a mausoleum dedicated to Fieldmarshal Baron Gideon Laudon (1717–90), a hero of the recent war against the Turks. Deym announced that 'on the stroke of each hour a funeral music will be heard, which will be different each week', and that music by Mozart would be played during the first week; it is not certain whether any other music was, in fact, performed in the mausoleum. The composition in question was almost certainly the Adagio and Allegro for mechanical organ K594 which Mozart had completed in December 1790. The Fantasia K608 and the Andante K616 were probably also composed for Deym.

Sophie Haibel* recalled, in a letter to Constanze* and Nissen* on 7 April 1825, that shortly after Mozart died, 'Müller' came to take his death mask. Neither the original nor a copy supposedly made for Constanze has survived. According to Ludwig Nohl, Constanze's copy was inadvertently broken many years later in Salzburg 'and she did not pick up the pieces'. In a later version of the story, related by Arthur Schurig, it was Constanze herself who let the mask slip out of her hands, whereupon she promptly expressed her satisfaction that 'the ugly old thing was smashed'.

In 1799 Deym married Countess Josephine Brunsvik (1779–1821) who bore him three children. After his death, she ran the gallery which had by then been moved to a specially constructed building near the Danube Canal. Some of the contents were sold in 1814 and the gallery was closed in 1819. After Deym's death Beethoven* had wanted to marry Josephine, but she turned him down, perhaps because of his insecure financial situation. In 1810 she married Baron Christoph Stackelberg. Josephine's older sister Countess Therese Brunsvik (1775–1861) was a very good friend of Beethoven.
(Deutsch[2], Krieg, Nohl, Schurig)

Doles, Johann Friedrich (b. Steinbach-Hallenberg, Thuringia, 23 April 1715; d.

Leipzig, 8 February 1797). German choirmaster and composer of church music. A pupil of J. S. Bach, he was himself Kantor at St Thomas's church in Leipzig from 1756 until 1789. Mozart met him more than once during his visit to Leipzig from 20 to 23 April 1789. When Mozart played the church organ on 22 April, Doles manipulated the stops for him together with the organist Karl Friedrich Görner (whose father Johann Gottlieb Görner had been organist there when Bach was Kantor). According to J. F. Rochlitz (*Allgemeine Musikalische Zeitung*, 1800), Mozart improvised for Doles the six-part Canon κAnh.4/572a later that same day. In 1790 Doles dedicated his cantata *Ich komme vor dein Angesicht*, on a text by Christian Fürchtegott Gellert (1715–69), jointly to Mozart and Johann Gottlieb Naumann (1741–1801), Kapellmeister at the Dresden court, whom Mozart had met there in 1789.
(Robinson)

Durazzo, Giacomo, Count (b. Genoa, 27 April 1717; d. Venice, 15 October 1794). Italian impresario and diplomat. Member of an eminent Genoese family which produced seven doges and two cardinals (his own brother Marcello was doge of Genoa, 1767–9). From September 1749 until June 1752 Durazzo served as ambassador of the Republic of Genoa in Vienna.

In 1752 he was appointed co-director, with Count Franz Esterházy (1729–1803), of the Burgtheater and Kärntnertor-Theater, and in 1754 assumed sole responsibility for them as Superintendent of Spectacles. It was in this capacity that he invited the Mozart children to play at a public concert during their visit in late 1762, but, as Leopold Mozart explained to Hagenauer* in his letter of 10 December, they were forced to decline for lack of time. Durazzo had himself some practical experience of the theatrical profession. On 17 January 1752 he took part at Count Taroucca's house in an amateur performance of Nivelle de La Chaussée's comedy *Le préjugé à la mode*, and he acted in various other private performances during the following two months. His own pastorella *Le cacciatrici amanti*, with music by Georg Christoph Wagenseil, was given at Schloss Laxenburg on 25 June 1755, and his comedy *La joie imprévue* was presented at Count Haugwitz's palace on 28 January 1756.

After controlling theatrical productions for ten years, during which he succeeded, with Gluck*'s co-operation, in re-establishing French *opéra comique* and Italian *opera seria* in Vienna, he resigned on 1 April 1764 – according to some contemporary rumours, because of the discovery of discrepancies in the theatre accounts, though the true reason may have been that his affair with the singer and dancer Louise Geoffroy-Bodin had lost him Maria Theresa*'s favour. In September 1764 he took up the post of Austrian ambassador in Venice, which he retained until 1784. On 3 March 1771 Mozart and his father were received by him during their first journey to Italy. While in Venice, Durazzo was able to render further services to the Burgtheater by arranging the engagement of several leading singers, among them Nancy Storace* and Michael Kelly*.
(Dean, Haas[1], Zechmeister)

Duschek [Dušek], Josepha, *née* Hambacher (baptized Prague, 6 March 1754; d. Prague, 8 January 1824). Czech soprano. She studied with the Czech composer, pianist and teacher Franz Xaver Duschek [Dušek] (1731–99), whom she married in

1776. Her maternal grandfather was the prominent Salzburg merchant Ignaz Anton von Weiser*. The Duscheks met the Mozarts while visiting their Salzburg relatives in August 1777. On that occasion Mozart wrote for Josepha the scena *Ah, lo previdi . . . Ah, t'invola agl'occhi miei* K272. The two families remained on friendly terms, and Mozart and Constanze* stayed at the Villa Betramka, the Duscheks' summer residence [later a Mozart museum] in the Prague suburb of Smichov, during part of their visit to that city in 1787 for the première of *Don Giovanni*. Mozart reportedly put the finishing touches to the opera while seated in the garden of the villa; and Josepha is supposed to have locked him in a room until he had composed the scena *Bella mia fiamma . . . Resta, o cara* K528 for her.

Mozart and Josepha collaborated professionally on more than one occasion: in March 1786 he accompanied her at a concert at the Viennese court, and in April and May 1789 she sang at concerts he gave in Dresden and Leipzig. She took part in memorial concerts for Mozart at St Nicolas Church in Prague (14 December 1791) and at the Prague National Theatre (13 June 1792). In 1797 Constanze loaned the Duscheks a sum of money, which was later repaid, probably from the proceeds of the sale of the villa by Josepha in 1799, following her husband's death.

Josepha Duschek's career as a concert singer lasted from the 1770s into the 19th century and took her, in addition to Salzburg and Vienna and several German cities, as far as Warsaw. Yet opinions were divided about her artistry. 'Mme Duschek sang to perfection,' Zinzendorf* noted in his diary on 27 March 1786, after hearing her sing at Prince Paar's in Vienna. And Schönfeld wrote in his *Jahrbuch der Tonkunst von Wien und Prag* that her beautiful voice and expressive singing secured for her everyone's approval. But Leopold Mozart was not among her admirers: in his letter to Nannerl* of 18–21 April 1786 he severely criticized what he considered her strident and overly dramatic rendering of an aria by Johann Gottlieb Naumann. (Postolka[2], Schönfeld)

Eberardi [Eberhardi], **Teresa.** Contralto who would have taken the part of Giacinta at the première of *La finta semplice* which Leopold Mozart tried to arrange in Vienna in 1768.

From 1760 to 1762 she had appeared at the King's Theatre, London, where her roles included Decio in Gioacchino Cocchi's *Tito Manlio*, Brigida in Domenico Fischietti's *Il mercato di Malmantile*, Lena in Baldassare Galuppi's *Il filosofo di campagna*, and Clarice in the same composer's *Il mondo della luna*. Later, at the Burgtheater in Vienna, she appeared as Emilia in Florian Leopold Gassman's *Il viaggiatore ridicolo* (25 October 1766), Angiolina in his *L'amore artigiano* (26 April 1767), and Lucinda in Galuppi's *Il vecchio geloso* (1767). Sonnenfels found her gestures too stiff and stilted, but concluded that 'as a singer, she is certain to please everybody'.
(*London Stage*, Sonnenfels, Zechmeister)

Eberlin, Johann Ernst (b. Jettingen, near Burgau, Bavaria, 27 March 1702; d. Salzburg, 21 [?19] June 1762). German composer and organist. He was educated at the Gymnasium in Augsburg, and in 1721 enrolled in the law faculty of Salzburg University; but he abandoned his studies two years later in order to join the court and cathedral Kapelle. He was named fourth organist in 1725, and court and cathedral organist in succession to Matthäus Gugl in 1729. On the death of Karl Heinrich von Bibern in 1749 he became court and cathedral Kapellmeister.

On 17 February 1727 he married Maria Josepha Cäcilia Pflanzmann (1698–1763) who bore him five daughters. The oldest, Maria Cäcilia Barbara-(1728–1806), is the one most frequently mentioned in the Mozarts' correspondence, where she is referred to as 'Waberl'; she married Joseph Meissner*. Another daughter, Maria Josepha Katharina, married Anton Cajetan Adlgasser*.

Eberlin composed numerous masses and oratorios, as well as three operas (all lost) to texts by Metastasio* and much music for school plays. Into the latter category falls the setting of the intermezzo *Tobias a Raguele cum gaudio excipitur*, which was performed together with the play *Sigismundus Hungariae rex* on 1 and 3 September 1761 (both texts were by Marian Wimmer). Among the dancers was the five-and-a-half-year-old Wolfgang; it was his first public appearance. Leopold Mozart is believed to be the author of a report on the state of music in Salzburg, published in Berlin in 1757, which expressed great admiration for Eberlin's mastery of the art of composition and compared him to Alessandro Scarlatti and Telemann. Mozart himself seems at first to have had a high regard for Eberlin's works, for on 10 April 1782 he asked his father to have copies made of Eberlin's toccatas and fugues, as he wished Baron van Swieten* to hear them. But on 20 April he cancelled the request, explaining that he had in the meanwhile got hold of the music – and realized that it was too trivial to merit a place beside Handel* and Bach (the only two composers normally performed at Swieten's).

Leopold Mozart had hoped to be named Kapellmeister in succession to Eberlin, but Giuseppe Francesco Lolli was appointed instead and Leopold had to be content with the position of vice-Kapellmeister.

(Haas², Pauly²)

Esterházy von Galántha, Franz ['Quin-Quin'], Count (b. 19 September 1715; d. Vienna, 7 November 1785). Imperial and royal chamberlain; royal Hungarian court chancellor. Son of Count Franz Esterházy von Galántha (1683–1754).

On 17 November 1785 Mozart's *Maurerische Trauermusik* K477/479a was performed at a double memorial celebration held at the 'Zur gekrönten Hoffnung' Lodge for the count and Major-General Georg August, Duke of Mecklenburg-Strelitz (1748–85), who had died in Hungary on 6 November. The music had apparently been composed originally for a quite different, non-memorial ceremony held on 12 August of that year at the 'Zur wahren Eintracht' Lodge, when a foreign Brother, Carl von König, was raised to Master Mason.

Count Esterházy von Galántha was a subscriber to Mozart's Trattnerhof concerts in March 1784 (*see* TRATTNER).

(Autexier, Landon³, Schuler¹³,¹⁵)

Esterházy von Galántha, Johann Baptist, Count (b. Vienna, 6 June 1748; d. Vienna, 25 February 1800), known in the family as 'Red John' because of the colour of his hair. Imperial and royal chamberlain and court councillor; one of the leading patrons of music in Vienna. Son of Count Michael Esterházy von Galántha (1711–64), ambassador to St Petersburg; nephew of Count Franz Esterházy von Galántha*. In 1772 he married Countess Maria Anna Pálffy (1747–99).

Ettore, Guglielmo d'

Mozart played at his palace on 12 March 1783, and gave nine further concerts there in March 1784. In addition, Esterházy was a subscriber to the Trattnerhof concerts (*see* TRATTNER). On 26 February and 4 March 1788, at Esterházy's, Mozart conducted an orchestra of eighty-six players and a choir of thirty singers in performances of Carl Philipp Emanuel Bach's oratorium *Die Auferstehung und Himmelfahrt Christi*; among the soloists were Aloisia Lange* and Johann Valentin Adamberger*. *Acis and Galatea*, in Mozart's revised orchestration K566, was performed at Esterházy's on 30 December 1788, and *Messiah*, with Mozart's orchestration K572, on 6 March and 7 April 1789 (*see* HANDEL).

Esterházy was a freemason and, like Mozart, a member of the 'Zur neugekrönten Hoffnung'* Lodge.

(Landon[3], *Mozart: Dokumente*)

Ettore, Guglielmo d' (b. *c.*1740; d. Stuttgart, 1771). Italian tenor who created the title role in *Mitridate**. He had sung Artaban at the première of Giuseppe Scarlatti's opera *Artaserse* in Vienna on 4 January 1763. Mozart met him in Milan early in 1770. In a letter from Bologna on 24 March of the same year, Leopold Mozart explained that he was called 'il Cavaliere Ettore, because he has received a certain decoration'. Charles Burney* reported that at performances of an opera by Antonio Sacchini given at Padua in June 1770 'a famous tenor, il Cavalier Guglielmi Ettori, in the service of the Duke of Württemberg . . . was more applauded than all the rest'. In the libretto of *Mitridate* published later that year, Ettore is stated to be '*virtuoso di camera* to His Serene Highness the Elector of Bavaria'.

Ettore has been identified by L. F. Tagliavini and J. H. Eibl as the troublemaker referred to in Leopold's statement, in his letter of 17 November 1770 written in Milan during rehearsals for *Mitridate*, that 'we have beaten off a second attack since yesterday'. The identification is based on the fact that four different drafts exist for Mitridate's cavata 'Se di lauri il crine adorno' and two for his recitative 'Respira alfin', while his aria 'Vado incontro al fato estremo' was set twice by Mozart. From this it has been argued that Ettore was a man not easily satisfied and likely to have made difficulties. The identification draws even stronger support from the following passage in Leopold's letter to Wolfgang of 29 April 1778: 'You must not allow any envious persons to get the better of you or upset you. It happens everywhere – think only of Italy, of your first opera [*Mitridate*] . . . of d'Ettore, etc.'

(Burney[4], Eibl in *Mozart: Briefe*, Tagliavini in *NMA* II/5/4)

Eybler, Joseph Leopold von (b. Schwechat, near Vienna, 8 February 1765; d. Vienna, 24 July 1846). Austrian composer and choirmaster. His family had contacts with the Haydns, since his grandfather hailed from Hainburg where Joseph Haydn*'s father was born. He received instruction in composition from Albrechtsberger* from 1777 to 1779, and he must have met Mozart before 27 March 1789, for in a letter written on that day Haydn asked him to give his warm regards to 'those two great men, Mozart and Albrechtsberger'. He reportedly assisted Mozart at rehearsals for *Così fan tutte**. On 30 May 1790 Mozart wrote out a testimonial praising his knowledge of composition and singing, as well as his skill as an organist and pianist. (In a testimonial dated 24 January 1793, Albrechtsberger was to claim that 'after Mozart, [Eybler] was the greatest musical genius Vienna possessed'.)

Shortly after Mozart's death, Constanze* asked Eybler to complete Mozart's Requiem. Eybler confirmed his acceptance in writing on 21 December 1791, but after some initial work he abandoned the task, which was eventually entrusted to Süssmayr*. Eybler's association with the Requiem did not end there, however, for he conducted it at the memorial service for Haydn at the Schottenkirche in Vienna on 15 June 1809; and on 23 February 1833 he suffered a stroke while directing a performance of it.

Eybler composed numerous masses, a Requiem, and an opera, *Das Zauberschwert*. He was appointed court vice-Kapellmeister in 1814, and on 16 June 1824 succeeded Salieri* as Kapellmeister. He was ennobled in 1834.
(Badura-Skoda/Herrmann, Haas[3])

Ferdinand (b. Vienna, 1 June 1754; d. Vienna, 24 December 1806). Austrian Archduke, son of Empress Maria Theresa* and Francis I. Governor and Captain-General of Lombardy from 1771 until 1796. On 15 October 1771, in Milan, he married Maria Beatrice Ricciarda d'Este (1750–1829), daughter of Ercole III Rainaldo (1727–1803), Duke of Modena. By this marriage, Ferdinand became the head of the Habsburg-Este family. His son Francesco was Duke of Modena from 1814 to 1846.

Mozart was presented to the young Ferdinand and his brother Maximilian Franz* on 16 October 1762, during his first visit to Vienna. In 1771 he was commissioned by Maria Theresa to contribute an opera (*Ascanio in Alba**) to the festivities planned to be held in Milan in celebration of Ferdinand's wedding. A general account of these festivities can be found in Giuseppe Parini*'s *Descrizione delle feste celebrate in Milano per le nozze delle LL. Altezze Reali l'Arciduca Ferdinando d'Austria e l'Arciduchessa Beatrice d'Este* (published in Milan in 1825).

After the success of Mozart's opera Ferdinand considered offering him an appointment at his Milanese court, but Ferdinand's mother poured cold water on the idea (*see* MARIA THERESA).

Ferraresi del Bene, Adriana: *see* GABRIELI, ADRIANA.

Fesemayr, Maria Anna (b. Salzburg, 20 February 1743; d. Salzburg, late 1782). Soprano; the original Weltgeist in *Die Schuldigkeit des ersten Gebots**, and, according to the libretto of *La finta semplice**, the first Ninetta. (*See also* RE PASTORE, II.) Like Adlgasser*, Maria Anna Braunhofer*, and Maria Magdalena Lipp*, she received a stipend from Archbishop Schrattenbach* for study in Italy. She left for Venice in January 1764, and on her return in December 1765 was appointed a court singer. Mozart and his father were witnesses at her wedding to Adlgasser on 19 June 1769.

Firmian, Karl Joseph, Count (b. Deutschmetz [Mezzocorona], Trentino, 6 August 1718; d. Milan, 20 July 1782). Son of Count of the Realm Franz Alphons Georg Firmian (1680–1748) and of his wife Barbara Elisabeth, *née* Countess Thun-Hohenstein; nephew of Leopold Mozart's first employer, Baron Leopold Anton Firmian, Archbishop of Salzburg from 1727 to 1744. After studies at the universities of Innsbruck, Salzburg, and Leyden, he subsequently travelled in Italy and France. He was appointed imperial ambassador to the Neapolitan court, and

Fischer, Ludwig

later served as governor-general of Lombardy from 1759 until 1782. A highly skilled diplomat, he was also a man of vast learning who took a profound interest in the arts. His library in Milan comprised 40,000 volumes. The famous art historian Johann Joachim Winckelmann (1717–68), in a letter to Hieronymus Dietrich Berendis on 15 May 1758, called Firmian 'a man of great intellect and quite prodigious erudition', and writing to Johann Michael Francke on 30 September 1758, he described him as 'the greatest and most learned man among all the persons of noble birth whom I know'. For Charles Burney*, who visited the count in July 1770, everything at his house 'breathed taste and affluence' and he himself appeared 'to have all the marks of a truely great man'.

To the young Mozart he proved a most generous patron. It may be presumed that Wolfgang had been recommended to him by his brother Count Franz Lactantius Firmian (1712–86), high steward at the Salzburg court, who was well disposed towards the Mozarts. On 7 February 1770, soon after their arrival in Milan, Wolfgang and his father were received by Firmian, who presented Wolfgang with a beautifully bound edition of Metastasio*'s works. On 17 February Leopold informed his wife* that 'the Duke and Princess of Modena' [Ercole III Rainaldo d'Este and his daughter Maria Beatrice Ricciarda d'Este, the fiancée of Archduke Ferdinand*] proposed to come to Firmian's palace the next day 'to hear Wolfgang'. They were also the guests of honour at a grand concert at Firmian's on 12 March, to which some 150 members of the higher aristocracy were invited. For the occasion Mozart composed several soprano arias on texts by Metastasio. Evidently the duke and the princess were as impressed by Mozart's talents as Firmian is known to have been, for the following spring he received a commission to write an opera (*Ascanio in Alba**) for the wedding festivities planned for October 1771. Firmian was no doubt also instrumental in obtaining for Mozart the contract (which was drawn up at his house on 13 or 14 March 1770) for the opera *Mitridate**, to be produced during the 1770–1 winter season at the Teatro Regio Ducal, Milan.

On 14 March Wolfgang and his father were invited to a farewell lunch by Firmian who not only gave Wolfgang a gold snuff box containing twenty gigliati, but also handed them letters of recommendation to leading patrons of the arts at Parma (Guglielmo du Tillot, Marchese di Felino) and Bologna (Field-Marshal Count Gian-Luca Pallavicini-Centurioni), as well as to Count Rosenberg-Orsini* in Florence. In his turn, Pallavicini-Centurioni (1697–1773) gave a concert on 26 March to present Mozart to the Bolognese nobility, and wrote letters of introduction to several important persons in Rome, among them his distant relative Cardinal Count Lazzaro Opizio Pallavicini (1719–85), who headed the State Secretariat at the Vatican. It was probably through the latter's influence that Mozart was awarded the Cross of the Golden Spur in June 1770 and granted an audience with Pope Clement XIV in July. Thus Firmian's patronage during Mozart's first journey to Italy had most important consequences, both directly and indirectly. He was to give Mozart further generous support on later occasions.

(Burney[3], *Mozart in Italia*)

Fischer, (Johann Ignaz) Ludwig (b. Mainz, 18 or 19 August 1745; d. Berlin, 10 July 1825). German bass; the original Osmin (*Die Entführung**). He first attracted attention with his singing while still at Mainz, but it was at Mannheim, where he studied with Anton Raaff* and was subsequently appointed a court singer, that his professional career flourished. In 1778 he moved with the court to Munich (*see* KARL THEODOR). There, on 6 October 1779, he married the actress and soprano Barbara Strasser. By 1780, when he and his wife were engaged in Vienna, he was considered the finest bass in Germany. There was universal praise for his interpretative skills and great admiration for the exceptional beauty of his voice which encompassed two-and-a-half octaves. According to the composer Johann Friedrich Reichardt (1752–1814), who was Kapellmeister for the Royal Berlin Opera under Frederick the Great and his successor Frederick William II* from 1775 to 1794 and, consequently, responsible for Fischer's eventual engagement in Berlin, his voice displayed 'the depth of a cello and the natural height of a tenor'. Another writer (in the Viennese journal *Meine Empfindungen im Theater*) stated that it remained perfectly pure over its entire range, down to the very lowest notes.

During his three highly successful years in Vienna (1780–83), he sang some twenty different roles, including Don Gonzales in Beecke*'s *Claudine von Villa Bella* (in which he made his début on 13 June 1780), Herr von Bär in Salieri*'s Singspiel *Der Rauchfangkehrer* (30 April 1781), Thoas in Gluck*'s *Iphigenie in Tauris* (in the German version, based on J. B. von Alxinger's text, which was presented on 23 October 1781), and the High Priest in Gluck's *Alceste*, in Italian (3 December 1781). Mozart appreciated Fischer's 'excellent bass voice' and his high standing with the public so greatly that, when composing *Die Entführung*, he added the big first-act aria 'Solche hergelauf'ne Laffen' to the original score, because, as he explained to his father on 26 September 1781, 'one must make good use of such a man, especially as he is such a great favourite with audiences here'; he added that the new aria would provide an opportunity for Fischer's 'beautiful low notes' to glow. A similar effect must have been achieved by Osmin's third-act aria 'O! wie will ich triumphieren', where, at one point, the low D is held over no fewer than eight bars. Mozart even contemplated making a German version of *Idomeneo** in which the tenor title role would be transposed into the bass register for Fischer. When the latter decided in 1783, apparently because of differences with Rosenberg-Orsini*, to leave Vienna (in which connection Mozart gave him a letter of introduction to Legros* in Paris), Mozart castigated the authorities, in a letter to his father on 5 February 1783, for their foolishness in permitting the departure of 'a man who will never be replaced'.

Fischer later sang with great success in Italy, Prague and various German cities. On 21 March 1787 he gave a concert at the Kärntnertor-Theater in Vienna, at which he sang the aria *Non so d'onde viene* K512, a bass version arranged for the occasion by Mozart of the soprano aria K294 which he had originally written for Aloisia Weber* (*see also* BACH). It was perhaps also for him that Mozart composed the scena *Così dunque tradisci . . . Aspri rimorsi atroci* K432/421a. In 1789 Fischer accepted a permanent appointment in Berlin, but continued to make guest appearances elsewhere. Thus he sang in London in 1794 and 1798, and in the latter year once more returned to Vienna. There, on 24 October, he again took the part of Osmin in a performance of *Die Entführung* at the Freihaus-Theater; at concerts at the same theatre on 27 October and 5 November he sang, among other arias, 'In diesen heil'gen Hallen' from *Die Zauberflöte**. In 1812, at the Haymarket Theatre in London, he appeared as the Count in *Le nozze di Figaro**.

Barbara Fischer, *née* Strasser (1758–after 1825) was herself an accomplished singer, although her voice, at the time of her Viennese engagement (1780–83), was judged by F. L. Schröder and by Gebler* to be already on the decline. Among her roles at the Burgtheater were Frau von Bieder in Grétry's *Die abgeredete Zauberei* [*La fausse magie*] (12 April 1780), Frau von Habicht in Salieri's *Der Rauchfangkehrer* (30 April 1781), Ismene in Gluck's *Alceste* (3 December 1781), and Donna Menzia de Rosalva in Maximilian Ulbrich's *Der blaue Schmetterling, oder Sieg der Natur über die Schwärmerei* (2 April 1782). The Fischers' son Joseph (1780–1862) and daughters Josepha (b. 1782) and Wilhelmine (b. 1785) also had successful careers as singers. (Deutsch[1], Gebler, Meyer, Michtner, Würtz[3])

Fränzl, Ignaz (Franz Joseph) (baptized Mannheim, 4 June 1736; d. Mannheim, 3 September 1811). German violinist and composer. He joined the Mannheim orchestra in 1747 and became its Konzertmeister in 1774. In 1768 he performed with great success at the Concert Spirituel in Paris. After hearing Fränzl play a concerto at Mannheim, Mozart (who had already met him at Schwetzingen in 1763) wrote to his father on 22 November 1777: 'I like his playing very much. As you know, I am not a great lover of difficulties. He plays difficult pieces, but one is not aware of their difficulty and one thinks that one could play them just as he does. That is true mastery. He has, moreover, a beautiful, round tone. He does not miss a note, one hears everything . . . He also possesses a fine staccato, which he plays with a single bowing, both up and down; and I have never heard a double trill such as he executes. In short, he may not be a wizard, but he is a very sound violinist.' In 1778, when part of the orchestra moved to Munich (*see* KARL THEODOR), Fränzl remained in Mannheim. Mozart met him there again in November 1778, on his return from Paris, and began writing the violin concerto KAnh.56/315*f* for him, which he did not, however, complete. In 1805 Fränzl became director of music at Mannheim. His own compositions included symphonies, violin concertos, and string quartets; most were published in Paris and London.

Ignaz Fränzl married Antonia Sibilla de La Motte (whose sister Marie Elisabeth was the wife of Christian Cannabich*) in 1765. Their son Ferdinand Fränzl (1767–1833) became a violinist with the Mannheim orchestra in 1782. In February 1786 Leopold Mozart met both father and son in Munich and on 2 March heard them play a concerto each at a concert there. The following month they both performed at a concert of the Tonkünstler-Societät in Vienna. In 1789 or 1790 Ferdinand Fränzl was appointed Konzertmeister of the Munich court orchestra, in 1792 Konzertmeister in Frankfurt am Main, and in 1806 he became director of music in Munich. He composed chamber music, songs and several works for the stage, including *Die Luftbälle, oder Der Liebhaber à la Montgolfier, Carlo Fioras, oder Der Stumme in der Sierra Morena* and *Hadrian Barbarossa*. (Komma[2], Würtz[1,4])

Frederick William II, King of Prussia (b. Berlin, 25 September 1744; d. Potsdam, 16 November 1797). Son of Prince Augustus William, second son of King Frederick William I (1688–1740), and of Louise Amalie of Brunswick. He succeeded his uncle Frederick the Great upon the latter's death on 17 August 1786. He was twice married: in 1765 to Elisabeth of Brunswick (d. 1841), from whom he was divorced in 1769; and, in 1769, to Frederika Louisa of Hesse-Darmstadt (1751–1805).

On 26 May 1789 Mozart played before Frederick William II and his consort at the royal palace in Berlin. It was on this occasion (or possibly already during Mozart's stay at Potsdam a few weeks earlier) that the king, who was an accomplished cellist, commissioned six string quartets, as well as six piano sonatas for his daughter Frederika (1767–1820). However, Mozart was to compose only three 'Prussian' quartets (K575, 589, 590 – see KOZELUCH), and only one of the sonatas (K576).

Freysinger. Family which Mozart came to know in Munich in 1777. The father, Franziskus Erasmus Freysinger, a court councillor, had attended St Salvator School at Augsburg together with Leopold Mozart. His two daughters, Juliana and Josepha, played the piano. Wolfgang undertook to write a sonata for Josepha; this may have been K311/284c which he is believed to have composed at Mannheim that autumn. In a letter from there on 3 December 1777 he informed his cousin Maria Anna Thekla Mozart* (who was living in Augsburg) that the promised sonata was not yet ready, but that he intended to write it soon; he would then send it to her with a covering note, for transmission to Munich. It is not known whether, in fact, he ever sent her this or any other sonata.

Freystädtler, Franz Jacob (b. Salzburg, 13 September 1761; d. Vienna, 1 December 1841). Composer, organist and pianist; pupil of Mozart. Son of Jacob Freystädtler, choirmaster at St Sebastian's Church in Salzburg. He was himself organist at St Peter's in that city from 1778 to 1784, subsequently spent two years in Munich and, in May 1786, moved to Vienna. There he received instruction from Mozart, reportedly in musical theory. Freystädtler composed various pieces for the piano (sonatas, sets of variations), chamber music and some songs. He became a successful music teacher, but eventually died in extreme poverty.

During their journey to Prague in January 1787 Mozart, Constanze* and Franz de Paula Hofer* coined nicknames for themselves and others (according to Mozart's letter to Gottfried von Jacquin* of 15 January). For Freystädtler they invented the sobriquet 'Gaulimauli' which would appear to be derived from the words 'Gaul' (= horse) and 'Maul' (= mouth), but is doubtless as meaningless as the names 'Punkitititi' and 'SchablaPumfa' chosen for Mozart and Constanze. Later that year Mozart wrote a canon to the text 'Lieber Freistädtler, lieber Gaulimauli' (K232/509a). This canon was very likely intended as incidental music for *Der Salzburger Lump in Wien*, a farce Mozart was planning to write in the summer of 1787 and of which an outline, in his hand, has survived. The model for the 'Lump' [= scoundrel] was clearly Freystädtler.
(Hamann¹, Orel¹)

Friedrich Wilhelm II: *see* FREDERICK WILLIAM II.

Gabrieli [Gabrielli], **(Francesca) Adriana** [known as 'Ferraresi (Ferrarese) del Bene'] (b. Ferrara *c.*1755; d. ?Venice, after 1799). Italian soprano; the original Fiordiligi (*Così fan tutte**). Charles Burney*, after hearing her in 1770 at the Conservatorio dei Mendicati in Venice where she was studying with Antonio Sacchini, considered that she 'sung very well, and had a very extraordinary compass of voice, as she was able to reach the highest E of our harpsichords, upon which she could dwell a considerable time, in a fair, natural voice'. Eventually she ran away from the Conservatorio and soon afterwards married Luigi del Bene, the son of the papal ambassador in Venice. She did not, however, live with him for very long.

In 1785 and 1786 she sang at the King's Theatre, London, with only mixed success, perhaps due in part to her frequent indisposition. About her London début in the pasticcio *Demetrio* on 8 January 1785 – not 21 January, as stated by W. T. Parke in his *Musical Memoirs* and repeated in *New Grove* – Parke wrote that she 'had a sweet voice, and sang with taste, but was not calculated to shine as a *prima donna*', adding, however, that she was 'much applauded'. He judged her 'not equal to the part of Euridice' at the performance of Gluck*'s *Orfeo ed Euridice* on 11 May 1785. On 10 July 1787 she appeared at the Scala, Milan, as Cimene at the première of Angelo Tarchi's *Il conte di Saldagna*; in 1788 she sang at the Teatro Communale at Trieste. From there she went to Vienna where she made a splendid début, on 13 October 1788, as Diana in Martín y Soler*'s *L'arbore di Diana*, establishing herself at one stroke as one of the most brilliant members of the Italian company. Zinzendorf* noted that she had sung 'enchantingly'. And the *Rapport von Wien* was equally enthusiastic about her voice: 'She has an unbelievable top and a striking lower register, and connoisseurs of music declare that no such voice has been heard in Vienna within living memory. It is only regrettable that the acting of this outstanding artist should not be up to her singing.'

During her engagement in Vienna Gabrieli won plaudits both in *buffa* and in dramatic coloratura roles. She triumphed as 'Donna Zuccherina, virtuosa di musica' in the pasticcio *L'ape musicale* (27 February 1789; Zinzendorf: 'La Ferrarese sang marvellously'), as Eurilla in Salieri*'s *La cifra* (11 December 1789), as Eurilla in Pietro Alessandro Guglielmi's *La pastorella nobile* (24 May 1790), and as Racchelina in Paisiello*'s *La molinara* (13 November 1790). For the revival of *Le nozze di Figaro** on 29 August 1789, at which she sang Susanna, Mozart specially wrote for her the aria 'Un moto di gioia mi sento' K579 and the rondo 'Al desio di chi t'adora' K577, to replace Susanna's original second and fourth act arias 'Venite inginocchiatevi' and 'Deh vieni non tardar'. The music which Mozart composed for Fiordiligi in *Così fan tutte* bears witness to Gabrieli's remarkable technique and range. Yet Mozart was not one of her greatest admirers. After attending a performance at the Dresden opera he reported to Constanze* on 16 April 1789: 'Allegradi [Maddalena Allegrante], the *prima donna*, is much better than La Ferrarese, which, admittedly, is not saying much'. And regarding 'Un moto di gioia', he wrote (on ?19 August 1789) that it ought to be a success, 'provided she is able to sing it in an unaffected manner, which, however, I greatly doubt'.

Her impetuous nature antagonized several members of the Italian company who resented, moreover, the preference shown her by her lover Da Ponte*. The latter wrote about her in his memoirs: 'She had indeed great merit. Her voice was delightful, and her manner of singing fresh and wonderfully moving. She did not have a particularly graceful figure and was not a very good actress; but with her two very beautiful eyes and her enchanting mouth, there were few operas in which she did not greatly please . . . Yet this lady, quite apart from arousing the envy of the other singers . . . possessed a somewhat violent character which tended to provoke malevolence rather than inspire friendship.' Eventually their enemies succeeded in having both her and Da Ponte dismissed by the new emperor, Leopold II*. They left for Trieste in June 1791.

Her career continued for several more years. In July 1797 she sang in the first Trieste performance of *Così fan tutte*.

(Burney[4], Da Ponte, *London Stage*, Michtner, Parke)

Galitsin [Galitzin], **Dmitry Michailovich**, Prince (b. Åbo [Turku], 15 May 1720 [?1721]; d. Vienna, 30 September 1793). Russian ambassador in Paris, subsequently from 12 January 1762 until 25 May 1792 Russian ambassador and minister plenipotentiary in Vienna; a notable music-lover. Son of Prince Michail Michailovich Galitsin (d. 1730), governor-general of Finland and later president of the War College in Moscow.

In March 1768 Mozart and Nannerl* performed at Prince Galitsin's house. On 16 March 1781, the day of Mozart's arrival in Vienna, Galitsin was among 'twenty persons of the highest nobility' who attended a concert given by Archbishop Colloredo* at the House of the Teutonic Order (according to Mozart's letter to his father the next day). On 17 March Mozart, with other musicians in the archbishop's service, performed at Galitsin's. The latter was to prove a generous patron to Mozart. 'I am engaged for all his concerts,' Mozart wrote to his father on 21 December 1782. 'I am always fetched in his coach and brought back in it, and am treated most magnificently at his house.' In his letter of 3 March 1784 Mozart mentioned that he was playing at Galitsin's on five Thursdays from 26 February to 25 March. Galitsin was also a subscriber to the Trattnerhof concerts (*see* TRATTNER) that year.

(Landon[3], Schuler[13])

Gamerra, Giovanni de (b. Leghorn [Livorno], 1743; d. Vicenza, 29 August 1803). Italian poet, librettist and dramatist (known particularly for his melodramas). He took minor orders, then studied law at Pisa, and eventually opted for a military career in the Austrian army (1765–70). He was subsequently appointed poet at the Teatro Regio Ducal, Milan (1770–74), and court poet in Vienna (1774–6). In the latter capacity, he wrote three librettos for Salieri*: *La calamità de' cuori* (produced on 31 October 1774), *La finta scema* (9 September 1775), and *Daliso e Delmita* (29 July 1776). He held the position of court poet in Vienna again from 1793 to 1802, during which period four more of his librettos were set by Salieri, and two (*Giulietta e Pierotto* and *L'amor marinaro*) by Joseph Weigl*.

In Milan in 1772, Gamerra wrote the libretto for Mozart's *Lucio Silla**, which Mozart then probably submitted for comments to Metastasio*. Gamerra also furnished the libretto for the second opera given at the Teatro Regio Ducal during the same carnival season, Paisiello*'s *Sismano nel Mogol*, the première of which Mozart attended on 30 January 1773. Eight years later Mozart wrote new music to a text taken from this latter libretto (*A questo seno deh vieni . . . Or che il cielo a me ti rende* K374), which was sung by the castrato Ceccarelli* at a concert in Vienna on 8 April 1781. After Mozart's death, Gamerra translated the text of *Die Zauberflöte** into Italian, and this version was performed in Prague in 1794.

(*ES*, Zechmeister)

Garibaldi [Caribaldi], **Gioacchino** (b. Rome, 1743; d. Rome, after 1792). Italian tenor who would have taken the part of Don Polidoro at the première of *La finta semplice** which Leopold Mozart tried to arrange in Vienna in 1768. After performing at various Italian opera houses, he was engaged at the Burgtheater in 1767 and took the part of Giannino at the première of Florian Leopold Gassmann's *L'amore artigiano* on 26 April of that year. He does not appear to have stayed in Vienna much more than three years.

Sonnenfels was delighted with Garibaldi's beautiful tenor voice, but less so with his acting, in which he accused him of rather clumsily seeking to ape Francesco Caratoli*. Burney*, after hearing him in the pasticcio *La lavandara astuta* in Milan in July 1770, judged him to have sung very well: 'He has a pleasing voice, and much taste and expression; was encored, *alla Italiana*, two or three times.'

Garibaldi continued to sing in Italy until at least 1792, but he achieved some of his greatest successes in Paris where, on 11 June 1778, he was much acclaimed for his interpretation of the part of Belfiore in Niccolò Piccinni's *Le finte gemelle*. Grimm*, in his *Correspondance littéraire*, extolled the singer's 'bewitching' voice ['la voix enchanteresse de Caribaldi']. Piccinni's opera was being presented in a double bill with Noverre*'s ballet *Les petits riens*, featuring music by Mozart (KAnh.10/299b). (Burney[4], Sonnenfels, Zechmeister)

Gebler, Tobias Philipp, Baron (b. Zeulenroda, 2 November 1726; d. Vienna, 9 October 1786). Senior Austrian government official whose appointments included that of vice-chancellor at the Austro-Bohemian chancellery; he was created a baron in 1768. Gebler played a leading role in the promotion of the sciences, in the reorganization of the police and the judiciary, and in the development of the educational system. He was also mainly responsible for the banning, in 1770, of improvised theatrical farces, which were frequently of low moral standard. He is furthermore believed to have been the author of the memorandum *Vorschlag zur Verbesserung der National-Schaubühne und des Theaters überhaupt*, probably written in 1775, which proposed that Joseph II* should assume direct control over the national theatre; the emperor did so that same year. Many of Gebler's ideas on different aspects of contemporary drama and opera (he was an early champion of German opera) found expression in the letters which he wrote between 1771 and 1786 to the Berlin bookseller and writer Christoph Friedrich Nicolai (1733–1811). The correspondence contains interesting judgments on various contemporary singers and actors; it was published in 1888.

Gebler was himself a successful playwright. However, of the numerous plays written by him and produced in Vienna during his lifetime, only *Thamos, König in Ägypten* is still generally known, at any rate by its title, and that only because of Mozart's music (K345/336a). The play, which is loosely based on the novel *Sethos* (Paris, 1731) by the Abbé Jean Terrasson (1670–1750), presents certain masonic ideals, especially in the portrayal of the young Thamos and the elderly King Sethos. It was published in Prague and Dresden in 1773, and in Vienna in 1774. The first performance was given by Karl Wahr's company at Pressburg [Bratislava] on 11 December 1773.

That same year Mozart composed choruses and incidental music for this 'heroic drama' by Gebler, who was apparently dissatisfied with the music previously provided by Johann Tobias Sattler (d. 19 December 1774). The play was presented at the Kärntnertor-Theater, Vienna, on 4 April 1774, with Mozart's choruses and probably also with his incidental music (the latter was revised by Mozart in 1776–7). In 1779–80 he reworked the choruses and added a final one, for which the text is believed to have been written by Johann Andreas Schachtner*. Mozart may have prepared this new version for Johann Böhm*'s theatrical company which played in Salzburg in April and May 1779 and again from September 1779 to March 1780. Later Böhm used Mozart's *Thamos* music in performances of Karl Martin Plümicke's tragedy *Lanassa* (based on Antoine Lemierre's *La veuve du Malabar*).

Gebler became himself a prominent freemason. In 1784 he joined the 'Zur gekrönten Hoffnung' Lodge and also became Grand Master of the 'Zum neuen Bunde' District Lodge. In 1786 he was elected Master of the newly formed 'Zur neugekrönten Hoffnung'* Lodge.

(Gebler/Nicolai, Grossegger, *NMA* II/6/1, Zechmeister)

Gemmingen-Hornberg, Otto Heinrich, Baron (b. Heilbronn, 5 [?15] November 1755; d. Heidelberg, 15 March 1836). Official at the palatine court (chamberlain, councillor) and diplomat; playwright. In Mannheim, where he lived until 1782, he published *Mannheimer Dramaturgien*, a journal devoted to the contemporary theatre. He befriended Mozart during his stay in Mannheim in 1777–8 and, and on his departure for Paris, provided him with a letter of introduction to the palatine ambassador Count Karl Heinrich Joseph Sickingen*, who received him on several occasions. In November 1778, at Mannheim, Mozart began the composition of a 'duodrama' based on Gemmingen-Hornberg's melodrama *Semiramis* (*see* SEMIRAMIS).

Gemmingen-Hornberg is known to have resided in Vienna from 1782 to 1786, but he is likely to have visited the city already earlier, for he was apparently responsible for the formation of the 'Zur Beständigkeit' Masonic Lodge which opened its doors on 18 August 1779. While in Vienna, he founded several further periodicals: *Der Weltmann* (1782), *Magazin für Wissenschaft und Kunst* (1784), and *Wiener Ephemeriden* (1786). In 1782 he joined the 'Zur gekrönten Hoffnung' Lodge, and in 1783 he became a founding member and Master of the 'Zur Wohltätigkeit'* Lodge, to which Mozart was admitted on 14 December 1784. Indeed, it may well have been Gemmingen-Hornberg who suggested to Mozart that he should become a mason. In 1786 he, like Mozart, became a member of the new 'Zur neugekrönten Hoffnung'* Lodge. He returned to Vienna in 1797 as ambassador of the Margravate of Baden, and remained in this post until 1801.

As a playwright, Gemmingen-Hornberg is best known for his moralizing domestic drama *Der deutsche Hausvater* (1780), based on Diderot's *Le père de famille*.
(*Brockhaus*, Kreutz, Schuler[11])

Gerl, Barbara, *née* Reisinger (b. Vienna or Pressburg [Bratislava], 1770; d. Mannheim, 25 May 1806). Soprano, actress and dancer; the original Papagena (*Die Zauberflöte**). By her early teens, she was touring with Georg Wilhelm's theatrical company in Austria and Moravia, playing children's roles and singing in operettas. In 1789 she joined Schikaneder*'s company in Regensburg, making her début as Kalliste in a German version of Pietro Alessandro Guglielmi's *La sposa fedele*. In the spring of that same year she, like Benedikt Schack* and her future husband Franz

Gerl, Franz Xaver

Xaver Gerl* (whom she would marry on 2 September 1789), joined Schikaneder's new company in Vienna, with which she appeared until 1793 or 1794. She sang Papagena at least until 29 September 1792. Mozart composed – or, more probably, simply orchestrated – the duet 'Nun, liebes Weibchen, ziehst mit mir' K625/592a which she and Schikaneder performed in the latter's Singspiel *Der Stein der Weisen, oder Die Zauberinsel* (music by Schack and F. X. Gerl). As for her personal relations with Mozart, no evidence has been discovered to substantiate the once current story of his infatuation with her. After leaving Vienna, she was under contract at theatres in Brünn [Brno] and Mannheim (*see* GERL, FRANZ XAVER).
(Orel[4,5])

Gerl, Franz Xaver (b. Andorf, Upper Austria, 30 November 1764; d. Mannheim, 9 March 1827). Austrian composer, actor and bass; the original Sarastro (*Die Zauberflöte**). By 1777 he was a chorister in Salzburg, where Leopold Mozart was almost certainly among his teachers. From 1782 to 1784 he studied logic and physics at Salzburg University. In 1785 he joined Ludwig Schmidt's theatrical company at Erlangen as singer and actor. There, on 20 May 1786, he sang Osmin in *Die Entführung**, later one of his most famous roles. He was then engaged by G. F. W. Grossmann, with whose troupe he performed in Cologne, Düsseldorf and Bonn as principal bass 'in comic roles in Singspiels and comedies'. By 1787 he had joined Schikaneder*'s company at Regensburg, making his début as the Count in a German version of Sarti*'s *Fra i due litiganti il terzo gode*; his other roles included 'servants in comedies and tragedies'.

Like his future wife Barbara Reisinger (*see* GERL, BARBARA), and Benedikt Schack*, he joined Schikaneder's new company in Vienna in the spring of 1789. During the next four years, he appeared at the Freihaus-Theater in more than thirty plays and operas. The latter included, in addition to *Die Zauberflöte* (he sang Sarastro at least until the eighty-third performance on 23 November 1792), the title roles in German versions of *Don Giovanni** (5 November 1792) and *Le nozze di Figaro** (28 December 1792). He furthermore composed the music, often in collaboration with Schack, for several plays and Singspiels presented by the company, starting with the opening production, Schikaneder's *Der dumme Gärtner aus dem Gebirge, oder Die zween Anton*, on 12 July 1789. Apart from the role of Sarastro, Mozart wrote for him the aria *Per questa bella mano* K612. Gerl was one of the persons – the others being Schack and Franz de Paula Hofer* – who joined Mozart in a sing-through of his uncompleted Requiem on the day before he died.

After leaving Vienna in 1793 or 1794, the Gerls were under contract at Brünn [Brno] from 1794 until 1801. In 1802 they were engaged at the court theatre in Mannheim, where Gerl performed until he retired on pension in 1826 (Barbara had died in 1806). On 12 April 1826 Gerl married his widowed sister-in-law Magdalena Dengler, *née* Reisinger (d. 1839).
(Orel[4,5])

Gieseke [Giesecke], **Karl Ludwig** [real name: Johann Georg Metzler] (b. Augsburg, 6 April 1761; d. Dublin, 5 March 1833). Actor and librettist; scientist. After studying law at Göttingen University, he embarked in 1783 on an acting career. He performed with several troupes in Germany and Austria before being engaged at the Freihaus-Theater in Vienna in early 1789. He was kept on by Schikaneder* and remained with the latter's company until 1800, when he set up as a dealer in minerals. In 1805 he worked as a councillor in the department of mines in Denmark. Later he undertook a research trip to Greenland, and in 1814 was appointed Professor of Mineralogy in Dublin. He became a member of the Royal Irish Academy in 1816, and later its vice-president. Having been ennobled by King Frederick VI of Denmark, he called himself Sir Charles Gieseke. Henry Raeburn painted his portrait in 1817.

In addition to his stage performances, mainly in minor roles (he took the part of First Slave at the première of *Die Zauberflöte**), he wrote, adapted or translated some twenty Singspiel librettos for Schikaneder's company. Little credence is, however, given nowadays to earlier suppositions that he made a significant contribution to the text of *Die Zauberflöte*. On the other hand, he is known to have prepared the German versions of *Le nozze di Figaro** and *Così fan tutte** which were produced at the Freihaus-Theater on 28 December 1792 and 14 August 1794 respectively.

In 1790 he joined the 'Zur neugekrönten Hoffnung'* Lodge, to which Mozart also belonged.

(Blümml, Deutsch[3])

Gilowsky von Urazowa. Salzburg family on intimate terms with the Mozarts, whose correspondence contains frequent references to the following persons: court surgeon Johann Wenzel Andreas Gilowsky (1716–99); his eldest daughter Maria Anna Katharina ['Katherl'] (1750–1802) who was Nannerl*'s close friend; and his only son Franz Xaver Wenzel (1757–1816), also a surgeon, who was Mozart's witness at his wedding to Constanze*, and who, in 1787, married the only daughter of the wealthy Salzburg surgeon Joseph Günther. When Mozart died, he owed some 600 gulden to Franz Xaver Wenzel.

The latter's cousin Johann Joseph Anton Ernst Gilowsky (1739–89), a high official at the Salzburg court, arranged the settlement of Leopold Mozart's estate between Wolfgang and Nannerl in 1787. In 1784 he had become Master of the Salzburg 'Zur Fürsicht' Lodge. He died by his own hand.

(Schuler[5])

Girelli (-Aquilar), Antonia Maria (fl. 1752–72). Italian soprano; the original Silvia (*Ascanio in Alba**). She appeared at the Teatro San Samuele, Venice, as a dancer in 1752, and as a singer by 1759. In 1760–61 she performed in Prague; on 14 May 1763 she assumed the title role at the première of Gluck*'s *Il trionfo di Clelia* at Bologna, on 24 August 1769 she sang in the same composer's *Le feste d'Apollo* at Parma, and in early 1771 she appeared in Ignazio Platania's *Berenice* at Turin.

The register of the Teatro Regio Ducal, Milan, described her in October 1771 as '*virtuosa di camera* to His Royal Highness the Duke of Parma and Piacenza' [i.e. Ferdinand (1751–1802), who had succeeded his father Philip as Duke in 1765]. At the third performance of *Ascanio in Alba* on 24 October, she had to repeat one of her arias (according to Mozart's letter to Nannerl* of 26 October), so her rendition of it must have been more than just competent. Yet when, barely a year later (14 November 1772), she made her London début in the pasticcio *Sofonisba*, Charles Burney* was far from impressed: 'Her style of singing was good, but her voice was in decay, and her intonation frequently false . . . However, it was easy to imagine from what remained, that she had been better.' During that London season she also sang in Antonio Sacchini's *Il Cid* and *Tamerlano* and in Tommaso Giordani's *Artaserse*. Her husband, a Spaniard called Aquilar (or Aguilar), was an accomplished oboist. (Burney[2], Croll[4], *London Stage*)

Gluck, Christoph Willibald (b. Erasbach, Upper Palatinate, 2 July 1714; d. Vienna, 15 November 1787). German composer. It is extremely doubtful that the fifty-four-year-old Gluck, highly regarded in Vienna and enjoying an international reputation on the strength of his numerous operas, intrigued to prevent the performance of the twelve-year-old Wolfgang's *La finta semplice** in 1768, as Leopold Mozart accused him of doing in his letter to Hagenauer* of 30 July 1768: 'All the composers, Gluck foremost among them, have made every effort to undermine progress with the opera.' Leopold was still suspicious of Gluck ten years later when, on 9 February 1778, he cautioned Wolfgang against having any more contact than was absolutely necessary with either Gluck or Niccolò Piccinni while in Paris. (Mozart did, in fact, meet Piccinni in Paris, but Gluck was away from early February until November 1778, by which time Mozart had left.) And Leopold surely overestimated the threat which his son then posed to these two well-established composers when he wrote on 13 August 1778, regarding Wolfgang's prospects of obtaining a commission for an opera in Paris: 'Piccinni and Gluck will do everything to prevent it.'

Quite to the contrary, Gluck was to show himself generously appreciative of Mozart's later success. 'My opera [*Die Entführung**] was given again yesterday, at Gluck's request,' Mozart informed his father on 7 August 1782. 'Gluck paid me many compliments. I shall dine at his house tomorrow.' And on 12 March 1783, following a concert at the Burgtheater the previous day at which Aloisia Lange* had sung Mozart's aria *Non so d'onde viene* K294 (*see* BACH), and he himself had played his Piano Concerto K175 and conducted the 'Paris' Symphony K297/300a, he wrote, with evident pleasure: 'Gluck had the box next to the Langes, where my wife* was sitting. He was lavish in his praise for the symphony and the aria, and invited all four of us to dine with him on Sunday.' Mozart's admiration for Gluck's music may be deduced from the statement in his letter of 24 October 1781 that he had attended nearly all the rehearsals of *Iphigenie in Tauris* (in the German version by J. B. von Alxinger) which had had its première the previous evening.

Mozart set two librettos by Metastasio* which Gluck, among other composers, had previously used: *Il re pastore** (Mozart in 1775, Gluck in 1756) and *La clemenza di Tito** (Mozart in 1791, Gluck in 1752).

Goethe, Johann Wolfgang von (b. Frankfurt am Main, 28 August 1749; d. Weimar, 22 March 1832). German poet. On 25 August 1763 he attended a concert given by Wolfgang and Nannerl* in Frankfurt am Main. Almost seventy years later, on 3 February 1830, he told J. P. Eckermann that he still remembered very clearly 'the little fellow with his wig and his sword'.

Goethe was a great admirer of the operas of Mozart, and compared him to Raphael and Shakespeare. During the period 1791–1817 when Goethe was its director, 280 performances of Mozart's operas were given at the Weimar theatre:

eighty-two of *Die Zauberflöte**, sixty-eight of *Don Giovanni**, forty-nine of *Die Entführung**, thirty-three of *Così fan tutte**, twenty-eight of *La clemenza di Tito**, and twenty of *Le nozze di Figaro**. When Goethe's Singspiel *Theatralische Aberteuer* – his text was a translation of G. M. Diodati's libretto for Domenico Cimarosa's opera *L'impresario in angustie* which Goethe had heard in Rome in 1787 – was produced at Weimar on 24 October 1791, he did not use the original score, but took the music from Mozart's *Der Schauspieldirektor**. Goethe even worked on a sequel to *Die Zauberflöte*, and tried to interest the composer Paul Wranitzky (1756–1808) in the project; but the text remained in fragmentary form. It was no doubt in recognition of Goethe's well-known reverence for Mozart's music that Ignaz E. F. K. Arnold dedicated his book *Mozart's Geist. Seine kurze Biographie und ästhetische Darstellung* ... (Erfurt, 1803), jointly to August Eberhard Müller (a pianist and composer who assisted in the posthumous publication of Mozart's collected works by Breitkopf & Härtel*) and to Goethe.

Mozart set only one of Goethe's poems: *Das Veilchen* K476. This, the most famous of Mozart's songs, was composed in 1785, its text being taken from another of Goethe's Singspiel librettos, *Erwin und Elmire*.

(Michtner, Orel², Weiss)

Goldhann [Goldhahn], **Joseph Odilo** [Odilio]. Wealthy Viennese iron-merchant who appears to have been involved in Mozart's financial affairs in 1791, if not before; he may well have lent Mozart money. Mozart's earliest extant reference to him, in a letter to Anton Stoll* in May 1791, indicates that Mozart's acquaintance with him dated at least from the previous year.

H. C. Robbins Landon and M. Boyd definitely identify Goldhann as the person referred to by Mozart as 'N.N.' in his letter to Constanze* of 12 June 1791, and with whom he said he was anxious to conclude a transaction (no doubt of a financial nature); J. H. Eibl merely states that Goldhann may be 'N.N.'. (The letters, which stand for 'nomen nescio', are used to denote a person whom one cannot or does not wish to name.)

Goldhann played a role in Mozart's affairs even after the latter's death, for he signed, as an 'invited witness', the list of Mozart's personal effects on 7 December 1791. Nissen* states, moreover, in his biography of Mozart, that Constanze was so distraught over Mozart's death that, for her own safety, she was taken first to the house of a 'Herr Bauernfeind' (probably Joseph von Bauernfeld, a financial associate of Emanuel Schikaneder*) and then to Goldhann's; the source of this information was no doubt Constanze herself.

In 1868 Gregor Wöber, a retired archivist, recalled in a letter to an unknown correspondent that his mother-in-law, Goldhann's daughter Nanette (d. 1862), 'frequently told me that Mozart came often to her parents' house, that she and he often played music for four hands together, and that, after his death, his widow received many kindnesses from her family'.

(Landon², Eibl in *Mozart: Briefe*, Boyd in *Mozart Compendium*; Wöber's letter is reproduced in Eibl's notes to *Anhang* A.IV in *Mozart: Briefe*)

Gossec, François Joseph (b. Vergnies, Hainaut, 17 January 1734; d. Passy, Paris, 16 February 1829). Flemish composer. In 1751 he moved to Paris where he was engaged by the financier Alexandre-Jean-Joseph Le Riche de La Pouplinière (1692–1762) as leader of his private orchestra; in 1762 he was put in charge of the private theatre of Prince Louis Joseph de Condé (1736–1818) at Chantilly. In 1769 he founded the Concert des Amateurs. After serving on the board of the Opéra (1782–4) and as director of the Ecole Royale de Chant (established in 1784), he was from 1795 until 1816 inspector of teaching and professor of composition at the Conservatoire. He wrote numerous symphonies, much chamber music, and several serious and comic operas.

Mozart, who met Gossec soon after arriving in Paris in March 1778, wrote to his father on 5 April: 'Er ist mein sehr guter freünd, und sehr trockner [literally: dry] Mann.' This has been translated in Emily Anderson's *The Letters of Mozart and his Family* (3rd edition revised by S. Sadie and F. Smart, London, 1985) as 'He is a very good friend of mine and at the same time a very dull fellow.' While this is a possible rendering of the German, Mozart's remark may have been simply a non-judgmental pun on the second syllable of Gossec's name: 'sec' = 'dry'. He had certainly good reason to be well disposed towards Gossec, for the latter had just told Legros* that a chorus composed by Mozart for insertion in a *Miserere* by Holzbauer* (κAnh.1/297a) was 'charming and certain to produce a good effect' and that the words were 'very well arranged and most excellently set to music'.
(Brook et al., Wangermée)

Gottlieb, (Maria) Anna ['Nanette'] (b. Vienna, 29 April 1774; d. Vienna, 4 February 1856). Austrian soprano and actress; the original Barbarina (*Le nozze di Figaro**) and Pamina (*Die Zauberflöte**). Both her father, Johann Christoph Gottlieb (1737–98), and her mother, Anna Maria, *née* Theiner (1745–97), were members of the Burgtheater. She started her career at a very early age and was barely twelve years old when she created the role of Barbarina at the Burgtheater. On 7 November 1789 she made her début at the Freihaus-Theater as Prinzess Amande in the Singspiel *Oberon, König der Elfen* by Paul Wranitzky (1756–1808). Two years later she sang Pamina at the première of *Die Zauberflöte*. In 1792 she joined the Theater in der Leopoldstadt, a well-known suburban establishment specializing in Singspiels, comedies and farces. There she performed until 1828. She achieved one of her greatest successes in the very popular *Das Donauweibchen* by Ferdinand Kauer (1751–1831).

She made a dramatic appearance at the festivities in Salzburg in 1842 (*see* SCHWANTHALER; MOZART, FRANZ XAVER WOLFGANG). William Kuhe described the incident in *My Musical Recollections*: 'There entered a very tall, thin and eccentric-looking woman, who at once exclaimed, as though addressing an audience: "Ich bin die erste Pamina" (I am the first Pamina). Naturally we thought her demented, but investigation established the truth of her assertion. This lady . . . had ostensibly come from Vienna to join in our homage to Mozart; but as a matter of fact she seemed to think that she had at least an equal claim with him to be an object of universal veneration . . . she expected deputations to wait upon her, and other extreme marks of attention.'

Anna's sister Josepha Gottlieb [later: Doppler] (1767–1825) was a member of the Burgtheater from 1785 until 1814. Another sister, Charlotte, also went on the stage. Their brother Christian was a cellist.
(Komorzynski[1], Kuhe, Raeburn[6], Schuler[14])

Graf, Friedrich Hartmann (b. Rudolstadt, 23 August 1727; d. Augsburg, 19 August 1795). German composer and flautist. He wrote a great deal of instrumental music, including four flute concertos. His career as soloist and concert director took him to Hamburg and Augsburg, and, in 1783–4, London. In 1779 he became a member of the Royal Swedish Academy of Music; in 1789 Oxford University conferred a doctorate on him.

In October 1777 Mozart was introduced to him by Johann Andreas Stein* in Augsburg, where Graf had been musical director for protestant churches since 1772. Mozart thought him pompous and unintelligent: 'He puts all his words on stilts,' he told his father in his letter of 14 October 1777. 'And usually he opens his mouth before he knows what he wants to say – and sometimes it closes again without having done anything.' He found Graf's music equally uninspiring: 'He often marches into his modulations far too – clumsily.'

Friedrich Hartmann's brother Christian Ernst Graf [Graaf] (b. Rudolstadt, 30 June 1723; d. The Hague, 17 July 1804) was a violinist and Kapellmeister at the Hague court. Mozart met him there in 1765–6, and composed eight Variations for the piano on his song 'Laat ons juichen, batavieren' (K24). Another brother, Friedrich Leopold Graf, was leader of the orchestra of the Zurich Musical Society, which may have performed at Wolfgang's and Nannerl*'s concerts in that city in October 1766.

(Layer³, Scharnagl/Haase)

Grimm, Friedrich Melchior, Baron (b. Regensburg, 26 December 1723; d. Gotha, 19 December 1807). Author and critic; diplomat. From 1749 he resided in Paris, where he frequented the *Encyclopédistes*. In 1753 he began the *Correspondance littéraire*, a chronicle of Parisian cultural events, which was to extend to the year 1773; it was circulated in manuscript to various European sovereigns and princes, including Catherine the Great, the Queen of Sweden, and the King of Poland. From 1775 to 1792 he served as envoy of the Duchy of Saxe-Gotha-Altenburg in Paris.

He prove an invaluable friend to the Mozarts during their stay in Paris in 1763–4, arranging Wolfgang's and Nannerl*'s appearance at court and organizing the two concerts which the children gave at Félix's theatre on 10 March and 9 April 1764. 'M. Grimm alone ... has done everything,' Leopold Mozart reported to Hagenauer* on 1 April. When Wolfgang published his op. I and op. II (two sets of violin sonatas, K6–7 and K8–9) in February 1764, it was Grimm who wrote the dedications to Louis XV's daughter Louise-Marie-Thérèse de Bourbon (Madame Victoire de France) and to the Comtesse de Tessé, which appeared over Wolfgang's name. In the *Correspondance littéraire*, on 1 December 1763, he lavishly praised Wolfgang's virtuosity as a pianist and improviser, as well as his supreme command of harmony and modulation, and marvelled at the genius of this 'extraordinary phenomenon'. When the Mozarts left Paris, he gave Nannerl a gold watch and Wolfgang a fruit knife set with gold and mother-of-pearl and fitted with one gold and one silver blade. On 15 July 1766, following the Mozarts' further, briefer visit to Paris, he wrote another highly eulogistic article in the *Correspondance* on both children, and particularly on Wolfgang: 'This marvellous child is now nine years old. He has hardly grown any taller; but he has made prodigious progress in music.' In yet another article, on 1 April 1772, he referred to Wolfgang as 'that charming and marvellous child'.

When the Mozarts decided, early in 1778, that Wolfgang should seek his fortune in Paris, they were delighted to learn that Grimm had recently returned there from his extensive travels. 'It is the only thing that comforts me, for we can assuredly rely on him, as he is a sincere and true friend to us,' Maria Anna Mozart* wrote to Leopold from Mannheim on 7 March. At first Grimm was as helpful as before, providing introductions to influential persons and inviting Wolfgang, after his mother's death, to stay in the Rue de la Chaussée d'Antin with his mistress Madame d'Epinay and himself. But Wolfgang became increasingly irritated by Grimm's firm belief in the superiority of Italian composers, and he found Grimm's attitude towards him less and less to his taste. 'M. Grimm may be able to help *children* [evidently a reference to their relationship in 1763–4] but not grown-up people . . .' he wrote to his father on 11 September, in a letter filled with complaints about his host. 'You must not imagine that he is the same as he was. If it were not for Mme d'Epinay, I would no longer be in this house.' Their final contacts were soured further by Grimm's insistence that Wolfgang set out on his return journey to Salzburg several days earlier than he himself wished. When Mozart proposed staying a few days at Count Sickingen*'s, Grimm was furious. In his letter of 26 October–2 November 1778 from Strasbourg, Mozart told his father that Grimm had threatened never to speak to him again should he leave his house before he left Paris, and that he had, unwillingly, complied with Grimm's wishes.

Guardasoni, Domenico (b. ?Modena, *c.*1731; d. Vienna, 13 or 14 June 1806). Italian tenor and impresario. In May 1764 he sang at the première of Antonio Boroni's *Sofonisba* at Venice; later that year he performed in Prague. In 1772 he was engaged in Vienna, and he appeared there as the Cavaliere di Ripafratta at the première of Salieri*'s *La locandiera* on 8 June 1773. He subsequently sang with Giuseppe Bustelli's company in Dresden, Leipzig and Prague, and with Joseph Felix von Kurz's troupe in Warsaw. From 1785 he was associated with Pasquale Bondini*'s company at the National Theatre in Prague as opera producer and impresario; he became first Bondini's co-director (1787) and later his successor.

Guardasoni supervised the première of *Don Giovanni** in October 1787. He presented the opera in Leipzig in 1788, and in 1789 he took the company to Warsaw where he remained until the spring of 1791, returning to Prague on 10 June. In July, while on a visit to Vienna, he commissioned Mozart to compose *La clemenza di Tito**, which was produced in Prague on 6 September of that year. Guardasoni's company also gave performances of *Le nozze di Figaro** and *Così fan tutte**. Its repertoire further included operas by Salieri, Stephen Storace (*see* STORACE, NANCY) and Niccolò Zingarelli, and *Rinaldo und Alcina* by Maria Theresia von Paradis*.
(*DEUMM*, Landon², Volek, Zechmeister)

Haffner. Salzburg family friendly with the Mozarts and frequently mentioned in their correspondence. Sigmund [Siegmund] Haffner (b. Imbach [Jenbach], Tyrol, 1699; d. Salzburg, 12 January 1772) was a prominent merchant, and mayor of Salzburg from 1768 to 1772. He married twice: in 1733 Anna Elenore Kaltenhauser (1712–44), and in 1745 Eleonora Mezger (1716–64). On the occasion of the ennoblement on 29 July 1782 of his son Sigmund [Siegmund] (1756–87) – who took the title 'von Imbachhausen' – Mozart composed the so-called 'Haffner' Symphony K385. (He later reworked the score for a concert at the Burgtheater, Vienna, on 23 March 1783.) For the wedding of the younger Sigmund's sister Maria Elisabeth (1753–81) to Franz Xaver Späth in 1776, Mozart had written the 'Haffner' Serenade K250/248*b*, which was first performed at the family's summer house in Loretogasse on 21 July 1776 (the villa burned down in 1818).

Hagenauer. Salzburg family friendly with the Mozarts. Johann Lorenz Hagenauer (b. 10 August 1712; d. 9 April 1792) was a prosperous merchant, and owner of the houses Nos 7 and 9 Getreidegasse, as well as of a house in the Nonntal. In 1738 he married Maria Theresia Schuster (d. 1800); they had eleven children. Late in 1747 the newly married Leopold Mozart rented the third-floor flat at No. 9 Getreidegasse; there Wolfgang was born on 27 January 1756. The house, first mentioned in documents in 1408, had been acquired by the Hagenauer family in 1703. A close friendship developed between the Hagenauers and the Mozarts which continued after the latters' move to the 'Tanzmeisterhaus' (*see* RAAB) in 1773. Hagenauer assisted Leopold Mozart in financial matters and granted him loans on several occasions. The almost seventy letters which Leopold addressed to Hagenauer between 1762 and 1768 contain a vast amount of invaluable information on Wolfgang's early travels.

As a child, Wolfgang appears to have been particularly fond of Hagenauer's fourth son, Kajetan Rupert (1746–1811); when told, while in London, that Kajetan had become a novice at St Peter's Abbey in Salzburg, he wept, fearing that he would never see Kajetan again (according to Leopold's letter to Hagenauer of 27 November 1764). When Kajetan was admitted to the priesthood (as 'Pater Dominicus'), Wolfgang wrote for him the so-called 'Dominicus' Mass K66, which was performed at St Peter's on 15 October 1769. In January 1786 Kajetan was elected abbot of that church.

Haibel, Sophie: *see* WEBER, SOPHIE.

Handel, George Frideric (b. Halle, 23 February 1685; d. London, 14 April 1759). German, later English, composer. Mozart came to know Handel's music at an early age. When he played before King George III and Queen Charlotte in the spring of 1764, the king, whose favourite composer Handel was, placed before him works by various contemporaries, including Handel (who had died in London just five years before Mozart's arrival). The eight-year-old Wolfgang played them all splendidly *prima vista* (as his father proudly informed Hagenauer* on 28 May 1764). He then improvised 'the most beautiful melody' on the basis of one of Handel's arias. Wolfgang is likely to have had other occasions to acquaint himself with Handel's music during his stay in London, for during Lent 1765 no fewer than seven of Handel's oratorios were performed at Covent Garden, in addition to *Acis and Galatea* at the Little Theatre in the Haymarket.

In 1782 Mozart began to take part in the regular Sunday concerts at Baron van Swieten*'s, where 'no music is played other than that of Handel and Bach' (according to Mozart's letter to his father of 10 April 1782). Swieten had the scores

of many of Handel's works in his personal library. At his suggestion, Mozart made adaptations of four of Handel's works. These versions were then performed in Vienna: *Acis and Galatea* K566, to a German text by Johann Baptist von Alxinger (1755–97), at Jahn's Rooms in [?] November 1788 and at Count Johann Baptist Esterházy*'s palace on 30 December 1788, with Cavalieri*, Johann Valentin Adamberger* and Tobias Gsur as soloists; *Messiah* K572, with Aloisia Lange*, Adamberger, Katharina Altomonte and Ignaz Saal, at Count Esterházy's on 6 March and 7 April 1789; the *Ode for St Cecilia's Day* K591 and *Alexander's Feast* K592 probably in the late autumn or winter of 1790.
(*Mozart: Dokumente*)

Hasse, Johann Adolph (baptized Bergedorf, near Hamburg, 25 March 1699; d. Venice, 16 December 1783). Prolific, highly successful and much-travelled German composer, admired in Italy and Germany especially for his operas, of which he wrote more than sixty (the first, *Antioco*, was performed at Brunswick in 1721, while the last, *Il Ruggiero, ovvero L'eroica gratitudine*, was produced in Milan in 1771). For many of these operas he used librettos by Metastasio*. In addition, he composed oratorios, cantatas, masses, quartets, trio sonatas, and works for the keyboard. He was himself a good singer and a proficient pianist.

He began his musical career as a tenor in Hamburg, before being engaged at the court of Brunswick in 1719. In 1721 he left for Italy where he lived, mainly in Naples, for some nine years, studying (his teachers included Alessandro Scarlatti) and composing, primarily operas and intermezzos. In 1730 he married the celebrated Italian soprano Faustina Bordoni (1700–81). In July 1731 he took up the post of Kapellmeister at the court of Elector Frederick Augustus of Saxony (who was also King Augustus II of Poland) at Dresden. While that city remained the centre of his activities for the next thirty years, he left it on several occasions to visit Italy (notably Venice) and Vienna. After leaving Dresden, he resided in Vienna from late 1760 until the summer of 1762, and again from 1764 until the end of 1772 when he retired to Venice. Many of his most important works were composed in Vienna.

There is plentiful evidence of the prominent position which Hasse occupied in European musical circles. In 1733–4 he gave lessons to the future Empress Maria Theresa*, whose favourite composer he later became. The famous castrato Carlo Broschi ['Farinelli'] was commanded by King Philip V to sing the same two arias ('Per questo dolce amplesso' and 'Pallido il sole') from Hasse's opera *Artaserse* (1730) each evening during his ten years' service at the Spanish court (1737–46). Charles Burney* writes of having met the 'admirable poet Metastasio*' and the 'no less admirable musician Hasse' during his visit to Vienna in 1772. And Leopold Mozart, in a letter to Hagenauer* on 30 July 1768, called him 'der Musick-Vatter' ['the father of music'], evidently a reference to his eminence as well as to his age.

Clearly the support of a man such as Hasse was eagerly sought, and he was generous in giving it. Leopold Mozart informed Hagenauer, in the same letter, that Hasse greatly admired Wolfgang's opera *La finta semplice*＊ and was ready to assure any 'slanderers' that it was superior to many operas which had been performed in Vienna. However, even Hasse's help was not sufficient to secure a performance of Wolfgang's opera in Vienna that year. Leopold must nonetheless have been delighted with Hasse's willingness to write letters of recommendation in connection with Wolfgang's first journey to Italy the following year. In his letter of 30 September 1769 to the Abbate Giovanni Maria Ortes (1713–99), a wealthy music-lover living in Venice, Hasse spoke highly of both father and son, declaring that Wolfgang's compositions were remarkable for a twelve-year-old boy and would be admirable even for an adult artist, while, on a personal level, his appearance and comportment were so pleasing that it was difficult for anyone who knew him not to love him. In a further letter on 4 October 1769, Hasse asked Ortes to regard Wolfgang and his father 'come miei amici'.

Mozart met Hasse again in Milan in 1771, both of them having been invited to write new works in celebration of Archduke Ferdinand*'s marriage to Maria Beatrice Ricciarda d'Este. In the event, Mozart's serenata *Ascanio in Alba** was far better received than Hasse's opera *Il Ruggiero*. Later Mozart set two librettos by Metastasio which Hasse, among other composers, had previously used: *Il re pastore** (Mozart, 1775; Hasse, 1755) and *La clemenza di Tito** (Mozart, 1791; Hasse, 1735). In addition, Hasse may have composed music (in ?1758) to Metastasio's *Il sogno di Scipione*, which Mozart set in 1771.

(Abert, Burney[5], Hansell S.[3])

Hässler, Johann Wilhelm (b. Erfurt, 29 March 1747; d. Moscow, 29 March 1822). German composer who was for many years a prominent organist, pianist, conductor and teacher at Erfurt; in 1780 he established a concert agency there and in 1784 opened a music shop. He performed successfully in various other German cities during the 1780s, and in London from 1790 until 1792 (on 30 May 1792 he played a piano concerto by Mozart there). In the latter year he was appointed court conductor at St Petersburg, and from 1794 was active as pianist and teacher in Moscow. Most of his compositions were for the keyboard.

Mozart met him at Dresden on 15 April 1789, on which occasion they engaged in an informal contest, first on the organ at the court church and later on the piano at the residence of Prince Alexander Michailovich Beloselsky (1757–1809), the Russian ambassador to Saxony. In a letter to Constanze* the next day, Mozart compared Hässler's skills as an organist unfavourably with those of Albrechtsberger*; as for his performance on the piano, 'I consider that [Josepha Barbara] Auernhammer* plays as well as he does'.

(Hoffmann, Norris)

Hatzfeld, August Clemens Ludwig Maria, Count (baptized Bonn, 10 November 1754; d. Düsseldorf, 30 January 1787). Son of Count Karl Ferdinand Franz Christoph Hatzfeld, high steward (later court councillor and high chamberlain) in the service of the Elector of Cologne, and of his second wife Maria Anna, *née* Baroness Venningen. Destined from an early age for the church, he was tonsured before he was ten years old and was later appointed a canon at Eichstätt Cathedral. From 1778 to 1780 he studied law at Mainz University. In 1781 he became a member of the cathedral chapter at Eichstätt, which was henceforth to be his official place of residence.

On 17 January 1786 he received permission to undertake a six weeks' pilgrimage to Mariahilf Church in Vienna; by early April he was back at Eichstätt. While in Vienna he became a close friend of Mozart. Hatzfeld was an accomplished violinist whose teachers included the well-known French violinist and composer Pierre Vachon (1731–1803). In Vienna, according to the obituary published in Karl Friedrich Cramer's *Magazin der Musik* (Hamburg) on 26 July 1787, Hatzfeld 'studied and played [Mozart's] celebrated quadros [quatuors] under their creator's guidance, and he grew so attuned to the spirit of their composer that the latter was almost disinclined to hear his masterpieces performed by anyone else.' For the performance of *Idomeneo** at Prince Auersperg's on 13 March 1786, Mozart wrote a violin obbligato for Hatzfeld as accompaniment to the aria 'Non temer, amato bene' (K490) which he composed specially for the occasion.

After his return to Eichstätt, Hatzfeld applied for a *cappelania honoris* [honorary curacy] which would have allowed him to reside in Vienna. But shortly after it was granted, he died suddenly from a pulmonary infection. In his letter of 4 April 1787, Mozart informed his father of the 'sad death of my best and dearest friend'.

Hatzfeld's brother Hugo Franz (b. 1755), a canon at Mainz, was a competent singer and composer. The most brilliant musician in the family was Countess Hortensia Hatzfeld*, the wife of Hatzfeld's half-brother Clemens August Johann Nepomuk.

(Hedler, Schmid[6])

Hatzfeld, (Maria Anna) Hortensia, Countess (b. 1750; d. 31 December 1813). Daughter of Count Johann Karl Zierotin (1719–76) and his wife Maria Josepha Theresia, *née* Countess Königsegg-Erps; niece of Count Maximilian Friedrich Königsegg (1704–84), Elector and Archbishop of Cologne from 1761; wife of Lieutenant-General Count Clemens August Johann Nepomuk Hatzfeld (1743–94), councillor to the Elector of Cologne, and half-brother to Count August Clemens Hatzfeld*.

She was a leading patroness of music, both in Bonn – where her protégés included the organist and composer Christian Gottlob Neefe (1748–98), as well as his pupil, the young Beethoven* – and in Vienna, where she was a subscriber to Mozart's Trattnerhof concerts in 1784 (*see* TRATTNER). The composers Franz Xaver Rigler and Leopold Kozeluch* dedicated piano sonatas to her. She was in contact with Gottfried von Jacquin*, and Mozart may have met her at the latter's house.

Moreover, having studied the piano and singing in Vienna during her youth, she was herself a brilliant pianist and a highly accomplished soprano. At the performance of *Idomeneo** at Prince Auersperg's palace on 13 March 1786 she sang Elettra. Previously, she had appeared there in the title roles of Vincenzo Righini's *Armida* (23 July 1782) and Gluck*'s *Alceste* (12 February 1786); according to Michael Kelly*, she sang 'inimitably well' in the latter performance, which was directed by the composer himself. She also took the role of Aspasia in Salieri*'s *Axur, re d'Ormus* at Prince Auersperg's on 18 November 1793. In his *Jahrbuch der Tonkunst von Wien und Prag* Schönfeld praised her great vocal agility and her 'marvellous trill', and judged that her execution 'surpassed in many respects the skills of the ordinary amateur'.

(Kelly, Schmid[3], Schönfeld)

Haydn, Joseph (b. Rohrau, Lower Austria, 31 March 1732; d. Vienna, 31 May

1809). Austrian composer. Maximilian Stadler* told Vincent Novello in 1829 that Haydn and Mozart had been 'like brothers', delighting in each other's music; moreover, Mozart had frequently acknowledged his debt to Haydn as a formative influence on his style, whilst Haydn had declared that Mozart was 'a God in music'. On 15 January 1785 Mozart and some friends (*see* Schmith) played for Haydn the six quartets k387, 421/417b, 428/421b, 458, 464 and 465 which Mozart later dedicated to him. The last three were again performed in Haydn's presence on 12 February, on which occasion Haydn told Leopold Mozart, then on a visit to Vienna: 'I say to you before God, as an honest man, that your son is the greatest composer I know, personally or by name: he has taste and, in addition, the most profound knowledge of composition' (Leopold's letter to Nannerl* of 16 February 1785). Nor was this mere polite hyperbole, for W. T. Parke recalled in his *Musical Memoirs* having 'heard Haydn, while he was in England, declare that Mozart was the most extraordinary, original, and comprehensive musical genius that was ever known in this or any age.' And Charles Burney* overheard Haydn say: 'He was truly a great musician. I have been often flattered by my friends with having some genius; but he was much my superior.' When news of Mozart's death reached Haydn in England, he wrote to Maria Anna von Genzinger on 20 December 1791: 'Posterity will not see such a talent again in a hundred years!' And to their mutual friend Puchberg* he confessed in a letter in January 1792: 'I was quite beside myself for a long time over his death and could not believe that Providence had so soon claimed such an irreplaceable man for the next world.'

When the aforementioned six quartets were published by Artaria* later in 1785, they carried an affectionate dedication (in Italian) to Haydn: 'A father having resolved to send his sons out into the great world, considers it desirable to entrust them to the protection and guidance of a very celebrated man, who happily has also been his best friend . . .' And the dedication is signed 'Il tuo sincerissimo amico'. Further evidence of their close friendship can be found in two letters from Mozart to Puchberg dating from 1789–90. In December 1789 he wrote, referring to a forthcoming rehearsal of *Così fan tutte**: 'I am inviting only you and Haydn'; and on 20 January 1790, concerning the first orchestral rehearsal: 'Haydn is coming with me.' Maximilian Stadler also told Novello that he had frequently participated with Haydn and Mozart in performances of the latter's quintets.

Mozart was much moved and saddened by Haydn's departure for England in mid-December 1790. 'We are probably saying our last farewell in this life,' he is reported by Haydn's biographer A. C. Dies to have murmured, with tears in his eyes, when they parted. Haydn apparently interpreted this remark as a reference to his own advanced age (he was, after all, approaching sixty), but he was, in fact, to survive Mozart by almost twenty years. At a memorial service for Haydn held at the Schottenkirche in Vienna on 15 June 1809, Mozart's Requiem was performed under Eybler*'s direction.

(Burney¹, Dies, Landon¹, Novello, Parke)

Haydn, (Johann) Michael (baptized Rohrau, Lower Austria, 14 September 1737; d. Salzburg, 10 August 1806). Austrian composer; younger brother of Joseph Haydn*. Like the latter, he was a chorister at St Stephen's Cathedral in Vienna, where he received a sound musical education. In 1757 he was appointed

Heina, Franz Joseph

Kapellmeister to the Bishop of Grosswardein in Hungary [Oradea in Romania]. By 1763 he was a court musician and Konzertmeister in Salzburg, where he was to reside for the rest of his life. On 17 August 1768 he married the singer Maria Magdalena Lipp*, whose father was an organist at court. After Adlgasser*'s death in 1777 Haydn became organist at the Dreifaltigkeitskirche [Trinity Church] and, after Mozart left Archbishop Colloredo*'s service, also cathedral organist.

He wrote many masses and other sacred music; in 1767 he collaborated with Adlgasser and the eleven-year-old Mozart in the oratorio *Die Schuldigkeit des ersten Gebots**. He was also a prolific composer of secular works (symphonies, concertos and chamber music). Both Mozart and his father recognized Haydn's talent, but their admiration for his compositions and musicianship appears to have been less than profound. It is true that Wolfgang – or Leopold – on one occasion praised Haydn and Adlgasser as 'excellent masters of counterpoint' (*see* ADLGASSER), but elsewhere Mozart's correspondence contains some more equivocal statements and, in one letter from Paris (18 July 1778), the ironic remark that he had played a 'galanterie' sonata 'in the style and with all the fire, spirit, and precision of Haydn' – those being evidently qualities which he missed in Haydn's compositions and playing. After hearing Haydn's opera *Andromeda e Perseo* (text by Varesco*), Leopold observed drily, in a letter to Nannerl* on 13 March 1787, that Haydn 'has no talent for writing music for the theatre'.

According to G. Croll, Haydn's sacred music had some influence on Mozart's; in particular, he believes that Mozart's (incomplete) Requiem owed certain of its essential characteristics to the Requiem that Haydn had written in 1771 after Archbishop Sigismund Schrattenbach*'s death – just as, in its turn, Mozart's Requiem was to leave a strong imprint on the (also uncompleted) Requiem which Haydn composed for the Empress Maria Theresia (d. 1807), consort of Emperor Francis II. Croll points out, furthermore, that in the final chorus of his oratorio *La Betulia liberata* K118/74c the young Mozart drew directly, in 1771, on Haydn's choral composition *Cantate Domino*, which had been performed in the Latin school play *Pietas christiana* in Salzburg on 31 August 1770.

On a more personal level, Leopold Mozart was at times critical of Haydn's behaviour, especially of what he regarded as his over-fondness for alcohol. Thus he wrote to Wolfgang on 29 December 1777: 'Who do you think has been appointed organist at the Dreifaltigkirche [i.e. in Adlgasser's place]? Herr Haydn. Everyone is laughing. He will be an expensive organist: after each Litany he swills a quart of wine, and to the other services he sends Lipp (*see* LIPP), who also likes to booze.' By 29 June 1778 Leopold had become even more censorious: 'We said that . . . Haydn would drink himself into dropsy within a few years, or, at any rate, since he is now too lazy to do anything, would continue getting more and more lazy, the older he gets'. (Croll[3], Croll/Vössing, Pauly/Sherman)

Heina [Haina], Franz Joseph [François-Joseph] (b. Mieschitz [Měšic], near Prague, 20 November 1729; d. Paris, February 1790). Horn player and music publisher. When Leopold Mozart met him in Paris in late 1763, he was *cor de chasse* in the service of the Prince de Conti (1717–76). Leopold also heard him play at the house of Baron Bagge (1722–91), an ardent music lover. To Wolfgang and his mother* he proved a true friend during their stay in Paris in 1778. He frequently visited them; his wife Gertrude also called on Wolfgang's mother; and the latter, writing to Leopold on 12 June, mentioned having been invited to lunch by the Heinas two days earlier. When she fell ill, it was Heina who found a German doctor for her (she did not trust French ones) and later sent a German priest. Apart from Wolfgang and the nurse, Heina was the only other person present when she died on 3 July; on the following day he attended the funeral at St Eustache. In the church register he is described as 'a trumpeter in the Household Cavalry in the Royal Guard, and a friend'. (According to F. Lesure, he had been discharged from the Guard in 1775.) In 1785 he joined the orchestra at the Comédie-Française.

Heina ran a music publishing firm at the Hôtel de Lille in the Rue de Seine. He issued the first editions of seven of Mozart's works: the variations for piano K179/189a, 180/173c, 354/299a, the Divertimento (Piano Trio) K254, and the piano sonatas K309/284b, 310/300d and 311/284c.

(Lesure)

Henneberg, Johann Baptist (b. Vienna, 6 December 1768; d. Vienna, 26 November 1822). Austrian musician. From 1790 until 1803 he was Kapellmeister and resident composer of Schikaneder*'s company in Vienna; among other Singspiels, he wrote the music for the very popular *Die Waldmänner* (14 October 1793), to a text by Schikaneder. In addition, he succeeded his father Andreas Henneberg (Hönneberg), on the latter's death in 1791, as organist and Kapellmeister at the Schottenstift. He gave up his Viennese appointments in 1804. Some years later he was appointed organist at the court of Prince Nikolaus Esterházy (1765–1833) at Eisenstadt, but after the dissolution of the latter's orchestra he returned to Vienna and became choirmaster at the Am Hof church. In 1818 he was named court organist.

In 1792 he married Maria Henriette Petit [Paty], who bore him eight children; Schikaneder was godfather to four of them. After her death in 1814 he remarried; he was survived by his second wife, Josepha.

During Mozart's absence in Prague from late August to mid-September 1791, Henneberg was responsible for rehearsals of *Die Zauberflöte**. He also directed performances after the first two, which were conducted by Mozart himself.

(Branscombe[3], Komorzynski[3])

Heufeld, Franz Reinhard von (baptized Mainau, Lake Constance, 13 October 1731; d. Vienna, 23 March 1795). Auditor of the court accounts; director of German theatrical productions in Vienna in 1769, and again from 1773 to 1775; playwright. In 1776 he married Maria Anna Zach von Hartenstein (1751–1803); they had seven children.

Heufeld was the author of a number of often satirical comedies, some of which were produced to acclaim in Vienna, starting with *Die Haushaltung nach der Mode, oder Was soll man für eine Frau nehmen?* on 16 February 1765 (Mozart saw a performance of the play in Munich on 29 December 1774). A companion piece, *Der Liebhaber nach der Mode, oder Was für einen Mann soll man nehmen?* was produced on 12 April 1766 and remained in the repertory until 1776. He furthermore translated Monvel's original French text for the Singspiel *Julie* (music by Nicolas Dezède) which was performed at the Burgtheater on 23 August 1779 (*see also* Mozart's Variations K264/315*d*).

But Heufeld is best remembered by historians of the theatre for his role in the first Viennese productions of *Romeo and Juliet* (12 September 1772) and *Hamlet* (16 January 1773). For the former, he based his text on the 'domestic tragedy' *Romeo und Julie* (1767) by Christian Felix Weisse (1726–1804), which differed considerably from Shakespeare's play; for the latter, he freely adapted the prose translation made by Christoph Martin Wieland (1733–1813) of Shakespeare's *Hamlet*. However, unlike their German models, Heufeld's versions provided both tragedies with a happy ending: the lovers awake from their apparent death, Hamlet does not die but becomes king. At the première of *Hamlet*, the title role was taken by Joseph Lange*, Ophelia was played by Marie Anna Teutscher, Oldenholm (Polonius) by Johann Gottlieb Stephanie*, and Gustav (Horatio) by Jautz*.

The Mozarts first met Heufeld in Vienna in 1767 or 1768. They subsequently corresponded, and Leopold and Wolfgang met him again during their visit to Vienna in 1773. In January 1778 Leopold asked Heufeld to obtain for Wolfgang a letter of introduction to Queen Marie Antoinette, and he also sought his help in securing for Wolfgang the post of Kapellmeister for German opera in Vienna. In his reply, Heufeld declared himself unable to comply with either request (*see also* JOSEPH II), but suggested that Wolfgang should compose a comic German opera and submit it for consideration to the emperor, an idea which Wolfgang dismissed scornfully in his letter to his father of 4 February: 'Does the fool really think that I will write a German opera, with no assurance of acceptance, just on the off-chance?' He was also annoyed because Heufeld had referred to him, in his letter to Leopold, as 'Ihr Sohn' rather than by the more respectful expression 'der Herr Sohn': 'He is just a Viennese boor; or he imagines that people remain twelve years old for ever'. Mozart nevertheless resumed contact with Heufeld after settling in Vienna in 1781. (Zechmeister)

Hilleprandt, Franz von (b. 1796; d. 1869 [?1871]). Salzburg lawyer. In 1841 he founded the *Dommusikverein und Mozarteum*, the forerunner of the *Internationale Stiftung Mozarteum* which continues to play such a significant role in the musical life of Salzburg and, at the same time, constitutes one of the foremost centres for Mozart scholarship.
(Eibl in *Mozart: Briefe*, Schneider)

Hofdemel, Franz (b. *c.*1755; d. Vienna, 6 December 1791). Clerk at the High Court of Justice in Vienna. In late March 1789 Mozart wrote to him, addressing him as 'Dearest friend' – so their first contacts evidently went back to an earlier period – and requesting a loan of 100 gulden (the money presumably being required for Mozart's forthcoming journey to Berlin). The request was granted and the bill of exchange signed on 2 April 1789. At that time Hofdemel was about to be admitted to the 'Zur neugekrönten Hoffnung'* Lodge, of which Mozart was himself a member.

On 6 December 1791, the day after Mozart's death, Hofdemel savagely attacked his pregnant twenty-five year-old wife Maria Magdalena with a razor, slashing her across the face, neck and shoulders. He then cut his own throat; his wife survived. The fact that she had been taking piano lessons with Mozart prompted rumours that the attempted murder and suicide had been the actions of a husband crazed by jealousy over his wife's affair with her teacher. From there it was but a short step to imagining that Mozart had been poisoned by Hofdemel. The emperor and empress patently believed in the wife's innocence, since Leopold II* granted her a generous pension, while Maria Luisa* publicly expressed sympathy for her. Maria Magdalena nevertheless left Vienna, probably because of the derogatory stories circulating about her morals, and returned to her father's home at Brünn [Brno] where, on 10 May 1792, she gave birth to a son. She died in 1804.

While the precise nature of Mozart's relations with Maria Magdalena Hofdemel cannot be established, the suggestion that Mozart's death might be attributable to her husband no longer finds any supporters among Mozart scholars. The possibility of a liaison between Mozart and Maria Magdalena has, however, inspired more than one work of fiction, such as the novellas *Mozart und seine Freundin* (1841) by Leopold Schefer (1784–1862) and *Franz Hofdemel: Eine Mozart-Novelle* (1932) by Wolfgang Goetz (1885–1955).

(Guggitz)

Hofer, Franz de Paula (b. Vienna, 9 January 1755; d. Penzing, near Vienna, 14 June 1796). Violinist. In 1780 Hofer was a member of the orchestra of St Stephen's Cathedral, and from 1787 he played in the court orchestra. On 21 July 1788 he married Constanze*'s sister Josepha Weber*.

Mozart appears to have been on friendly terms with Hofer even before he became his brother-in-law, for Hofer was among those who accompanied Mozart and Constanze on their journey to Prague in January 1787. In May 1789, in a letter announcing his return from a trip to Berlin, Mozart expressed the hope that Constanze would come to meet him at the first post-stage outside Vienna, together with Hofer 'whom I embrace a thousand times'. Hofer was again Mozart's companion on the journey to Frankfurt in September 1790. Together with Gerl* and Schack*, Hofer sang through the uncompleted Requiem with him on the day before he died.

(Blümml)

Hofer, Josepha: *see* WEBER, JOSEPHA.

Hoffmeister, Franz Anton (b. Rothenburg am Neckar, 12 May 1754; d. Vienna, 9 February 1812). Austrian music publisher and composer. He arrived in Vienna in 1768 to study law, but subsequently made his career in music. A prolific and popular composer, he wrote over sixty symphonies, some sixty concertos, an enormous amount of chamber music, and several Singspiels. The most successful of these, *Der Königssohn aus Ithaka* (to a libretto by Emanuel Schikaneder*), was first produced at the Freihaus-Theater on 27 June 1795 and by the end of that year had reached twenty-nine performances there; by 1803 it had been presented also in Germany and in Budapest, Prague and Warsaw.

Mozart was, of course, familiar with many of Hoffmeister's compositions. An entry in his hand, in Nannerl*'s diary, records that quartets by Hoffmeister were played at the Mozarts' on 31 August 1780; the first movement of Mozart's Flute Quartet K298 consists of a set of variations on Hoffmeister's song *An die Natur* (to a text by Wilhelm Gottfried Becker); and the inventory of Mozart's estate included the score of a piano concerto by Hoffmeister, as well as twenty-two issues of the *Prénumération pour le Forte Piano ou Clavecin*, a monthly publication launched by Hoffmeister in November 1785, which presented, notably, works by Mozart, Joseph Haydn*, Vanhal* and Hoffmeister himself.

Hoffmeister founded his publishing business in January 1784 and ran it, somewhat fitfully and at various Viennese addresses, until 1806. His list included also Albrechtsberger*, Beethoven*, Carl Ditters von Dittersdorf and Ignace Joseph Pleyel. Among the first editions of Mozart's works for which he was responsible were those of the Piano Quartet K478 (published in 1785); the Piano Trio K496, the so-called 'Hoffmeister' Quartet K499, and the Violin Sonata K481 (all in 1786); and the Violin Sonata K526 (1787). He later sold a number of publications, including some of Mozart's compositions, to Artaria*.

In Leipzig in 1800 he established, together with the organist Ambrosius Kühnel (1770–1813), a *Bureau de musique* whose publishing activities were conducted over the next few years in rather loose association with the Viennese firm. After Hoffmeister returned to Vienna in 1805, Kühnel remained in sole charge of the *Bureau de musique* until his death. It was then bought by the Leipzig bookseller Carl Friedrich Peters (1779–1827) who published several of Mozart's works, including, for the first time, the bass aria *Non so d'onde viene* K512 (*see* FISCHER). The publishing house C. F. Peters acquired an outstanding reputation in the 19th century, which it has maintained to the present time. As for Hoffmeister, he withdrew from his publishing ventures in 1806.

In 1790 he had married Theresia Haas (d. 1831), who may have helped him run his business. The couple had no children.

(Weinmann[1,4,7])

Holzbauer, Ignaz (Jakob) (b. Vienna, 17 September 1711; d. Mannheim, 7 April 1783). Austrian composer and conductor. Essentially self-taught in music, he held appointments in Bohemia, Vienna and Stuttgart, and, from 1753 until 1778, was Kapellmeister at Mannheim. When part of the orchestra moved to Munich in the latter year (*see* KARL THEODOR), he elected to remain behind. His wife Rosalie, *née* Andreides, whom he married in 1737, was an opera singer; she sang Cimene in Hasse*'s *Leucippo* at the Burgtheater, Vienna, on 5 September 1748.

Holzbauer composed church, chamber and ballet music, but is best remembered for his opera *Günther von Schwarzburg* (first produced at Mannheim on 5 January 1777) which, by treating a German subject seriously in a Singspiel, played a significant role in the development of that genre. Mozart was greatly impressed when he attended a performance at Mannheim on 5 November 1777: 'Holzbauer's music is very beautiful,' he wrote to his father on 14 November. 'The text [by Anton Klein] does not deserve such music. What amazes me especially is that a man as old as Holzbauer should still possess so much spirit; for you cannot imagine what fire there is in this music.' Mozart also thought highly of a mass by Holzbauer which he heard at Mannheim.

Shortly after Mozart's arrival at Mannheim in late October 1777, Holzbauer presented him to Count Savioli, the Director of Music. He was also helpful in other respects, thus bearing out Leopold Mozart's statement, in his letter of 10 November

1777, that 'Holzbauer has always been a decent and honest man'.

In 1778 in Paris, Mozart wrote, at Legros*'s request, additional music (ĸAnh.1/297a) for a *Miserere* by Holzbauer which was to be performed at the Concert Spirituel (*see* GOSSEC).

(Grave, Zechmeister)

Hornung, Joseph von Arimathia. Bass; according to the libretto of *La finta semplice**, the original Don Cassandro. He was born at Ramelzhofen in Swabia, was a chorister at St Peter's Abbey in Salzburg from *c.*1757, and sang with the court orchestra from 1768; but, despite several applications, he was never offered a fixed appointment. After the death of Felix Winter* (also a bass), Leopold Mozart observed in a letter to his wife* on 14 November 1772 that Hornung 'should now be able to land a job, unless they decide to bring a bass over from the West Indies'. Presumably he was not engaged even then, for in a letter from Munich, on 1 March 1775, Leopold wrote that Hornung was considering offers from Cadiz, Alexandria (in Piedmont), and Milan.

Hübner, Beda [baptismal name: Georg] (b. Temesvar, 18 December 1740; d. Salzburg, 2 April 1811). His mother, Maria Elisabeth Hübner, was a sister of Beda Seeauer (1716–85) who became abbot of St Peter's, Salzburg, in 1753. After his parents' early death Hübner was educated at Steyr and Salzburg. He entered St Peter's Abbey in 1757, was consecrated a priest in 1763, and served as librarian and as secretary to his uncle. From 1786 to 1798 he was a curate at Abtenau, near Salzburg. In 1798 a serious foot ailment obliged him to retire to the abbey where he spent his remaining years teaching and writing.

From the beginning of 1764 until 8 September 1767 Hübner kept a diary, partly in Latin and partly in German, in which, among other matters, he reported Nannerl*'s and Wolfgang's early exploits. In an entry on 26 April 1766, he called them 'veritable wonders of the world'. On 29 November 1766, the day on which the Mozarts returned from their long European journey, he recorded their experiences and also mentioned a strong rumour that they 'will not remain here for very long, but will shortly visit the whole of Scandinavia and the whole of Russia, and may even travel as far as China'. An entry on 8 December 1766 described some of the splendid presents which the family had received during their travels; it also had an interesting passage on the considerable progress which Wolfgang had made as a pianist during his prolonged absence from Salzburg.

(Klein)

Hummel, Johann Nepomuk (b. Pressburg [Bratislava], 14 November 1778; d. Weimar, 17 October 1837). Composer, and one of the outstanding pianists of his time, famous for his improvisations. Son of Johannes Hummel (d. 1828), a conductor at the Freihaus-Theater in Vienna.

He was reportedly introduced to Mozart by the latter's friend and pupil Franz Jacob Freystädtler*. He lodged with the Mozarts while receiving instruction, probably in 1786–7. During this time, Johannes Hummel later wrote, Mozart looked after the young Johann Nepomuk like a father and Constanze* 'cared for him like a mother'. He subsequently undertook an extended tour of northern Europe;

Ippold, Franz Armand d'

Mozart heard him play in Berlin on 23 May 1789. Later Hummel studied with Clementi* in London and also received instruction in composition from Salieri*, Albrechtsberger* and Joseph Haydn* in Vienna. For some years he was Konzertmeister to Prince Nikolaus Esterházy (1765–1833) at Eisenstadt. In 1816 he was appointed Kapellmeister at Stuttgart, and in 1817 Kapellmeister at Weimar, where he remained until his death. He made several highly successful concert tours which took him as far as Russia. His pupils included three future piano virtuosi: Carl Czerny (1791–1857), Adolph von Henselt (1814–89), and Sigismond Thalberg (1812–71). He also taught Mozart's younger surviving son Franz Xaver Wolfgang*.

Constanze appears to have entertained some expectations of payment from Hummel, for on 23 January 1838, three months after his death, she wrote to his sons Eduard and Karl: 'Did this great man really not think of me, his former *foster-mother*, at his death? After he had so often promised, in *speaking* to me, that once he was successful he would not fail to recompense me richly for all the trouble I took, for the love and care he received and the cost of his board and lodging, and for the lessons my late husband Mozart gave him.' When her letter produced no response, Constanze tried to put pressure on Hummel's widow and sons by legal means, but she was obliged to withdraw her claim for compensation the following year.

Hummel wrote much piano music, as well as ballets, Singspiels and chamber music. His compositions were very highly regarded in his day, as is shown by a letter Chopin wrote to the pianist Anne Caroline de Belleville-Oury (1808–80) in 1840, in which he congratulated her on her marvellous interpretation of 'such great masters as Mozart, Beethoven and Hummel, the masters of all of us'.

(Sachs, Zimmerschmied)

Ippold, Franz Armand d' (b. Doxan, near Leitmeritz, 1729 or 1730; d. Salzburg, 25 February 1790). A friend of the Mozarts. From 1775 he was director of the Collegium Virgilianum, a school for the sons of noblemen in Salzburg. He held the rank of captain, and in 1777 was appointed court military councillor. He was in love with Nannerl*, but although she returned his feelings, she did not marry him (*see* MOZART, MARIA ANNA WALBURGA IGNATIA). In 1784 she became the wife of Johann Baptist Franz von Berchtold zu Sonnenburg*.

Ippold remained friendly with Leopold Mozart and took particular delight in playing with Nannerl's son Leopold, who was living with his grandfather in Salzburg. Ippold is frequently mentioned in Leopold Mozart's letters to Nannerl. Moreover, a reference by Wolfgang, in his letter to Nannerl of 2 June 1787, to a communication he had received from Ippold led O. E. Deutsch and J. H. Eibl to conclude that it was Ippold who had informed Wolfgang of his father's death on 28 May. In the aforesaid letter to his sister Wolfgang described Ippold as 'our true and good friend' and expressed the hope that 'since he has on so many occasions shown himself a friend to our family', he would be prepared to represent his [Wolfgang's] interests in the division of their father's inheritance. Wolfgang enclosed a letter (since lost) to be handed to Ippold, which presumably contained a request to that effect. However, there is no mention of Ippold in Mozart's subsequent correspondence regarding the inheritance, and it may be inferred that Ippold had declined to assume a responsibility which might have brought him into conflict with Nannerl's own interests.

(Deutsch in *Mozart: Dokumente*, Eibl in *Mozart: Briefe*)

Jacquin, (Emilian) Gottfried von (b. 1767; d. Vienna, 24 January 1792). Official at the Austro-Bohemian court chancellery in Vienna; composer and amateur singer. He was the younger son of the distinguished botanist Nikolaus Joseph von Jacquin (1727–1817) who designed the municipal botanical gardens in Vienna. Gottfried was a friend of Mozart, whose close contacts with the Jacquin family probably dated from before 1783.

In March 1787 Mozart wrote for Gottfried the aria *Mentre ti lascio, o figlia* K513. On 26 March 1791 Gottfried published, presumably with Mozart's agreement, six songs supposedly written by himself (*Des Herrn von Jacquin 6 deutsche Lieder beym Klavier zu singen*), but of which the following two had in fact been composed by Mozart: *Als Luise die Briefe ihres ungetreuen Liebhabers verbrannte* K520 and *Das Traumbild* K530. On the other hand, the Berlin publisher Concha later printed, under Mozart's name, the song *Vergiss mein nicht* (KAnh.246/C8.06) which had probably been written by Gottfried von Jacquin (or possibly by W. Ehlers).

As far as the bass aria *Io ti lascio, oh cara, addio* KAnh.245/621a is concerned, it has not so far been possible either to confirm or to disprove conclusively Constanze*'s statement, in her letter to Breitkopf & Härtel* of 25 May 1799, that the piece was composed by Jacquin and that Mozart merely added the violin parts. However, Christian Esch advanced fresh arguments in 1991 against attributing the melody to Jacquin. Some uncertainty has also surrounded the five notturni K436–439, 346/439a. In a letter to Johann Anton André* on 31 May 1800, Constanze indicated that Mozart had done no more than add an accompaniment to the music which Jacquin had composed for the voice.

It was for Gottfried's sister Franziska (1769–1850), who studied the piano with him, that Mozart wrote the Piano Trio K498 and the Sonata K521.
(Esch, Kraus)

Jautz, Dominik Joseph (b. Prague, 1732; d. 1806). Actor; the original Pasha Selim (*Die Entführung**). From 1772 to 1793 he was a member of the Burgtheater, where he made his début on 29 February 1772 as Clarendon in Beaumarchais's *Eugénie*; thereafter he usually appeared in secondary roles. In the first Viennese production of *Hamlet* in 1773 (*see* HEUFELD) he played Gustav (Horatio). Prior to *Die Entführung*, he had already taken speaking roles in several Singspiels. In 1796 his daughter Therese, herself an actress, married the popular actor and singer Friedrich Baumann (1764–1841), for whom Mozart had written the aria *Ich möchte wohl der Kaiser sein* K539.
(Michtner, Zechmeister)

Joseph II (b. Vienna, 31 March 1741; d. Vienna, 20 February 1790). Eldest son of Empress Maria Theresa* and her husband Francis I. Archduke; after his father's death (18 August 1765) he became emperor, and at the same time he acted as co-regent with his mother in the Austrian dominions until her death on 29 November 1780, after which date he ruled alone. He married twice: on 6 October 1760, Isabella (1741–63), daughter of Philip, Duke of Parma and Piacenza; and on 23 January 1765, Maria Josepha (1739–67), sister of Maximilian III Joseph, Elector of Bavaria.

Joseph was passionately fond of music. He received instruction in singing and dancing at an early age, and played several instruments competently, often participating in private music-making at the palace (*see also* MAXIMILIAN FRANZ). He frequently attended concerts and was regularly seen at the opera. He even tried his hand at composition. In 1774 Maria Theresa entrusted him with the supervision of the court theatres, and from that time until his death he determined their artistic policy (notably the establishment of a German opera company at the Burgtheater in 1778 and the return of Italian opera in 1883) and closely controlled the engagement of the artists. He was, indeed, a good judge of singers. During his several journeys to Italy, he was constantly searching for new talent, sending back reports on the singers he had heard and, on occasion, entering into direct negotiations with them. Thus, while in Naples in 1784, he invited the soprano Celeste Coltellini* to sing in Vienna on the conclusion of her current contract, and on another journey the following year he recruited the mezzo-soprano Rosalinda Marconi-Molinelli. After attending the première of Pietro Alessandro Guglielmi's *Le vicende d'amore* in Rome in 1783, he dispatched the score and libretto to Vienna; the opera was duly produced at the Burgtheater on 16 June 1784 and performed before the court at Schloss Laxenburg the next day.

Although an accessible and benevolent ruler, he was nonetheless an autocrat, as Heufeld* explained to Leopold Mozart, who had asked for his help in obtaining the post of conductor of German opera for Wolfgang: 'To recommend anyone to the emperor would simply ensure that he was not appointed,' Heufeld wrote on 23 January 1778. 'Nor are there any intermediaries through whom he could be approached, since, being himself a connoisseur of music, he determines and decides everything according to his own ideas and preferences . . . I could also cite you the examples of several persons who addressed themselves directly to the sovereign and were unsuccessful.'

Joseph's reign almost entirely encompassed Mozart's career. No doubt Joseph first saw him when the Mozarts were received at court on 13 October 1762. At an audience in 1768 (probably on 19 January), Joseph – by then emperor – suggested that Wolfgang should write an opera, a remark which led to the composition of *La finta semplice**. Mozart's later efforts to secure a court appointment, especially after settling in Vienna in 1781, eventually met with some success: on 7 December 1787 he was named chamber musician, at the relatively modest salary of 800 gulden. There is evidence that Joseph was by no means insensitive to the special quality of Mozart's compositions (*see* DON GIOVANNI), although his own tastes ran more toward the light, sparkling Italian *opere buffe* of a Paisiello*, Cimarosa*, or Martín y Soler*. Carl Ditters von Dittersdorf recalled in his autobiography that Joseph once compared Mozart's compositions to a gold snuffbox manufactured in Paris, and Joseph Haydn*'s to one finished off in London.

(Dittersdorf, Michtner, Payer, Zechmeister)

Karl Theodor (b. Drogenbos Castle, near Brussels, 11 December 1724; d. Munich, 16 February 1799). Elector Palatine from 1742, following the death of Karl Philipp of Pfalz-Neuburg; in addition, Elector of Bavaria from 30 December 1777, in succession to his cousin Maximilian III Joseph (b. 1727). Son of Duke Johann Christian of Pfalz-Sulzbach (1700–32) and of his wife Maria Anna (1708–28), daughter of Duke Franz Egon de La Tour d'Auvergne. He was twice married:

in 1742 to Elisabeth Maria Auguste (1721–94), a daughter of Prince Joseph Karl Emanuel of Pfalz-Sulzbach, and in 1795 to Maria Leopoldine (1776–1848), a daughter of Archduke Ferdinand*.

Under Karl Theodor, who was himself an accomplished flautist and cellist, Mannheim, the capital of the Palatinate, became an outstanding centre for music in the 1760s and 1770s. The Mannheim court orchestra, Leopold Mozart wrote to Hagenauer* on 19 July 1763, was 'beyond doubt the best in Germany'. Charles Burney* was equally enthusiastic about 'this extraordinary band', in which 'there are more solo players, and good composers . . . than perhaps in any other orchestra in Europe; it is an army of generals, equally fit to plan a battle, as to fight it.'

On 18 July 1763 Wolfgang and Nannerl* displayed their talents at Schwetzingen, Karl Theodor's summer residence near Mannheim; according to Leopold Mozart, the elector and electress 'were delighted beyond words, and everybody was amazed'. Fourteen years later Wolfgang and his mother* spent over four months (30 October 1777 – 14 March 1778) at Mannheim. The length of their stay was due in part to Wolfgang's growing attachment to Aloisia Weber*, but mainly to his efforts to secure a post at court, if only as music teacher to Karl Theodor's illegitimate children. On his return journey from Paris he once more stayed at Mannheim (6 November–9 December 1778), again in the vain hope of an appointment, even though Karl Theodor had by then moved to Munich with his court and most of the orchestra. While in Munich (25 December 1778 – mid-January 1779), Mozart presented to the electress a copy of six violin sonatas which had recently been published by Jean-Georges Sieber in Paris and were dedicated to her (κ301/293a, 302/293b, 303/293c, 304/300c, 305/293d and 306/300l).

Mozart met Karl Theodor again while in Munich for the production of *Idomeneo** (6 November 1780–12 March 1781), and was warmly complimented by him at the first rehearsal with full orchestra, which was held at the palace on 23 December 1780. 'After the first act, the Elector called out "Bravo" very loudly,' Mozart reported to his father on 27 December; and after hearing parts of Act II, '[he] said, with a laugh: "Who would have believed that such great things could lodge in so small a head!"' Later Karl Theodor praised the opera most highly at court, and declared (according to Mozart's letter of 30 December 1780) that no music had ever made so great an impression on him.

Mozart was to stay in Munich once more (29 October – 6 or 7 November 1790) after attending Leopold II*'s coronation in Frankfurt. On that occasion Karl Theodor invited him to perform at a concert given at court on 4 or 5 November before King Ferdinand IV and Queen Maria Karolina (a daughter of Empress Maria Theresa*) of Naples. 'This is really a great honour,' Mozart wrote to Constanze*, adding that it did little credit to the Viennese court that the king should have had to visit a foreign country to hear him – a peevish reference to the fact that Mozart had not been invited to perform during the royal couple's visit to Vienna in September of that year.

(Burney[5], Heigel, *LDG*)

Kelly [also O'Kelly or, as in Mozart's own catalogue of his compositions on 29 April 1786, Occhely], **Michael** (b. Dublin, 25 December 1762; d. Margate, 9 October 1826). Irish tenor, particularly successful in *buffo* roles; composer, theatre manager, and music publisher; the original Don Basilio and Don Curzio (*Le nozze di Figaro**). Son of Thomas Kelly, master of ceremonies at Dublin Castle and a well-known wine merchant.

He received piano and singing lessons in Dublin (his teachers included Rauzzini*), and made his first operatic appearances in that city in Niccolò Piccinni's *La buona figliuola* and Charles Dibdin's *Lionel and Clarissa*. In 1779 he left Ireland to study singing in Naples and Palermo. In 1781, at Leghorn [Livorno], he made the acquaintance of Stephen and Nancy Storace*. He sang at various Italian opera houses before being engaged by Count Durazzo*, the Austrian ambassador in Venice, for the new Italian company in Vienna.

Like Benucci*, Bussani* and Nancy Storace, he made his Viennese début on 22 April 1783 in Salieri*'s *La scuola de' gelosi* (in which he appeared as the Conte di Bandiera). His other roles in Vienna, apart from those in *Le nozze di Figaro*, included Sumerse in Domenico Cimarosa's *L'italiana in Londra* (5 May 1783), Masotto in the Viennese première of Sarti*'s *Fra i due litiganti il terzo gode* (28 May 1783), Almaviva in Paisiello*'s *Il barbiere di Siviglia* (in succession to Stefano Mandini*), Gafforio in the same composer's *Il re Teodoro in Venezia* (23 August 1784), Valente in Stephen Storace's *Gli sposi malcontenti* (1 June 1785), and Corrado at the première of Martín y Soler*'s *Una cosa rara* (17 November 1786). He established himself as an excellent and highly popular *buffo* tenor. When he was granted a leave of absence of several months in 1787, Joseph II* wrote to Rosenberg-Orisini* that, were Kelly to depart for good, 'it would be a real loss for the Italian opera company, for he is excellent in several roles and never less than good in any of them'. Kelly left for London in February 1787, together with the Storaces and Thomas Attwood*. He did not return to Vienna.

Over the next twenty-five years he enjoyed a highly successful singing career in England and Ireland. James Boaden, in *Memoirs of the Life of John Philip Kemble* (1825), described him as 'a very kind and friendly man, and a very able and scientific singer', adding that 'his voice had amazing power and steadiness, his compass was extraordinary'. In addition, Kelly became stage manager at the King's Theatre, London, and director of music at Drury Lane; he also put on Italian opera seasons in Dublin. Of his own operas, *Blue Beard* (1798) proved the most enduring, remaining in the repertory some twenty-five years. In 1801 he opened his Music Saloon in Pall Mall, where he published music and also sold wine. The business venture eventually failed and he was declared bankrupt on 5 September 1811, the very day on which, in Dublin, he made his final appearance on an operatic stage.

Kelly's *Reminiscences* (1826) contain some interesting pages on musical life in Vienna and are valuable for his recollections of Mozart: 'He was a remarkably small man, very thin and pale, with a profusion of fine fair hair, of which he was rather vain . . . He was remarkably fond of punch, of which beverage I have seen him take copious draughts . . . He was kind-hearted, and always ready to oblige; but so very particular, when he played, that if the slightest noise were made, he instantly left off . . . His feeling, the rapidity of his fingers, the great execution and strength of his left hand, particularly, and the apparent inspiration of his modulations, astounded me . . . Mozart was very liberal in giving praise to those who deserved it; but felt a thorough contempt for insolent mediocrity.'

(Kelly, King[1], Michtner, Payer)

Kirchgässner [Kirchgessner], **Maria Anna Antonia** ['Marianne'] (b. Bruchsal, 5 June 1769; d. Schaffhausen, 9 December 1808). German armonica player, blind from the age of four. She toured widely in Germany and other European countries; from 1794 to 1796 she was in London, and in 1798 she spent seven months at St Petersburg. (On the popularity of the armonica in the 18th century, *see* DAVIES.)

In 1791 she performed in Austria, playing on an armonica made by the Karlsruhe Kapellmeister Joseph Aloys Schmittbaur (1718–1809), whose pupil she had been. On 24 April 1791 she was heard in Linz, and she subsequently gave three concerts in Vienna, on 10 June at the Burgtheater, on 19 August at the Kärntnertor-Theater, and on 8 September at Jahn's Rooms. At the second concert, she played the Adagio and Rondo for armonica, flute, oboe, viola and violoncello K617 which Mozart had written for her. (She is known to have played the piece also at a concert at Königsberg on 14 November 1798.) No doubt the Adagio K356/617a was likewise composed for her.

In 1806 she returned to Vienna and, at a concert at the Burgtheater on 1 April, she performed music specially composed for her by Antonín Reicha (1770–1836) as accompaniment to a speech from Schiller's play *Die Jungfrau von Orleans*, declaimed by the actress Betty Roose (1778–1808), the leading tragedienne of the National Theatre (who had played Johanna at the Viennese première on 27 January 1802). (Pisarowitz[4], Ullrich[2])

Köchel, Ludwig Alois Ferdinand von (b. Stein, near Krems, 14 January 1800; d. Vienna, 3 June 1877). Austrian botanist, mineralogist and music bibliographer. In 1862 Breitkopf & Härtel* published his *Chronologisch-thematisches Verzeichnis sämtlicher Tonwerke Wolfgang Amadé Mozarts* (now usually designated as 'K', 'KV', or 'K¹'). It was dedicated to Otto Jahn and contained references to the latter's comprehensive four-volume biography *W. A. Mozart*, issued by the same firm between 1856 and 1859. Köchel arranged Mozart's compositions chronologically and identified them by numbers; where appropriate, he provided particulars of autograph and other manuscript sources, as well as of first editions. Fragmentary and lost works he consigned to an appendix [*Anhang*]. Köchel's catalogue came quickly to be regarded as the most authoritative source in its field.

In 1905 the same publishers brought out a second edition [K²] prepared by Count Paul Waldersee, who took account of certain emendations suggested by Köchel himself as well as of the results of more recent research, but did not revise the list in any major respect. On the other hand, the third edition [K³] by Alfred Einstein (Leipzig, Breitkopf & Härtel, 1937, followed by Einstein's supplement published by J. W. Edwards at Ann Arbor in 1947) proposed significant changes in the dating of many works, while at the same time inserting into the main list many of the fragments and lost works which Köchel had relegated to his appendix. The original numbers were retained, but accompanied where necessary by distinguishing letters ('*a*' '*b*', etc.). No further substantial changes were made until the sixth edition [K⁶], prepared by Franz Giegling, Alexander Weinmann and Gerd Sievers (Breitkopf & Härtel, Wiesbaden, 1964), which incorporated all the latest findings; it was accompanied by a 64-page thematic survey of the opening bars of all compositions. The so-called seventh and eighth editions merely reproduce the sixth. (King[2], Köchel)

Kozeluch, Leopold

Kozeluch [Kotzeluch, Koželuh], **Leopold** [Jan Antonín, Ioannes Antonius] (b. Velvary, 26 June 1747; d. Vienna, 7 May 1818). Bohemian composer, pianist, teacher and publisher. He received his musical training at Velvary and, from 1765, in Prague, where he studied with his cousin, the composer Jan Antonín Kozeluch (1738–1814) and with Franz X. Duschek (*see* DUSCHEK, JOSEPHA).

In 1778 he moved to Vienna and there enjoyed a successful career as pianist and teacher. In 1781 he refused an offer to become court organist at Salzburg – mainly, he told his friends (who must have informed Mozart of the remark, since he reported it to his father on 4 July), because of the manner in which Archbishop Colloredo* had treated Mozart: 'If he lets such a man go, what might he not do to me?' On 14 November 1782 Kozeluch married Maria Anna (Allmayr) von Allstern, a niece of Ignaz von Born*. In 1785 he founded a publishing firm which, in June 1789, printed Mozart's piano Variations on 'Je suis Lindor' K354/299a (*see also* HEINA). On 12 July 1789 Mozart informed Puchberg* that Kozeluch would publish the six quartets which he was then writing for the King of Prussia (*see* FREDERICK WILLIAM II); in the event, he composed only three (K575, 589 and 590), and these were not published until after his death, on 28 December 1791, by Artaria*. Kozeluch was himself a composer of symphonies, piano music and several operas. He also wrote a Homage Cantata on the occasion of Leopold II*'s coronation in Prague in September 1791; a setting of a text by August Gottlieb Meissner (*see* MARIA LUISA), it was sung by Josepha Duschek on 12 September, in the presence of Leopold and his consort.

Kozeluch must have regarded Mozart as a formidable rival, both as a pianist and a composer. Indeed, a report on musical life in Vienna printed in the Salzburg periodical *Pfeffer und Salz* on 5 April 1786 stated baldly: 'It is well known that Herr Leopold Kozeluch competes with Mozart.' It has even been alleged that Kozeluch intrigued against Mozart. In a letter to Breitkopf & Härtel* in 1799, Niemetschek* stated that he had deliberately refrained from mentioning Kozeluch's name in his biography of Mozart 'because of the petty jealousy with which he always pursued Mozart in Prague. At the time of the coronation of Emperor Leopold II, he calumniated him in the most villainous manner, and even maligned his character.' (Hitzig, Postolka[3], Wessely[1])

Kronauer, Johann Georg (b. Winterthur, Switzerland, *c*.1743; d. Vienna, 2 March 1799). Teacher of languages, especially French, residing in Vienna. In 1782 Mozart, who was planning a concert tour which was to include London, began to study English. In a letter to his father on 17 August 1782, he mentioned having already taken three lessons and expressed the hope that he would be able to read books in English within three months.

Mozart's teacher may have been Kronauer, in whose album he made the following entry in English on 30 March 1787: 'Patience and tranquillity of mind contribute more to cure our distempers as the whole art of medecine.' The sentence does not necessarily indicate Mozart's command of English at the time, since he might have found the maxim in a book such as the following, found among his possessions after his death: *An Attempt to Facilitate the Study of the English Language by Publishing in the Present Cheap Manner a Collection of some Letters, Anecdotes, Remarks and Verses Wrote by several Celebrated English Authors* ... (Ronneburg, 1774) by

Friedrich Wilhelm Streit. Mozart probably never became very proficient in English. It is true that he addressed a short note in fairly correct English to his pupil Thomas Attwood* in 1785; but on 24 April 1787 he wrote in the album of Gottfried von Jacquin*'s brother Joseph Franz: 'Don't never forget your true and faithfull friend . . .'

Kronauer was a freemason; in 1790 he was, like Mozart, a member of the 'Zur neugekrönten Hoffnung'* Lodge.

(*Mozart: Bibliothek*, Schuler[12])

Kymli, Franz Peter Joseph (b. Mannheim, *c*.1748; d. Paris, *c*.1813). Portraitist and miniaturist. He studied painting in Mannheim and, from June 1775, in Paris. By 1776 he had been appointed court painter by the Elector Palatine Karl Theodor*. In that year he exhibited at the Salon du Colisée in Paris; between 1779 and 1787 he repeatedly showed his paintings at the Salon de la Correspondance. His subjects included Emperor Joseph II*, the Prince de Ligne (1735–1814), and Pierre Pomme, Louis XVI's personal physician; he also painted three self-portraits.

Mozart was introduced to him in Paris in 1778 by their mutual friend Anton Raaff*. 'He is a most amiable fellow,' Mozart wrote to his father on 18 July 1778, 'an upright and honest man, and a good Christian.' But what particularly endeared Kymli to Mozart was that he knew Fridolin Weber* and his family well. 'He had the good fortune and the pleasure of carrying you about in his arms on many occasions and of kissing you hundreds of times when you were still very small . . .' Mozart informed Aloisia Weber on 30 July. 'He never tires of speaking about you, and as for myself, I cannot stop doing so.'

In 1789 Kymli became a councillor at the palatine legation in Paris. He continued to reside in the French capital after being dismissed from his post in 1799 by the new Elector, Maximilian IV Joseph.

(*ALBK*)

Lange, Aloisia: *see* WEBER, ALOISIA.

Lange, (Johann) Joseph (b. Würzburg, 1 April 1751; d. Vienna, 17 September 1831). German actor who played Herz (or perhaps Puf) at the première of *Der Schauspieldirektor**. After his father, Johann Bartholomäus Lange, had died on 1 September 1760, he came under the benevolent care of Johann Philipp Christoph von Reibelt (1686–1766), a prominent official at the Würzburg court and a distant relative. In the summer of 1767 or early the following year, he went to live with Reibelt's son-in-law, Baron Egyd Valentin Felix Borie (1719–93), who was a well-known jurist in Vienna.

By 1770 Lange had embarked on his acting career. He was to be a member of the Burgtheater until 1810 and again from 1817 to 1821, with guest appearances between the two periods. A very handsome man, with an expressive face and a sonorous voice, he was idolized by the Viennese, who greatly admired his noble style of acting. He was particularly successful as Romeo and Hamlet (*see* HEUFELD); in the former role he was often partnered by Johanna Sacco* as Juliet. Joseph II* wrote to Rosenberg-Orsini* on 29 September 1786 that, were Lange to leave Vienna, it would be the 'most irreparable' loss for the German theatre company.

Laschi, Filippo

On 24 September 1775 he married the singer Anna Maria Elisabeth Schindler (b. 1757); she died on 14 March 1779. On 31 October 1780 he married Aloisia Weber*; as a result, he became Mozart's brother-in-law on Mozart's own marriage to Constanze* in 1782. The two couples maintained friendly contacts. After Lange and Aloisia separated *c.*1795, he lived with Theresia Vogel (d. 1851), a lady-in-waiting, who bore him three children (he also had three by his first wife and six by Aloisia). He was still acting as late as 1822.

Lange was also a gifted painter (he had studied at the Academy of Drawing and Copper Engraving in Vienna) and he was frequently commissioned to make portraits of actors and to record scenes from plays for various theatrical publications. In a letter to Nannerl* on 25 March 1785 Leopold Mozart praised as an excellent likeness a sketch (since lost) which Lange had made of him during a visit to Salzburg. Lange's portrait of Mozart (probably painted *c.*1789–90) remains, though uncompleted, the most celebrated in existence; Constanze assured Vincent Novello* that 'it exactly resembled him'. It hangs today in the museum at Mozart's birthplace in Salzburg. Lange also painted Constanze.

Lange's older brother Joseph Michael (baptized Würzburg, 25 October 1742; d. Vienna, 29 July 1771) was likewise a very talented actor. He made a very successful début at the Kärntnertor-Theater on 20 August 1770 as Marcius in the tragedy *Brutus* by Joachim Wilhelm von Brawe (1738–58). At the same performance Joseph Lange made his first appearance on the Viennese stage in the much smaller part of a tribune.

(Blümml, Landon³, Novello, Schuler¹, Payer)

Laschi, Filippo (b. ?Florence; d. after ?1776). Italian tenor who would have taken the part of Fracasso at the première of *La finta semplice** which Leopold Mozart tried to arrange in Vienna in 1768. Father of Luisa Laschi*. He sang in London from 1748 until 1750, also in Brussels in 1749 and in Turin in 1754. In 1765 he appeared as Messer Ridolfo in Baldassare Galuppi's *Li tre amanti ridicoli* at the Burgtheater, where his subsequent roles included Ruggiero in Antonio Sacchini's *La contadina in corte* in [?]1766, and Apollo as well as the High Priest at the première of Gluck*'s *Alceste* on 26 December 1767. In 1770 he sang Sempronio in the opera *Amor non ha bisogno di maestro* (by an unidentified composer). Joseph von Sonnenfels, writing in 1768, praised Laschi's intelligence and good taste which made him avoid cheap effects, and described him as still one of the outstanding Italian operatic singers, even though his voice had lost some of its quality; he was 'a noble *buffo*'.

In a letter from Venice on 13 February 1771, Leopold Mozart informed his wife* that Laschi had recently died; but according to R. Angermüller, he was still singing in Florence in 1777.

(Angermüller¹⁵, *London Stage*, Sonnenfels, Zechmeister)

Laschi [Mombelli], **Luisa** (b. Florence, 1760s; d. *c.*1790). Italian soprano; the original Countess (*Le nozze di Figaro**), and Zerlina in the first Viennese production of *Don Giovanni**. Daughter of Filippo Laschi*. She was engaged in Vienna from August 1784 to February 1785 and again, following performances in Naples, from April 1786 until 1790. She made a brilliant début as Giannina in Domenico Cimarosa's *Giannina e Bernardone* on 24 September 1784. Her other roles included

Rosina in Paisiello*'s *Il barbiere di Siviglia* (21 January 1785), Isabella in Martín y Soler*'s *Una cosa rara* (17 November 1786), Amore in the same composer's *L'arbore di Diana* (1 October 1787), Carolina in Salieri*'s *Il talismano* (10 September 1788), and Amarilli in his *Il pastor fido* (11 February 1789). A writer in the *Kritisches Theaterjournal von Wien* described her performance in *L'arbore di Diana* as 'grace personified', adding: 'Mombelli's Amor: ah, who would not be enchanted by it, what painter has ever depicted a mischievous smile more perfectly, what sculptor has portrayed more graceful gestures, what other singer is capable of producing such melting, marvellously smooth singing with such simplicity and genuine emotion?'

On 2 November 1786 she married the well-known Italian tenor Domenico Mombelli (1751–1835), who had joined the Burgtheater company at the beginning of that season (he made his début as Milord Arispinghe in Cimarosa's *L'italiana in Londra* on 12 May 1786). She thereafter sang under her married name. Their first joint appearance was probably in Sarti*'s *I finti eredi* on 1 August 1786. At the Viennese première of *Don Giovanni* (7 May 1788) she was seven months' pregnant; the child died shortly after birth, as an earlier one had done the previous year. On 27 February 1789 Luisa appeared as 'Donna Farinella, virtuosa di musica' and her husband as 'Don Capriccio, virtuoso di musica' in the pasticcio *L'ape musicale*, both roles being evidently designed to display their vocal brilliance.

Their names are no longer mentioned by Michtner for the 1789–90 season at the Burgtheater, and nothing further is known about Luisa. Perhaps she died soon after their return to Italy. Domenico Mombelli remarried, probably in 1791. His second wife, the ballerina Vincenza Viganò, belonged to a well-known family of dancers (Onorato Viganò was her father and Salvatore her brother); she was also a niece of Luigi Boccherini. From June 1794 to July 1795 Domenico sang again in Vienna, with great success. In 1805 he settled in Bologna, where he formed a small touring company. On 18 May 1812 he sang, with his daughters Ester and Anna, at the première in Rome of Rossini's first opera *Demetrio e Polibio*, which he had himself commissioned and for which Vincenza had written the libretto.
(Michtner, Raeburn[7], Weinstock)

Lausch, Laurenz (fl. late 18th century). Austrian music copyist and publisher. He established a prominent copying business in Vienna in the 1780s and later himself issued some publications. His numerous announcements of manuscript music in the *Wiener Zeitung* regularly included works by Mozart, frequently in arrangements, especially for the piano. Thus he offered for sale, on 1 July 1786, the complete score of *Le nozze di Figaro**, as well as a version 'skilfully arranged to be sung at the pianoforte' and a setting of the numbers for string quartet. A similar announcement appeared on 24 May 1788 regarding *Don Giovanni**. Another one, on 14 January 1792, offered arrangements for voice and piano, as also for string quartet, of various numbers from *Die Zauberflöte**, billed as 'the last work of this world-famous composer . . . Wolfgang Amade Mozart, the darling of the Muses'.
(*Mozart: Dokumente*, Weinmann[8])

Legros, Joseph (b. Monampteuil, near Laon, 7 or 8 September 1739; d. La Rochelle, 20 December 1793). French tenor and composer. He sang at the Paris Opéra from 1764 until 1783, during which time he created roles in four of Gluck*'s

Leopold II

operas: Achille in *Iphigénie en Aulide* (19 April 1774), Orphée in the revised *Orphée et Eurydice* (2 August 1774), Admète in the revised *Alceste* (23 April 1776), and Pylade in *Iphigénie en Tauride* (18 May 1779). Legros himself composed an opera, *Anacréon*, and some songs. From 1777 to 1790 he was director of the Concert Spirituel, the famous concert series founded by the composer Anne Danican Philidor (1681–1728) in 1725.

Mozart saw a great deal of Legros in Paris in 1778. Having been invited to use Legros's piano for his composing, he spent many days at Legros's house, where he also frequently conversed with Anton Raaff* who was staying there. For the Concert Spirituel, Mozart composed the so-called 'Paris' Symphony K297/300*a* which was played to great acclaim on 18 June and repeated on 15 August (*see also* HOLZBAUER). In addition, he wrote a sinfonia concertante for Punto*, Ramm*, Ritter* and Wendling* (KAnh.9/297*B*) but, to his annoyance, it was never played at the Concert Spirituel. (Mozart suspected Giovanni Giuseppe Cambini [1746–1825], an Italian violinist and composer then living in Paris, of having prevented its performance.) Before his departure, Mozart sold both the symphony and the sinfonia concertante to Legros. He also tried to persuade Legros to invite Aloisia Weber* to Paris for the following winter, but learned that the soprano Franziska Dorothea Lebrun (1756–91) had already been engaged.

In August 1782 Mozart wrote to Legros from Vienna concerning the possibility of a contract for himself for Lent 1783. Legros's reply is not known; Mozart never returned to Paris.

(Rushton)

Leopold II (b. Vienna, 5 May 1747; d. Vienna, 1 March 1792). Son of Empress Maria Theresa* and her husband Francis I. Archduke; Grand Duke of Tuscany, 1765–90; King of Austria, Bohemia and Hungary upon the death of his brother, Joseph II* (20 February 1790); crowned Roman Emperor at Frankfurt am Main on 9 October; crowned King of Bohemia in Prague on 6 September 1791. In August 1765 he married the Spanish infanta Maria Luisa*; they had sixteen children. (*See also* VILLENEUVE.)

Leopold almost certainly met the Mozarts on their visit to Vienna in late 1762. During their first Italian journey, Wolfgang and his father were received in audience by him at the Pitti Palace in Florence on 1 April 1770. On the following day Wolfgang played before him and the Grand Duchess at the Villa (del) Poggio Imperiale, on which occasion, according to Leopold Mozart's letter to his wife* of 3 April, he sight-read the 'most difficult' fugues and improvised on the 'most difficult' themes 'as easily as one eats a piece of bread'. After his father had failed to obtain an appointment for Wolfgang at Archduke Ferdinand*'s court at Milan, he hoped to secure a post for him at Leopold's court in Florence, but in that respect also he was unsuccessful. Little is known about Leopold's taste in music, but he evidently had a liking for Italian *opera buffa*, for after the première of Domenico Cimarosa's *Il matrimonio segreto* in Vienna on 7 February 1792 he ordered a repeat performance that same evening.

Mozart travelled to Frankfurt for Leopold's coronation, though at his own expense and not as a member of the official retinue. During his stay, *Die Entführung** was performed on 12 October and he himself gave a concert on 20 October, but instead of *Don Giovanni**, announced for 5 October, the Mainz theatre company presented Carl Ditters von Dittersdorf's *Die Liebe im Narrenhaus*. On the other hand, *Don Giovanni* was performed in Prague on 2 September 1791, in the presence of Leopold and his consort, as part of the celebrations of Leopold's coronation as King of Bohemia. Mozart, who had come to Prague with Constanze*, probably conducted himself; he certainly directed the première of the festival opera *La clemenza di Tito** on 6 September.

On 11 December 1791 Constanze submitted a petition for a pension to Leopold. She was eventually granted one on 13 March 1792 by his successor, Francis II, who awarded her some 266 gulden annually, starting that year.

Leutgeb [Leitgeb]**, Joseph** (b. Vienna, 8 October 1732; d. Vienna, 27 February 1811). Austrian horn player; a friend of the Mozarts. On 2 November 1760 he married Barbara Plazzeriani (1732[?3]–85), the daughter of an Italian cheese and sausage merchant, Blasius Plazzeriani.

Between 27 November 1761 and 28 January 1763 Leutgeb played horn concertos at fourteen concerts at the Burgtheater, Vienna. In 1762 or 1763 he joined the Salzburg court orchestra, but was evidently granted frequent leaves of absence. In January 1770 he played in Frankfurt am Main, where he was well known, and in April and May of the same year he gave concerts in Paris. In a letter from Milan on 13 February 1773, Leopold Mozart mentioned the possibility of a concert being arranged for Leutgeb, who had recently arrived in Milan where he was 'extraordinarily popular'.

In 1777 Leutgeb moved back to Vienna, where he set up as a cheesemonger, or, more probably, took over his late father-in-law's shop in what is now Vienna's 8th district. He must have fallen on hard times, for Mozart, who renewed contact with the Leutgebs after settling in Vienna, wrote to his father on 8 May 1782, in reference to a loan the latter had made them: 'I beg you to be patient a little while longer with poor Leutgeb; if you knew his circumstances and saw how he has to struggle to make ends meet, you would, I am sure, feel sorry for him.' After his wife's death, Leutgeb married, on 15 January 1786, Franziska Hober (or Huber; 1733[?43]–1828).

Mozart wrote for Leutgeb the Quintet K407/386c, the incomplete Rondo K371, the horn concertos K417, 447 and 495, and probably also the two movements K412 and 514 (later completed by Süssmayr*) which together make up the first horn concerto K386b. The horn parts in certain other works may also have been composed for him. Some of the autographs contain jocular comments by Mozart: K417 is headed 'Wolfgang Amadé Mozart has taken pity on Leutgeb, ass, ox, and fool, at Vienna, 27 March 1783,' while on K495 he wrote remarks in different coloured inks. In their personal contacts, also, Leutgeb appears to have served as a butt for Mozart's jokes. Thus he is likely to have been the victim of the 'surprise' described by Mozart in his letter to Constanze* of 25 June 1791: at his instigation, a message was delivered to the person in question (whose name was later deleted by Nissen*), falsely announcing the arrival of a close acquaintance from Rome: 'The poor man put on his best Sunday clothes and dressed his hair most splendidly – you can imagine how we made fun of him – it's true, I always need to make a fool of someone.' While Constanze was taking the cure at Baden, Mozart sometimes slept at Leutgeb's house. Their friendship continued until the end of Mozart's life. (Heartz[2], Pisarowitz[5])

Lichnowsky, Karl

Lichnowsky, Karl (Alois Johann Nepomuk Vinzenz Leonhard), Count [later Prince] (b. Vienna, 21 June 1761; d. Vienna, 15 April 1841). Prominent Austrian patron of the arts, especially music; said to have been a pupil of Mozart. Son of Prince Johann Karl Lichnowsky (1730–88) and his wife Maria Carolina, *née* Countess Althann (1741–1800). He studied law at Göttingen, and later became court councillor at the Austro-Bohemian court chancellery in Vienna and court chamberlain. A freemason, he joined in 1783 the 'Zur Wohltätigkeit'* Lodge, to which Mozart was himself admitted the following year. In 1785 Lichnowsky transferred to the 'Zur wahren Eintracht' Lodge, and in 1786 he became a member of the 'Zur Wahrheit' Lodge (*see* 'Zur neugekrönten hoffnung'). In 1788 he married Countess (Maria) Christiane Thun-Hohenstein (1765–1841), a daughter of Mozart's great benefactress Countess Wilhelmine Thun-Hohenstein*.

In April 1789 Mozart travelled with Lichnowsky, doubtless at the latter's invitation, via Prague to Dresden and Leipzig, where they parted company in May. Mozart went to stay in Berlin from 19 to 28 May, before returning to Vienna by himself. The reason for Lichnowsky's journey is not known; perhaps he was on his way to his estate at Grätz, near Troppau in Upper Silesia (where, in 1806, Beethoven* would write most of his Fourth Symphony). There is no information available, either, regarding the precise circumstances which led Mozart to accompany him.

A further mystery surrounds Mozart's later relations with Lichnowsky. In a note dated 9 November 1791, the court of justice for Lower Austria reminded the court treasury that Prince Karl Lichnowsky had obtained an order against Mozart for the recovery, by means of the seizure of his property and the withholding of one half of his official salary, of a debt amounting to some 1435 gulden (and legal costs of twenty-four gulden). Nothing is known about the date of the loan or the circumstances in which it was granted, nor about the legal proceedings leading to the court order. There is no indication that the latter had been executed, even in part, when Mozart died a few weeks after the above-mentioned communication. No mention of the debt was made in any of the documents pertaining to his estate which are known to have been drawn up after his death, and in due course Constanze* received in full the still-outstanding salary instalments for the months of November and December 1791.

Lichnowsky later became a most generous friend to Beethoven, who dedicated to him the piano trios op. 1, the 'Pathétique' Piano Sonata op. 13, the Piano Sonata op. 26, the Second Symphony op. 36, and the variations on 'Quant' è più bello' WoO 69. He dedicated the ballet score *Die Geschöpfe des Prometheus* op. 43 and the Variations on 'See the conqu'ring hero comes' WoO 45 to Princess Christiane.

(Brauneis, Forbes, Schuler[11])

Linley, Thomas (b. Bath, 5 May 1756; d. Grimsthorpe, Lincolnshire, 5 August 1778). English composer and violinist. His father, also named Thomas (1733–95), was a well-known composer, harpsichordist, concert director and singing teacher. Thomas Jr. played a violin concerto at a concert in Bristol shortly after his seventh birthday. He studied music with William Boyce in London and, from 1768 to 1771, was a pupil of Pietro Nardini in Florence. After his return to England he frequently played at concerts in Bath and also became leader of the Drury Lane orchestra. He composed both sacred and secular works; the latter included at least twenty violin concertos (only one of which survives) and music for the stage. He died in a boating accident.

Mozart met Linley in Florence in April 1770, at the house of Corilla Olympica [real name: Maddalena Morelli-Fernandez], a poetess celebrated for improvising poems which she sang to the guitar or other string instruments. The two children took a great liking to each other and made music together on several occasions: 'They took turns at playing the whole afternoon, not like boys, but like men,' Leopold Mozart reported to his wife* on 21 April from Rome. He described Linley as 'a very charming boy' who played 'most beautifully'. On the day of the Mozarts' departure (probably 6 April), Linley had presented Wolfgang with a poem in Italian, written at his request by Corilla Olympica, proclaiming his admiration and affection.

Linley's sister Elizabeth Anne (1754–92) was a well-known soprano. After her marriage to Richard Brinsley Sheridan in 1773 she withdrew from public performance, but still gave private concerts.
(Beechey)

Lipp, Maria Magdelena (b. Eggenfeld, Bavaria, 1745; d. Salzburg, 10 June 1827). Soprano; the original Göttliche Barmherzigkeit (*Die Schuldigkeit des ersten Gebots**) and, according to the libretto of *La finta semplice**, the first Rosina. (*See also* RE PASTORE, IL.) Daughter of Franz Ignaz Lipp (1718–98), a native of Eggenfeld, who was appointed third organist at the Salzburg court in 1754. He composed a certain amount of sacred music. The Mozarts seem to have thought little of his musicianship: 'You can easily imagine how abysmal the standard now is, for Lipp has been accompanying at court since Adlgasser*'s death,' Leopold Mozart wrote on 11 June 1778. And Wolfgang, in a letter from Paris on 18 July 1778, reported that he had been playing fugues 'with all the skill of a Lipp' – a remark which, as J. H. Eibl points out, should clearly be read as a jocular allusion to Lipp's pedestrian style.

On Maria Magdalena's studies and career, *see* BRAUNHOFER. She married Michael Haydn* on 17 August 1768. They had a daughter, Aloisia Josepha, who was born on 31 January 1770 and died a year later. The various references to Maria Magdalena in the Mozarts' correspondence reflect no particular affection. Her sister Maria Josepha Judith caused a minor scandal in 1778 by giving birth to an illegitimate daughter whose father was the court Konzertmeister Antonio Brunetti. The child died after five weeks; the parents were married later that year.
(Aigner, Croll[6], Eibl in *Mozart: Briefe*)

Lodron, Antonia Maria Josepha Felicitas, Countess (b. Salzburg, 13 October 1738; d. Salzburg, 14 December 1780). Daughter of Count Johann Georg Anton Felix Arco*; sister of Count Karl Joseph Arco*. On 4 April 1758 she became the second wife of Hereditary Marshal Count Ernst Maria Joseph Nepomuk Lodron (1716–79); she bore him three sons and five daughters.

There are numerous references to the family in the Mozarts' correspondence. For the countess's name day on 13 June, Mozart composed the Divertimento K247 in 1776, and the Divertimento K287/271H in 1777. Also in 1776, he wrote the Concerto for three pianos K242 for her and her two eldest daughters, Maria Aloysia (b. 1761) and Maria Josepha (b. 1764), who both became Leopold Mozart's pupils in 1778. Two younger daughters, Maria Antonia (b. 1767) and Maria Anna Aloysia (b. 1769) received instruction from Nannerl*.

Leopold does not appear to have liked the countess much, for in a letter to Wolfgang on 5 January 1778 he referred to 'her usual false friendliness' and on 28 May 1778 he observed tartly, in connection with the sudden death of the Lodrons' administrator: 'Now I know at last how weeping becomes Countess Lodron, and that she is even capable of weeping.'
(Schuler[8])

Lolli, Giuseppe (fl. 1770–91). Italian bass; the original Commendatore and Masetto (*Don Giovanni**). He was again in the cast at the gala performance of *Don Giovanni* in Prague on 2 September 1791.

Little is known about his career. In 1772 he sang Don Pompeo in Agostino Accorimboni's *L'amante nel sacco* in Rome; in 1777 he appeared at Florence as Fabio in Anfossi*'s *Il principe di Lago Nero* and as Prospero in the same composer's *Il curioso indiscreto*. During the 1780–81 season he performed at Parma.
(Angermüller[15])

Lugiati, Pietro (b. Verona, 26 January 1724; d. Verona, 19[?1] November 1788). Member of a prominent and wealthy Veronese family; his father Francesco was district treasurer, and he himself became a high official in the service of the Venetian Republic, to which Verona was subject at the time. He was also a great lover of music and of the theatre.

During Leopold and Wolfgang Mozart's first stay at Verona (27 December 1769 – 10 January 1770) he invited Wolfgang to play before guests at his house, and attended Wolfgang's concert at the Accademia Filarmonica on 5 January. He also arranged for Wolfgang's portrait to be painted. The artist was formerly identified as Lugiati's cousin Giambettino Cignaroli, but is now believed to have been the latter's nephew Domenico Saverio dalla Rosa (1743–1821). Lugiati appears to have been in contact with cultural circles in other Italian cities, for in a letter on 22 April 1770 he informed Wolfgang's mother* that he had put her son in touch with the 'most illustrious persons' in Rome. Wolfgang and his father stayed with the Lugiatis again in 1771 and 1772 (and perhaps also in 1773).
(*Mozart in Italia*)

Mandini, Maria, *née* de Vesian (fl. 1780s). Soprano; the original Marcellina (*Le nozze di Figaro**). Daughter of Antoine François de Vesian, a court official at Versailles; wife of Stefano Mandini*.

She was engaged in Vienna in 1783, at the same time as her husband, and made her début as Madama Brillante in Domenico Cimarosa's *L'italiana in Londra* on 5 May. Her other roles during her five years in Vienna included the Contessa di Belfiore in Sarti*'s *Fra i due litiganti il terzo gode* (28 May 1783), Marina in Martín y Soler*'s *Il burbero di buon cuore* (4 January 1786), Olimpia in Cimarosa's *Le trame deluse* (7 May 1787), Livietta in Paisiello*'s *Le due contesse* (28 July 1787), and Britomarte in Martín y Soler's *L'arbore di Diana* (1 October 1787). She also sang in numerous concerts, in oratorios and at private functions. If she was not quite as highly regarded as her husband in Vienna, her talents and looks did not go unappreciated. Zinzendorf* wrote of her performance as Olimpia: 'La Mandini excelled herself'; and of her appearance in *Il burbero*: 'La Mandini showed us her beautiful hair.'

She left Vienna with her husband for Italy in 1788. In June 1789 both were highly acclaimed for their performances in Francesco Bianchi's *La villanella rapita* at the Théâtre de Monsieur in Paris. Arthur Young, an Englishman who heard her at this time, wrote in his *Travels during the Years 1787, 1788, and 1789* ... (London, 1792) that she was 'a most fascinating singer, – her voice nothing, but her grace, expression, soul, all strung to exquisite sensibility'.

Maria's older sister Marianna Piccinelli, known as 'La Francesina', was engaged at the Burgtheater, Vienna, for the 1784 season, making her début as Bettina in Sarti's *I contrattempi* on 26 April. She met with scant success in Vienna and left in September of the same year.
(Michtner)

Mandini, Stefano (1750–*c.*1810). Italian baritone; husband of Maria Mandini*. The original Count Almaviva (*Le nozze di Figaro**); Mozart also intended him to sing Don Asdrubale (*Lo sposo deluso**). He had a successful career in Italy before being engaged in 1783 in Vienna, where he became one of the stars of the new Italian opera company, much admired both as a singer and an actor.

According to O. Michtner, Mandini made his Viennese début as Milord Arispinghe in Domenico Cimarosa's *L'italiana in Londra* on 5 May 1783. Over the next five years he distinguished himself in a variety of roles. Of his Mingone in Sarti*'s *Fra i due litiganti il terzo gode* (28 May 1783), Zinzendorf* wrote: 'Mandini performed the role of Mingone to perfection.' Joseph II* was so delighted with his Almaviva in Paisiello*'s *Il barbiere di Siviglia* (13 August 1783) that he ordered the Act III duet in which the Count, disguised as a student of theology, sanctimoniously wishes Bartolo 'peace and joy' ['Gioia e pace sia con voi'] to be repeated. As Count Zefiro in Gazzaniga's *La dama incognita, ossia Le vendemmie* (13 April 1784) Mandini, according to Zinzendorf, 'sang like an angel'. In Paisiello's *La contadina di spirito* (6 April 1785), Benucci* and Mandini, appearing as the Marchese Tulipano and his son Giorgino, were, in Zinzendorf's opinion, 'extraordinarily funny'. And the anonymous author of a scathing review (quoted by Michtner) of Martín y Soler*'s *L'arbore di Diana* (1 October 1787), while condemning the role (Doristo) assigned to Mandini as morally pernicious and musically inadequate, nevertheless judged that he had acquitted himself well, 'for he is a first-rate artist who performs all his roles well'. (*See also* BENUCCI.)

Other parts taken by Mandini in Vienna included Teodoro in Paisiello's *Il re Teodoro in Venezia* (23 August 1784), Artidoro in Stephen Storace's *Gli sposi malcontenti* (1 June 1785), Pippo in Francesco Bianchi's *La villanella rapita* (25 November 1785 – *see* CALVESI), the Poet in Salieri*'s *Prima la musica, poi le parole* (Schönbrunn Palace, 7 February 1786), Marone in Anfossi*'s *Il trionfo delle donne* (15 May 1786), Lubino in Martín y Soler's *Una cosa rara* (17 November 1786), and Biscroma in Salieri's *Axur, re d'Ormus* (8 January 1788).

Mandini's departure in early 1788 for Naples, where he had been invited by Queen Maria Karolina, was greatly regretted by the Viennese public, which gave him an ovation at his farewell concert on 15 February 1788. The following year he sang with considerable success in Paris. After his appearance as Pippo in Bianchi's *La villanella rapita* on 15 June (*see also* MANDINI, MARIA), the critic of the *Mercure de France* wrote (on 27 June): 'Signor Mandini's voice is very beautiful and quite unforced, with a wide compass, capable of singing even tenor . . . His acting is full of wit and subtlety and comic invention, yet always natural.' His Almaviva in Paisiello's *Il barbiere di Siviglia* on 22 July was no less favourably reviewed in the *Mercure de France* of 1 August. In 1794–5 Mandini performed in Venice. Negotiations for a new extended contract in Vienna came to nothing, but he did sing there in performances of Niccolò Piccinni's *La Griselda* and Paisiello's *La molinara* in June 1795. At the time he was on his way to St Petersburg, where he was to score fresh triumphs. 'He was handsome, he was a splendid actor and he sang marvellously,' the French painter Elisabeth Vigée-Lebrun, who had seen and heard him in St Petersburg, recalled in her memoirs.

Mandini's younger brother, Paolo Mandini (1757–1842), a tenor, was a member of Joseph Haydn*'s opera company at Eszterháza in 1783–4. He was subsequently engaged at the Burgtheater, Vienna, for the 1785–6 season and again in 1789. (*Mercure de France*, Michtner, Raeburn[8], Vigée-Lebrun)

Manservisi, Rosa (fl. 1770s–1790s). Italian soprano; the original Sandrina (*La finta giardiniera**). Charles Burney* was quite favourably impressed when he heard her sing in Munich in 1772: 'Her figure is agreeable, her voice, though not strong, is well-toned, she has nothing vulgar in her manner, sings in tune, and never gives offence.'

She was engaged in Vienna from 1 October 1783 and made her début on 14 November 1783 as Berenice in Felice Alessandri's *La finta principessa*. Her other roles included Donna Stella in *La frascatana* (8 December 1783), Camilletta in *La finta amante* (20 June 1784), and Belisa in *Il re Teodoro in Venezia* (23 August 1784), all by Paisiello*; Carlotta in Sarti*'s *I contrattempi* (26 April 1784); and Lauretta in Salieri*'s *Il ricco d'un giorno* (6 December 1784). She proved herself a useful and generally competent member of the Italian company, without, however, evoking great enthusiasm. Zinzendorf* was far from enchanted with her: after her début, he wrote that she was ugly and that she bellowed; her performance in *La finta amante* he described as 'execrable'. She left Vienna in the spring of 1785 for the Teatro San Moisè in Venice, where she was to meet with greater success. Later she was engaged in Dresden, and it was there that Mozart met her again in 1789. 'You can imagine how delighted she was to see me,' he wrote to Constanze* on 16 April 1789. She became a prominent singing teacher in Dresden.

Her sister Teresa also appeared in that first Munich production of *La finta giardiniera*, either as Serpetta or Armida.
(Burney[5], Michtner)

Manzuoli, Giovanni (b. Florence, *c.*1720; d. Florence, 1782). Italian castrato who created the title role in *Ascanio in Alba**. After singing at various Italian theatres, he was engaged in 1749 by the famous castrato Farinelli (*see* HASSE) to perform in Madrid. He resided there until 1753 and returned for a shorter period in September 1755, by which time his fame was well established throughout Europe. He was among several prominent singers invited to appear in David Perez's *Alessandro* *nell'Indie* at the opening of the Teatro de los Paços Ribeira in Lisbon on 31 March 1755.

In October 1760 he became, according to Metastasio*, 'the idol' of Vienna after his performance in Hasse's *Alcide al bivio* (for which Metastasio had supplied the libretto). While in Vienna, Manzuoli also sang at the premières of Giuseppe Scarlatti's *Issipile* (25 November 1760) and Tommaso Traetta's *Armida* (3 January 1761). In 1763 he created the role of Horatz in Gluck*'s *Il trionfo di Clelia* at the opening of the Teatro Communale at Bologna. During the 1764–5 season he sang at the King's Theatre in London. His opening performance in the pasticcio *Ezio* on 24 November 1764 was a spectacular success, as Charles Burney* later recalled: 'Manz[u]oli's voice was the most powerful and voluminous soprano that had been heard on our stage since the time of Farinelli; and his manner of singing was grand and full of taste and dignity . . . The applause was hearty, unequivocal, and free from all suspicion of artificial zeal; it was a universal thunder.' Among his other roles at the King's Theatre was Farnaspe at the première of Johann Christian Bach*'s *Adriano in Siria* on 26 January 1765.

During his stay in London Manzuoli became friendly with the Mozarts and reportedly gave Wolfgang some singing lessons. They met again in April 1770 in Florence, where Manzuoli had become a court singer, and their contacts grew still closer in Milan in 1771, when Manzuoli came out of retirement to sing in the two theatrical spectacles put on in celebration of Archduke Ferdinand*'s wedding: Hasse's *Il Ruggiero* and Mozart's *Ascanio in Alba*. Burney had noted, after hearing Manzuoli in Florence in 1770, that the castrato's voice 'seemed less powerful . . . than when he was in England'. But Manzuoli must have acquitted himself well enough of his role in Mozart's 'festa teatrale', for at the third performance he had to repeat one of his arias. A dispute then arose over his fee. His contract having stipulated a payment of 500 cigliati for the opera, with no mention of the 'festa teatrale', he now demanded a further sum of 500 cigliati. When he received instead a total of 700 cigliati and a gold snuff-box ('quite enough, I think,' Mozart observed in his note to Nannerl* of 23 or 24 November 1771), he returned both the money and the box, and left Milan in a huff. He had behaved, Mozart told his sister, 'like a true castrato'.

(Burney²,⁴, Hansell², *London Stage*, Zechmeister)

Marchand. A very talented family, on friendly terms with the Mozarts. Theobold Hilarius Marchand (baptized Strasbourg, 21 November 1746; d. Munich, 22 November 1800) was a singer and actor who had joined Sebastiani's company in the Rhineland in the 1760s and taken it over in 1770. He was director of the German court theatre under Karl Theodor* from May 1777 to 1793, first in Mannheim and from 1778 in Munich. He was married to the actress Maria Magdalena Brochard (1748[?9]–94). They had three children: Anna Maria Margaretha ['Gretl'] (b. ?Frankfurt, *c.*1768; d. Munich, 11 June 1800), Heinrich Wilhelm Philipp (baptized Mainz, 4 May 1769; d. ?Mannheim, after 1811), and Daniel Ernst Lambert (baptized Mainz, 15 December 1770).

Mozart made Marchand's acquaintance during his stay at Mannheim in 1777–8, and met him again in Munich in 1780 while preparing *Idomeneo*. When Leopold Mozart arrived in Munich with Nannerl* in late January 1781 to attend the première, he must have quickly established cordial relations with Marchand, for the latter's two older children came to live and study with him in Salzburg, Heinrich from 1781 until 1784 and Margaretha from 1782 to 1784; to the boy he gave instruction in composition, piano and violin playing, to the girl piano and singing lessons. Mozart's letters to his father frequently contain affectionate greetings to the two children. In 1783 they were joined by Marchand's niece, Maria Johanna Brochard (1775–1824), the daughter of Eva Margaretha Brochard, née Ihlein (b. 1752), an actress and singer married to the dancer Georg Paul Brochard. The young girl probably studied singing and the piano with Leopold.

The three children returned to Munich in early September 1784, shortly after Nannerl's marriage and departure for St Gilgen. However, in February 1785 Leopold Mozart took Heinrich with him to Vienna, where Heinrich played at Wolfgang's concert on 18 February and at another one given by the Tonkünstler-Societät on 15 March; in between he himself gave two concerts at the Burgtheater on 2 and 14 March. The following year Leopold Mozart negotiated a contract for him as pianist and violinist at the Salzburg court, where he probably remained until 1789. In that year Heinrich entered the service of Prince Thurn und Taxis at Regensburg as a pianist. In 1798–9 he undertook some concert tours. In 1805 he visited Paris and, while there, resigned his post at Regensburg from June 1806. A critic writing in the *Allgemeine Musikalische Zeitung* (*see* BREITKOPF & HÄRTEL) in 1798 described him as a brilliant pianist, 'especially with his right hand, for with the left he is not quite as accurate'.

Margaretha began to sing in public in 1784 and made her début at the Munich court opera in 1787 in Vogler*'s *Castore e Polluce*. In 1790 she married the composer and conductor Franz Danzi (1763–1826). After appearances with Domenico Guardasoni*'s company in Germany and Prague (1792–3) and performances in Italy (1794–5), she and her husband returned to Munich in 1796. During the next three years she was one of the most admired singers there; her roles included the Queen of Night in *Die Zauberflöte**, Donna Anna in *Don Giovanni**, Susanna in *Le nozze di Figaro**, and Blonde in *Die Entführung**. Her final appearance was as Canzade in Danzi's *Der Kuss* on 27 June 1799.

Of her brother Daniel, Leopold Mozart wrote to Nannerl on 8 September 1786 that he was an 'incomparable' cellist whose playing was deeply moving. He was expected to visit Salzburg with his sister and father at the end of that month: 'By then another new fortepiano will have been finished which will be placed in our large room [at the 'Tanzmeisterhaus' – *see* RAAB], since it belongs to Marchand. So there will be nothing but music, with the five of us here [Heinrich was by then already in the archbishop's service], always ready to make music.' Leopold's letter bears witness to the continuing close relations between the two families. The fact that both Leopold and Theobald Marchand were freemasons no doubt created a further bond between the two men. Apart from periodically meeting in Salzburg or Munich, they corresponded regularly.

Mozart saw the Marchands for the last time in Munich in November 1790. At that time he also met Maria Johanna Brochard again. 'Her looks have unfortunately been spoiled by smallpox,' he wrote to Constanze*: 'What a pity! She never stops talking about you. She plays the piano very nicely.' Her lack of looks did not hamper her career. She made her début as an actress at the Munich court theatre in 1790, and as a singer the following year as Azemia in *Die Wilden*, a German version of Nicolas d'Alayrac's *Azémia, ou Le nouveau Robinson* (Paris, 1786, subtitled *Les sauvages* in 1787). She married the dancer Franz Renner, and in 1797 both left Munich for Mannheim. Maria Johanna subsequently lived with and eventually married the actor, playwright and theatre manager Franz von Holbein (1779–1855), a descendant of the famous painter. She died in Prague on 24 April 1824. (Nothing is known about Daniel Marchand's later life.)

Theobald Hilarius Marchand was, of course, well acquainted with Fridolin Weber* and his family; in fact, he gave acting lessons to Aloisia Weber* while in Mannheim. In 1784 Mozart wrote to him in an (unsuccessful) effort to arrange an engagement for Josepha Weber* in Munich.
(Branscombe⁴, Münster¹,³, Schuler⁴, Würtz/Alexander, Zenger)

Marchetti-Fantozzi, Maria (b. 1767; d. after 1807). Italian soprano; the original Vitellia (*La clemenza di Tito**). She married the tenor Angelo Fantozzi in 1788. After performing with great success in Naples and Milan, she was engaged in Prague where she remained until the end of September 1791; later she sang in Venice and also in Berlin. She had a beautiful voice, a pleasing appearance and an imposing stage presence. According to Zinzendorf*, Leopold II* found her enchanting in *La clemenza di Tito*.

The soprano Josepha Marchetti-Fantozzi who was engaged at the Munich opera in 1806 was presumably a daughter of Maria Marchetti-Fantozzi. In 1808 Josepha sang at the première of the opera *Antigonus* by Baron Johann Nepomuk Poissl (1783–1865); in 1809 she appeared as Sesto in *La clemenza di Tito*. That same year she married the tenor Georg Weixelbaum; the couple left Munich in 1816.
(Kutsch/Riemens, Zenger)

Maria Luisa [Ludovica] (b. Naples, 24 November 1745; d. Vienna, 15 May 1792). Daughter of King Charles VII of the Two Sicilies (reigned 1734–59, from 1759 to 1788 King Charles III of Spain) and of his wife Anna Amalia of Saxony. She married Archduke Leopold [later Emperor Leopold II*] in 1765 and bore him sixteen children. She was, in turn, Grand Duchess of Tuscany (1765–90) and Empress (from 1790).

On 6 September 1791, in Prague, Maria Luisa attended with her husband the first performance of *La clemenza di Tito**, specially composed by Mozart to celebrate Leopold's coronation as King of Bohemia. In his *Rococobilder – nach den Aufzeichnungen meines Grossvaters* (Gumbinnen, 1871), Alfred Meissner stated that the empress afterwards described the opera as 'una porcheria tedesca' ['German trash']. The grandfather cited in the title of his book as the source of the anecdotes was August Gottlieb Meissner (1753–1807), a writer and a professor at Prague University, who was involved in the coronation festivities as author of the text of Kozeluch*'s Homage Cantata. Some doubt has been expressed about the authenticity of the remark he attributed to Maria Luisa, but O. Jahn, in the fourth volume (1859) of his biography of Mozart (*see* BREITKOPF & HÄRTEL.), mentioned a story then still current in Prague, according to which the empress had indeed used the term 'porcheria' about *La clemenza di Tito* (and, perhaps, about German music in general). It is in any case certain that Maria Luisa greatly disliked the opera, for on

the day following the performance she wrote to her daughter-in-law Maria Theresia (the wife of Archduke Franz, the future Emperor Francis II) that the music had been so bad that 'almost all of us fell asleep'.
(Eibl³, Eisen)

Maria Theresa [in German: Maria Theresia] (b. Vienna, 13 May 1717; d. Vienna, 28 November 1780). Eldest daughter of Emperor Charles VI (1685–1740); on 12 February 1736 she married her cousin Francis (1708–65), then Duke of Lorraine, later Grand Duke of Tuscany (1737–65) and Emperor Francis I (1745–65). In 1765, on the accession of her son Joseph II*, she became Dowager Empress.

The Mozarts' first audience with Maria Theresa and her husband at Schönbrunn on 13 October 1762 (described in Leopold Mozart's letter to Hagenauer* of 16 October) is famous for the fact that the six-year-old Wolfgang jumped on her lap, threw his arms round her neck and kissed her warmly. Two days later, the empress sent sumptuous clothes to the two children and 100 ducats to Leopold. She received the Mozarts graciously on several other occasions, but did nothing to further Wolfgang's career beyond commissioning a dramatic work for Archduke Ferdinand*'s marriage festivities in 1771 (*see* ASCANIO IN ALBA). In fact, she ruined his chances of an appointment at Ferdinand's court when she wrote to the latter as follows on 12 December 1771: 'You ask my permission to take the young man from Salzburg into your service. I do not know in what capacity, since I do not believe that you have need of a composer or of useless persons. However, if it gives you pleasure, I do not wish to prevent you from doing so. I just want to warn you against burdening yourself with useless persons; and do not ever give them any official positions. Moreover, it lowers the standing of your court when these persons wander all over the world like beggars. Besides, he has a large family.' The archduke did not engage Mozart.

Martini, Giovanni Battista [Padre] (b. Bologna, 24 April 1706; d. Bologna, 3 August 1784). Franciscan monk. He was a prolific composer of sacred and secular works, an internationally renowned musical scholar, and a famous teacher of composition whose pupils included many of the leading musicians of the time. Mozart and his father called on him at least twice during their stay at Bologna in March 1770, and he was present at the concert held at Field-Marshal Count Pallavicini-Centurioni's house on 26 March, for the purpose of presenting Wolfgang to the cream of local society. Moreover, Martini thoroughly tested Wolfgang's musical skills, with significant consequences: 'The fact that Padre Martini, who is the idol of the Italians, himself conducted all the tests and that he speaks of Wolfgang with such great admiration has increased his reputation throughout Italy,' Leopold wrote to his wife* on 27 March.

The contacts were resumed during Wolfgang's longer stay at Bologna later that same year. 'We are the best of friends,' Leopold reported on 6 October 1770, adding that they visited Martini each day and discussed musical history with him. It has been suggested that Martini was instrumental in securing Wolfgang's admission to the celebrated Accademia Filarmonica, although the precise nature of his help has not been determined. (Erich Schenk states, in his biography of Mozart, that Martini substituted his own version of the test piece for Wolfgang's.) Martini also provided Wolfgang with a testimonial (dated 12 October 1770) affirming his excellence as a composer and performer, and praising especially the skill with which he had improvised on the cembalo upon themes proposed by Martini himself. Leopold was to urge Wolfgang on several later occasions to make use of this testimonial in his efforts to obtain appointments.

Martini seems to have been a most lovable man. Charles Burney* wrote of him: 'Upon so short an acquaintance I never liked any man more; and I felt as little reserve with him after a few hours' conversation, as with an old friend or beloved brother.' And Mozart wrote to Martini in an oft-quoted letter on 4 September 1776: 'I do not cease to grieve at finding myself so far from the person I love, revere and esteem most in this world.' (While these may indeed have been Mozart's sentiments, it should be pointed out that, apart from the signature, this letter was written entirely in Leopold's hand and is therefore likely to have been drafted by him.) Enclosed with the letter was the score of the *Offertorium de tempore 'Misericordias Domini'* K222/205a which Mozart had composed and performed in Munich the previous year and upon which Martini was now asked to pronounce judgement. In his reply of 18 December 1776, he praised the composition, declaring that it had 'all the qualities that modern music requires'.

In the summer of 1777, in response to Martini's request for a portrait, Leopold arranged for Wolfgang to be painted by a Salzburg artist, wearing the Order of the Golden Spur. Leopold subsequently sent the painting to Martini; it hangs now in the Civico Museo Bibliografico Musicale in Bologna. In a letter to Martini on 22 December 1777, Leopold described it as an excellent likeness.
(Brofsky[1], Burney[4], Schenk)

Martín y Soler, Vicente (b. Valencia, 2 May 1754; d. St Petersburg, 11 February 1806). Spanish composer. He received his musical training mainly in Valencia and Madrid, but probably also studied composition with Padre Martini* in Bologna. From 1777 to 1779 he was in the service of the Infante Carlos [later King Charles IV]. He soon made his name as a composer of Italian operas, having some ten works produced in Naples, Turin, Venice, Lucca and Parma between 1779 and 1785.

He began his career by writing *opere serie* (*Ifigenia in Aulide, Andromaca*), but was to achieve his greatest successes in *opere buffe*, especially those composed in Vienna where he arrived in late 1785. There he found his ideal librettist in Da Ponte*. Their collaboration resulted in three operas: *Il burbero di buon cuore*, produced on 4 January 1786, with Benucci* (Ferramondo), Maria Mandini* (Marina), and Nancy Storace* (Angelica); *Una cosa rara, ossia Bellezza ed onestà* (17 November 1786), with Benucci (Tita), Dorotea Bussani* (Ghita), Michael Kelly* (Corrado), Luisa Laschi* (Isabella), Stefano Mandini* (Lubino), and Nancy Storace (Lilla); and *L'arbore di Diana* (1 October 1787), with Luisa Laschi (Amore), Anna Morichelli-Boselli (Diana), and Stefano Mandini (Doristo). The last two works proved particularly successful, far outshining Mozart's operas in popularity. Mozart's quotation, in the supper scene of *Don Giovanni**, of the fragment 'O quanto un sì bel giubilo' from the first act finale of *Una cosa rara* clearly testifies to the great success of the latter opera, which portrayed that 'rare' creature, a woman both beautiful and virtuous; its subject was thus the opposite of that of Da Ponte's (and Mozart's) *Così fan tutte**. The opera even inspired a sequel: the Singspiel *Der Fall ist noch weit seltener* (the 'much rarer thing' being male fidelity), with text by Schikaneder* and

Maximilian Franz

music by Benedikt Schack*, was produced at the Freihaus-Theater, Vienna, on 10 May 1790. As for *L'arbore di Diana*, it achieved the greatest number of performances (sixty-six) of any opera in Vienna during the decade 1781–91.

From December 1788 until 1794, Martín y Soler was attached to the court of Catherine the Great at St Petersburg, where he composed two Russian comic operas, one to a libretto partly written by the empress herself (*The Unfortunate Hero Kosometovich*, 1789). He was subsequently engaged at the King's Theatre in London; there he once more collaborated in *opere buffe* with Da Ponte (*La scuola de' maritati*, *L'isola del piacere*). By 1796 he was back in St Petersburg; from 1800 until 1804 he served as superintendent of the Italian court theatre there.
(Michtner, *Mozart Compendium*, Wessely[3])

Maximilian Franz (b. Vienna, 8 December 1756; d. Hetzendorf, near Vienna, 26 or 27 July 1801). Austrian archduke, youngest son of Empress Maria Theresa* and Francis I. Mozart was presented to Maximilian and his brother Ferdinand* on 16 October 1762, during his first visit to Vienna. On 23 April 1775 Mozart's *Il re pastore* was performed in Maximilian's honour at the archbishop's palace in Salzburg. The following evening Maximilian played the violin in the court orchestra. He also used to participate with his brother Joseph II* in private chamber music performances. In 1781 he proposed that Mozart be engaged as piano teacher to the young Princess Elisabeth Wilhelmine Louise of Württemburg (1767–90), who was then staying in Vienna with her parents (she was to become engaged to Archduke Franz on 4 March 1782 and was to marry him on 6 January 1788). However, Joseph II urged the engagement of Salieri* instead (in the end Georg Summer was appointed).

Maximilian appears to have felt genuine admiration for Mozart, who hoped to receive tangible proof of it one day. 'He thinks the world of me,' Mozart wrote to his father on 23 January 1782. 'He is always singing my praises, and I am almost certain that if he were already Prince Elector of Cologne, I would be his Kapellmeister by now' – an appointment which, he added, was 'not to be despised'. At the same time, Mozart was not over impressed by Maximilian himself: 'Stupidity stares out of his eyes,' he wrote on 17 November 1781. 'He talks and pontificates incessantly, and always in falsetto.' In the event, Maximilian, who became coadjutor of the Archbishop and Elector of Cologne, Count Maximilian Friedrich Königsegg, in 1780, was not to succeed him until April 1784. There is no further reference in Mozart's published correspondence to the possibility of a post at Cologne. Shortly after Mozart's death, Maximilian, who was in Vienna at the time, made Constanze* a gift of twenty-four ducats.
(Braubach)

Mazzolà, Caterino (b. Longarone, near Belluno, ?1745; d. ?Venice, 1806). Italian librettist. From 1780 until 1798 he held the post of poet to the Italian theatre at the Dresden court of the Elector Frederick Augustus III [later King Frederick Augustus I] of Saxony. In 1791 he abridged for Mozart Metastasio*'s libretto (1734) for *La clemenza di Tito**.

The following operas based on his librettos received performances at the Burgtheater, Vienna, in Mozart's day: Salieri*'s *La scuola de' gelosi*, which inaugurated the new era of Italian opera on 22 April 1783 (the text had been written by Mazzolà in collaboration with Giovanni Bertati); Giacomo Rust's *Il marito indolente* (25 October 1784); Joseph Weigl*'s *Il pazzo per forza* (14 November 1788); Franz Seydelmann's *Il turco in Italia* (28 April 1789); and Pierre Dutillieu's *Il trionfo d'amore* (14 November 1791). Mazzolà also furnished the text for Salieri's *Il mondo alla rovescia* (13 January 1795).

It was a letter from Mazzolà recommending Da Ponte* to his friend Salieri which led to Da Ponte's appointment as poet to the Italian company in Vienna.
(Michtner)

Meissner, Joseph (Dominikus) Nikolaus (b. Salzburg, *c*.1725; d. Salzburg, 12 March 1795). Salzburg court singer and singing teacher; son of Salzburg court musician Nikolaus Meissner (*c*.1691–1760). While officially described as a bass, he possessed a vocal range embracing also the regular tenor register. A report on the state of music in Salzburg published in F. W. Marpurg's *Historisch-Kritische Beyträge zur Aufnahme der Musik* in Berlin in 1757 and believed to have been written by Leopold Mozart pays tribute to the 'quite exceptionally pleasing quality' of his voice, as well as to its astonishing compass. In a letter to his father from Paris on 12 June 1778, Wolfgang, after extolling Raaff*'s 'beautiful and very pleasing' voice, wrote: 'When I shut my eyes as I listen to him, I find many similarities between his and Meissner's voice, but I find Raaff's even more pleasing.' Wolfgang went on to praise Meissner's cantabile, but criticized his 'bad habit of deliberately making his voice tremble' at times, which was 'entirely contrary to nature'. He acknowledged, however, that he had not heard Meissner in his prime.

At the first performance of *Die Schuldigkeit des ersten Gebots** in 1767, Meissner sang the tenor part of the 'Lukewarm, later zealous Christian', a character who did not appear in the section composed by Wolfgang. The libretto of Wolfgang's *La finta semplice** assigns to him the tenor role of Fracasso. He enjoyed an international reputation (Hübner* claimed that he could have few, if any, equals as a bass in Europe) and frequently accepted engagements elsewhere. Thus the Mozarts met him at Donaueschingen in November 1766, and in May 1770 in Rome (where he had just arrived from Naples). There he and Wolfgang performed on 2 May 1770 at a concert at the Collegio Germanico. He was perhaps identical with the 'Giuseppe Meisner' who sang at the Burgtheater in 1755–6 and 1763.

In 1751 Meissner married Maria Cäcilia Barbara Eberlin (1728–1806), a daughter of the Salzburg court organist Johann Ernst Eberlin*. Meissner's sister Maria Elisabeth Sabina (1731–1809) was also a court singer at Salzburg.
(Angermüller[11], Klein)

Mesmer, Franz Anton (b. Iznang, near Lake Constance, 23 May 1734; d. Meersburg, 5 March 1815). He studied medicine in Vienna, where he subsequently practised as a physician and became known for his treatment of patients by 'animal magnetism', which he believed to be transmitted by the hypnotist to the subject. He achieved some striking successes, especially with hysterical patients, but his methods met with growing opposition from conventional doctors. He was forced to leave Vienna in 1778, after being accused of fraudulent practice and expelled from the medical faculty following his – initially beneficial but ultimately unsuccessful – treatment of the blind Maria Theresia von Paradis*.

He subsequently established a flourishing practice in Paris, but his fortunes declined when a commission of physicians and scientists set up by the French government in 1784 reported adversely on his methods. He retired to Versailles, later went to Switzerland, revisited Vienna on several occasions in the early 1790s, and eventually returned to Germany. Although he was himself largely discredited, 'Mesmerism' continued to fascinate medical men and was widely used; it was, however, not until the 19th century that its psychological nature was properly recognized.

On 10 January 1768 Mesmer married Maria Anna von Bosch (1724–90), the wealthy widow of Councillor Ferdinand Konrad von Bosch. The Mesmers entertained lavishly at their splendid house in the Rauchfangkehrergasse in the Landstrasse suburb [later Rasumofskygasse, in the 3rd district]. It was there, according to Nissen*'s biography of Mozart, that *Bastien and Bastienne** received its first performance in 1768. Mesmer was himself an accomplished performer on the violoncello, cembalo and armonica (on the last instrument, *see* DAVIES).

The Mozarts were also on friendly terms with Joseph Conrad Mesmer (1735–1804), the director of St Stephen's Cathedral School and a relative of Franz Anton Mesmer. In January 1778, informed of Wolfgang's efforts to seek his fortune outside Salzburg (he was by then at Mannheim), Joseph Conrad wrote to Leopold: 'Why didn't you send your son straight to Vienna? And why won't you do so even now? I promise you most faithfully that he can have free board, lodging and everything else in my house as long as he wishes, and that I and all his other friends will try to obtain a good appointment for him quickly' (quoted in Leopold's letter to Wolfgang of 29 January 1778).

It is not known whether Wolfgang met Franz Anton Messmer again during the latter's visits to Vienna in 1790 and 1791. There is an amusing reference to 'Mesmerism' in the Act I finale of *Così fan tutte**, when Despina, disguised as a doctor, waves a magnet over the supposedly poisoned Ferrando and Guglielmo, declaring that it is a piece of Dr Mesmer's magnetic stone ('Questo è quel pezzo di calamita Pietra Mesmerica'), which, she explains, was first discovered in Germany and later became famous in France as well. In reality, Mesmer used an artificial magnet in his 'cures'.

(Deutsch[4], Steptoe)

Metastasio, Pietro [real name: Antonio Domenico Bonaventura Trapassi] (b. Rome, 3 January 1698; d. Vienna, 12 April 1782). The most celebrated librettist of the 18th century. His adoptive parent, the Roman jurist and critic Gian Vincenzo Gravina, left him financially independent at his death in 1718. Metastasio promptly abandoned the legal profession for which he had been trained and made a name for himself as a poet and, from 1723, as a librettist, working mainly in Rome and Venice. In 1730 he accepted an invitation to become court poet in Vienna in succession to Apostolo Zeno. He took lodgings in the house of Niccolò Martinez, the master of ceremonies of the papal nuncio, at the corner of Michaeler-Platz and Kohlmarkt opposite the imperial palace, and there he lived until his death over fifty years later.

Metastasio wrote librettos for some thirty three-act heroic operas, for several shorter dramatic works of the 'azione teatrale' type, for eight oratorios, and for numerous serenatas and poems. His librettos were set more than 800 times in the 18th and early 19th centuries, some of them (*Adriano in Siria, Alessandro nell'Indie, Artaserse, Didone abbandonata, Olimpiade*) by twenty-five or more composers. When Mozart wrote *Il re pastore** in 1775, the libretto had already been used by at least eight other composers, including Bonno*, Sarti*, Hasse*, Gluck*, Niccolò Piccinni and Nicolò Jommelli. Among Mozart's predecessors in setting *La clemenza di Tito** were Hasse, Gluck, Jommelli, Giuseppe Scarlatti, and Sarti. Mozart further used librettos by Metastasio in *Il sogno di Scipione** and in the oratorio *La Betulia liberata* K118/74c. He also wrote several concert arias to texts taken from Metastasio's librettos, notably *Alcandro, lo confesso . . . Non so d'onde viene* K294 (K512), *Basta vincesti . . . Ah, non lasciarmi, no* K486a/295a, and *Ah se in ciel, benigne stelle . . .* K538 (*see also* FIRMIAN). While working on *Lucio Silla** in Milan in 1772, he probably sent Gamerra*'s text to Metastasio for revision.

Mozart's only documented meeting with Metastasio occurred in July 1768 when Leopold, seeking to rout all opposition to the hoped-for Viennese production of *La finta semplice**, arranged for Wolfgang to demonstrate his skill as a composer before various eminent persons, Metastasio among them; the latter then publicly declared his admiration for the opera (according to Leopold's letter to Hagenauer* of 30 July 1768).
(Apollonio, Robinson M.F.²)

Mölk, von. Salzburg family on friendly terms with the Mozarts. Franz Felix Anton von Mölk (b. Buxheim, near Memmingen, Swabia, 1714; d. Regensburg, 20 January 1776) was court chancellor in Salzburg and court councillor; he was ennobled in 1752. He and his wife Anna (*c.*1718–99), *née* Wasner von Wasenau, had six children, of whom the oldest, Franz (*c.*1748–1800), and the only girl, Maria Anna Barbara ['Waberl'] (1752–1823), were most frequently mentioned in the Mozarts' correspondence. In 1792 the second son, Albert (1749–99), who was a canon at Salzburg Cathedral and inspector of the St Johannis Hospital in the city, acted as an intermediary between Schlichtegroll* and Nannerl*, forwarding the biographer's questions about Mozart to her and sending back her answers.

Morella, Francesco. Lyrical tenor; Ottavio in the first Viennese production of *Don Giovanni**. In preparing the latter role, he apparently felt so daunted by the coloratura aspects of 'Il mio tesoro . . .' that the aria was omitted and Mozart composed for him a new number, 'Dalla sua pace . . .' K540a.

Morella had made his Viennese début on 31 March 1788 as Almaviva in Paisiello*'s *Il barbiere di Siviglia*. He also appeared as Canciano in Weigl*'s *Il pazzo per forza* (14 November 1788) and as Don Riccardo in Anfossi*'s *Le gelosie fortunate*, a role he had already sung at Venice in 1786 and in which he alternated in Vienna with Domenico Mombelli (*see* LASCHI, LUISA). Overall, he failed to fulfil the expectations placed in him; he left at the end of the 1788–9 season.
(Michtner)

Mozart, Anna Maria (b. Vienna, 16 November 1789; d. Vienna, 16 November

Mozart, Carl Thomas

1789). Fifth child of Mozart and Constanze*. She died of intestinal cramp an hour after birth.
(Blümml)

Mozart, Carl Thomas (b. Vienna, 21 September 1784; d. Milan, 31 October 1858). Second and older surviving child of Mozart and Constanze*; his godfather was Johann Thomas von Trattner*. After attending school in Vienna and in Prague (where he stayed with Niemetschek*), he was apprenticed to a commercial firm at Leghorn [Livorno] in 1797 or 1798. In 1805 he moved to Milan and studied with the court Kapellmeister Bonifazio Asioli (1769–1832), having decided to pursue a musical career. 'I leave everything to your judgment and shall certainly not advise you against doing so,' Constanze wrote to him on 5 March 1806. 'But always bear in mind this warning which I give you with the greatest affection: any son of Mozart's who is no more than mediocre will bring more shame than honour upon himself.' Her son eventually heeded the caution: in 1810 he became an official in the service of the Viceroy of Naples in Milan, and thereafter channelled his love for music into private music making (*see also* WALTER).

He attended the unveiling of his father's statue in Salzburg in 1842 (*see* SCHWANTHALER, TAUX, and MOZART, FRANZ XAVER WOLFGANG) and also the centenary celebrations in 1856. After his death, at a commemorative ceremony in Salzburg on 12 November 1858, his friend Alois Taux conducted Mozart's Requiem.
(Hummel²)

Mozart, Constanze: *see* WEBER, CONSTANZE.

Mozart, Franz Xaver Wolfgang (b. Vienna, 26 July 1791; d. Carlsbad [Karlovy Vary], 29 July 1844). Austrian composer, pianist and Kapellmeister. Sixth and younger surviving child of Mozart and Constanze*; his godfather was Johann Thomas von Trattner*. He was known as 'Wolfgang' or 'Wolfgang Amade(us)' (on occasion 'Wolfgang Gottlieb'), and later signed himself 'W. A. Mozart', sometimes adding 'Sohn' ['son'].

He soon appeared in public: the programme of a Mozart memorial concert held in Prague on 15 November 1797, at which Constanze was to sing in a trio and a quartet by Mozart, announced that 'little Wolfgang, just six years old' would perform the aria 'Der Vogelfänger bin ich ja' from *Die Zauberflöte**. He studied with Albrechtsberger*, Hummel*, Salieri*, Johann Andreas Streicher (*see* STEIN) and Vogler*. Success came early: his op. 1, a piano quartet, was published in 1802; and he first appeared as a pianist at a concert at the Theater an der Wien in Vienna on 8 April 1805, when he played Mozart's Piano Concerto K467 in a programme which also featured his own cantata for three solo voices, chorus and orchestra, composed in honour of Joseph Haydn*'s seventy-third birthday. On 30 March 1807 Salieri declared in a testimonial that 'il giovine Signor Wolfango [*sic*] Amadìo Mozart' possessed a rare talent for music and predicted for him a future as brilliant as his father's.

On 22 October 1808 Wolfgang left Vienna to became tutor in the household of Count Viktor Baworowski at Podkamien, 100 km east of Lemberg [Lvov], which was then in the Austrian empire. From 1811 to 1813 he was tutor in the home of the imperial chamberlain Count Janiszewski at Sarki, outside Lemberg. Subsequently he settled in Lemberg itself, where his pupils included Julie Baroni von Cavalcabò [later de Webenau] (1813–87), who became a well-known pianist and composer; Schumann dedicated his *Humoreske* op. 20 to her. She was the daughter of Councillor Ludwig Kajetan Baroni von Cavalcabò (1765–1847) and his wife Josephine, *née* Countess Castiglioni (1788–1860). The latter was to occupy a very special place in Wolfgang's life, as is shown by the fact that he named her his sole heiress. The most explicit reference to their relationship occurs in a note made by Vincent Novello* after a conversation with Constanze in 1829: 'Young Mozart's mistress in Poland is a countess who is, unfortunately, married to a man she does not esteem. He is so much attached to her that his mother feared he would never leave Poland for any length of time without her and as he cannot take her with him on account of the husband Madame Mozart begins to despair of his ever establishing himself in Vienna or other large capital where his parts might be better known and appreciated.'

Encouraged by the artistic and financial success of a concert he gave at Lemberg on 17 December 1818, Wolfgang undertook a lengthy tour which took him to Russia, Poland, Denmark, Prague (where he had spent some six months in 1795–6; – *see* NIEMETSCHEK), Switzerland, Northern Italy, and to many cities in Germany and Austria, and concluded with a recital in Vienna in the summer of 1821. In May of that year, at Salzburg, he had met his aunt Nannerl* for the first time. In 1822 he went back to Lemberg. In August 1826 he visited Constanze in Salzburg and, while there, conducted Mozart's Requiem at a memorial service for his stepfather, Georg Nikolaus Nissen*, who had died on 24 March of that year. On 29 August he played his own Piano Concerto in E flat major at a concert at the Salzburg town hall. He then returned to Lemberg, and in 1834 was appointed Kapellmeister at the local theatre. He finally left that city in 1838 to move to Vienna, at the same time as the Baronis.

In 1841 he was made honorary Kapellmeister of the newly founded *Dommusik-verein und Mozarteum* (*see* HILLEPRANDT). The following year he participated in the festivities accompanying the unveiling of Mozart's statue in Salzburg (*see* SCHWANTHALER). At the ceremony on 4 September 1842 he conducted a chorus he had written for the occasion, whose musical themes were taken from *La clemenza di Tito**; at a festival concert he played a concerto by Mozart (probably K466). In the spring of 1844, in failing health, he went to Carlsbad where he died on 29 July, in the arms of his pupil Ernst Pauer. Josephine Baroni von Cavalcabò was present at his funeral. Commemorative ceremonies were held in Carlsbad (1 August), Salzburg (19 August), Vienna (5 September), and Lemberg (6 September); each included a performance of Mozart's Requiem.

Wolfgang was an excellent pianist and a competent composer; his Second Piano Concerto, in E flat, which he repeatedly performed at concerts, proved particularly popular. He was, however, unable to free himself of the heavy shadow which his father's reputation cast over his career. In this respect, he was assuredly ill-advised to adopt permanently the name 'Wolfgang Amadeus (Gottlieb) Mozart', under which Constanze, no doubt for reasons of publicity, had presented him at the outset of his career. It can only have drawn attention to the difference between his own talent and his father's genius.

Mozart, Johann Thomas Leopold

Like his father, Wolfgang was a freemason.
(Angermüller[6], Goldinger, Hummel[2], Hurwitz, Novello)

Mozart, Johann Thomas Leopold (b. Vienna, 18 October 1786; d. Vienna, 15 November 1786). Third child of Mozart and Constanze*; his godfather was Johann Thomas von Trattner*. Cause of death: suffocation.
(Blümml)

Mozart, (Johann Georg) Leopold (b. Augsburg, 14 November 1719; d. Salzburg, 28 May 1787). Composer and violinist; Wolfgang's father. Son of the Augsburg bookbinder Johann Georg Mozart (1679–1736) and of his second wife, Anna Maria, *née* Sulzer (1696–1766).

After receiving his basic education in Augsburg he enrolled on 26 November 1737 at the university in Salzburg, where he studied philosophy and jurisprudence; however, in 1739 he was expelled for poor attendance. He was then taken on as valet and musician by Count Johann Baptist Thurn-Valsassina und Taxis (1706–62), a Salzburg canon who was president of the consistory. It was to him that Leopold dedicated, in 1740, his op. 1, six trio sonatas. During the next three years, he wrote two German Passion cantatas (*see* WEISER), as well as music for a Latin drama performed at the university. In 1743 he was accepted into the court orchestra as fourth violinist, advancing to second violinist in 1758 and being appointed vice-Kapellmeister in 1763. In addition, he became violin instructor to the choirboys in 1744, and in 1757 was made court and chamber composer. In the course of his forty-four years with the orchestra, he played under several court Kapellmeisters: Karl Heinrich von Bibern (1743–9), Johann Ernst Eberlin* (1749–62), Giuseppe Francesco Lolli (1763–78), Domenico Fischietti (1772–83), Giacomo Rust (1777), and Luigi Gatti (appointed 1783). He served five archbishops: Baron Leopold Anton Firmian (1727–44), Count Jakob Ernst Liechtenstein (1745–7), Count Andreas Jakob Dietrichstein (1747–53), Count Siegmund Christoph Schrattenbach* (1753–71), and Count Hieronymus Colloredo* (elected 1772).

On 21 November 1747 he married Maria Anna Pertl, who bore him seven children (for particulars, *see* MOZART, MARIA ANNA). Only two children, Nannerl* and Wolfgang, reached adulthood. Once their exceptional talents had become apparent, Leopold devoted all his energy and spare time to their education and to promoting their careers, especially and with increasing single-mindedness that of his son. As a result, he composed little after 1762 (his output up to that time had been considerable, but unfortunately much of it has been lost) and he ceased composing altogether in 1771. He undertook several journeys designed to display his prodigies to the world, travelling at first with his wife and both children, and, from 1769, with Wolfgang alone. Since he was unable to accompany Wolfgang to Munich and Mannheim in 1777, his wife took his place, but Leopold kept a sharp eye on their progress, demanded constant reports on Wolfgang's activities and plans, and sent back a steady stream of suggestions, advice and, frequently, criticism.

Towards Wolfgang, in particular, he was often reproachful and censorious, rebuking him for being indolent, thoughtless, frivolous, impractical, irresponsible, too easily swayed by new acquaintances. At the same time, there were repeated declarations of affection. 'If your tears, your sadness and your profound anxiety have no other cause than that you doubt my love and tenderness for you, then you may sleep peacefully – eat and drink peacefully, and return home still more peacefully,' he wrote on 31 December 1778 (in fact, Wolfgang's distress was due to his rejection by Aloisia Weber*). Their relations grew strained when, against Leopold's advice, Wolfgang left Archbishop Colloredo's service in 1781, and they were not improved by his marriage to Constanze* the following year. A letter written by Leopold to Baroness Waldstätten* on 23 August 1782, shortly after that marriage, throws a revealing light on his attitude towards his son: 'Having done my duty as a true father, having in my numerous letters made the clearest and most lucid representations to him on all matters, and feeling convinced that he realizes under what burdensome conditions I am living, especially arduous for a man of my advanced years, and that he is aware of the snubs that are inflicted on me at Salzburg – for he must know that I am made to suffer both morally and physically for his conduct – all I can do now is to leave him to his own resources, as he wished, and to pray God to bestow on him His paternal blessing and not to withdraw His divine grace from him . . . I should be quite easy in my mind, had I not detected a major fault in my son: he is either too *easy-going* and *lethargic*, too *indolent*, at times perhaps too *proud* . . . or he is too *impatient*, too *precipitate*, incapable of biding his time. His actions are determined by two opposing impulses – to do too much, or to do too little: he knows no middle way.'

In 1785 Leopold paid Wolfgang and Constanze a prolonged visit (11 February – 25 April), during which he heard Wolfgang play on several occasions and met various members of his circle. While in Vienna Leopold was admitted on 6 April as an Entered Apprentice to the 'Zur Wohltätigkeit'* Lodge, of which Wolfgang was a member. On 16 April Leopold was raised to the grade of Fellow Craft Mason (Journeyman) at the 'Zur wahren Eintracht' Lodge, and on 22 April, at the same lodge, to that of Master. Wolfgang's *Lied zur Gesellenreise* K468 ('Geselle' = 'Journeyman') was probably performed at the ceremony on 16 April.

Leopold's long visit may well have resulted in greater intimacy between father and son, and Leopold must have been delighted by Haydn's flattering tribute to Wolfgang (*see* HAYDN, JOSEPH). However, their relations suffered a further strain in the autumn of 1786 when Wolfgang, having learned that his father had been taking care of Nannerl's son Leopold since his birth some fifteen months earlier, enquired if he would be willing to look after his own two children Carl* and Johann*, while he and Constanze travelled to Germany and England during the coming carnival season. Leopold refused in most decided terms. 'You will readily appreciate that I had to write a very *emphatic* letter . . .' he told Nannerl on 17 November 1786. She, unlike her brother, maintained a very close relationship with her father, even after she moved to St Gilgen following her marriage to Johann Baptist Franz von Berchtold zu Sonnenburg* in August 1784. This is evidenced by the tone and the frequency of Leopold's letters to her: during the remaining thirty-three months of his life he wrote to her no fewer than 130 times (unfortunately her replies have not been preserved.) After his visit to Vienna in 1785, he did not see Wolfgang again.

Leopold enjoyed an international reputation, largely as a result of his highly regarded didactic work, *Versuch einer gründlichen Violinschule*, which was published at Augsburg in 1756 (with a second edition in 1769–70 and a third, enlarged one, in

1787) and subsequently translated into Dutch (1766) and French (1770). However, his professional life at Salzburg was not entirely successful; he was, for instance, disappointed in his hope of becoming Kapellmeister after Eberlin's death. Later, Wolfgang's defection from Colloredo's service certainly did not make his life in Salzburg any easier. On 28 May 1787 Kajetan [Dominicus] Hagenauer (*see* HAGENAUER), wrote in his diary: 'Leopold Mozart . . . who died today, was a man of great intelligence and wisdom, who would have been capable of rendering good services to the state even apart from music . . . He was born at Augsburg and spent most of his life in the service of our court, but he had the misfortune of being always persecuted and he did not by any means enjoy the same favour here as in other, larger cities in Europe.'
(Plath[3], Schmid[3])

Mozart, Maria Anna Thekla [known as 'das Bäsle', i.e. 'the cousin'] (b. Augsburg, 25 September 1758; d. Bayreuth, 25 January 1841). Daughter of Leopold's brother Franz Alois Mozart (1727–91) and his wife Maria Viktoria, *née* Eschenbach (1727–1808).

Wolfgang struck up a friendship with her during his stay at Augsburg with his mother* in October 1777. 'Our Bäsle is beautiful, intelligent, charming, clever, and merry,' he wrote to his father on 16 October. 'We get on very well together . . . We pull everyone's leg and have great fun together.' When he reached Mannheim, they exchanged portraits by post. They also started a correspondence which has become notorious for the coarse jokes and scatalogical terms which, side by side with much light-hearted word-play, abound in Wolfgang's letters (it should, however, be emphasized that there are no sexual obscenities).

This matter needs to be considered in the context of contemporary attitudes. In the first place, there was undoubtedly less squeamishness then about mentioning bodily functions than in later periods. Moreover, examples of this type of humour occur also in letters from Wolfgang to his father, and even in a note from his mother to her husband. Furthermore, in a letter to his father on 14 November 1777, Wolfgang describes an evening spent at Christian Cannabich*'s house in Mannheim, when he was encouraged to invent rhymes on similarly scabrous words and expressions, in order to amuse the company which included Cannabich himself, his wife and his daughter Rosina, as well as 'treasurer' Gres and two musicians from the Mannheim orchestra. It is, in any case, evident that, far from objecting to these jokes, the Bäsle (whose replies have not been published and have presumably not survived) must have been entertained by them, since they extended over a series of letters. Finally, it is worth noting that Constanze* made no attempt later to suppress the letters; on the contrary, she sent them to Breitkopf & Härtel* in 1799, when that firm was collecting material for a new biography of Mozart, with the comment: 'These admittedly tasteless but nonetheless very witty letters doubtless also merit some mention, although they obviously cannot be printed in full' (letter of 28 August 1799).

Wolfgang's letters to his cousin were playful in tone and at times mildly flirtatious, but indicate no feeling deeper than affection. In January 1779 she met him, at his suggestion, at Munich and probably visited Salzburg shortly afterwards. The Mozarts' published correspondence contains only three further letters from

Wolfgang to her, written in May 1779, April 1780, and October 1781 (though there appear to have been others). The first of these is very much in the vein of the earlier letters, but the last two are entirely devoid of any coarseness.

In 1784 the Bäsle gave birth to an illegitimate child which was baptized Maria Josepha on 22 February. The mother's name was entered in the register as 'Trazin' and the father's as 'Ludwig Berbier'. It was later established that the latter was in reality Baron Theodor Franz de Paula Reibeld (1752–1807), a canon at Augsburg Cathedral. (It will be noted that the second syllable of his assumed name reproduces, in reverse order, the first four letters of his true name. Similarly, the first four letters of the Bäsle's fictitious name invert the last four of her real one. This recalls the joke played by Mozart on J. A. Stein* at their meeting in Augsburg in 1777, when – as he informed his father on 14 October 1777 – he introduced himself as 'Trazom'. Leopold thereupon signed his own letter of 1 November 1777 with the same name.)

On 31 May 1802 Maria Josepha married Franz Joseph Streitel (1771–1854). When the couple moved to Kaufbeuren in 1812, and from there to Bayreuth in 1814, the Bäsle went with them. Maria Josepha died in Bayreuth on 6 April 1842, a little over a year after her mother.

(Eibl/Senn, Wegele)

Mozart, Maria Anna Walburga, *née* Pertl (baptized St Gilgen, 25 December 1720; d. Paris, 3 July 1778). Mozart's mother. Daughter of Wolfgang Nikolaus Pertl (1667–1724), from 1716 deputy prefect of the Hüttenstein–St Gilgen district, and of his wife Eva Rosina Barbara Euphrosina (1681–1755), *née* Altmann, the widow of Ignaz Franz Puxbaum. The couple, who married on 22 November 1712, had three daughters: Clara Elisabeth Rosina, born on 4 July 1713 and buried two days later; Maria Rosina Erntrudis (1719–28); and Maria Anna Walburga. After Pertl's death in 1724, his widow moved with her two surviving daughters to Salzburg.

Maria Anna became the wife of Leopold Mozart* in Salzburg on 21 November 1747. They had seven children, of which only the fourth, Nannerl*, and the last, Wolfgang, reached adulthood. The others were Johann Leopold Joachim (b. 18 August 1748; d. 2 February 1749), Maria Anna Cordula (b. 18 June 1749; d. 24 June 1749), Maria Anna Nepomucena Walpurgis (b. 13 May 1750; d. 29 July 1750), Johann Karl Amadeus (b. 4 November 1752; d. 2 February 1753), and Maria Crescentia Franziska de Paula (b. 9 May 1754; d. 27 June 1754).

Maria Anna Mozart accompanied Leopold and the two children to Vienna in 1762, on the long journey to Paris and London (1763–6), and once more to Vienna in 1767. In September 1777 she and Wolfgang set off together for Munich, Mannheim, and eventually Paris; there she died after a short illness.

Not enough information is available to allow a full assessment of the nature of her relationship with her son. What is evident is that, unlike her husband, she had little authority over Wolfgang once he was grown up. On 5 February 1778, in a postscript to a letter from Wolfgang to his father, she commented on Wolfgang's new friendship with Fridolin Weber* and his family, and on Wolfgang's earlier intention to travel to Paris with Johann Baptist Wendling* and Friedrich Ramm*: 'I never liked his being in the company of Wendling and Ramm, but he did not permit me to voice any objections and never took any account of what I said. However, no sooner had he struck up an acquaintance with the Webers than he promptly changed his mind. In other words, he would rather be with other people than with me, for I remonstrate with him about matters that are not to my taste and he does not like that. So you will have to think over yourself what should be done . . . I am writing this in the greatest secrecy, while he is at dinner, and I shall close now, for I do not want him to catch me.'

The baptismal register of the Parish of St Gilgen, on 25 December 1720, gave her names as 'Anna Maria Walburga'. However, they appear as 'Maria Anna' in the entry relating to her wedding in the register of marriages of Salzburg Cathedral, and also in six out of seven entries relating to the births of her children in the register of births (the seventh mentions only the name 'Maria').
(Valentin[3])

Mozart [later Berchtold zu Sonnenburg], **Maria Anna Walburga Ignatia** ['Nannerl'] (b. Salzburg, 30 or 31 July 1751; d. Salzburg, 29 October 1829). Fourth child of Leopold Mozart and his wife Maria Anna Mozart*; Wolfgang's sister. She was a brilliant pianist when still very young, and Leopold displayed the exceptional talents of both children on the early visits to Munich (January – February 1762) and Vienna (October – December 1762), on the grand tour to Paris and London (June 1763 – November 1766), and on the second journey to Vienna (September 1767 – January 1769). Thereafter Nannerl was left at home, to make music in private.

In 1781 she was in love with Franz Armand d'Ippold*, who returned her feelings. Arguing that their prospects were brighter in Vienna than in Salzburg, Wolfgang proposed, in a letter to his sister on 19 September 1781, that they should move to the Austrian capital, where Nannerl could make a reasonable income from teaching and performing at private concerts, while Ippold stood a good chance of obtaining a well-paid position, with Wolfgang's help. This suggestion was not taken up, but Nannerl's diary indicates that Ippold was still a frequent visitor in the summer and autumn of 1783 when Wolfgang and Constanze* were staying in Salzburg. However, Nannerl did not marry him, probably because of her father's opposition to the match. Instead, on 23 August 1784 at St Gilgen, she married Johann Baptist Franz von Berchtold zu Sonnenburg* and became step-mother to his five children. The couple had three children of their own: Leopold Alois Pantaleon (b. Salzburg, 27 July 1785; d. Innsbruck, 15 May 1840); Johanna [Jeanette] (b. St Gilgen, 22 March 1789; d. Salzburg, 1 September 1805); and Maria Babette (b. St Gilgen, 17 November 1790; d. St Gilgen, 29 April 1791).

In October 1801, eight months after her husband's death, Nannerl moved with her two surviving children back to Salzburg, where she lived in the house of her friends, the Barisanis*, and gave piano lessons. In 1825 she became blind. When Vincent Novello* visited her on 15 July 1829, for the purpose of presenting to her a gift of sixty guineas subscribed by himself and other English musicians, he found her very feeble and almost incapable of speech. She died some three months later.

Her relations with Wolfgang, once so close, grew more distant once he had settled in Vienna, and particularly following his marriage to Constanze, for whom Nannerl felt little affection. She did not see him again after his and Constanze's visit to Salzburg in 1783. Later, tensions developed between them concerning the division of their father's small estate (*see also* GILOWSKY). Writing to Breitkopf & Härtel* in

February 1800, she explained that it was not until she read Niemetschek*'s biography that she learned of the 'wretched [financial] situation in which my brother found himself'.

After Wolfgang's death there appears to have been little, if any, communication between Nannerl and Constanze. In another letter to Breitkopf & Härtel, in March 1800, Nannerl severely criticized the manner in which Constanze was disposing of Wolfgang's compositions. Even when Constanze took up residence in Salzburg with Nissen* in 1821, contacts are unlikely to have been more than formal.

In her will of 20 October 1823, Nannerl left instructions to be buried in her father's grave at St Sebastian's cemetery in Salzburg (the grave also contained the remains of Nannerl's daughter Johanna and of Constanze's aunt Genovefa, the mother of the composer Carl Maria von Weber). However, after Constanze had arranged for the interment of her husband Nissen in the same grave in 1826 and for the erection of a tombstone bearing his name alone, Nannerl, apparently angered by this action, added a codicil to her own will on 1 July 1827, stating that she now wished to be buried at St Peter's cemetery – which, in due course, she was.

Nannerl's son lived with his grandfather Leopold Mozart until the latter's death in May 1787. He made his career in government service, mainly in the Tyrol. On 16 April 1816, at Bregenz, he married Josephine Fuggs (b. 1795); they had two children: Henriette (1817–90), who married Franz Forschter (1806–71) in 1841, and Cäsar August Ernst (b. and d. 1822). Franz and Henriette Forschter also had two children: a son, Gustav (1841–75), who followed a military career; and a daughter, Bertha (b. 1842), who died in 1919 in a mental asylum near Graz, where she had been confined during much of her life.

(Angermüller[12], Goldinger, Hitzig, Hummel[1], Novello, Rieger)

Mozart, Raimund Leopold (b. Vienna, 17 June 1783; d. Vienna, 19 August 1783). First child of Mozart and Constanze*, named after Baron Raimund Wetzlar von Plankenstern*, who had offered to be godfather, and after Leopold Mozart. 'Congratulations, you are a grandpapa!' Wolfgang wrote to his father on 18 June. 'Yesterday, the 17th, at half-past-six in the morning, my dear wife was safely delivered of a big and sturdy boy, as round as a ball.' On 5 July: 'Little Raimund looks so much like me that everyone immediately remarks on it. He is the spitting image of me. My dear little wife is absolutely delighted, as this is what she always wanted.'

The baby died of intestinal cramp while staying with a foster mother during his parents' absence in Salzburg. They may not have learned of his death until they returned to Vienna in late November 1783.

(Blümml)

Mozart, Theresia Constanzia Adelheid Friederike Maria Anna (b. Vienna, 27 December 1787; d. Vienna, 29 June 1788). Fourth child of Mozart and Constanze*; her godmother was Maria Theresia von Trattner (*see* TRATTNER). Cause of death: intestinal cramp.

(Blümml)

Müller, Johann Heinrich Friedrich (b. Halberstadt, 20 February 1738; d.

Mysliveček, Joseph

Vienna, 8 August 1815). Playwright and actor; member of the Vienna court theatre from 1763 to 1801. He first made his mark as Sever in a German version of Corneille's *Polyeucte* on 13 September 1763; his final appearance was on 15 December 1801 in a play by Kotzebue. He specialized in character roles, such as servants and pedants.

Müller assisted Weiskern* in the translation of the French comedy *Les amours de Bastien et Bastienne* (*see* BASTIEN UND BASTIENNE). In September 1776 he was sent by Joseph II* on a tour of the leading German theatres, with instructions to recruit fresh talent for Vienna; for this purpose he was empowered to negotiate terms and conclude contracts as he deemed fit. The four-months' shopping trip resulted in the engagement of several excellent singers and actors, among them Johann Franz Hieronymus Brockmann*, Friedrich Ludwig Schröder, and Johann Joseph Nouseul*. A detailed account of the journey can be found in Müller's book *Abschied von der k.k. Hof- und National-Schaubühne* ... , published in Vienna in 1802. Subsequently Müller was in charge of the newly established German opera company (*see* BÖHM). In 1783 he wrote some doggerel verses for a carnival masquerade devised by Mozart.

He was a generous host. On 20 February 1785, Leopold Mozart (and no doubt Wolfgang and probably also Constanze*) were among twenty-one guests at a luncheon at his house. In a letter to Nannerl* the next dday, Leopold described the meal as 'splendid'. Several of Müller's children (according to Leopold, he had eight) became actors. One daughter, Josepha Hortensia (1766–1808), was also a pianist; on 17 February 1785 she played at a concert at the Burgtheater.

(Michtner, Müller, Zechmeister)

Mysliveček, Joseph (b. Horní Sárka, near Prague, 9 March 1737; d. Rome, 4 February 1781). Czech composer. In addition to oratorios and instrumental music, he wrote many operas, mostly for theatres in Italy where he was much admired and known as 'Il divino Boemo'. Mozart made his acquaintance in March 1770 during his visit to Bologna where Mysliveček was supervising the production of his opera *La Nitteti*. They met again during Mozart's further stay at Bologna in the summer of that year: 'Herr Mysliveček frequently visited us in Bologna and we often called on him,' Leopold Mozart wrote to his wife* from Milan on 27 October 1770. 'He is a man of honour and we have become very good friends.' Mysliveček had been admitted to the Accademica Filarmonica of Bologna on 15 May, an honour which was accorded to Mozart on 10 October (*see* MARTINI). Their contacts were resumed in the autumn of 1771 in Milan where Mozart had gone for the production of *Ascanio in Alba** and Mysliveček for the première of his opera *Il gran Tamerlano* at the Teatro Regio Ducal on 26 December 1771 (after Mozart's departure). They met yet again in Milan during the following winter.

Their final encounter, in Munich in the autumn of 1777, took place in more pathetic circumstances, for Mysliveček was then undergoing treatment for venereal disease, in the course of which his nose had been cauterized. In his letter of 30 September, Leopold Mozart suggested an excuse which Wolfgang could use, should he not wish to see Mysliveček whom 'everyone must be shunning and loathing'. But Wolfgang was more charitable: 'What, I should know that my very good friend Mysliveček resided in a city or in some corner of the world where I was staying, and not go to see him, not speak to him? That I cannot do,' he replied on 11 October. He twice visited Mysliveček at the Herzogsspital, on the second occasion with his mother. He was greatly moved by the sight of the disfigurement which Mysliveček had suffered, and even had to be comforted by the patient himself, who seems to have adopted a stoical attitude towards his misfortune. Mysliveček advised Wolfgang to seek his fortune in Italy and undertook to obtain for him a commission to write an opera for the Teatro San Carlo in Naples. This offer was repeatedly discussed in Mysliveček's correspondence with Leopold over the following months, but nothing ever came of it. Mysliveček himself returned to Italy at Easter 1778. His career there declined after the failure of his opera *Armida* (Milan, 1779), and he died indigent.

Mozart thought quite highly of Mysliveček's compositions for the piano. His sonatas, he wrote to his father on 13 November 1777, 'are sure to please everyone, they are easy to memorize and effective if played with the proper accuracy'. (DiChiera[1,2])

Nannerl: *see* MOZART, MARIA ANNA WALBURGA IGNATIA.

Niemetschek, Franz Xaver [Niemeczek; Němeček, František Xaver (Petr)] (b. Sadska, Bohemia, 24 July 1766; d. Vienna, 19 March 1849). Biographer of Mozart. After teaching at schools in Pilsen and, from 1792, in Prague, he was appointed professor of theoretical and practical philosophy at Prague University in 1802. In 1820 he accepted a post at the university of Vienna, but was forced to retire the following year for reasons of ill-health. He was married to Therese Schnell (1765–1828).

Niemetschek was introduced to Mozart, perhaps by Josepha Duschek*, during Mozart's stay in Prague from late August to mid-September 1791. 'My wife saw him every day,' he informed Breitkopf & Härtel* in 1799. Some time after Mozart's death, the latter's older son Carl Thomas* went to live with the Niemetscheks in Prague (*see* SWIETEN). 'Carl slept in my room and was under my supervision for more than three years,' Niemetschek wrote to the same publishers on 21 March 1800, apparently referring to the period 1794–7. Carl himself, in a letter to Adolf Popelka in 1856, stated mistakenly that he had lodged with Niemetschek from 1792 until 1797. Constanze* also left her younger son Franz Xaver Wolfgang Mozart* with the Niemetscheks for some six months while she carried out a concert tour with her sister Aloisia Lange* in Germany in 1795–6. Later, in Vienna, Franz Xaver Wolfgang gave piano lessons to Niemetschek's grandchildren.

Niemetschek's *Leben des k.k. Kapellmeisters Wolfgang Gottlieb Mozart* was the first important biography of Mozart. It appeared anonymously in 1797 (Prague, Widtmann) and under the author's name – spelt 'Niemtschek' – in 1798 (Prague, Herrl); a second, augmented edition was published in 1808 (Prague, Herrl). Constanze supplied Niemetschek with various letters and notes, which he used, however, with some circumspection, for, as he explained to Breitkopf & Härtel in the above-mentioned letter of 21 March 1800, 'I do not believe everything Madame Mozart says or shows.' In addition to writing Mozart's life, Niemetschek played an important part in the publication of his collected works by Breitkopf & Härtel. (Favier, Hitzig, Hummel[2])

Nissen, Georg Nikolaus (b. Haderslev, 22 January 1761; d. Salzburg, 24 March 1826). Danish diplomat, biographer of Mozart; Constanze*'s second husband. On joining the diplomatic service in 1790, he was posted to Regensburg as assistant to Friedrich von Eyben, ambassador of Holstein-Glückstadt to the Imperial Diet. In February 1793 he was transferred to the Danish Embassy in Vienna with the rank of legation secretary; he became legation councillor in 1802 and *chargé d'affaires* in 1805.

He made Constanze's acquaintance not later than 1797. By September 1798 they were living at the same address in the Judengässchen in Vienna, but it was not until 26 June 1809 that they were married in the cathedral at Pressburg [Bratislava], to which city Nissen, like other diplomats, had moved during Napoleon's second siege of Vienna. The couple returned to Vienna on 13 August, following the conclusion of a truce. In February 1810 Nissen resigned from his post, and he and Constanze spent the next eleven years in Copenhagen, where Nissen was appointed censor of political journals and, in October 1810, elected councillor of state. He retired in 1820; the following year he and Constanze went to live in Salzburg.

From an early stage in their relationship, Nissen helped Constanze in business matters. Many letters signed and dispatched by her are, in fact, in his hand and were composed by him. Shortly before his death he confided to his stepson Franz Xaver Wolfgang Mozart* that she had trusted him so completely that 'rarely did she look at the letters I had written except to sign them'. In 1798–9, he and the Abbé Maximilian Stadler* examined the musical autographs left by Mozart. Around 1823 Nissen began to collect material for a comprehensive biography of Mozart. In this task he was assisted by Anton Jähndl (1783–1861), a choirmaster at a convent in Salzburg, and by Maximilian Keller (1770–1855), an organist at Altötting, who, when he was ten years old, had heard Mozart play the organ at Seeon Abbey. After Nissen's death Constanze invited Dr Johann Heinrich Feuerstein (d. Dresden, 2 January 1850), a physician living at Pirna, near Dresden, to complete the book. It was published by Breitkopf & Härtel* in Leipzig in 1828, with the following title: *Biographie W. A. Mozart's. Nach Originalbriefen, Sammlungen alles über ihn Geschriebenen, mit vielen neuen Beylagen, Steindrücken, Musikblättern und einem Facsimile*. Although the author's name is given as 'von Nissen', he was not entitled to the particle (and had in fact not used it himself), since the Danebrog Order which he was awarded in 1809 did not carry ennoblement. A supplement [*Anhang*], likewise dated 1828, offered, among other items, a study of Mozart's operas. A second edition of the biography appeared in 1849 and a French translation in 1869. (Münster², Valentin¹)

Nouseul, Johann Joseph (b. 1742; d. Vienna, 8 December 1821). Actor, singer and theatre manager; the original Monastatos (*Die Zauberflöte*). After acting with Marchand*'s company, he moved to Munich in 1774, and in 1776 he performed at Rastatt, where he married the actress Maria Rosalie Lefebre (1750–1804). Later he founded his own company in Hanover. The couple subsequently held well-paid appointments in Munich, which they left in 1779 to join the Burgtheater. Nouseul first appeared there on 17 January 1780, as Reichenthal in Gottlieb Stephanie*'s *Die abgedankten Offiziere, oder Standhaftigkeit und Verzweiflung*, whilst Rosalie made her début two days later as Madame Murer in Beaumarchais's *Eugénie*. She was to remain a highly valued member of the Burgtheater until her death on 24 January 1804. Nouseul himself, however, left the company in 1781.

In 1782 he and Friedrich Gensicke were joint managers of the Kärntnertor-Theater, and the following year Nouseul was in charge of the theatre at Graz. He was a member of Johann Friedel's company at the Freihaus-Theater in Vienna when it was taken over by Schikaneder* in 1789. In 1800 he rejoined the court theatre and appeared there until 1814.
(Schuler[14])

Novello, Vincent (b. London, 6 September 1781; d. Nice, 9 August 1861). English musician (especially famous in his day as organist and choirmaster at the Portuguese Embassy chapel in London) and music publisher. On 17 August 1808 he married Mary Sabilla Hehl (b. c.1789; d. Nice, 25 July 1854) who bore him eleven children; one of the daughters, Clara (1818–1908), became a very well-known singer.

In 1829 Novello travelled to Austria with his wife, for the double purpose of presenting to the ailing Nannerl* a sum of sixty guineas subscribed by a group of London musicians (who included Mozart's pupil Thomas Attwood*) and of collecting material for a biography of Mozart which he intended to write, no doubt stimulated by Nissen*'s book published the year before. (He never carried out this project; it was his pupil Edward Holmes who, in his *Life of Mozart* [1845], wrote the first comprehensive biography in English.) In Salzburg, in addition to Nannerl, the Novellos met Constanze*, her sister Sophie Haibel*, and Franz Xaver Wolfgang Mozart*, who happened to be visiting his mother. In Vienna they conversed with Eybler*, the Abbé Maximilian Stadler* and the Streichers (*see* STEIN), among others; and Mary Novello spoke with Aloisia Lange*.

Both Vincent and Mary kept diaries during this journey. These were discovered after the Second World War in the villa at Fermo, in Italy, where Clara Novello had lived with her husband Count Giovanni Battista Gigliucci from 1843 to 1849 and again from 1861 on. They were transcribed by Clara's granddaughter Nerina Medici di Marignano and, edited by Rosemary Hughes, were published in London in 1955 – appropriately enough, by Novello & Co. The Novellos met Constanze again in 1838 while passing through Salzburg on their way to Italy.
(Hughes, Novello)

Noverre, Jean-Georges (b. Paris, 29 April 1727; d. St Germain-en-Laye, 19 October 1810). Dancer and choreographer of French–Swiss extraction (his father served in the Swiss Guard attached to the French court). He played a seminal role in the development of the dramatic ballet and was the author of highly influential studies of the dance, notably *Lettres sur la danse et sur les ballets* (Lyons and Stuttgart, 1760, revised in 1783, enlarged in 1803).

Noverre subscribed to the aesthetic philosophy proclaimed by the 18th-century *Encyclopédistes* that art should imitate nature, and accordingly sought to eliminate various traditional features and routines which he considered irrelevant or contrary to this aim. He furthermore insisted on unity of conception in the creation of ballets. He was, on the whole, less successful in imposing his ideas in France than abroad, and as a result the most productive periods of his career were those spent in other countries, in particular in Stuttgart (1760–67), Vienna (1767–74, 1776), and

Paisiello, Giovanni

London, where he was engaged for several seasons during the period 1755–94. His appointment as ballet master at the Paris Opéra (1776–81) was to involve him in much controversy which eventually led to his resignation.

If Mozart had not already made Noverre's acquaintance during his second journey to Vienna (September 1767 – January 1769), he would undoubtedly have done so during the festivities accompanying Archduke Ferdinand*'s wedding in Milan in October 1771, which included both Mozart's *Ascanio in Alba** and Noverre's ballet *Roger et Bradamante*. The contacts were renewed during Mozart's visit to Vienna with his father in the summer of 1773; in a letter to his wife* on 28 August, Leopold mentioned that they should be dining at Noverre's the following day. And as soon as Mozart reached Paris with his mother in 1778, he received an invitation from Noverre to dine at his house whenever he wished. In addition, Noverre tried, unsuccessfully, to obtain for him a commission for an opera. There was also talk of a new ballet by Noverre, for which Mozart would write the music. It is not certain whether this was a reference to the revised version of *Les petits riens* or to a different, ultimately unrealized, project.

The ballet *Les petits riens* was originally performed at the Burgtheater, Vienna, on 5 January 1768, to music probably composed by Franz Aspelmayr (1728–86). Now, in Paris, Mozart contributed several numbers to a new production which was presented at the Opéra on 11 June 1778, in a double bill with Niccolò Piccinni's opera *Le finte gemelle (see also* GARIBALDI). Of the twenty-one pieces which made up the revised ballet κAnh.10/299*b*, the overture and seven numbers have now, on stylistic grounds, been definitely attributed to Mozart, while eight other numbers are thought to be almost certainly by another composer; the authenticity of the remaining ones has not yet been determined.

(Hansell[3], Lynham, *NMA* II/6/2)

Paisiello, Giovanni (b. Roccaforzata, near Taranto, 9 May 1740; d. Naples, 5 June 1816). Prominent Italian composer of secular and sacred music, best known for his comic operas. His earliest operas were produced at various north Italian theatres, but it was during his residence in Naples from 1766 to 1776 that he made his reputation as a gifted composer of *opere buffe*. In 1776 he accepted the post of director of the Russian court theatres at St Petersburg, where he remained eight years. He then returned to Naples to take up the position of court composer to King Ferdinand IV; in 1787 he was also placed in charge of all secular music. He lived in Naples for the remainder of his life, except for the years 1802–4, which he spent in Paris as Napoleon's director of music. His fortunes in Naples continued to flourish under the reigns of Joseph Bonaparte (1806–8) and Joachim Murat (1808–15), but he was deprived of most of his court appointments upon the return of King Ferdinand in 1815; he died in relative poverty.

Paisiello composed more than eighty operas, many of which had considerable success in Vienna. With a total of 294 performances, he was by far the most popular composer at the court theatres in the period 1781–91 (Salieri* was next, with 185). *La frascatana* achieved thirty-five performances between 29 April 1775 and 5 February 1777, and was revived on 8 December 1783, with Nancy Storace* in the title role; *Il barbiere di Siviglia* became an enduring favourite following its Viennese première on 13 August 1783, with Stefano Mandini* as Almaviva, Benucci* as

1 Mozart: oil painting by Barbara Krafft, 1819

2 The Mozart family: group portrait
by Johann Nepomuk della Croce

3 Leopold Mozart: portrait by
Pietro Antonio Lorenzoni, 1765

4 Constanze Mozart:
oil painting by
Joseph Lange, 1782

5 Franz Xaver and Carl
Thomas Mozart: oil painting
by Hans Hansen, *c.* 1798

6 Mozart: unfinished portrait by
Joseph Lange, *c.* 1789

7 First page of the autograph MS of the
second 'Haydn' String Quartet, K421

8 Archbishop Count
Hieronymus Colloredo

9 Empress Maria Theresa:
portrait by Michael
Christian Emanuel Hagelgans

10 Emperor Joseph II with
his two sisters,
Archduchesses Anna and
Elizabeth: portrait by
Joseph Hauzinger

11 Elector Karl Theodor holding a transverse flute:
portrait by Johann Georg Ziesenis

12 Countess Wilhelmine Thun-Hohenstein: anonymous portrait

13 Ignaz von Born: portrait by Johann Baptist Lampi

14 Abbé Maximilian Stadler: engraving by Johann Balthasar Pfister

15 Antonio Salieri: portrait by
Joseph Willibrod Mähler

16 Joseph Haydn: portrait by
Thomas Hardy

17 Christian Cannabich: engraving by Egid Verhelst

18 Pietro Metastasio:
pastel by Rosalba Carriera

19 Lorenzo da Ponte: engraving by
Michele Pekenino after Nathaniel Rogers

20 Emanuel Schikaneder:
engraving by Philipp Richter

21 Anton Raaff:
portrait by Moritz von
Kellerhoven

22 Elisabeth Augusta
('Lisl') Wendling:
anonymous pastel

23 Aloisia Lange (née Weber) as
Zemire in *Zemire und Azor:* etching by J. E. Nilson

24 Josepha Duschek: engraving by
August Clar after J. F. Haake

25 Francesco Benucci: engraving by
Friedrich John after Dorffmeister

26 Anna (Nancy) Storace: engraving by
Pietro Bettelini

27 Michael Kelly: engraving by Neagle from a watercolour by Thomas Lawrence

Bartolo, Bussani* as Figaro, and Nancy Storace as Rosina; *Il re Teodore in Venezia*, first produced on 23 August 1784, was given almost sixty more times over the next six-and-a-half years; and *La molinara*, first performed in Vienna on 13 November 1790, remained in the repertory until the end of the century.

Mozart made Paisiello's acquaintance during his visit to Naples in May–June 1770, and he met him again in Turin in January 1771. They renewed contact when Paisiello spent several months in Vienna on his return journey from Russia in 1784. On 13 June Mozart took Paisiello to a private concert at which he was playing with his pupil Barbara von Ployer*. On 23 August he attended the première of Paisiello's opera *Il re Teodoro in Venezia*, which was specially written for Vienna.

Mozart wrote new settings for the following arias from operas by Paisiello: in 1777, for Josepha Duschek*, *Ah, lo previdi . . . Ah, t'invola agl'occhi miei* K272, from *Andromeda*; in 1781, for Ceccarelli*, *A questo seno deh vieni . . . Or che il cielo a me ti rende* K374, from *Sismano nel Mogol* (Mozart had heard the opera in Milan in January 1773); in 1787, for Gottfried von Jacquin*, *Mentre ti lascio, o figlia* K513, from *La disfatta di Dario*. Furthermore, at a concert on 23 March 1783, Mozart improvised the Variations K398/416e on the aria 'Salve tu, Domine' from *I filosofi immaginari*; and in 1789 he wrote the aria 'Schon lacht der holde Frühling' K580 for Josepha Hofer* to sing in a German-language version of *Il barbiere di Siviglia*, which, however, does not appear to have been produced as planned.
(Michtner, *Mozart Compendium*, Robinson M.F.[3])

Panzachi, Domenico de' (b. 1733; d. after 1805). Italian tenor; the original Arbace (*Idomeneo**). Mozart explained in a letter to his father on 5 December 1780 that, in order to please the 'worthy old fellow', he had acceded to Panzachi's request to lengthen the recitative 'Sventurata Sidon' in Act III. He had done so all the more readily, he added, because the change was likely to prove dramatically effective, since Panzachi was such a good actor. Panzachi had been performing in Munich since 1762.

Paradis [Paradies], Maria Theresia von (b. Vienna, 15 May 1759; d. Vienna, 1 February 1824). Austrian pianist and composer. Daughter of Joseph Anton von Paradis (1739–1808), secretary in the Department of Commerce, from 1785 councillor in the Lower Austrian government service.

Blind since the age of three, she became a patient of Dr Mesmer* in 1776, and in January 1777 moved into the clinic which he had set up at his house. After three weeks' intensive treatment her sight was partly restored. In the end, however, for reasons which seem to have been as much of a psychological as a physiological nature, the initial progress was not maintained and blindness returned. She left his clinic in June 1777.

Despite her serious handicap, she became an excellent pianist. Between 1783 and 1786, accompanied by her mother, she carried out two successful European concert tours, the second of which took her to Paris and London. Thereafter she devoted herself mainly to teaching and composition. She wrote some sonatas, concertos and other pieces for the piano, a number of songs, and three works for the stage: *Ariadne und Bacchus* (performed at Schloss Laxenburg on 20 June 1791), *Der Schulkandidat* (given at the Marinelli-Theater in Vienna on 5 December 1792), and *Rinaldo und*

Parini, Giuseppe

Alcina (produced by Guardasoni*'s company in Prague on 30 June 1797). The scores of the first and third of these Singspiels have been lost, as have those of several others of her works.

Mozart is known to have met her in Salzburg in August 1783; he may, of course, have made her acquaintance already earlier in Vienna. He composed a piano concerto (probably K456) for her; he later performed it himself at a concert at the Burgtheater, Vienna, on 13 February 1785, and also in Leipzig on 12 May 1789. (Angermüller[7], Deutsch[4], Komorzynski[2], Ullrich[1])

Parini, Giuseppe (b. Bosisio, 22 or 23 May 1729; d. Milan, 15 August 1799). Italian poet. He wrote the text for *Ascanio in Alba**, as well as two other, uncompleted, librettos, *L'amorosa incostanza* and *Iside salvata*. He is better known, however, for his satirical epic *Il giorno* and for his sonnets (*Per Caterina Gabrielli cantatrice*, *Il lamento d'Orfeo*) and odes (*La musica*, *In morte del Maestro Sacchini*). He was a member of two prominent academies, the Arcadia in Rome and the Accademia dei Trasformati in Milan. (*See also* FERDINAND.)

His libretto for Mozart's *Ascanio in Alba* was later also set by the Portuguese composer António Leal Moreira (1758–1819), whose opera was performed at Queluz Palace, near Lisbon, on 5 July 1785 in honour of King Peter III's birthday. (Allorto)

Pergmayr, Johann Gottlieb (b. Grieskirchen, Upper Austria, 1709; d. Salzburg, 14 December 1787). Salzburg town councillor; joint owner of the firm Gottlieb Pergmayr & Georg Lürzer. Mozart's godfather. In fact, either he or his first wife Maria Cordula (d. 1755) is named in the cathedral baptismal register as godfather or godmother in the case of each of the seven children of Leopold and Maria Anna Mozart*. Maria Cordula had previously been married to Pergmayr's employer, the merchant Johann Kaufmann von Söllheim (1691–1735); she was the daughter of Michael Wenger, who was the mayor of Salzburg from 1732 to 1741. Pergmayr's second name usually appears in the Latin entries in the cathedral register as 'Amadeus' (or 'AmaDeus'), but in the record of Wolfgang's baptism it takes the Greek form 'Theophilus' – which is also listed as one of Wolfgang's own names. In a letter from Paris to Hagenauer* on 16 May 1766, Leopold remarks that Pergmayr 'must surely be very moved at the thought that he held these children who are causing such a sensation in the world over the baptismal font'. Actually, only his wife's name is mentioned in the register in Nannerl*'s case.

On 10 February 1756 Pergmayr married Anna Maria Thün (d. 1778). He was a witness at the wedding of Michael Haydn* and Maria Magdalena Lipp* in 1768. (Breitinger[2])

Petrosellini, Giuseppe (b. Corneto Tarquinia, 19 or 29 November 1727; d. Rome, after 1799). Italian librettist who is now regarded as the probable author of the libretto used by Mozart in *La finta giardiniera**. He served as secretary to Prince Giustiniani and as valet to Pope Pius VI; he was a member of several Italian academies. His most famous libretto was written for Paisiello*'s opera *Il barbiere di Siviglia*, first produced at St Petersburg in 1782. His other librettos include *L'incognita perseguitata* (set by Niccolò Piccinni in 1764 and by Anfossi* in 1773), *Il*

barone di Rocca antica (set by Anfossi in 1771 and by Salieri* in 1772), *La dama pastorella* (set by Salieri in 1780, and presented by him in a textually and musically revised version as *La cifra* in Vienna in 1789), and *L'italiana in Londra* and *Il pittor parigino* (set by Domenico Cimarosa in 1778 and 1781).
(Angermüller², Mondolfi)

Pichler, Karoline, *née* von Greiner (b. Vienna, 7 September 1769; d. Vienna, 9 July 1843). Austrian novelist, playwright and literary hostess. She was the daughter of Franz Sales von Greiner (1730–98), councillor in the Austro-Bohemian chancellery and a member the Education Commission, and of his wife Charlotte, *née* Hieronymus (1739–1815). There was much music-making at the Greiners' house, Mozart being one of several well-known performers who regularly played in quartets there. From an early age, Karoline studied singing and the piano with Joseph Anton Steffan (1726–97) and eventually became a much admired amateur pianist, guitarist and singer; Schönfeld considered her one of the finest women pianists in Vienna. Her engagement to Johann Baptist von Häring (1761[?2]–1818), an excellent amateur violinist, was broken off in 1788; on 25 May 1796 she married Andreas Pichler (1764–1837), a civil servant.

She was a prolific writer, and her complete works, published between 1828 and 1844, ran to sixty volumes; but she is remembered today almost solely for her memoirs *Denkwürdigkeiten aus meinem Leben*, which were published by her daughter Caroline von Pelzeln in 1844. This chronicle of the intellectual and cultural life of the time contains interesting reminiscences about Mozart, whom she knew quite well and often heard play. Although she was not his pupil, he gave her some informal instruction. Her father was among the subscribers to Mozart's Trattnerhof concerts in 1784 (*see* TRATTNER).
(Blümml, Pichler, Schönfeld)

Pierron, (Marie) Therese (baptized Mannheim, 27 December 1761; d. after 1798). Pupil of Mozart. On 12 or 13 December 1777 Mozart and his mother* moved from the *Pfälzischer Hof*, the inn where they had been staying since their arrival in Mannheim on 30 October, to the house of Councillor Anton Joseph Serrarius. There they were offered free lodging, wood and light, in exchange for piano lessons to be given by Mozart to Serrarius's stepdaughter, Therese. Her father, Dominik Pierron, a valet in the service of Karl Theodor*, had been murdered, sometime before June 1764, by the elector's personal physician, Dr Bechtel. When Mozart met Therese, she had been playing the piano for eight years.

At a musical evening held at Serrarius's house on 14 January 1778, she performed a concerto she had been studying with Mozart; this was probably the same concerto which she played at a concert on 23 February, namely K246. On 12 March she partnered Rosina Cannabich* and Aloisia Weber* in a performance at the Cannabichs' of the Triple Concerto K242. Mozart dedicated to her the Violin Sonata K296 which he composed while in Mannheim (and which he was to publish in Vienna in 1781, together with five other violin sonatas, in an edition dedicated to Josepha Auernhammer*).

August Wilhelm Iffland (1759–1814), later one of Germany's most celebrated actors, was engaged in 1779 at the Mannheim theatre. He met Therese and fell in

Ployer, Maria Anna Barbara von

love with her. In a letter to his sister Louise, on 8 November 1780, he described her in the following terms: 'Demureness and grace in every movement. Blonde hair, dressed very simply. Big blue eyes; a nose which is not pretty, *almost* a snub nose; a splendid mouth; dimpled cheeks; a splendid chin. A smile – such as could induce a starving tiger to release its prey. A complexion of milk and roses.' Therese later married Georg Heinrich Schwendel.

A photograph of Serrarius's house, which was destroyed in the Second World War, can be seen at the Reiss Museum in Mannheim. Moreover, the Mannheim artist Hanns Maria Barchfeld (1895–1953) made a drawing of the house in 1941. This was reproduced, apparently from a copy printed in a newspaper, by W. Herrmann in his 1977 article on Therese Pierron; the fate of the original is unknown.
(Herrmann, Höft)

Ployer, Maria Anna Barbara ['Babette'] **von** (b. Sarmingstein, Upper Austria, 2 September 1765; d. before 1811). Excellent amateur pianist; a pupil of Mozart. Daughter of Franz Kajetan von Ployer (1734–1803), a tax-collector and timber merchant, and of his wife Maria Barbara, *née* Gartenmüller (d. 1779). From 1780 she lived in Vienna with her father's cousin Gottfried Ignaz von Ployer (*c.*1743–97), a senior civil servant (he was ennobled in 1773) who, among other appointments, served on the Education Commission and at the high court of justice and was treasury representative to the department for the mint and mines; he was also the Viennese agent for the Salzburg court. He was a subscriber to Mozart's Trattnerhof concerts in 1784 (*see* TRATTNER).

Barbara studied with Mozart in 1784. He dedicated to her the piano concertos K449 ('she has paid me well for it,' he wrote to his father on 20 February 1784) and K453. She is known to have performed the latter, in Paisiello*'s presence, at a private concert held at the lodgings of Gottfried Ignaz von Ployer in the Viennese suburb of Döbling on 13 June 1784. At the same concert she also played the Sonata for two pianos K448/375a with Mozart. Zinzendorf*, after hearing her on 23 March 1785, described her as a 'marvellous' pianist. Mozart also composed for her a funeral march of sixteen bars (K453a) which was pasted, written in his own hand, into her album (lost in 1945); the title *Marche funèbre del Sigr Maestro Contrapunto* is, however, in a different hand and may not have been chosen by Mozart himself.

In some lines in Latin written in Mozart's album on 28 June 1787, Franz Kajetan von Ployer proclaimed his undying gratitude to Mozart – 'who surpasses all in divine Apollo's art' – for having brought glory to his daughter.

Barbara married Kornelius Bujanovics von Agg-Telek (*c.*1770–1844), whose father, Karl Bujanovics, was the representative of the Transylvanian court in Vienna. Kornelius owned an estate at Kreuz [Krizevci], north-east of Agram [Zagreb] in Croatia. According to Constanze*'s letter to Johann Anton André* of 31 May 1800, Barbara was living there at that time. The couple had at least one son, Ladislaus, who was still alive in 1844. Barbara herself died some time before 16 April 1811; on that day her husband was married in Vienna to Karoline Schott, *née* von Auernhammer, perhaps a relative of Mozart's pupil Josepha Barbara Auernhammer*.
(Schuler¹³, Senn²)

Poggi, Domenico (d. after 1790). Italian bass who would have taken the part of Simone at the première of *La finta semplice** which Leopold Mozart tried to arrange in Vienna in 1768. He was engaged in Vienna from 1767 until 1775 and appeared as Oracolo at the première of Gluck*'s *Alceste* on 26 December 1767. According to Sonnenfels, he had a rich and very pleasing voice and was a first-rate actor. Michael Kelly*, in his *Reminiscences*, called him 'the most celebrated *buffo* singer of his day'. (*See also* BAGLIONI, CLEMENTINA.)
(Kelly, Sonnenfels)

Ponziani, Felice. The original Leporello (*Don Giovanni**). He is known to have sung at Parma during the 1784–5 season. In 1786 he took the title role in the highly successful production of *Le nozze di Figaro** in Prague. The *Prager Oberpostamtszeitung* of 9 January 1787 described him as 'a man who here, and wherever else he has appeared, has been the favourite of connoisseurs and of all who have heard him'. He again sang Leporello when *Don Giovanni* was performed in Prague on 2 September 1791 in the presence of Leopold II*. In 1792 he performed in Venice.

Puchberg, Johann Michael von (b. Zwettl, Lower Austria, 21 September 1741; d. Vienna, 21 January 1822). Viennese merchant; a good friend of Mozart, and his chief creditor during the final period of his life. From 1768 Puchberg was in the employ of the Viennese textile manufacturer Michael Salliet, eventually becoming manager of the firm. In 1780, three years after Salliet's death, Puchberg married his widow Elisabeth (1748–84); in 1787 he married Anna Eckart. His flat in Hohe Markt square was in a house owned by Count Franz Walsegg-Stuppach*. Like Mozart, Puchberg was a freemason, a fact frequently alluded to by Mozart in his requests for financial assistance. He was ennobled in 1792, but is reported to have died a poor man.

The first mention of Puchberg in Mozart's extant correspondence occurs in a letter to his brother-in-law Johann Baptist Franz von Berchtold zu Sonnenburg* on 29 September 1787, in which Mozart, who was about to set out for Prague, requested that the 1000 gulden due to him from his father's estate be sent to Puchberg (*see also* GILOWSKY). The first of the surviving nineteen 'begging' letters dates from June 1788 (but a reference in it to an already existing debt makes it clear that Puchberg's generosity had commenced earlier); the last letter dates from June 1791. Puchberg seems to have responded regularly to Mozart's appeals for help, if not always with the full amount requested. The largest single payment, according to the notes made by Puchberg on Mozart's letters, amounted to 300 gulden, the smallest to ten gulden; he did not accede to Mozart's request, in June 1788, for a larger loan of 1000 or 2000 gulden for a period of one to two years. The total money advanced by Puchberg was in excess of 1415 gulden (the equivalent, in 1990, of *c*.£3000 or US$5100). After Mozart's death Constanze* appointed Puchberg as her representative in the official assessment of Mozart's estate. According to Nissen*'s biography, Mozart owed Puchberg some 1000 gulden when he died, but it was not until several years later that Puchberg demanded repayment, which Constanze duly made.

Mozart's letters to Puchberg frequently expressed great anguish. On 27 June 1788 he wrote: 'If you, dearest Brother, do not help me in my present predicament, I shall lose my honour and my good repute, which are the only things that I wish to preserve. I rely entirely on your true friendship and brotherly love, and I confidently expect that you will come to my aid with word and deed . . .' On 12 July 1789: 'Dear God! I am in a predicament which I would not wish on my worst enemy. If you, dearest friend and Brother, abandon me now, I am lost, wretched as I am, together with my poor sick wife and my child, and through no fault of mine.' In late March or early April 1790: 'Just once more and for the last time I appeal to you, at this time of my greatest need, to help me as best you can, confident as I am in your proven friendship and brotherly love.' And on or before 17 May 1790: 'Since I can find no true friends, I am obliged to turn to usurers. But as [this] takes time . . . I am so destitute at present that I must beseech you most earnestly, dearest friend, to let me have whatever you can spare . . . If you only knew what sorrow and concern all this causes me. It has prevented me all this time from finishing my quartets.' This was evidently a reference to the set of quartets commissioned by King Frederick William II* of Prussia in 1789; Mozart completed only three (K575, 589, 590) of the six he had undertaken to write (see also KOZELUCH).

Mozart appears to have felt genuine affection for Puchberg. In a letter to Constanze on 23 May 1789 announcing his imminent return from Berlin, he wrote 'I hope that you will drive out to meet me at the first stage-post . . . I hope that Hofer*, whom I embrace a thousand times, will accompany you. If Herr und Frau von Puchberg were to drive out with you too, then all the friends I want to see will be there.' During his absence Constanze had been staying with the Puchbergs.

Mozart's reference in his correspondence to a trio he had written for Puchberg appears to relate either to the Piano Trio K542 or to the Divertimento for violin, viola and cello K563. In a letter to Constanze from Dresden on 16 April 1789 he mentioned having performed the 'Puchberg' trio there with Anton Teyber (see TEYBER) and the cellist Nikolaus Kraft (1778–1853).
(Eibl[2], Komorzynski[4])

Pufendorf, Anna von, née Baroness Posch (b. c.1757; d. Vienna, 7 April 1843). Wife of Councillor of the Realm Konrad Heinrich von Pufendorf (1743–1822). A great music-lover and an excellent amateur singer, she regularly arranged concerts at her house which were entirely devoted to vocal music (incuding choruses, fugues, and sacred pieces). At the performance of *Idomeneo** at Prince Auersperg's palace on 13 March 1786 she took the part of Ilia. According to Schönfeld's *Jahrbuch der Tonkunst von Wien und Prag*, her voice was not particularly big, 'but she sings with enchanting style, refinement and feeling'. She was a subscriber to Mozart's Trattnerhof concerts in 1784 (see TRATTNER).
(Schönfeld, Schuler[13])

Pulini, Antonio. Writing to Hagenauer* on 30 January 1768, Leopold Mozart mentioned that there were then several excellent singers available in Vienna for an *opera buffa* such as he wished Wolfgang to write; among them he named a 'Sgr. Polini'. Leopold was presumably referring to the Antonio Pulini who had sung at the Burgtheater in Florian Leopold Gassmann's *Il viaggiatore ridicolo* in October 1766, and in Niccolò Piccinni's *Le contadine bizzarre* and Giuseppe Pasqua's *L'albagia smascherata* in early 1767.

According to J. H. Eibl, he was the same person as the 'Baron Pulini' who sang Idamante at the private performance of *Idomeneo** conducted by Mozart at Prince Auersperg's palace on 13 March 1786, and for whom, on that occasion, Mozart wrote the tenor parts in K489 and K490.
(Eibl in *Mozart: Briefe*, Zechmeister)

Punto, Giovanni [real name: Jan Václav (Johann Wenzel) Stich] (b. Zehušice, near Čáslav, Bohemia, 28 September 1746; d. Prague, 16 February 1803). Horn virtuoso, violinist and composer. He was a bondman of Count Johann Joseph Anton Thun-Hohenstein*, who had him trained in music and in whose private orchestra in Prague he played from 1763 to 1766. He subsequently fled from Prague and, to cover his tracks, changed his name to 'Giovanni Punto'. He was a member of the Mainz court orchestra from 1769 to 1774, and later performed in many of the leading European music centres. Beethoven wrote for him his Horn Sonata op. 17, which they played together at Punto's concert at the Burgtheater, Vienna, on 18 April 1800. Punto himself composed a number of horn concertos and a considerable amount of chamber music featuring the horn.

When Mozart heard him in Paris in 1778, he was greatly impressed: 'Punto blows magnifique,' he wrote to his father on 5 April 1778. Mozart composed for Punto the horn part in the (lost) Sinfonia Concertante for flute, oboe, horn, and bassoon KAnh.9/297B (*see* LEGROS).
(Morley-Pegge/Fitzpatrick)

Raab, Maria Anna ['Mitzerl'] (b. Salzburg, 1709 or 1710; d. Salzburg, 5 April 1788). A close friend of the Mozarts, frequently mentioned in their correspondence, invariably under her pet name 'Mitzerl', and at times as 'die Tanzmeister Mitzerl', in reference to her ownership of the so-called 'Tanzmeisterhaus' on the Hannibal-Platz [later Makart-Platz].

The house, which was built no later than 1617, probably took its name from an early occupant, the French-born dancing-master Johann Pastier (or Pastir) who married Rosina Franziska Hämmerl, a native of Salzburg, in 1672. In 1711 the then owner, Count Maximilian Johann Preisgott Kuefstein, sold the property to Anna Eva Waglhofer, wife of the dancing-master Lorenz Spöckner (or Speckner). She, in turn, transferred the title to the house in 1739 to her son Karl Gottlieb Spöckner (1707–67), who was likewise a dancing-master. He was a witness at Leopold Mozart's wedding in 1747.

Upon Spöckner's death on 13 May 1767 the house became the property of his cousin, 'Mitzerl Raab'. It was she who, in 1773, rented an eight-room flat on the first floor to the Mozarts. Leopold resided there for the rest of his life, while Wolfgang lived in the house for more than seven years, until close to his twenty-fifth birthday. From Munich, where he was rehearsing *La finta giardiniera**, he wrote to Nannerl* on 30 December 1774: 'Please give my best regards to Fräulein Mitzerl. She has no reason to doubt my love, I see her constantly before me in her charming negligée [i.e. with her hair undressed]; I have seen many pretty girls here, but none as beautiful as she is.' To several commentators this passage proved that 'Mitzerl' was one of the great loves of Wolfgang's youth – until it was discovered that the register of deaths gave her age in 1788 as seventy-eight, so that she must have been sixty-four in 1774.

Raaff, Anton

On 23 August 1787, some three months after Leopold's death, 'Mitzerl' ceded the house to her cousin Ignaz Raab (1743–1811), a well-to-do lawyer in Vienna. He sold it on 15 April 1795 to Franz Xaver Oberer, who installed his printing-works in the large room on the first floor which the Spöckners had used for balls and masquerades and the Mozarts for small concerts.

The 'Tanzmeisterhaus' survived intact until 16 October 1944 when two-thirds of it were destroyed in an air raid. Of the Mozarts' flat, the music room alone survived. Post-war plans to restore the house to its original form were frustrated by the sale of the property to an insurance company which proposed to put up a five-storey office block. Eventually this was constructed on the site of the destroyed part of the house only. The section spared by the bombs was acquired in 1955 by the *Internationale Stiftung Mozarteum*, which duly restored it, including the aforementioned music room. Since 1956 the latter has been used for exhibitions, conferences, concerts and other cultural events; on 12 June 1981 a Mozart Museum was established there. (Angermüller[10], Breitinger[1], Rech[1])

Raaff, Anton (baptized Gelsdorf, near Bonn, 6 May 1714; d. Munich, 28 May 1797). Celebrated German tenor who created the title role in *Idomeneo**. After studying with Giovanni Ferrandini in Munich in 1736–7 and then with the well-known castrato Antonio Bernacchi in Bologna, he embarked on a highly successful international career which, during the first twenty years, took him to Italy, Bonn, Vienna, Lisbon, Madrid and, in 1759, back to Italy. In Vienna, in 1749–50, he sang the title role at the première of Nicolò Jommelli's *Catone in Utica* (16 April 1749), as well as appearing in the same composer's *Merope*, *Achille in Sciro* and *Didone abbandonata*. Metastasio* wrote to Carlo Broschi [Farinelli] on 28 May 1749 that Raaff sang 'like a seraph'. (On 22 January 1761, in a letter to Princess Belmonte, he would call him 'our incomparable Signor Raaff'.) During the decade following his return to Italy he established himself as the leading tenor on the Neapolitan and Florentine stage. In 1770 he was engaged at Mannheim and in 1778 moved with the court to Munich (*see* KARL THEODOR). Among the prominent composers who wrote leading roles for him was Johann Christian Bach*.

An unnamed biographer in the *Allgemeine Musikalische Zeitung* (*see* BREITKOPF & HÄRTEL) in 1810 claimed that Raaff's voice 'has never had its equal for compass and beauty'. In addition, according to the same writer, he possessed a technique which enabled him to overcome the greatest difficulties with complete ease, and a diction of such clarity, in German as well as Italian, that 'not a syllable was lost even when he was accompanied by the most dazzling instrumentation, in the very largest theatre'.

In his letter of 18–20 October 1777 Leopold Mozart advised Wolfgang, who was about to seek his fortune in Mannheim, to confide in no one but Raaff, who 'is a god-fearing and honest man . . . and can give you much advice and assistance'. Wolfgang was introduced to Raaff by the violinist Christian Franz Danner (1757–1813), whose father, also a violinist and a member of the Mannheim court orchestra, was an old friend of the Mozarts. But despite his sincere efforts on Wolfgang's behalf, Raaff was unable to secure an appointment for him, either at Mannheim or later in Munich. (He may, however, have helped him eventually to get the commission for *Idomeneo*.)

Mozart was disappointed when he heard Raaff in Ignaz Jakob Holzbauer*'s opera *Günther von Schwarzburg* at Mannheim on 5 November 1777: 'Anyone hearing him begin an aria, who does not remember at the same moment that it is Raaff, the once so famous tenor, who is singing, would be sure to burst out laughing,' he wrote on 14 November. However, when, a few months later, he attended one of Raaff's concerts in Paris, he realized that the tenor still possessed, though in diminished form, some of the qualities which had made him such an outstanding singer: 'His voice is beautiful and most agreeable . . . In bravura singing, longer passages and roulades, [he] is superb, and then there is his good, clear diction . . . and his Andantinos' (letter of 12 June 1778).

In Mannheim Mozart had composed the aria *Se al labbro mio non credi* K295 for Raaff. Now, in Paris, their personal relations grew increasingly affectionate: 'He is very fond of me, and we are the best of friends,' Mozart wrote in the same letter. His mother* was even more enthusiastic: 'Herr Raaff visits us every day,' she informed her husband on 12 June. 'And each time he comes, he sings something for me. I am quite in love with his singing. He is such a decent, honest man, and sincerity itself; if you knew him, you would love him with all your heart.' At the concert on 18 June, at which the 'Paris' Symphony K297/300a was first performed (*see* LEGROS), Raaff sang Johann Christian Bach's aria 'Non so d'onde viene' (which Mozart called his 'favourite piece' – *see* BACH).

During rehearsals for *Idomeneo* in Munich in 1780, Mozart's feelings towards Raaff were as warm as ever ('Raaff is my best and dearest friend,' he wrote to his father on 15 November 1780), but he was concerned about Raaff's vocal deficiencies ('he is, after all, an old man . . .'). He was also dismayed by his poor acting: 'Raaff is just like a statue,' he declared on 8 November. On 27 December Mozart complained that Raaff and Dal Prato* were 'the most wretched actors who have ever stood on a stage', and he added: 'Raaff is the best and most honest of fellows, but he is so set in his sloppy old routines that it drives one absolutely crazy'. However, Mozart willingly fulfilled Raaff's request for an additional aria ('Torna la pace al core') in Act III. Raaff was particularly delighted with the Act II aria 'Fuor del mar ho un mar in seno': 'The fellow is as enamoured of his aria as an ardent young lover might be of his sweetheart,' Mozart wrote on 1 December, 'for he sings it at night before going to sleep and in the morning when he wakes up.'

When Michael Kelly*, with Nancy Storace* and her brother Stephen, called on Raaff in Munich in 1787, he sang for them 'Non so d'onde viene' (see above). 'Though his voice was impaired,' Kelly recalled in his *Reminiscences*, 'he still retained his fine *voce di petto* and sostenuto notes, and pure style of singing.' Raaff was then seventy-three years old.

(Freiberger, Heartz[1], Kelly, Raaff, Zechmeister)

Ramm, Friedrich (1744–?1811). German oboist. A member of the Mannheim court orchestra from the age of fourteen, he was among the players who moved to Munich in 1778 (*see* KARL THEODOR). Mozart made his acquaintance shortly after arriving at Mannheim on 30 October 1777. In his letters to his father of 4 November and 3 December Mozart expressed admiration both for the musician ('he plays very well, with a pleasingly pure tone') and the man ('he is a very decent, cheerful and honest fellow'). Ramm, in his turn, was greatly impressed by Mozart's Oboe

Rauzzini, Venanzio

Concerto K271*k*. Mozart wrote on 14 February that at a concert at Christian Cannabich*'s house the previous day, Ramm had played it for the fifth time: it had become his 'cheval de bataille'. Mozart considered accompanying Ramm and Wendling* to Paris the following summer, but eventually travelled independently, with his mother*. In Paris, he wrote the oboe part in his Sinfonia Concertante KAnh.9/297*B* for Ramm (*see* LEGROS).

Mozart met Ramm again while staying in Munich for the production of *Idomeneo** (for which Ramm expressed the greatest admiration). It was at that time (early 1781) that Mozart composed his Oboe Quartet K370/386*b* for Ramm. They met on several later occasions, in Vienna in 1787 (Ramm's concert at the Kärntnertor-Theater on 14 March included a symphony by Mozart and also one of his arias, sung by Aloisia Lange*), in Prague in April 1889, and, no doubt for the last time, during Mozart's stay in Munich in October–November 1790.

Rauzzini, Venanzio (baptized Camerino, near Rome, 19 December 1746; d. Bath, 8 April 1810). Italian male soprano, composer and teacher; the original Cecilio (*Lucio Silla**). He made his début in Niccolò Piccinni's *Il finto astrologo* in Rome in 1765 and subsequently sang in Munich (1766–72), Vienna (1767), and Italy (1772–4). Charles Burney*, who met him in Munich in 1772, wrote that he was 'not only a charming singer, a pleasing figure, and a good actor; but a more excellent contrapuntist, and performer on the harpsichord, than a singer is usually allowed to be'. In 1774 Rauzzini moved to England, where he spent the remainder of his life. Until he settled in Bath in 1777, he appeared regularly and with considerable success at the King's Theatre, London, both in his own and in other composers' works. At Bath he organized concerts, at which he often sang himself. He was buried in Bath Abbey.

Rauzzini composed a number of operas and other vocal works, as well as some instrumental music. The best-known of the operas is *Piramo e Tisbe* (Munich, 1769; revived London, 1775). Several of his pupils had highly successful careers, notably Elizabeth Billington, John Braham, Charles Incledon, Michael Kelly* (whom he taught in Dublin in 1778), Gertrud Mara and Nancy Storace*.

Mozart and his father heard Rauzzini in Hasse*'s *Partenope* in Vienna in September 1767, but they were apparently not over-impressed, to judge by Leopold's remark in his letter to Hagenauer* on 29 September that the singers were 'nothing special'. Five years later, Leopold formed a far more favourable view of Rauzzini's musicianship during rehearsals for *Lucio Silla*. On 28 November 1772 he wrote to his wife* from Milan: 'Wolfgang has so far composed only the first aria [presumably 'Il tenero momento'] for the *primo uomo*, but it is an admirable one and he sings it like an angel.' At the première Rauzzini aroused the jealousy of the *prima donna* Anna Lucia de Amicis* when he was warmly applauded by Archduchess Maria Beatrice Ricciarda (*see* FERDINAND) at his first appearance. The reason, Leopold explained to his wife in his letter of 2 January 1773, was that Rauzzini had made the archduchess believe that he suffered from acute stage-fright and needed encouragement. 'A typical castrato's trick,' Leopold called it.

While in Milan, Mozart composed the motet *Exsultate jubilate* K165/158*a* for Rauzzini, who sang it at the Theatine Church on 17 January 1773.
(Burney[5], Hansell[4])

Ritter, Georg Wenzel (b. Mannheim, 7 April 1748; d. Berlin, 16 June 1808). German bassoonist. A member of the Mannheim court orchestra since 1764, he moved to Munich in 1778 (*see* KARL THEODOR). In 1788 he joined the court orchestra of King Frederick William II* of Prussia in Berlin.

Mozart first met Ritter at Schwetzingen in 1763, and again at Mannheim in 1777. He praised Ritter's playing in a letter to his father on 3 December 1777; the following year, in Paris, he wrote the bassoon part of the Sinfonia Concertante κAnh.9/297B for him (*see* LEGROS).

Robinig von Rottenfeld. Salzburg family friendly with the Mozarts and frequently mentioned in their correspondence. Georg Joseph Robinig von Rottenfeld (1710–60), a prosperous ironmonger ennobled in 1752, and his wife Viktoria (1716–83) had four children: Maria Josepha (1743–67), Maria Elisabeth ['Lisl'] (1749–92), Maria Aloisia Viktoria ['Louise'] (1757–86), and Georg Siegmund [Sigismund] (1760–1823). The family owned a house in Salzburg [later No. 14 Sigmund-Haffner-Gasse], as well as a property outside the town. They also possessed a scythe factory near Thalgau, north of Salzburg.

In January 1775 Nannerl* travelled to Munich with Frau Robinig von Rottenfeld and Louise to attend the première of *La finta giardiniera**. When Mozart met the mother again in Munich in January 1779, on his return journey from Paris, he was less than delighted. 'You have no idea how I suffered during Madame Robinig's visit here,' he wrote to his father on 8 January, 'for it is indeed a long time since I have talked to such a foolish woman.' She also attended, together with her three surviving children, the première of *Idomeneo** in January 1781. The Divertimento κ334/320b and the March κ445/320c may have been commissioned by Georg Siegmund.

Rodolphe, Jean Joseph [Rudolph, Johann Joseph] (b. Strasbourg, 14 October 1730; d. Paris 12 August 1812). Horn player, violinist and composer (especially of ballets and *opéras comiques*). From 1760 to 1765 he was a member of the Württemberg court orchestra at Stuttgart. In *c*.1766 he settled in Paris, where he at first played in the orchestra of the Prince de Conti (1717–76) and then, from 1773, in the royal court orchestra. According to Mozart's letter to his father of 14 May 1778, Rodolphe offered him the post of organist at Versailles, at a yearly salary of 2000 livres. Leopold, though doubtful that Rodolphe was empowered to do so, urged Wolfgang to consider the advantages of such a position, should it be made available to him. But Mozart did not feel tempted to look seriously into the matter, and his father, still hoping to attract him back to Salzburg, did not insist. (Moroda, Stiefel²)

Rosenberg-Orsini, Franz Xaver Wolf, Count [from 1790, Prince] b. Vienna, 6 April 1723; d. Vienna, 14 [?24] November 1796. Austrian diplomat. Son of Count Wolf Sigmund Rosenberg-Orsini and his wife Maria Eleonore, *née* Countess Hohenfeld. After postings in London, Milan, Copenhagen (1750–57) and Madrid (1757–65), he served from 1766 until 1770 as high chamberlain at the court of Leopold, Grand Duke of Tuscany [later Leopold II*]. From April 1774 to March 1775 he accompanied Archduke Maximilian* on a European tour. From 1776 until 1791 he was high chamberlain and director of court theatres in Vienna; in 1791, under Leopold II, he was replaced as director by Count Johann Wenzel Ugarte, but was reinstated in that position by Francis II in 1792. He retired in 1794.

Two days after their arrival in Florence on 30 March 1770, Mozart and his father called on Rosenberg, who arranged an audience with Grand Duke Leopold. Later, in Vienna, Mozart naturally had frequent contacts with Rosenberg. To judge by Mozart's letters, Rosenberg proved helpful and encouraging, particularly in connection with the composition and production of *Die Entführung**. He also urged Mozart to compose an Italian opera (*see* OCA DEL CAIRO, L'). Since Rosenberg wanted Giambattista Casti, whom he had known in Florence, to be appointed court poet in Vienna in place of Da Ponte*, he was somewhat hostile towards the latter. In his memoirs, Da Ponte even asserts that Rosenberg tried to undermine his professional standing in various ways, for instance by intervening in the rehearsals of *Le nozze di Figaro** (*see* BUSSANI, FRANCESCO).

(Da Ponte, Michtner, Wandruszka)

Rossi, Felice. Bass-*buffo*. He may have sung the role of Roberto at the première of *La finta giardiniera**, for he is known to have been in Munich in 1774–5 (the suggestion that he sang Don Anchise is less plausible since that is a tenor part). Mozart met him in Munich in September 1777 and again later in Vienna, probably in March 1780 and certainly in the summer of 1781, since in a letter to his father on 1 August 1781 he mentioned having provided Rossi, who was about to visit Prague, with a letter of introduction to Josepha Duschek*. Mozart added that he was all the more ready to oblige Rossi since the latter had written the text for a cantata which Mozart was himself planning to perform at a concert during Advent. However, Mozart does not appear to have composed his cantata, nor is anything known about the proposed concert.

Rumbeke [Rumbeck, Rombeck], **Marie Karoline,** Countess, *née* Cobenzl (1755–1812). Mozart's first Viennese pupil. Daughter of Count Johann Karl Philipp Cobenzl (1712–70), since 1753 minister plenipotentiary for the Austrian Netherlands (whom the Mozarts met in Brussels in 1763), and of Maria Theresa, *née* Countess Pálffy d'Erdödy (d. 1771). Marie Karoline was a cousin of Count Johann Philipp Cobenzl*. On 12 July 1778, at Huysinghen Castle near Halle, south of Brussels, she married Count (Chrétien) Charles Rumbeke (b. Ghent, 14 December 1758), the son of Count Charles-Louis-Albert Rumbeke (1732–58). Her young husband was appointed a chamberlain at the Viennese court in December 1778. His full title was Count Thiennes et Rumbeke, but his wife was normally referred to, by Mozart and others, simply as Countess Rumbeke.

Within a week of Mozart's arrival in Vienna on 16 March 1781, the countess began taking piano lessons with him. He may have written the variations K359/374*a* and 360/374*b* for her. Schönfeld, in his *Jahrbuch der Tonkunst von Wien und Prag*, placed her among the very greatest performers on the piano, which, he stated, 'she plays in masterly fashion, with accuracy, taste and speed'. The painter Elisabeth Vigée-Lebrun described Countess Rumbeke's salon in her memoirs as an exceptionally brilliant one. Vigée-Lebrun also paid tribute to her good works on behalf of the Viennese poor.

Marie Karoline's brother Count Johann Ludwig Joseph Cobenzl (1753–1809) had a distinguished career as a statesman and diplomat, notably as Austrian ambassador to the court of Catherine the Great at St Petersburg from 1779 until 1795. It was to his wife Theresia Johanna (*née* Countess Montelabate), whom he had married in 1774, that Mozart dedicated the first edition of the sonatas K284/205*b*, 333/315*c* and 454, published together by Christoph Torricella* in Vienna in 1784. (Goethals, Schönfeld, Vigée-Lebrun)

Sacco, Johanna, *née* Richard (b. Prague, 16 November 1754; d. Vienna, 21 December 1802). The leading Viennese actress of her time; she played Madame Krone (or perhaps Madame Pfeil) at the première of *Der Schauspieldirektor*. She began her stage career at the age of eight and first made a name for herself in Hamburg where she was engaged in 1771; in 1774 she acted in Warsaw.

She made her Viennese début on 10 June 1776 in the title role of *Eugénie* (based on Beaumarchais's French play), and remained a valuable member of the court theatre for the next seventeen years. She was a highly acclaimed Juliet, and famous for her interpretation of the title roles in Christian Heinrich Spiess's *Maria Stuart* and Lessing's *Minna von Barnhelm* and *Emilia Galotti*. On 14 February 1778 she played Ophelia opposite Joseph Lange*'s Hamlet. On 5 December 1778 she appeared in Benda*'s *Medea*, and on 4 January 1780 in his *Ariadne auf Naxos*. The Gotha Theatre Almanach for 1778 called her 'the incomparable Sacco'; and Joseph II*, who had himself arranged her engagement at the Burgtheater, wrote to his brother Leopold, Grand Duke of Tuscany [later Leopold II*]: 'The German theatre company with Madame Sacco constantly delights the Viennese and I derive benefit from that, for the box-office, which used to be considered bankrupt, now shows only profit.' At her own request she retired on a pension in 1793, explaining that she considered herself 'no longer young enough to portray youthful romantic girls . . . while, on the other hand, feeling little inclination to play mothers'. (Häussermann, Wlassack, Wurzbach)

Salieri, Antonio (b. Legnago, 18 August 1750; d. Vienna, 7 May 1825). Italian composer and teacher. He spent most of his life in Vienna, having been taken there in 1766, as a young orphan, by the court composer Florian Leopold Gassmann (1729–74). After completing his education under Gassmann's guidance, he was, by 1769, directing operatic rehearsals at the court theatres. In 1774, after Gassmann's death, he became himself court composer and conductor of Italian opera. In 1775 he married Theresia von Helferstorfer (1755–1807), who bore him eight children, two of whom had for their godmother his former pupil and reputed mistress, the singer Catarina Cavalieri*. In 1788 he succeeded the late Giuseppe Bonno* as court Kapellmeister. He was also president, from 1788 to 1795, and subsequently vice-president, of the Tonkünstler-Societät (a well-known musicians' benevolent society). In 1790 he was, at his own request, released from his responsibilities at the opera by the new Emperor Leopold II*, whose feelings towards him were considerably less warm than those of Joseph II*. He remained court Kapellmeister, but, as his health and mental state deteriorated, his functions were assumed by Joseph Eybler* in 1824. His pupils included Beethoven*, Hummel*, Schubert, Süssmayr*, and Weigl*.

Of Salieri's more than forty comic and serious operas, only nine did not receive their first performance in Vienna: five were produced in Italy during a leave-of-absence lasting from 1778 until 1780 (La Scala, Milan, opened on 3 August 1778 with his *Europa riconosciuta*); three were written for Paris (among them, the highly successful *Tarare* [1787], later extensively revised for Vienna as *Axur, re d'Ormus*); and one of his late works, *Annibale in Capua*, was produced at Trieste in 1801. His career as an operatic composer spanned over thirty years: the earliest surviving work, *Le donne letterate*, was produced in Vienna in 1770, the last, *Die Neger*, in 1804. It was his *La scuola de' gelosi* (first produced in Venice in 1778 and specially revised for Vienna) which inaugurated the new era of Italian opera on 22 April 1783, an event especially memorable for the first appearance in Vienna of the recently engaged Benucci*, Francesco Bussani*, Kelly*, and Nancy Storace*. It was also Salieri who arranged Da Ponte*'s appointment as poet to the Italian opera company. He himself collaborated with Da Ponte in several operas, although, after the comparative failure of their first common venture, *Il ricco d'un giorno* (6 December 1784), he did not call on Da Ponte again for several years. Instead, he turned to Giambattista Casti who, among other texts, provided him with the libretto of *Prima la musica, poi le parole*, the 'divertimento teatrale' performed at Schönbrunn on 7 February 1786, after Mozart's *Der Schauspieldirektor*.

During the decade 1781–91 when Mozart was struggling for official recognition and financial security, Salieri was clearly a dominant figure in the musical life of Vienna: his operas were regularly performed and generally well received, he occupied important official positions, he derived considerable benefit from his close relations with his mentor and friend Gluck*, and, above all, he enjoyed the confidence and protection of Joseph II. Yet he appears to have been jealous of Mozart, who was convinced that Salieri was hostile to him. In December 1789 Mozart wrote to Puchberg*, with reference to the rehearsals for *Così fan tutte*: 'When I see you I will tell you about Salieri's intrigues, which have, however, all come to nothing.' Vincent Novello* wrote in his diary after a conversation with Constanze* and Mozart's younger son Franz Xaver Wolfgang Mozart* in 1829: 'Salieri first tried to set this opera but failed, and the great success of Mozart in accomplishing what he could make nothing of is supposed to have been the first origin of his enmity and malice towards Mozart.' This statement is surely incorrect. In the first place, nothing is known about Salieri's supposed attempt at setting *Così fan tutte*; and secondly, his intrigues against Mozart appear to have started well before 1789–90. As early as 2 July 1783 Mozart complained to his father about 'a trick of Salieri's which has injured poor Adamberger* more than myself'. And Leopold wrote to Nannerl* on 28 April 1786, with reference to the imminent première of *Le nozze di Figaro*: 'It will be remarkable if he [Wolfgang] has a success, for I know that extraordinarily powerful cabals are ranged against him. Salieri and all his supporters will again move heaven and earth to prevent it.'

However, by 1791 such tensions as may have existed earlier between Mozart and Salieri seem to have disappeared, despite the fact that Mozart was able to pick up an important commission that year which Salieri had apparently been obliged to refuse (*see* CLEMENZA DI TITO, LA). On 13 October 1791 Mozart called for Salieri and Catarina Cavalieri in his carriage and took them to the theatre for a performance of *Die Zauberflöte*. The next day he described to Constanze with manifest pleasure their enthusiastic response to the spectacle: 'They both said that it was an opera worthy to be performed at the grandest festival and before the greatest monarch . . .

He listened and watched most attentively, from the overture to the final chorus, and there was not one number that did not elicit a "bravo" or "bello" from him.' Nor can Constanze have harboured any resentment against Salieri after Mozart's death, since she arranged for her younger son Franz Xaver Wolfgang to be taught by him. And on 30 January 1807 she wrote to her other son, Carl Thomas Mozart*, who was then living in Milan: 'Your brother now goes for lessons with Salieri and Hummel. Both feel great affection and friendship for him . . . He is now studying with three great masters, Salieri, Albresberger [i.e. Albrechtsberger*], and Hummel. How happy I would be if I could offer you just one of these men . . .' On 30 March 1807 Salieri furnished Franz Xaver Wolfgang with a testimonial affirming his considerable musical talent and predicting that he would be as successful as his father. Lastly, no credence is nowadays given to the once widely accepted story that Mozart was poisoned by Salieri. It provided the subject of Pushkin's well-known verse drama *Mozart and Salieri* (1831), on which Rimsky-Korsakov based his identically titled opera (Moscow, 7 December 1898).

Salieri's growing fame prompted one of Mozart's early works. In 1773 he composed, presumably with the intention of ingratiating himself with Salieri, six Variations for the piano K180/173c on the aria 'Mio caro Adone' from the latter's opera *La fiera di Venezia*.

(Angermüller[8], Braunbehrens, Michtner, Novello)

Sallaba, Mathias von (b. Prague, 1764 [?1766 or ?1767]; d. Vienna, 8 March 1797). Physician practising in Vienna. He qualified in 1786 and, after some further training under Dr Maximilian Stoll (1742–87), set up his own practice. He was consulted by Dr Closset* during Mozart's final illness.

(Werner, Wurzbach)

Salomon, Johann Peter (baptized Bonn, 20 February 1745; d. London, 28 November 1815). German violinist, composer and impresario. After holding appointments as court musician at Bonn and Rheinsberg, he moved to London; his first professional appearance there was at a concert at Covent Garden on 23 March 1781. Except for some journeys to the Continent, he resided for the remainder of his life in England, where he turned increasingly to conducting and the promotion of concerts. In particular, he was responsible for arranging Joseph Haydn*'s visits to London in 1790–91 and 1794–5. At a farewell dinner held in Vienna for Haydn on 14 December 1790, on the eve of his first journey to London, Salomon reportedly offered Mozart a similar contract for London for the following winter season.

Franz Xaver Wolfgang Mozart* told Vincent Novello* in Salzburg in 1829 that it was Salomon who had coined the name 'Jupiter' for the Symphony in C major K551. Salomon's own compositions include a number of pieces for the violin and some songs. He also wrote a few works for the stage, among them a comedy, *Le séjour du bonheur*, which was performed in Berlin in 1773, and an opera, *Windsor Castle, or The Fair Maid of Kent* (in collaboration with Reginald Spofforth), which was produced at Covent Garden in 1795.

(Badura-Skoda[1], Novello, Unverricht)

Saporiti [later Codecasa], **Teresa** (b. Milan, 1763; d. Milan, 17 March 1869).

Sarti, Giuseppe

Soprano; the first Donna Anna (*Don Giovanni**). She was engaged by Bondini* in 1782 and sang with his company in Leipzig and Dresden, and later in Prague. She seems to have left the company sometime in 1788, for on 26 December 1788 she sang in Pietro Alessandro Guglielmi's *Arsace* in Venice, and on 28 January 1789, in the same city, in Guglielmi's *Rinaldo*; she furthermore performed at the première of Francesco Bianchi's *Nitteti* in Milan on 20 April 1789. In subsequent years she sang in Milan, Bologna, Parma, and Modena. In 1795–6 she appeared in Domenico Cimarosa's *L'italiana in Londra* and Paisiello*'s *Il barbiere di Siviglia* in St Petersburg; in 1796 she also sang at a concert in Moscow. In the latter year she published two arias, *Dormivo in mezzo al prato* and *Caro mio ben, deh senti*. Also in 1796, and in 1797, she sang Alphonsine in Silvestro Palma's *La pietra simpatica* in Vienna.

Teresa may have been a sister of Caterina Bondini*. Teresa's older sister Antonia (d. 1787) was also, at one time, a singer with Bondini's company.
(*DEUMM*, *ÖBL*, Raeburn[9])

Sarti, Giuseppe (baptized Faenza, 1 December 1729; d. Berlin, 28 July 1802). Italian composer and teacher (among his pupils were Cherubini and King Christian VII of Denmark). After studying at Padua and with Padre Martini* at Bologna, he became organist at Faenza Cathedral (1748–52) and director of the local theatre, for which, in 1752, he wrote his first opera, *Pompeo in Armenia*. The second, *Il re pastore*, was performed with great success at Venice the following year. From 1755 until 1765, and again from 1768 to 1775, he occupied various important positions in the musical life of Copenhagen. Subsequently he became director of the Conservatorio dell' Ospedaletti in Venice (1775–9), and *maestro di capella* at Milan Cathedral (1779–83). In 1784, at the invitation of Catherine the Great, he went to St Petersburg, where he remained until 1801, initially as director of Italian opera, later as head of the new conservatory. He died in Berlin while on his way back to Italy. In Copenhagen Sarti had married Camilla Passi, who bore him two daughters.

He composed some seventy works for the stage, several of which were performed in Vienna, including *Le gelosie villane* (first in 1777), *Fra i due litiganti il terzo gode* (28 May 1783), *Giulio Sabino* (4 August 1785), and *I finti eredi* (1 August 1786). The most successful was *Fra i due litiganti*, which achieved sixty-three performances in Vienna during the decade 1781–91, outstripping all but Martín y Soler*'s *L'arbore di Diana*. In May 1784 a benefit performance of *Fra i due litiganti* was arranged for Sarti, who had broken his journey to Russia in Vienna. Mozart met him at this time: 'Sarti is a good honest fellow,' he wrote to his father on 12 June. 'I played many pieces for him, and finally some variations on an aria of his, which pleased him greatly.' The aria is believed to have been Mingone's 'Come un' agnello' from Act I of *Fra i due litigante* (but the authenticity of the surviving partial manuscript of K460/454a has been contested). The same aria is cited in the supper scene of *Don Giovanni**, in evident tribute to the popularity of Sarti's opera. In 1791 Mozart composed a final chorus, K615, for an amateur performance of *Le gelosie villane*.

A mystery surrounds the harshly critical analysis (*Esame acustico fatto sopra due frammenti di Mozart*) which Sarti made of certain passages from the two 'Haydn' quartets K421/417b and 465. Sarti's original manuscript, which has been lost, was undated and apparently written privately for a Milanese lady; it was never published,

but a partial German translation of a copy of the manuscript appeared in the *Allgemeine Musikalische Zeitung* (*see* BREITKOPF & HÄRTEL) in 1832. In his analysis Sarti accused the composer of totally neglecting the rules of counterpoint, and detected nineteen 'errors' in thirty-six bars. The music, he asserted, was of the kind that 'makes one put one's fingers in one's ears', and its creator was one of those 'barbarians with no ear whatsoever for music, who fancy themselves as composers'. One of the most curious aspects of the document is Sarti's statement that he does not know the composer nor wish to know him – yet the six 'Haydn' quartets were not published until September 1785 (the composition of K465 is dated 14 January 1785 by Mozart in his own catalogue), whereas, as indicated above, Sarti had met Mozart in the spring of 1784. It is therefore difficult to believe that Sarti could have been unaware of the identity of the composer he was thus disparaging.
(Badura-Skoda[3], Deutsch[9], DiChiera/Libby, Fischer[1,2], Michtner, *Sarti*)

Schachtner, Johann Andreas (b. Dingolfing, Bavaria, 9 March 1731; d. Salzburg, 20 July 1795). German musician and writer. After studying at Ingolstadt University, he moved to Salzburg where he received instruction from the court trumpeter Johann Caspar Köstler. In January 1754 he was appointed court and army trumpeter. He was a versatile musician, for, in addition to the trumpet, he played the violin and the violoncello. During Wolfgang's childhood, he visited the Mozarts almost daily and frequently joined in their music-making. He also published a volume of poetry, *Poetischer Versuch in verschiedenen Arten von Gedichten* (1765), and wrote the text for Adlgasser*'s oratorio *Die wirkende Gnade Gottes, oder David in der Busse* (1756). On 12 November 1754 he married Maria Franziska Rosalia Stain (1732–94); Leopold was a witness at the wedding. The couple had nine children, only two of whom outlived the parents.

Schachtner's collaboration with Mozart is thought to have extended to several works, but has not been definitely established in every case. He is known to have revised and augmented the Weiskern*–Müller* libretto of *Bastien und Bastienne*. Nor is there any doubt about his authorship of the German version of Varesco*'s libretto of *Idomeneo*, for quite apart from various references in Mozart's correspondence to his translation, it was published under his name in Munich in early 1781. He is furthermore generally believed to have supplied the text for the Singspiel later published under the title *Zaide*, and to have written the words of the final chorus which Mozart set in the 1779–80 version of his music to Gebler*'s *Thamos, König in Ägypten*. He is also thought to have been responsible for one of the German versions of *La finta giardiniera*. Finally, he may have written the text for the *Grabmusik* K42/35*a*.

In April 1792, at Nannerl*'s request, Schachtner wrote down his recollections of Mozart's childhood. Nannerl then made his account available to Schlichtegroll*, who quoted from it, at times verbatim, in his 1793 obituary of Mozart, as he did also from Nannerl's own far more lengthy statement.
(Schuler[2])

Schack [Žák, Schak], Benedikt (Emanuel) (b. Mirotice, 7 February 1758; d. Munich, 10 December 1826). Tenor and composer, of Bohemian origin; the original Tamino (*Die Zauberflöte*) and first German-language Don Ottavio (*Don*

Giovanni*, Vienna, 5 November 1792). He was a chorister at Prague Cathedral; from 1775 he studied philosophy and medicine in Vienna, but he soon made music, and especially singing, his career. In 1780 he became Kapellmeister to Prince Heinrich Schönaich-Carolath at Gross-Glogau in Silesia. In 1786 he joined Schikaneder*'s theatrical company and, in late May, appeared with it in Salzburg as Nardone in *Das Mädchen von Frascati*, a German version of Paisiello*'s *La frascatana*. He greatly impressed Leopold Mozart, who wrote to Nannerl* on 26 May 1786: 'He sings excellently, has a beautiful voice, an easy and flexible throat, and a very fine technique . . .'

Schack later became a valuable member of Schikaneder's company at the Freihaus-Theater, Vienna, singing leading tenor roles and composing the music – in some cases, together with Franz Xaver Gerl* – for a number of Singspiels, mostly to texts by Schikaneder (in particular, the 'Anton' operas beginning with *Der dumme Gärtner aus dem Gebirge, oder Die zween Anton*, presented on 12 July 1789). In 1793 he went to Graz, and from 1796 until 1814, when he retired on a pension, he was engaged at the Munich court theatre, where his daughter Antonie (1784–1851) also sang from 1800 or 1801 to 1806. His wife, the Silesian-born contralto Elisabeth Schack, *née* Weinhold, sang the Third Lady at the première of *Die Zauberflöte*.

Schack quickly formed a warm friendship with Mozart. When Constanze* asked him in 1826 for his recollections of the latter, she wrote: 'I can think of no one who enjoyed such constant and intimate contact with him, no one who knew him better and to whom he was more devoted than to yourself, especially during the important final years of his life and right up to his death, and during his residence in Vienna.' Schack was one of the three friends who sang through Mozart's unfinished Requiem with him at his bedside, just a few hours before he died. (The others were Gerl and Franz de Paula Hofer*.)

Mozart composed – or collaborated in – several numbers in Schack's and Gerl's scores, in particular the comic duet 'Nun, liebes Weibchen, ziehst mit mir' κ625/592a for *Der Stein der Weisen, oder Die Zauberinsel* (text by Schikaneder, produced 11 September 1790). He also wrote eight Variations for the piano κ613 on 'Ein Weib ist das herrlichste Ding auf der Welt' from Schack's and Gerl's *Die verdeckten Sachen*, the second 'Anton' Singspiel (produced 26 September 1789). A mass which Schack wrote in Munich may contain 'additions' by Mozart (κAnh.235*f*/C1.02).
(Deutsch[1], Branscombe[5])

Schiedenhofen [Schidenhofen] auf Stumm und Triebenbach, (Johann Baptist Joseph) Joachim Ferdinand von (b. 20 March 1747; d. 31 January 1823). Son of Kaspar Joachim Schiedenhofen von und zu Stumm (1697–1763), Salzburg court councillor and syndic of the cathedral chapter. Educated at the Gymnasium in Kremsmünster and at Salzburg University, he himself became a court councillor in 1771 and served as district chancellor from 1791 until 1812. On 9 February 1778 he married the far wealthier Anna Daubrawa von Daubrawaick (1759–1818), the daughter of Virgil Christoph Daubrawa von Daubrawaick (1725–87), Director of the Mint and councillor at the treasury.

The Schiedenhofens, and particularly Joachim Ferdinand and his sister Maria Anna Aloisia, were on friendly terms with the Mozarts. On more than one occasion, during Leopold's and Wolfgang's journeys to Italy, Nannerl* and her mother*

stayed at the Schiedenhofens' country estate at Triebenbach [Trübenbach], near Laufen in Upper Bavaria. The family also owned a house in Salzburg (No. 1 Getreidegasse). Joachim Ferdinand von Schiedenhofen's diary for the period from 10 October 1774 to 18 April 1778, which was discovered in 1956, contains numerous entries relating to Leopold and Wolfgang, and to performances of Wolfgang's music.
(Deutsch[5])

Schikaneder, Emanuel [real name: Johann Joseph Schickeneder] (b. Straubing, 1 September 1751; d. Vienna, 21 September 1812). Playwright, theatre manager, actor, singer, dancer, composer. Librettist of *Die Zauberflöte**, which was first produced by his own company at the Freihaus-Theater in Vienna, with himself taking the part of Papageno.

He was educated at the Jesuit high school at Regensburg. By the mid-1770s he was well launched in his stage career, performing as a dancer and actor at Innsbruck, and writing both text and music for his first comic opera, *Die Lyranten*, which was produced in 1775 or 1776. In the latter year the Innsbruck company, under its joint directors Andreas Schopf and Theresia Schimann, moved to Augsburg. There, on 9 February 1777, Schikaneder married the actress Maria Magdalena ['Eleonore'] Arth (1751–1821). In the spring of 1777 the couple joined Franz Joseph Moser's company in Nuremberg. In January 1778, after the death of Moser's wife, Schikaneder took over the company, which was then performing at Augsburg. During the following years, the troupe toured extensively, mainly in southern Germany and Austria. When it performed in Salzburg from mid-September 1780 until late February 1781, Schikaneder met the Mozarts and quickly formed a warm friendship with them. 'The good honest fellow even came with you as far as the mail coach, just to say good-bye,' Leopold recalled in a letter on 20 November 1780, referring to Wolfgang's departure to Munich to supervise the première of *Idomeneo**. From Munich, Wolfgang sent Schikaneder, at his request, the aria 'Zittre, töricht Herz, und leide' κAnh.11a/365a, which Frl. Adelheid, a member of the company, was to sing in August Werthes's comedy *Die zwey schlaflosen Nächte, oder Der glückliche Betrug* (based on Carlo Gozzi's *Le due notti affannose*).

Mozart and Schikaneder doubtless met again when the latter, together with Hubert Kumpf (a former tenor, current theatre director, and future police informer), took over the Kärntnertor-Theater in Vienna for a three-months' season in 1784; they opened on 5 November with *Die Entführung** (*see also* NOZZE DI FIGARO, LE). For the 1785–6 season Schikaneder was engaged at the Burgtheater, where he made his début on 1 April 1785 as Schwindel in Gluck*'s Singspiel *Die Pilgrime von Mekka*. In the meantime, his wife, with her friend Johann Friedel (1751–89), either formed an independent company or took charge of her husband's. After touring for some two years, they settled at Easter 1788 into the Freihaus-Theater in Vienna, which they ran until Friedel's death on 31 March 1789, when the theatre closed.

Schikaneder himself had founded a new company in 1786, and in May of that year he returned with it to Salzburg, where he immediately renewed his friendship with Leopold Mozart. The company moved on to Augsburg in June, and from 1787 to 1789 performed in the service of Prince Carl Anselm Thurn und Taxis at

Regensburg. However, after Friedel's death Schikaneder was reunited with his wife in Vienna. On 12 July 1789 he reopened the Freihaus-Theater with his own comic opera *Der dumme Gärtner aus dem Gebirge, oder Die zween Anton*, with music by Schack* and Gerl*, who had both followed him to Vienna from Regensburg. Among the members of Friedel's company who were kept on by Schikaneder were Nouseul* and Josepha Hofer*. Those newly engaged by him included Anna Gottlieb* and Jakob Haibel, a tenor, comic actor and Singspiel composer who was to marry Mozart's sister-in-law Sophie Weber* in 1807.

Schikaneder wrote numerous other librettos, especially for Singspiels, which were performed both at his own and at other theatres. Of particular interest, apart from Mozart's *Die Zauberflöte*, are the highly popular six further 'Anton' operas; *Der Fall ist noch weit seltener* (a sequel to Martín y Soler*'s highly successful *Una cosa rara*), which was produced, with music by Schack, in 1790; *Der Tiroler Wastel*, with music by Haibel, which was given 118 times at the Freihaus-Theater between 1796 and 1801; and *Das Labyrinth, oder Der Kampf mit den Elementen*, an opera by Peter von Winter (1754–1825) billed as '*Die Zauberflöte: Part II*', which had its première on 12 June 1798 and received over thirty performances in that year alone.

In 1799 the management of the Freihaus-Theater was taken over by a wealthy merchant, Bartholomäus Zitterbarth, while Schikaneder remained artistic director. The theatre closed on 12 June 1801, and on the following day Schikaneder opened the newly built Theater an der Wien, on a site close to the Freihaus-Theater, with a performance of the opera *Alexander*, for which he had himself written the libretto and Franz Teyber (*see* TEYBER) the music (Beethoven* having declined the invitation to set the text). Within a year, however, Schikaneder sold the licence to Zitterbarth who, in his turn, was obliged to sell the theatre some two years later. Schikaneder served again as artistic director from September 1804 to the end of 1806. From 1807 to Easter 1809 he was director of the Brünn [Brno] theatre. His final years in Vienna were increasingly sad ones, marked by financial ruin and mental illness. In 1812, while on his way to Budapest where he was to manage a new German theatre, he was stricken with insanity from which he did not recover. His wife survived him by nine years.

Schikaneder was a versatile actor as well as a prolific dramatist. On 19 December 1777 he played the title role in the first Munich production of *Hamlet*, and he appeared in the same part, to considerable acclaim, at Stuttgart in July 1778. A critic described him at that time as 'a very promising actor and, furthermore, a charming singer'. Above all, Schikaneder was a showman, with an excellent feeling for what would amuse and please his audience. Thus he staged several open-air productions, with horses and carriages and real soldiers, of Heinrich Ferdinand Möller's play *Der Graf von Waltron, oder Die Subordination*, which had a military subject. And in 1794 he was working on a scheme for reviving the Olympic Games in the Vienna Prater.

Two other members of Schikaneder's family performed at the première of *Die Zauberflöte*: his older brother Urban (b. Straubing, 2 November 1746; d. Vienna, 11 April 1818) as First Priest, and Urban's daughter Anna [Nanny, Nanette] (1767–1862) as First Boy; she later sang at the Theater in der Leopoldstadt and appeared there as the Queen of Night in July 1811. Her brother Joseph Carl Schikaneder (1770–1845) was a member of the Freihaus-Theater company from 1790 to 1793. He later performed at the Theater in der Leopoldstadt (1811, 1816–19), and worked as an opera producer in Prague (1819–34); he was also a dramatist and composer.

(Blümml, Branscombe[6], Honolka, Komorzynski[1])

Schlichtegroll, Friedrich Adolph Heinrich von (b. Waltershausen, near Gotha, 8 December 1765; d. Munich, 4 December 1822). German scholar. He was educated at the Gymnasium at Gotha, studied law at Jena University from 1783, and subsequently switched to theology and classical languages at Göttingen University. From 1787 he taught religious studies, German, Hebrew and Latin at his old school in Gotha; he retired in 1800 to devote himself to research. In 1807, having made an international reputation with various learned publications, particularly in the area of numismatics, he accepted the post of director and permanent secretary of the Munich Academy of Sciences, at the invitation of its president, the philosopher Friedrich Heinrich Jacobi (1743–1819). He was ennobled in 1808.

Between 1790 and 1806 Schlichtegroll published, with the assistance of contributors, thirty-four volumes of obituaries, each dealing with a six-months' period. His obituary of Mozart appeared in the second part of the *Nekrolog auf das Jahr 1791* (Gotha, Julius Perthes, 1793). Through an intermediary, Albert von Mölk (*see* MÖLK), he had, in March 1792, submitted a questionnaire to Nannerl*, to which she had replied with a long statement. Schlichtegroll, again through Mölk, sent further questions. At that point Nannerl enlisted the help of Johann Andreas Schachtner* who had been a close family friend. She then sent on his recollections, together with her own notes. In the obituary Schlichtegroll drew extensively on these documents.

In 1794 the Graz bookbinder Joseph Georg Hubeck (1755–1818) brought out a publication entitled *Mozarts Leben*. Constanze*, in a letter to Breitkopf & Härtel* on 13 August 1799, stated that it merely reproduced Schlichtegroll's obituary, and then revealed that she had bought up all 600 copies of the book 'in order to destroy at least those, since I cannot destroy the relevant issue of the *Nekrolog*'. She added that it should be possible to write a satisfactory biography of Mozart using the very numerous documents in her own possession, Niemetschek*'s study, and the 'good part' of the *Nekrolog*. H. H. Hausner has suggested that the Graz reprint of Schlichtegroll's obituary may have been financed by Mozart's great admirer Franz Deyerkauf*.

This obituary, together with Niemetschek's book and Nissen*'s biography, remained the principal sources of information on Mozart's life until Otto Jahn published his *W. A. Mozart* in Leipzig in 1856–9 (*see* BREITKOPF & HÄRTEL).

(Deutsch[10], Favier, Hafner[2], Hausner)

Schmith, Anton (d. ?Kiev, after 1820). Physician, with a large practice in Vienna; an excellent amateur violinist, and a friend of Mozart. On 31 October 1789 he made an entry in Latin, signed 'tuus sincerus amicus', in Mozart's album. According to Schubert's friend Joseph von Spaun (quoted by Deutsch), he played quartets with Mozart. He is likely to have attended (or may even have participated in) the performance on 15 January 1785, in Joseph Haydn*'s presence, of the six quartets K387, 421/417b, 428/421b, 458, 464 and 465 which Mozart subsequently dedicated to the latter. Schmith was percipient enough to discern Schubert's genius when shown some early minuets in 1812. The following year he was among the fifty persons charged with drafting the constitution of what was to become the Gesellschaft der Musikfreunde; in 1815 he played first violin in that society's amateur orchestra.

Very little is known about his personal life. In *c.*1802 he married a widow, Helene Mayrhofer; in 1803 she bore him a daughter whom they named Marie. Some time after 1815, having lost his considerable wealth as a result of ill-conceived speculations, he left Vienna to escape from his creditors and settled in Kiev, where he was well received by a Russian aristocrat whom he had treated in Vienna. Schmith's wife and daughter are said to have visited him in Lemberg [Lvov] in 1821. Four years later Nissen*, who had occasionally met him in Vienna, tried to obtain material for his Mozart biography from him through Albert Stadler (1794–1888), a mutual acquaintance who is now best known for his friendship with Franz Schubert. In a letter to Stadler on 23–4 October 1825, Nissen called Schmith an 'intimate friend' of Mozart. The latter may have presented Schmith with the autograph of *Ein musikalischer Spass* K522; subsequently it came into Franz Schubert's possession. (Deutsch[7])

Schrattenbach, Siegmund Christoph, Count (b. ?Graz, 28 February 1698; d. Salzburg, 16 December 1771). Member of an aristocratic family of Styrian origin, which also had a Moravian branch. He was educated at Maria Rast, near Marburg, and subsequently attended Salzburg University before studying theology in Rome. While still a child, he was appointed a canon at the cathedrals of Eichstätt and Augsburg, and in 1731 also at Salzburg. In 1750 he was elected dean of Salzburg Cathedral. On 5 April 1753 he was chosen by the cathedral chapter to succeed the late Archbishop Count Andreas Jakob Dietrichstein (b. 1689; archbishop, 1747–53).

He proved himself a generous patron of music. He sent Maria Anna Braunhofer*, Maria Anna Fesemayr* and Maria Magdalena Lipp* to finish their training in Italy, apparently at his own expense. (*See also* ADLGASSER.) In December 1769 he not only granted a request by Leopold Mozart – whom he had appointed vice-Kapellmeister in 1763 – for a leave of absence for the purpose of taking Wolfgang to Italy, but even subsidized their journey with a gift of 600 gulden; and, shortly before their departure, he named the thirteen-year-old Wolfgang third (unpaid) Konzertmeister of the court orchestra. (*See also* SOGNO DI SCIPIONE, IL..)

In December 1767 the Mozarts were very hospitably received in Brünn [Brno] by the archbishop's brother, Count Franz Anton Schrattenbach (1712–83), who was governor of Moravia. (Martin)

Schwanthaler, Ludwig von (b. Munich, 26 August 1802; d. Munich, 14 November 1848). German sculptor, prominent representative of Bavarian neoclassicism; creator of the Mozart monument in Salzburg. Many of his works were executed for palaces and museums in Munich, where his enormous figure of Bavaria on the Theresienhöhe has become one of the best-known sights of that city.

The erection of a statue of Mozart was first proposed in Salzburg in 1835. The following year an international appeal was launched for donations, and by early 1840 the fund had reached some 20,000 gulden. The site chosen for the statue was the Michaelis-Platz where, as it happened, Constanze* was then living with her sister Sophie Haibel* in the so-called 'Domherrstöckl' [later No. 8 Mozart-Platz]. Schwanthaler's model was cast in bronze by Johann Baptist Stiglmaier (1791–1844) in Munich on 22 May 1841. The plinth of the monument was erected in Salzburg in the spring of 1842 and the statue itself, which arrived on 10 August, was unveiled on 4 September. Among those present were Mozart's two surviving sons, Carl Thomas* and Franz Xaver Wolfgang*; Constanze had died six months earlier. The ceremonies and festivities extended over three days and included performances of Mozart's Mass in C major K317 and his Requiem at the Cathedral, concerts, and a torchlight procession. (*See also* MOZART, FRANZ XAVER WOLFGANG and TAUX.)

On the Mozart statue in Vienna, *see* TILGNER.

(Angermüller[1,16], Spatzenegger)

Seeau, Joseph Anton, Count (b. Linz, 10 September 1713; d.? Munich, 25 March 1799). From 1753, when he succeeded Count Joseph Ferdinand Maria Salern (1718–1805), he was for forty-six years (with only a short break in 1756) supervisor of entertainments at the Bavarian court in Munich. J. H. F. Müller*, whom Joseph II* sent on a four-months' tour of German theatres in 1776, noted that Seeau had complete control over the Italian opera and German theatre companies, with power to engage and dismiss performers, whose salaries he paid out of the receipts from the spectacles and from a yearly sum of money placed at his disposal by the elector. In 1778, after Karl Theodor* had decided to move his court from Mannheim to Munich, Seeau was appointed intendant for both cities. To Mozart's delight, he offered Aloisia Weber* a contract in Munich, where Fridolin Weber* was also engaged.

Seeau had served in the Austrian army, had fought several duels, and had the reputation of being a glutton for food and drink, as well as a libertine; Leopold Mozart informed Nannerl* in October 1785 that Seeau had a new mistress, the singer Elisabeth Augusta ['Gustl'] Wendling*. His features and manner of speech were described by one contemporary as a 'bizarre caricature'.

Mozart made Seeau's acquaintance on 9 December 1774, two days after his arrival in Munich for the première of *La finta giardiniera**. Their initial contacts must have been agreeable enough, for Mozart was able to assure his mother* on 11 January 1775 that Seeau was 'certainly a pleasant and courteous gentleman, possessed of greater *savoir-vivre* than many persons of his social position in Salzburg'. While staying in Munich in September – October 1777, Mozart had several further conversations with Seeau, who appeared sympathetic to his request for an appointment, but none was offered. Mozart's attitude subsequently grew more hostile when he learned that Seeau had falsely stated, on a visit to Mannheim, that *La finta giardiniera* had been booed in Munich.

After meeting Seeau again in Munich in 1780, during the preparations for *Idomeneo**, Mozart reported to his father that his comportment had changed dramatically: 'Seeau has been melted down like wax by the Mannheim people [i.e. the court officials whom Karl Theodor had brought with him from Mannheim],' he wrote on 8 November; and three days later he told his father that he would not recognize Seeau now, 'so completely have the Mannheimers transformed him'.

This clearly indicates that Seeau had not always in the past lived up to Mozart's favourable first impressions. It turned out that even now his manner was not always as agreeable as Mozart had imagined: 'I had a terrible row with Seeau the other day . . .' Mozart wrote on 27 December. 'In the end, when I shouted at him angrily, he gave in.'

Less than a month after the accession of Elector Maximilian IV Joseph on 16 February 1799, Seeau resigned; he died on 25 March.

(Müller, Zenger)

Sickingen, Karl Heinrich Joseph, Count (b. 1737; d. Paris [?Vienna], 13 July 1791). Son of Count Karl Sickingen (1702–85) and his wife Maria Charlotte Maximiliane, *née* Countess Seinsheim (d. 1747). Palatine minister to France from December 1768 to 30 December 1777 (on which day Karl Theodor* became also Elector of Bavaria), thereafter minister of the Palatinate and Bavaria in Paris until his death.

Mozart, who arrived in Paris in March 1778 with letters of introduction to the count provided by Baron Gemmingen-Hornberg* and Christian Cannabich*, was frequently entertained by him to lunch, the first time in the company of Anton Raaff* and Johann Baptist Wendling*. On 29 May Mozart informed his father that on the previous day he had again visited the count, whom he described as 'a charming man, a passionate lover of music and a true connoisseur'. On this occasion he had spent eight hours alone with him: 'We were at the piano morning, afternoon and evening until ten o'clock. We played all kinds of music – praising, admiring, analysing, discussing, and criticizing. He owns nearly thirty operatic scores.' By 12 June Mozart had lunched at Count Sickingen's no fewer than six times: 'One always stays from one o'clock until ten in the evening. But time passes so quickly there that one simply does not notice it. He is extremely fond of me, and I, for my part, like very much being with him, for he is a most friendly and intelligent man, with very sound judgment and a real insight into music.'

Sickingen even offered, should Mozart be unable to find employment in Karl Theodor's service, to ask his brother Wilhelm (1739–1818), who was then living at Mainz (see below), to find a position for him in that city (according to Mozart's letter to his father of 31 July). However, there is no further mention of that proposal in Mozart's correspondence, although he remained on friendly terms with Sickingen until his departure. In fact, when Baron Grimm* was pressuring him to leave earlier than he himself wished, he considered staying with Sickingen for a few days (*see* Grimm).

Unbeknown to Mozart, Sickingen was involved in an extraordinary personal drama, for he and his brother Wilhelm had, since 1771, kept their father, Count Karl Sickingen, imprisoned on the family estate at Sauerthal – mainly, it seems, because, being a fanatical alchemist, he was squandering the family fortune (Mozart's friend, the 'Paris' Sickingen, was himself conducting experiments on platinum, though with less financially disastrous consequences). In 1775, the poet Christian Friedrich Daniel Schubart (1739–91) published in the *Schwäbisches Magazin* a novella entitled *Zur Geschichte des menschlichen Herzens* which contained guarded allusions to the affair. In turn, this story partly inspired Friedrich Schiller (1759–1805) to write his play *Die Räuber* which was first performed at Mannheim in

1782. Shortly afterwards Count Wilhelm Sickingen, who since 1774 had been in the service, latterly as prime minister, of his cousin Baron Friedrich Karl Joseph Erthal, Elector of Mainz from 1774 to 1792, was relieved of his post and thereupon moved back to Vienna (where he died in 1818).

It is not clear who the 'Count Sickingen' was to whom Mozart, as he wrote to his father on 24 December 1783, intended to play *Idomeneo** on the piano. There is no evidence of any contacts between Mozart and Count Wilhelm Sickingen. Perhaps his brother Karl Heinrich Joseph, who had received Mozart so cordially in Paris and who is known to have visited Vienna in August 1784, had also stayed there the previous December.

(Baser, Lepsius, *Repertorium*)

Spitzeder, Franz (de Paula) Anton (b. Traunstein, Bavaria, 2 August 1735; d. Salzburg, 19 June 1796). Tenor; the original Christen-Geist (*Die Schuldigkeit des ersten Gebots**), and, according to the libretto of *La finta semplice**, the first Don Polidoro. At the performance of *Il re pastore** on 23 April 1775 he probably sang Alessandro or Agenore.

In 1722 his father Franz Spitzeder (d. 1753), a native of Innsbruck and by trade a weaver, married Christina Gebhart [Göbhart] at Traunstein; she bore him nine children. Probably shortly after her death (12 April 1743), Franz Anton became a choirboy at St Zeno's Monastery near Reichenhall. In December 1748 he enrolled at the Gymnasium in Salzburg and, concurrently with his academic studies, he received instruction in music (singing, organ, piano and violin). During the 1750s he spent three years in Italy, and from 1760 to 1796 he held the appointment of court tenor at Salzburg. He was much praised for the beauty of his voice, and was highly valued and well paid by Archbishop Schrattenbach* who, in 1764, became godfather to a son of his. He was also a highly respected singing and piano teacher.

In 1760 he married Maria Elisabeth Payerhueber (d. 1769), and in 1770 Maria Anna Englhart. He had seven children by his first wife, and eight more by his second. Spitzeder was on very friendly terms with the Mozarts, at any rate until the mid-1770s, after which their relations appear to have been less warm.

(Rainer, Schuler[3])

Stadler, Anton (Paul) (b. Bruck an der Leitha, 28 June 1753, d. Vienna, 15 June 1812). Austrian clarinettist and basset-horn player, as his brother Johann Nepomuk Franz (1755–1804). Before joining the Vienna court orchestra in 1787, Anton Stadler had been in the service of the Russian ambassador, Prince Dmitry Michailovich Galitsin*. Between 1791 and 1796 he toured Europe as a virtuoso. In 1799 he retired from the court orchestra on a pension, but continued to play both in the opera orchestra and as a soloist for several more years. In 1780 he had married Franziska Bichler (or Pichler); he left his family in 1801 and for the remainder of his life lived with Friederika Kabel, a needlewoman by profession.

After hearing Stadler play the clarinet at a concert at the Burgtheater, Vienna, on 23 March 1784, the critic and playwright Johann Friedrich Schink wrote in *Litterarische Fragmente* (Graz, 1785): 'My thanks to you, noble virtuoso! Never before have I heard such music drawn from this instrument. Never would I have imagined that a clarinet could imitate the human voice as perfectly as yours does.

Stadler, Mathias Franz de Paula

Your instrument has so soft and lovely a tone that no one with a heart can resist it, and I have a heart, dear virtuoso. My sincere thanks!' In addition to excelling as a performer on the clarinet, Stadler also strove to perfect it as an instrument, in particular by extending its lower range.

Stadler was a close friend of Mozart, and a fellow-mason. He probably accompanied Mozart and Constanze* to Prague in January 1787 (during the journey Mozart coined for him the nickname: 'Nàtschibinìtschibi' – cf. FREYSTÄDTLER). He was certainly in the Mozarts' party when they again travelled to Prague in August 1791 for the production of *La clemenza di Tito**. In fact, he played in the orchestra at the première. Mozart had written the clarinet and basset-horn obbligatos in Sesto's aria 'Parto, ma tu ben mio' and in Vitellia's rondo 'Non più di fiori vaghe catene' for Stadler, who performed them to great applause. Mozart also composed for Stadler his Clarinet Quintet K581 and the Clarinet Concerto K622.

(Hess, Pisarowitz[6], Weston[1,3])

Stadler, Mathias Franz de Paula (b. Schnaitsee, Bavaria, *c*.1744; d. Salzburg, 20 April 1827). Tenor and violinist; the original Oebalus (*Apollo et Hyacinthus**). He was a pupil at Salzburg Gymnasium in 1761–2, subsequently studied philosophy and, from 1764 to 1767, canon law. In 1768 he applied to Archbishop Schrattenbach* for a fixed position as tenor with the court orchestra, pointing out that he had sung both with the latter and with the cathedral orchestra on various occasions during the preceding year. He was listed as a tenor in the court calendars from 1776 until 1807. In 1787, one month after Leopold Mozart's death, he succeeded him as violin teacher to the boy choristers.

On 22 January 1770 Stadler married Maria Anna Sulzer. For some years, from 1774, the couple lived at the 'Tanzmeisterhaus' (*see* RAAB) where the Mozarts also had their flat. There are several references to Stadler in Leopold's letters.

Stadler, Maximilian [Abbé] [baptismal names: Johann Karl Dominik] (b. Melk, Lower Austria, 4 August 1748; d. Vienna, 8 November 1833). Austrian theologian, musician and musicologist. In 1758 he became a choirboy at Lilienfeld monastery, where he received instruction in classical languages and learned to play the violin, clavichord and organ. In 1762 he continued his studies in Vienna. In 1766 he was admitted as a novice to Melk monastery; there, on 13 October 1772, he celebrated his first mass. From 1775 to 1782 he taught dogmatics, ethics, church history and ecclesiastical law at Melk. He served as prior of the monastery from 1784 to 1785, then as commendatory abbot of the monasteries at Lilienfeld, Lower Austria (1786–9) and Kremsmünster, Upper Austria (1789–90); from early 1791 until 1796 he acted as consistorial adviser to the Bishop of Linz. Thereafter he lived in Vienna in a private capacity, devoting much of his time to music. In 1803 he was granted permission to transfer to the secular priesthood. That same year he took charge of the parish of Altlerchenfeld, a suburb of Vienna, and in 1809 of the parish of Böhmisch Krut [Grosskrut] in Lower Austria. In 1815 he retired on a pension and moved to Vienna, where he applied himself to collecting material for a history of Austrian music up to the death of Joseph II*. His own compositions included much church music, and also instrumental works and songs; the oratorio *Die Befreyung von*

Jerusalem was first performed at the university of Vienna on 9 May 1813. Stadler also arranged several operas for sextet, among them Gluck*'s *Orfeo ed Euridice* and Mozart's *Idomeneo**, *Der Schauspieldirektor** and *Die Zauberflöte**.

On 14 December 1767 Stadler heard Mozart play the organ at Melk monastery (at that time Mozart was not in his eighth, as Stadler stated in his memoirs, but in his twelfth year). He knew Mozart personally by November 1781, when he accompanied him to a play-through of the violin sonatas which Artaria* was to publish later that month (*see* AUERNHAMMER). In his autobiography he stated that he had repeatedly met Joseph Haydn* and Mozart, and he told Vincent and Mary Novello*, when they visited Vienna in 1829, that he used to spend many evenings with Albrechtsberger*, Haydn and Mozart, and that he often played with Haydn and Mozart in performances of the latter's quintets. There is, however, no mention of him in Mozart's extant correspondence.

On the other hand, Stadler's later contacts with Constanze* are quite well documented. In 1798, at her request, he began to examine the musical autographs left by Mozart (*see also* NISSEN). While engaged on this task, he completed a number of fragments, with a view to rendering them suitable for publication, and also made piano arrangements of certain pieces. In addition, he prepared a catalogue of the fragments and sketches. This catalogue appeared, substantially unchanged, in the supplement to Nissen's biography.

In 1826, in response to an article casting doubt on Mozart's authorship of the Requiem, Stadler strongly affirmed its authenticity in a tract, *Vertheidigung der Echtheit des Mozartischen Requiem* (Vienna, 1826, with two supplements in 1827). Constanze was delighted: 'How can I ever express to you the very sincere gratitude and joy I felt on reading your masterly text,' she wrote to him in February (?March) 1827. Constanze's deep appreciation of Stadler's various efforts to promote Mozart's reputation is reflected in another letter, probably dating from the late 1820s, in which she addressed him as 'My most esteemed and still more beloved friend'.

(Croll[1], Freeman[2], Haas[4], Hellmann, Novello)

Stein, Johann Andreas (b. Heidelsheim, 6 May 1728; d. Augsburg, 29 February 1792). Celebrated Augsburg organ and piano maker. After gaining experience in organ-building through working with Johann Andreas Silbermann (1712–83) in Strasbourg and Franz Jakob Späth (1714–86) in Regensburg, he settled in Augsburg in 1750.

Wolfgang first met Stein in the summer of 1763, when Leopold Mozart bought a practice piano from him. He renewed acquaintance with Stein in 1777, on which occasion he presented himself, as a joke, under the name 'Trazom' (*see also* MOZART, MARIA ANNA THEKLA). In a letter to his father on 17 October 1777 he discussed the outstanding features of Stein's pianos: 'It is true that he will not sell this type of piano for less than 300 gulden, but no money can pay for the care he takes and the work that goes into the making of it. His instruments have the special advantage over others of being made with an escape action . . .' Stein was also a competent pianist, and at a concert on 22 October he took part with the cathedral organist Johann Michael Demmler* and Mozart himself in a performance of the Triple Concerto K242.

Stephanie, Gottlob

Stein's pianos enjoyed an international reputation. In 1773 he demonstrated his 'Melodika' (an instrument producing flutelike tones) in Paris before Louis XV and Marie Antoinette, and in 1777 he displayed his 'Vis-à-vis' model at the Viennese court. He reportedly made over 700 pianos. Archbishop Colloredo* owned one, as did his sister Countess Maria Theresia Schönborn. For his contest with Clementi* before the Viennese court on 24 December 1781, Mozart borrowed the Stein piano owned by Countess Thun-Hohenstein*. And Count Ludwig Bentheim-Steinfurt noted in his diary that at his concert in Frankfurt am Main on 15 October 1790, Mozart had used 'a fortepiano by Stein of Augsburg which must be supreme of its kind'; it belonged to Baroness de Frentz.

In 1760 Stein married Maria Regina Burkhart (1742–1800), who bore him fifteen children, of whom only six survived their parents. Their daughter Maria Anna [Nanette] (1769–1833), herself an excellent pianist, married the pianist and teacher Johann Andreas Streicher (1761–1833) in 1794. Shortly afterwards the couple moved to Vienna, and there Maria Anna set up as a piano maker in partnership with her brother Matthäus Andreas (1776–1842), under the name 'Frère et soeur Stein'. Her husband also assumed an important role in the firm which quickly became famous for the beautiful and pure tone of its instruments (*see also* WALTER). In 1802, after Matthäus had left to set up his own business, the name was changed to 'Nanette Streicher, *née* Stein', and in 1823, when the Streichers' son Johann Baptist (1796–1871) joined the firm, to 'Nanette Streicher und Sohn'; after he became sole proprietor following his parents' death in 1833, it was renamed 'Johann Baptist Streicher'. The firm was eventually closed down by Johann Baptist's son Emil Streicher (1836–1916) in 1896.

Among Johann Andreas Streicher's pupils was Mozart's younger son Franz Xaver Wolfgang*.

(Cranmer, Fischer K. A., Göthel, Meisel/Belt[1], Schönfeld)

Stephanie, Christian Gottlob (b. Breslau, 1734; d. Vienna, 10 April 1798), usually known as 'Stephanie der Ältere' [the Elder], to distinguish him from his half-brother Johann Gottlieb Stephanie*. Playwright and actor. After making his acting début at Breslau in 1755, he accepted engagements at Altona in 1758 and at Mitau [Jelgava] in 1759. In 1760 he was offered a contract in Vienna. A dramatist in his own right, he also translated and adapted numerous comedies and tragedies for the Viennese stage. As an actor his most successful roles included Mellefont in Lessing's *Miss Sarah Sampson* and Arsace in Voltaire's *Sémiramis*. He was the first Viennese Tellheim in Lessing's *Minna von Barnhelm*.

He founded a periodical for the young, called *Gesammelte Schriften zum Vergnügen und Unterricht*, which was followed in 1766 by a further series entitled *Neue Sammlung zum Vergnügen und Unterricht*; the periodical was published by Rudolph Gräffer (1734–1817) in Vienna. In the *Neue Sammlung*, in 1768, Stephanie printed the songs 'Daphne, deine Rosenwangen' K52/46e (which appears as 'Meiner Liebsten schöne Wangen' in *Bastien und Bastienne**) and *An die Freude* K53/47e. (As well as being a publisher and printer, Rudolph Gräffer ran a well-known bookshop in Vienna from 1768 until 1793; he was a freemason.)

(Zechmeister)

Stephanie, Johann Gottlieb (b. Breslau, 19 February 1741; d. Vienna, 23 January 1800). Dramatist, librettist and actor. Librettist of *Die Entführung** and *Der Schauspieldirektor**; the original Frank in the latter Komödie. He is usually known as 'Stephanie der Jüngere' [the Younger], to distinguish him from his half-brother Christian Gottlob Stephanie*, and that is how he referred to himself in a postscript to Leopold Mozart's letter to his wife* of 12 August 1773 ('Stephanie der Jüngere and his beautiful wife send their greetings').

After studying law at Halle, he fought in the Seven Years War, first on the Prussian side and later, following his capture by the Austrians in 1760, in the Austrian army, from which he was discharged in 1765. In 1768 the banker Baron Bender was favourably impressed when he saw him act in an amateur performance at Dr Mesmer*'s. In 1769 – the year in which Bender became joint manager of the theatres (*see* AFFLIGIO) – Stephanie was offered a contract at the Kärntnertor-Theater, where he made his début in Brandes's comedy *Der Graf von Olsbach, oder Die Belohnung der Rechtschaffenheit* on 1 April 1769. He was to remain a member of the court theatre until 1799. Two of his most famous roles were in plays by Lessing, Tellheim in *Minna von Barnhelm* and the Prince in *Emilia Galotti*. In the Viennese première of *Hamlet* (*see* HEUFELD) he played Oldenholm (Polonius); in performances of *Romeo und Julie* he was Herr von Capellet (Capulet).

Stephanie also became one of the most successful and popular dramatists of his time. By the year 1776 some twenty of his plays had been performed at the Vienna court theatre, and between 1776 and 1846 thirty-two of his plays received 393 performances there. The comedy *Die abgedankten Offiziere, oder Standhaftigkeit und Verzweiflung*, first produced on 2 May 1770, was given no fewer than eighty times between 1776 and 1846. His German version of *Macbeth* (3 November 1772) – in which Lady Macbeth, in her madness, fatally stabs her husband – was also well received. His collected plays, published between 1774 and 1787, ran to six volumes.

Last but not least, Stephanie proved himself a prolific and competent librettist of Singspiels, providing texts, often adapted from foreign models, for various composers, among them Carl Ditters von Dittersdorf (*Der Apotheker und der Doktor*), Joseph Barta (*Da ist nicht gut zu raten*), and Ignaz Umlauf* (*Die schöne Schusterin, oder Die pücefarbenen Schuhe*). He furthermore turned a number of Italian and French comic operas into German Singspiels, including Anfossi*'s *L'incognita perseguitata* [*Die verfolgte Unbekannte*]; Paisiello*'s *I filosofi immaginari, ossia I visionari* [*Die eingebildeten Philosophen*]; Antonio Sacchini's *Il finto pazzo per amore* [*Der verstellte Narr aus Liebe*]; and André-Ernest-Modeste Grétry's *La fausse magie* [*Die abgeredete Zauberei*], *Silvain* [*Silvain*], and *Les deux avares* [*Die beiden Geizigen*].

Mozart may have met Stephanie as early as 1768, through Dr Mesmer. By 1781, when he was trying to launch his career in Vienna, Stephanie was in sole charge of German opera there. When Stephanie promised to write a libretto for him, Mozart was at first wary, for, as he wrote to his father on 16 June 1781, 'this man has a terrible reputation throughout Vienna as a rude, false, and slanderous fellow who treats people most unfairly'. However, his suspicions proved unfounded, as he acknowledged on 1 August: 'The day before yesterday Stephanie the Younger handed me a libretto to set to music. For all I know, he may behave very badly towards others, but I must say that he has been a very good friend to me. The text is quite good. The subject is Turkish and is called *Bellmont und Konstanze, oder Die Verführung [sic] aus dem Serail.*'

On 16 July 1771 Stephanie married the actress Maria Anna Mika [Myka] (*see* STEPHANIE, MARIA ANNA).

(Branscombe[7], Michtner, Zechmeister)

Stephanie, Maria Anna, *née* Mika or Myka (b. Stahlau, Bohemia, 1751; d. Vienna, 2 February 1802). Actress; wife of Johann Gottlieb Stephanie*. She played Madame Pfeil (or perhaps Madame Vogelsang) at the première of *Der Schauspieldirektor**. She made her début at the Kärntnertor-Theater on 27 April 1771 in a German version by C. H. Schmidt of *Fayel*, a tragedy by the French playwright François de Baculard d'Arnaud (1718–1805). She remained a member of the court theatre company until 1802.

(Zechmeister)

Stich, Jan Václav: *see* PUNTO, GIOVANNI.

Stoll, Anton (1747–1805). Schoolteacher and choirmaster at Baden, near Vienna; on friendly terms with Mozart. It was for him that Mozart wrote the motet *Ave verum corpus* K618, of which Stoll directed the first performance at Baden parish church on 23 June 1791. Mozart presented him with the autographs of this and other church compositions. In 1790 Stoll had performed one of Mozart's masses (probably the 'Coronation' Mass K317) with his choir and orchestra; in July 1791 they performed the *Missa brevis* in B flat major K275/272*b*.

Stoll also rendered some personal services to Mozart, such as finding rooms for Constanze* for her stay at Baden in the summer of 1791. Later he was to show great kindness to Joseph Haydn*'s wife Maria Anna during the final period of her life. She died at his house in Baden on 20 March 1800.

Storace, Ann [Anna] **Selina** ['Nancy'] (b. London, 27 October 1765; d. London, 24 August 1817). English soprano. The first Susanna (*Le nozze di Figaro**); Mozart also wrote for her the part of Eugenia in the unfinished *Lo sposo deluso**. Her father, Stephen [Stefano] Storace (*c*.1725 – *c*.1781) was an Italian double bass player who, after spending some ten years in Dublin, settled in London in 1758. There, in 1761, he married Elizabeth Trusler, the daughter of the proprietor of Marylebone Gardens. Nancy studied with Rauzzini* in London, and in 1778 she travelled with her parents to Naples, where her brother Stephen (1762–96), who would later become a popular composer, had been receiving musical instruction at the Conservatorio San Onofrio since 1776. When she appeared at the Teatro allo Pergola, Florence, in 1780, she had, according to Michael Kelly*, so great a success that the famous castrato Luigi Marchesi, who was singing in the same opera (probably by Francesco Bianchi), insisted on her immediate dismissal. She subsequently performed at Lucca, Leghorn [Livorno], Parma and Milan, and during the 1782–3 season at the Teatro San Samuele in Venice where, Michtner states, she was heard by Count Durazzo*, who recommended her to the Burgtheater.

For four years, from 1783 to 1787, she was one of the stars of the newly formed

Italian company, excelling in *buffa* parts. She delighted her audiences with her fine voice, good technique and spirited acting. Initially her dramatic gestures, developed on the Italian stage, were considered excessive in Vienna, but she quickly adapted to the local taste. Zinzendorf*, not usually the most indulgent of critics, nearly always declared himself enchanted by her performances, and comments such as 'La Storace se surpassa' and 'La Storace chanta comme un ange' appear regularly in his diary. 'Storace, the beautiful singer, delighted the eye, the ear and the soul,' wrote the Hungarian poet Ferencz Kazinczy (1759–1831).

After her successful début on 22 April 1783 as the Contessa in Salieri*'s *La scuola de' gelosi*, Nancy's roles included Livia in Domenico Cimarosa's *L'italiana in Londra* (5 May 1783), Dorina in Sarti*'s *Fra i due litiganti il terzo gode* (28 May 1783), Bettina in Anfossi*'s *I viaggiatori felici* (29 December 1783), Angelica in Martín y Soler*'s *Il burbero di buon cuore* (4 January 1786), and Lilla in the same composer's *Una cosa rara* (17 November 1786). She also took leading parts in several operas by Paisiello*, notably Rosina in the first Viennese production of *Il barbiere di Siviglia* (13 August 1783), Violante in *La frascatana* (8 December 1783), and Lisetta in *Il re Teodoro in Venezia* (from 6 October 1784). On 7 February 1786 she appeared at Schönbrunn in Salieri's *Prima la musica, poi le parole (see* SCHAUSPIELDIREKTOR, DER), in which she had to sing some arias from Sarti's *Giulio Sabino*; she caused much amusement by cleverly mimicking her old antagonist Luigi Marchesi, who had starred in that opera in Vienna the preceding summer. Lastly, she sang in two operas which her brother Stephen had been commissioned to write for the Burgtheater: *Gli sposi malcontenti* (1 June 1785) and *Gli equivoci* (27 December 1786).

At the première of the former work she suddenly lost her voice and did not return to the stage for almost four months. So great was her popularity that her reappearance on 26 September 1785 (in *Il barbiere*) prompted Da Ponte* to write a poem, *Per la ricuperata salute di Ophelia*, which was set to music jointly by Salieri, Mozart and Cornetti (perhaps Alessandro Cornet). The cantata is unfortunately lost; the name 'Ophelia' in the title was a reference to the character Ofelia in Salieri's new opera *La grotta di Trofonio* – a role which Nancy was then rehearsing and would sing at the première on 12 October. Shortly afterwards she asked to be released, but her request was not immediately accepted and she remained for a further season. Her final appearance at the Burgtheater was in *Il burbero di buon cuore* on 19 February 1787, and it was followed by a farewell concert at the Kärntnertor-Theater on 23 February. On the latter occasion, according to Thomas Attwood*, writing to an unidentified correspondent some forty years later (and quoted by Eisen), she sang the scena *Ch'io mi scordi di te? . . . Non temer, amato bene* K505, accompanied by Mozart, who had composed it for her; in addition, he played his Concerto in D minor K466.

While highly successful in her professional activities, Nancy was less fortunate in her private life. She married, against the advice of her friends, the far older English composer and violinist John Abraham Fisher (1744–1806), who arrived in Vienna during a concert tour in July 1783. The precise date of the marriage is not known, but it must have taken place in 1783 or 1784, for Joseph II* refers to Nancy's 'wretched husband' in a letter to Rosenberg-Orsini* on 3 October 1784; O. Edwards states that the marriage had already broken down by that year. Joseph II* reportedly ordered Fisher, who was said to have mistreated Nancy, to leave Vienna.

She had a daughter (presumably by Fisher) who died in July 1785.

In 1786 Nancy had an affair with Benucci*, who had been her frequent partner on the stage and was then singing Figaro to her Susanna, but this relationship likewise proved of short duration. If Zinzendorf is to be believed, she left Benucci for 'Lord Bernard' [i.e. William Harry (Vane), Lord Barnard (1766–1842), who was to become the Earl of Darlington in 1792 and Duke of Cleveland in 1833]. On the other hand, the conclusion drawn by some writers that Joseph II got rid of Fisher because he wanted Nancy for his own mistress appears to be entirely speculative, nor is there any evidence to support the suggestion, which has occasionally been made, that Mozart was himself in love with her. There is no doubt, however, that he maintained friendly relations with her, as well as with her brother, who came to Vienna for the production of each of his operas. In his *Reminiscences* Michael Kelly recalls an evening of quartet-playing hosted by Stephen Storace, at which the violins were played by Joseph Haydn* and Carl Ditters von Dittersdorf, the viola by Mozart, and the cello by the Czech composer Johann Baptist Vanhal*. It has been suggested (for instance, by R. Fiske) that Mozart may have given Stephen Storace some lessons, and may even have helped with the scoring of the two operas.

Nancy left Vienna towards the end of February 1787, together with Kelly, Thomas Attwood, and her mother and brother. They arrived in Salzburg on 26 February; Leopold Mozart showed them the sights the following day. He gathered that Nancy would be returning to Vienna in a year's time. That evening she sang three arias at a concert at Archbishop Colloredo*'s palace; at midnight she and her party left for Munich. The Storaces and Attwood hoped, on their return to London, to obtain a commission for Mozart to compose an opera for the London stage and thus offer him an opportunity to visit England, but nothing came of this project.

In the spring of 1788 Nancy corresponded with Count Rosenberg-Orsini regarding the possibility of a new contract for Vienna, but the negotiations did not bear fruit. Instead, she successfully continued her career at the King's Theatre and at Drury Lane in London (*see also* BENUCCI). In 1797 she undertook a continental tour with the tenor John Braham, who became her lover and with whom she lived until 1816, when they quarrelled. A son, Spencer, was born in 1802. She last appeared on the London stage on 30 May 1808, as Margaretta in her brother's *No Song, No Supper*.

(Edwards, Eisen, Fiske, Geiringer, Kelly, Michtner, *NMA* II/5/14, Payer)

Strack, Johann Kilian (baptized Mainz, 30 March 1724; d. Vienna, 16 January 1793). He was employed at the Austrian court from January 1758, first as personal valet to the three-year-old Archduke Ferdinand*, and, from 1765, in the service of Joseph II*. He was responsible for arranging the private chamber-music performances regularly held in the emperor's music-room, at which Strack himself played the cello. He was married three times. His last wife, Anna Katharina Popp, whom he married in 1775, bore him eight children.

Mozart probably met Strack in 1781 at the house of the court painter Joseph Hickel (who, among some 3000 portraits, did one of Joseph Lange* as Hamlet). Because of Strack's constant access to the emperor, Mozart set out discreetly to cultivate him. On 3 November 1781 Mozart informed his father that he had composed a serenade (K375) in honour of the name day of Hickel's sister-in-law

Therese on 15 October, 'but the principal reason why I wrote it was so that Herr von [sic] Strack, who is daily visitor there, could hear one of my compositions, and I therefore took some care over it'. On 10 April 1782 Mozart wrote: 'I have several times called on Herr von Strack [at his lodgings in the Graben]; he is certainly a good friend of mine . . . But I do not go too often, so as not to inconvenience him and in order to give him no reason for believing that I have an ulterior motive.' On one occasion only (23 January 1782) did Mozart sound a more wary note: 'He seems to be very well-disposed towards me . . . but one should never trust these court toadies.' His momentary caution may have been justified: C. F. Pohl, in his biography of Haydn*, alleges that Strack deliberately kept Haydn's and Mozart's music out of the emperor's private concerts.

In Albert Lortzing's Singspiel *Scenen aus Mozarts Leben* (composed c.1833), 'Fräulein von Strack' – presumably Strack's older daughter Maria Anna Katharina – is described as a pupil of Mozart. No evidence has yet come to light to show that this is anything but fiction.
(Pisarowitz², Pohl)

Strinasacchi, Regina (b. Ostiglia, near Mantua, 1764; d. Dresden, 11 June 1839). Italian violinist. After receiving her musical training in Venice (and perhaps also in Paris), she toured Italy as a soloist, quickly establishing herself as an outstanding artist. In 1784 she visited Vienna. 'She plays with great taste and feeling,' Mozart informed his father on 24 April 1784. He wrote the Sonata for violin and piano K454 for her, which they performed together at a concert at the Kärntnertor-Theater on 29 April (reportedly only the violin part was fully written out at the time). When Leopold heard her in Salzburg on 7 December 1785, he was greatly impressed: 'She plays not a single note without feeling . . .' he wrote to Nannerl* that same day. 'No one could play an Adagio with greater feeling or more movingly than she does. She puts her whole heart into the melody she is playing.'

In 1785 she married the cellist Johann Conrad Schlick (1759–1825) who was a member of the Duke of Gotha's orchestra. She herself thereafter played in the orchestra; she also continued to give concerts. After her husband's death she left Gotha and moved to Dresden where her son resided. In 1787 her brother Antonio Strinasacchi, also a violinist – though, according to Leopold Mozart, a far less brilliant one – was engaged to play in the Salzburg court orchestra for two years.

The celebrated soprano Teresa Strinasacchi, who was a prominent member of the Prague opera from 1793 to 1797 (she sang Sesto in *La clemenza di Tito** in December 1794), was probably related to Regina.
(White)

Strobach, Johann Joseph (b. Zwittau, 2 December 1731; d. Prague, 10 December 1794). Czech musician. After studying theology in Prague he switched to music, and for thirteen years played the violin in the orchestra of the church of the Holy Cross in that city. From 1765 he served as choirmaster in several other local churches. In addition, he later became conductor of the National Theatre orchestra. In that capacity he directed the enormously successful production of *Le nozze di Figaro** in late 1786. In a letter now lost but cited in Niemetschek*'s biography, Mozart, who came to Prague in January 1787 as a result of the furore created by these

performances, warmly congratulated Strobach on his skilful conducting of the opera. In November of the same year, Strobach took over from Mozart the conducting of *Don Giovanni** after the early performances.
(Favier, Fétis, Wurzbach)

Süssmayr, Franz Xaver (b. Schwanenstadt, Upper Austria, 1766; d. Vienna, 17 September 1803). Austrian composer. Son of a teacher and choirmaster who gave him his initial musical instruction. He was educated at Kremsmünster Abbey school from 1779 to 1784, and subsequently studied philosophy and law at the local Ritterakademie until 1787. He also received instruction in composition from Maximilian Piessinger (1753–1826) and Georg von Pasterwiz (1730–1803). In July 1788 he arrived in Vienna, where he at first earned his living giving private lessons. He made Mozart's acquaintance in 1791 (or perhaps already in 1790) and studied composition with him. After Mozart's death he became a pupil of Salieri*.

In June 1791 Süssmayr went to stay at Baden, presumably so that he might be of assistance to Constanze* who was taking the cure there during the final weeks of her pregnancy. At the same time he appears to have been kept busy copying music for Mozart. 'Please tell that fathead Süssmayr to send me my score for the first act [of *Die Zauberflöte**], from the introduction to the first Finale, so that I can orchestrate it,' Mozart wrote to Constanze on 2 July. Mozart's letters of this period contain numerous jocular and ribald, but patently affectionate references to Süssmayr. The fact that the son born on 26 July was named 'Franz Xaver Wolfgang' may well bear witness to their friendship.

Süssmayr accompanied the Mozarts to Prague in August 1791, but there is no evidence of his having written the recitatives for *La clemenza di Tito**, as has sometimes been alleged. He closely followed the composition of the Requiem, and Sophie Haibel* recalled hearing Mozart explain to him on the night before his death how it should be completed. Rather surprisingly, it was not Süssmayr but Eybler* whom Constanze originally asked to finish the work – 'I was annoyed with Süssmayr just then (I don't know why) and Mozart himself had felt a high regard for Eybler,' she wrote to the Abbé Maximilian Stadler* on 31 May 1827. But when Eybler abandoned the task, she turned to Süssmayr. He duly finished the Requiem, although the precise extent of his contribution is still a matter for conjecture. For C. Wolff, 'the Süssmayr score . . . is the only document that represents the genuine musical truth of the unfinished work'.

In 1794 Süssmayr was appointed Kapellmeister of German opera at the court theatre, with which he had been associated for some time. His own compositions comprised sacred as well as secular music. The latter included some thirty works for the stage, of which several achieved considerable popularity. Most successful were the Singspiel *Der Spiegel von Arkadien* (with text by Schikaneder*) which was produced at the Freihaus-Theater on 14 November 1794, and the ballet *Il noce di Benevento . . . , oder Die Zauberschwestern*, first performed at the Kärntnertor-Theater on 14 January 1802. Beethoven* wrote piano Variations (WoO76) on the trio 'Tändeln und scherzen' from Süssmayr's comic opera *Soliman der Zweite, oder Die drei Sultaninnen* (Kärntnertor-Theater, 1799).
(Wessely[2,4], Wolff)

Swieten, Gottfried (Bernhard), Baron van (b. Leyden, 29 October 1733; d.

Vienna, 29 March 1803). Diplomat and civil servant; composer; friend of Mozart. He was the oldest son of Dr Gerhard van Swieten (1700–72), who, soon after arriving in Vienna in 1745, became personal physician to Maria Theresa* and, in addition, occupied several administrative posts, including that of director of the court library. Gottfried van Swieten served as a diplomat in Brussels (1755–7), Paris (1760–63), Warsaw (November 1763 – middle of 1764), and as ambassador extraordinary at the Prussian court in Berlin from 1770 to 1777. After his return to Vienna he became director of the court library in November 1777 (the post had been vacant since his father's death), and in 1782 was appointed president of the Education and Censureship Commission. On 5 December 1791, the day of Mozart's death, he was relieved of his official duties by Leopold II*. Preoccupation with this sudden change in his fortunes has been cited as the reason for his not arranging a suitable funeral for Mozart.

The Mozarts met him during their stay in Vienna in 1767–8. In his petition of 21 September 1768 to Joseph II* Leopold Mozart states that the agreement he entered into with Affligio* concerning the composition and production of *La finta semplice** was concluded in the presence of, among others, the 'young Baron van Swieten'; and furthermore that, in order to lay malicious rumours alleging that the finished work was 'unsingable', Wolfgang had played the whole opera through on the piano in Swieten's apartment before various *cognoscenti* who were all 'greatly moved'. Later, in Berlin, Swieten frequented the circle of Frederick the Great's sister, Princess Anna Amalia of Prussia (1723–87), where the music of Handel* and J. S. Bach was greatly admired; he himself thereafter held these composers in particular veneration. 'Every Sunday at midday I go to Baron von Suiten's [*sic*],' Mozart wrote to his father on 10 April 1782, 'where no music is played other than that of Handel and Bach.' Swieten had the scores of many of Handel's works in his personal library (which Haydn* estimated to be worth 10,000 gulden); at his suggestion, Mozart re-orchestrated four of them, which were subsequently performed in Vienna (*see* HANDEL). In his *Jahrbuch der Tonkunst von Wien und Prag* Schönfeld pays tribute to Swieten's excellent taste in music: 'When he is present at a concert, our would-be connoisseurs do not take their eyes off him, so that they may read in his facial expression . . . the judgement which they should pronounce on what they hear.'

Swieten was among the subscribers to Mozart's Trattnerhof concerts in 1784 (*see* TRATTNER), and his name was the only one to appear on the new subscription list circulated by Mozart five years later. He seems, moreover, to have actively supported Mozart's efforts in 1790 to obtain the post of Second Kapellmeister. After Mozart's death, Constanze*'s correspondence contains several references to Swieten's 'generosity'. It was, in fact, Swieten who arranged the first performance in Vienna of Mozart's Requiem, on 2 January 1793, for the benefit of Constanze, who received the proceeds of more than 300 golden ducats. And according to the *Prager Neue Zeitung* of 9 April 1794, Swieten was instrumental in arranging for Carl Thomas Mozart* to be educated in Prague (*see also* NIEMETSCHEK).

During his stay in Berlin in the 1770s, Swieten reportedly studied composition with Princess Anna Amalia's musical adviser, the well-known Kapellmeister Johann Philipp Kirnberger (1721–83). Swieten wrote a vaudeville, *Les talents à la mode*, and a comic opera, *Colas, toujours Colas*, which was inspired by Pierre Alexandre Monsigny's *Rose et Colas*. The programme of a concert in the Augarten in Vienna, on

Taux, Alois

26 May 1782, included a symphony by him, as well as one of Mozart's. Swieten also wrote the text for Haydn*'s oratorios *The Creation* and *The Seasons*.
(Olleson[1,2], Schmid[5], Schönfeld)

Taux, Alois (b. Baumgarten, near Frankenstein, Silesia, 5 October 1817; d. Salzburg, 17 April 1861). German composer, Kapellmeister and choirmaster. After studying at the Prague conservatory, he became Kapellmeister at the theatre in Linz, and in 1839 was appointed to a similar position in Salzburg. In 1842 he was made artistic director of the festivities accompanying the unveiling of the Mozart monument (*see* SCHWANTHALER, and MOZART, FRANZ XAVER WOLFGANG). Carl Thomas Mozart*, who made his acquaintance on that occasion, soon became a close personal friend, at least partly out of gratitude for the kindness which Taux had shown Constanze* during the final period of her life.

Taux played, furthermore, a significant role in the development of the Salzburger Liedertafel, a choral society founded in 1847. He also conducted important choral concerts at the Mozart festivals of 1852 and 1856. After the death of Karl Flögel (1816–58), Taux succeeded him as choirmaster of the Liedertafel. Besides thus making many valuable contributions to the musical life of Salzburg, Taux was also more specifically, in G. Croll's words, 'responsible for giving the cult of Mozart's music a new and decisive impetus'. At the Stadttheater he conducted performances of *Don Giovanni**, *Die Entführung**, *Le nozze di Figaro**, *Der Schauspieldirektor**, and *Die Zauberflöte**.

Lastly, his contacts with many leading musicians and numerous music lovers of his time enabled Taux to establish a remarkable collection of autographs which is today one of the prize possessions of the Salzburger Liedertafel. He obtained most of these autographs during an extensive journey through Germany in 1845, in the course of which he met Berlioz, Lortzing, Mendelssohn, Schumann and Spohr.

Taux was married to Anna Dubsky von Wittenau (d. 1907). After his death he was interred in the same grave in St Sebastian's cemetery as Constanze's sisters Aloisia Lange* and Sophie Haibel*. In 1895 his remains were exhumed, at the same time as theirs, and reburied in the municipal cemetery.
(Angermüller[14], Croll[5], Schneider)

Tenducci, Giusto Ferdinando (b. Siena, *c.*1735; d. Genoa, 1790). Italian male soprano and composer. In 1758, after appearances in Venice and Naples, he arrived in London, where he first made his mark in Gioacchino Cocchi's *Ciro riconosciuto*; in 1762 he scored a great success as Arbaces at the première of Arne's *Artaxerxes*. He lived and performed in England, Scotland and Ireland for close on thirty years. Unusually for a castrato, he married – at Cork, in 1766, an Irish girl called Dora Maunsell, whose furious family promptly kidnapped the bride and had the bridegroom thrown into gaol; even more unusually, he is said to have fathered two children.

Tenducci's voice, while of relatively modest range, was exceptionally beautiful. According to Charles Burney*, his performance in *Artaxerxes* 'had a rapid effect upon the public taste, and stimulated to imitation all that were possessed of good ears and flexible voices'. Concerning Tenducci's rendition of Scottish songs, for which he won a new popularity, George Thomson (1757–1851), the well-known editor of Scottish folksongs who also published many of Robert Burns's songs, declared that '[his] singing was full of passion, feeling and taste and ... his articulation of the words was no less perfect than his expression of the music'. Probably Tenducci's last engagement in London was at the King's Theatre in May–June 1785 when he sang opposite Adriana Gabrieli* in several performances of Gluck*'s *Orfeo ed Euridice*. His own compositions – mainly some operas, all of them adaptations – were of little merit.

The Mozarts met Tenducci in London in 1764. Wolfgang ran across him again at Saint Germain in the summer of 1778 ('he was absolutely delighted to see me again,' Wolfgang informed his father on 27 August). On this occasion he undertook to write an aria for Tenducci, with four concertante solo parts for piano, oboe, horn and bassoon, to be performed by members of the Duc d'Ayen's orchestra. This composition (KAnh.3/315b) has been considered lost, but C. Esch suggested in 1991 that it might, in fact, be identical with the version of KAnh.245/621a (*see* JACQUIN) which he had recently discovered.

(Burney[2], Esch, Fiske[3], Hadden)

Teyber [Teuber]. A remarkable Austrian musical family, on friendly terms with the Mozarts. The father, Matthäus (*c.*1711–1785) was a violinist and, from 1757, a court musician in Vienna. In 1741 he married Therese Ried(e)l. Several of their children enjoyed highly successful careers in music (there may have been some confusion among scholars regarding the daughters' engagements, since programmes did not normally indicate the singers' first names).

Therese Teyber* was a very popular soprano at the Burgtheater throughout the 1780s (*see* separate entry).

(Anna) Elisabeth Teyber (1744–1816), her older sister, also a soprano, sang various roles in Vienna in the 1760s, including Pallade in Florian Leopold Gassmann's *Il trionfo d'amore* (1765), Circe at the première of Gluck*'s *Telemaco* (30 January 1765), Psiche in Gassmann's *Amore e Psiche*, and Elpicine in Hasse*'s *Partenope* (both in 1767). She later performed to great acclaim in various Italian cities and is reported to have sung at St Petersburg in the 1770s.

Barbara Teyber (?1750–1832), another daughter, is said to have participated in the first performances of Haydn*'s oratorio *Il ritorno di Tobia* II XXI:1 which the composer conducted in Vienna on 2 and 4 April 1775. P. Branscombe states that she sang Sara, whereas H. C. Robbins Landon believes that the role of Sara was taken by Magdalena Friberth and that Barbara Teyber sang Azaria/Raffaele.

Anton Teyber (1756–1822), a son who was a pupil of Padre Martini*, had a successful career as composer, pianist, and organist; after performing in Italian and other European musical centres, he was appointed court organist in Dresden in 1787, assistant Kapellmeister and composer at the court theatre in Vienna in 1791, and, two years later, court chamber musician (the post occupied by Mozart and left vacant since his death).

Franz Teyber (1758–1810), another son, also an outstanding all-round musician, had frequent professional contacts with Emanuel Schikaneder*. In 1784 he composed, for a production of *Die Entführung** by the Schikaneder–Kumpf company at the Kärntnertor-Theater (*see* SCHIKANEDER), a replacement for 'Martern aller Arten', the latter aria having, according to the *Wiener Kronik*, proved too difficult for the orchestra. From 1786 to 1788 he was attached as conductor and composer to Schikaneder's touring company. After working in Germany and Switzerland, he returned to Vienna in 1798; there he wrote the opera *Alexander* (to a text by Schikaneder) for the opening of the Theater an der Wien on 13 June 1801. He was appointed court organist in 1810.

Friedrich Teyber (1748–1829), yet another son, was a gifted amateur violinist.

The Mozarts knew the Teyber family well, perhaps since 1767. In a letter to his wife* from Vienna on 21 August 1773 Leopold describes an excursion he and Wolfgang made with the Teybers and another couple to Baden. During the same visit to Vienna Wolfgang borrowed a violin from them, on which he played a concerto at St Cajetan's monastery on 7 August. In 1783 Anton, newly returned from Italy, took part in the private concerts arranged by Swieten*, where, Wolfgang informed his father on 12 March, 'Van Swieten sings treble, I sing alto and at the same time play the piano, Starzer [the composer Joseph Starzer (1726[?7]–87)] sings tenor, and young Teyber from Italy sings bass.' In April 1789 Mozart met Anton Teyber again in Dresden, and, together with the cellist Nikolaus Kraft (1778–1853), they played the 'Puchberg*' Trio (K542 or K563) at a private concert at the Hotel de Pologne where Mozart was staying. As for Franz Teyber, Leopold described him in a letter to Nannerl* on 5 May 1786, on the occasion of his arrival with Schikaneder's company in Salzburg, as 'my very good friend from Vienna; a thorough and excellent musician, a good composer, organist and cellist'. Franz Teyber visited Leopold more than once and took part with him in private performances of Mozart's quartets.

(Branscombe[8,9,10,11], Landon[1], Michtner, Pfannhauser, Zechmeister)

Teyber [Teuber], Therese (baptized Vienna, 15 October 1760; d. Vienna, 15 April 1830). Austrian soprano; daughter of Matthäus Teyber (*see* TEYBER). The original Blonde (*Die Entführung**); Mozart furthermore intended her to sing Metilde in *Lo sposo deluso**. She was a pupil of the famous Italian contralto and singing teacher Vittoria Tesi-Tramontini (1700–75), who had resided in Vienna since 1748.

Therese was a member of the Burgtheater from 1778 until 1791, specializing in soubrette and *ingénue* roles. She made her début on 8 September 1778 as Fiametta in *Frühling und Liebe* by Maximilian Ulbrich (1752–1814). Thereafter she appeared in numerous Singspiels, frequently in servant roles, as in Gluck*'s *Die Pilgrime von Mekka* (26 July 1780), Salieri*'s *Der Rauchfangkehrer* (30 April 1781), and *Die Entführung* (16 July 1782). On 23 March 1783, she sang Giunia's aria 'Parto, m'affretto' from *Lucio Silla** at Mozart's concert at the Burgtheater, while he played his Piano Concerto K415/387b and a free fantasia at her concert on 30 March. In a letter to the poet and dramatist Anton Klein in May 1785, Mozart bracketed Teyber with Cavalieri* and Johann Valentin Adamberger* as singers of whom Germany had cause to be proud;, he regretted that they had been attached to the Italian company, to the detriment of German opera. In Italian *opera buffa* Teyber continued to sing the type of role which had made her so popular. Thus she was the 'cameriera' Carlotta in Salieri's *La scuola de' gelosi* (22 April 1783), Livietta in Sarti*'s *Fra i due litiganti il terzo gode* (28 May 1783), and the 'serva di locanda' Lisetta in Paisiello*'s *La frascatana* (8 December 1783). In 1788 she replaced Luisa Laschi* as Zerlina in some performances of *Don Giovanni**.

In 1785 (or 1787) she married the tenor Ferdinand Arnold. He was a member of the Burgtheater company from 1 May to 30 September 1778, and again from 1785 to 1788, but was not highly regarded in Vienna. The couple reportedly later sang with success in Hamburg, Berlin, Warsaw and Riga.
(Branscombe[12], Michtner, Pfannhauser)

Thiennes et Rumbeke: *see* RUMBEKE.

Thorwart, Johann (Franz Joseph) von (b. Vienna, 14 June 1737; d. Vienna, 26 August 1813). Austrian court official, increasingly responsible for the financial management of the National Theatre. The son of a tavern keeper, he became a valet to Prince Johann Friedrich Joseph Lamberg (1737–97), and, probably with his assistance, entered court service in *c.*1761. On 9 September 1760 he married Franziska Schnock (d. 1820), whose father had been a well-to-do surgeon. In 1764 he was placed in charge of the stalls at the German theatre; this proved a lucrative appointment, for it enabled him to purchase a house in 1767 and another one in 1769. By 1779 he was auditor of the National Theatre and, with short breaks, he continued to occupy various influential positions in the administration until his retirement on a pension in 1806. He was ennobled by Francis II in 1793.

Very little is known about Mozart's professional contacts with Thorwart, but they are likely to have been frequent, since, as he explained to his father on 16 January 1782, everything connected with the theatre had to pass through the hands of Thorwart, who had great influence with Count Rosenberg-Orsini* and his deputy, Baron Kienmayr. Mozart had, for instance, to apply to him for permission to give the concert which eventually took place on 3 March of that year. On 7 December 1787 Thorwart, in his capacity as secretary in the high chamberlain's office, countersigned the decree appointing Mozart 'chamber musician'.

At the same time Thorwart, who had been appointed Constanze*'s guardian on the death of her father Fridolin Weber* in 1779, played an important role in Mozart's personal life. In a letter to his father on 22 December 1781, Mozart related at length how, as a condition for having any further contact with Constanze, he had been forced by Thorwart to provide a written undertaking either to marry her within three years or thereafter pay her an annual compensation of 300 gulden (*see also* WEBER, CAECILIA). The document, he added, was subsequently torn up by Constanze, as a token of her trust in him. It was Thorwart who, on 29 July 1782, applied to the court marshal's office for permission for Constanze's marriage to Mozart, and on 3 August signed the marriage contract as her guardian. The next day he was named as a witness in the register of St Stephen's Cathedral. He was also a witness at the wedding of Constanze's sister Josepha Weber* to Franz de Paula Hofer* on 21 July 1788.

Da Ponte*, towards the end of his stay in Vienna, came to regard Thorwart as one of his worst enemies – which is hardly surprising since, as he records in his memoirs, he once accused Thorwart to his face of having misused public funds for his own gain.
(Blümml, Da Ponte)

Thun-Hohenstein, Johann Joseph Anton, Count (1711–88). Imperial chamberlain. Son of Count Johann Franz Joseph Thun-Hohenstein (1686–1720) and his wife Philippine Aloysia, *née* Countess Harrach; great-nephew of Count Ernst Thun, Archbishop of Salzburg from 1687 to 1709. He was married four times, and by his first three wives had twenty-four children; he was the father-in-law of Countess Wilhelmine Thun-Hohenstein*.

He possessed several palaces, including one in Linz and another in Prague, for the family owned property in Bohemia. His place in Prague's Malá Strana district was the site for concerts and operatic performances (Bondini*'s Italian company regularly performed there from 1781), and he himself had a private orchestra which included such accomplished musicians as the horn player Jan Václav Stich (*see* PUNTO).

Thun-Hohenstein offered Mozart hospitality both in Linz and in Prague. While staying with Constanze* at the count's palace in Linz in 1783, Mozart composed the 'Linz' Symphony K425, which received its first performance at the local theatre on 4 November 1783. 'I really cannot describe to you all the kindnesses which are showered on us in this house,' he assured his father on 31 October. And no sooner had they arrived in Prague in January 1787 than the count offered them quarters, into which 'quite a good piano' was promptly moved. 'After lunch the count entertained us with some music performed by his own people, which lasted about an hour and a half,' Mozart wrote to Jacquin* on 15 January. 'I can enjoy such *pure entertainment* every day.' The count's generosity was similarly extended to Leopold Mozart when he and the young violinist Heinrich Marchand (*see* MARCHAND) stopped at Linz on their journey from Vienna to Salzburg in April 1785. While staying at an inn, because all rooms at the count's house were occupied by his sons, they took the main meals with the family: 'Even breakfast is sent over here every day,' Leopold wrote to Nannerl* on 30 April. 'We wanted to leave this afternoon, but they won't let us go.'
(Preihs)

Thun-Hohenstein, (Maria) Wilhelmine, Countess (b. Vienna, 12 June 1744; d. Vienna, 18 May 1800). One of Mozart's principal patrons in Vienna. She was the daughter of Count of the Realm Anton Corfiz Ulfeld (1699–1770), holder of various high political and court appointments (minister for external affairs in 1742, prime minister in 1745, high steward from 1753), and of his second wife, Maria Elisabeth, *née* Princess Lobkowitz (1726–86). On 30 July 1761 Wilhelmine married Count Franz Joseph Anton Thun-Hohenstein (1734–1801), a son of Count Johann Joseph Anton Thun-Hohenstein* and his first wife, Princess Maria Christina Hohenzollern-Hechingen. Wilhelmine's husband became an imperial chamberlain and a court councillor.

The Mozarts may have met the countess and her husband when Wolfgang and Nannerl* played at Count Ulfeld's house in October 1762. In any case, Wolfgang was already well-acquainted with them when he arrived in Vienna in mid-March 1781. On 24 March he wrote to his father: 'I have already lunched twice at Countess Thun's and go there almost every day. She is the most charming and delightful lady I have met in my whole life, and she also thinks highly of me. Her husband is still the same peculiar but decent and honourable gentleman.' The countess's house, in her late father's residence near the Minoritenkirche, was a focal point of the aristocracy's social and musical life. The German traveller and author Georg Forster (1754–94) wrote: 'Almost every evening, between 9 and 10 o'clock, these persons meet at Countess Thun's. There is much witty conversation, piano-playing, singing in German or Italian, and, if they feel particularly animated, dancing.' Everybody of importance in the elegant society of the town attended her soirées, from Joseph II* down. One of Mozart's earliest frustrations after arriving in Vienna in March 1781 was having to refuse an invitation to play at her house – it made him 'quite desperate', he complained to his father on 11 April – because Archbishop Colloredo* required his services that evening: 'And who was [at the countess's]? The emperor.' Charles Burney* described her as 'a most agreeable and accomplished lady of very high rank, who, among many other talents, possesses as great skill in music as any person of distinction I ever knew . . . She is a chearful [sic], lively, and beneficent being, whom every one here seems to love as a favourite sister.' At Burney's request, she introduced him to Gluck*.

Her name frequently figures in Mozart's letters in 1781 and 1782. In May 1781 he played *Idomeneo** to her on her piano, in the presence of Count Rosenberg-Orsini* and Baron van Swieten*. In December 1781 she lent him her 'beautiful Stein* piano' for his contest with Clementi* at court. The following year, he played for her the different acts of *Die Entführung** as he finished them. On 17 August 1782 he wrote to his father: 'You cannot imagine what efforts Countess Thun, Baron van Swieten and other eminent persons are making to keep me here.' On 14 December 1782, Zinzendorf* heard Mozart play at her house. The fact that Mozart's extant correspondence contains no further reference to the countess after 1782 does not signify that she ceased to support him, for her name was on the list of subscribers to the Trattnerhof concerts in 1784 (*see* TRATTNER) – as were those of her sister, Countess Maria (Anna) Elisabeth Waldstein (1747–91), and the latter's husband, Count Georg Christian Waldstein (1743–91). Moreover, Mozart's appointment as 'chamber musician' on 7 December 1787 may well have owed something to her influence with Joseph II.

She had six children, two of whom died young. Her son Count Joseph Johann Thun (1767–1810) carried the family name forward into the next generation. In 1788 her oldest daughter, Maria Elisabeth (1764–1806), married Count [later Prince] Andrei Kyrillovich Rasumovsky, who was Russian ambassador in Vienna from 1793 until 1799. That same year the second daughter, (Maria) Christiane (1765–1841), married Prince Karl Lichnowsky*; she was a fine pianist. The third daughter, Maria Karolina (1769–1800), who excelled as a singer and guitarist, married Baron Gillford [later the Earl of Clanwilliam] in 1793.

(Burney[5], Orel[3], Preihs, Schönfeld)

Tibaldi, Giuseppe (Luigi) (b. Bologna, 22 January 1729; d. *c.*1790). Italian tenor and composer; the original Aceste (*Ascanio in Alba**). He studied composition with Padre Martini*, became a member of the Accademia Filarmonica in Bologna in 1747, and in 1751 was appointed *maestro di cappella* at San Giovanni in Monte in that city. Later he had a successful career as a singer. He also composed some church music and sixteen *Duetti notturni* for two sopranos and continuo.

Tibaldi sang various leading roles in Vienna between 1762 and 1767, most notably Porsenna at the première of Hasse*'s *Il trionfo di Clelia* on 27 April 1762,

Tilgner, Viktor Oskar

and Admeto at the première of Gluck*'s *Alceste* on 26 December 1767 (the title role was created by Antonia Bernasconi*). He often sang in the same opera as his wife, Rosa Tartaglini, whom he had married in 1753. Thus they appeared together in Vienna in Tommaso Traetta's *Ifigenia in Tauride* in 1763, in Gluck's *Ezio*, Hasse's *Egeria* and Florian Leopold Gassmann's *L'Olimpiade* in 1764, and in Gluck's *Telemaco* and Gassmann's *Il trionfo d'amore* in 1765. Tibaldi's numerous performances in Italy included roles in Vincenzo Ciampi's *Gianquir* in Venice in 1760, Niccolò Piccinni's *Didone abbandonata* in Bologna in 1772, Gregorio Sciroli's *Solimano* in Venice in 1776, and Admeto in Gluck's *Alceste* at Bologna in 1778.

Mozart came to know Tibaldi well while he was completing *Ascanio in Alba* in Milan. 'Signor Tibaldi . . . does my son the honour of calling every morning to watch him compose,' Leopold Mozart wrote to Count Gian-Luca Pallavicini-Centurioni on 30 October 1771.

(Brofsky², *DEUMM*, Zechmeister)

Tilgner, Viktor Oskar (b. Pressburg [Bratislava], 25 October 1844; d. Vienna, 16 April 1896). Sculptor; creator of the Mozart statue in Vienna. His enormous output comprised large figures for several state buildings (Neue Hofburg, Natural History Museum, Museum of the History of Art, Burgtheater), funerary monuments, ornamental fountains, busts (of royalty, aristocrats, artists, musicians), and statues – notably those of the composer Johann Nepomuk Hummel* (in Bratislava), of the painter Hans Makart (Vienna, Stadtpark), and of Mozart (Vienna). The latter statue was unveiled on the Albrechts-Platz on 21 April 1896, just a few days after Tilgner's death; in 1953 it was moved to the Burggarten.

On the Mozart statue in Salzburg, *see* SCHWANTHALER.

(Pollak, Wurzbach)

Torricella, Christoph (b. Switzerland, *c.*1715; d. Vienna, 24 January 1798). Swiss music publisher and art dealer (in an advertisement in the *Wiener Zeitung* on 7 July 1784 he described himself as a 'publisher of art, copper engravings, and music'). He began trading in Vienna in the early 1770s, sold music imported from England, the Netherlands and Paris, and, in 1781, started publishing his own editions of music. After some initial success, the latter venture appears to have run into difficulties, and in 1786 most of his plates were acquired by Artaria*.

Torricella's catalogue included works by J. C. Bach*, Clementi*, Joseph Haydn*, Hoffmeister*, Kozeluch*, Salieri*, Sarti*, and Vanhal*. In 1784 he issued the first editions of Mozart's piano sonatas K284/205*b* and 333/315*c*, and of the Violin Sonata K454 (*see* RUMBEKE); he also published the Variations for piano K265/300*e*, 398/416*e* and 455.

(Weinmann³'⁹)

Traeg, Johann (b. Gochsheim, Lower Franconia, 20 January 1747; d. Vienna, 5 September 1805). Austrian music publisher and copyist. Son of the musician Johann Veit Traeg and his wife Sophia Carolina, *née* Hoffmann. The family had moved to Vienna by 1779 (presumably after the father's death).

Johann Traeg's first known advertisement offering copies of music appeared in the *Wiener Zeitung* on 10 August 1782. In a further announcement in the same journal on 21 December of that year he offered for sale, among other items, manuscript copies of symphonies and piano concertos by Mozart. Various similar announcements of music by Mozart appeared during the following decade (in many instances, however, it has not been possible to identify with certainty the pieces advertised). In 1794 Traeg founded his own publishing firm, the first item being three quartets by Joseph Eybler*. On 22 October 1803 the firm was renamed 'Johann Traeg und Sohn*; the son (b. Vienna, 15 September 1781; d. after March 1831) also bore the name Johann. Some time after the elder Traeg's death, the firm's name was changed to 'Johann Traeg'. Business flourished for several years, but in 1817 most of the firm's publications were acquired by Artaria*, and it was liquidated in 1820. Its list had included works by such prominent composers as C. P. E. Bach, Beethoven*, Luigi Cherubini, Joseph Haydn*, Michael Haydn*, Hummel*, Ignace Joseph Pleyel and Vanhal*. It issued first editions of, among other works, Joseph Haydn's Piano Trio 11 XV:31, Mozart's String Quintet in B flat K174 (in 1798), Mozart's Fantasia K608 (in 1799, arranged for the piano, for four hands), Beethoven's songs *Zärtliche Liebe* WoO123 and *La partenza* WoO124, and several of Beethoven's sets of variations, including those on 'Ein Mädchen oder Weibchen' from Mozart's *Die Zauberflöte*, op. 66. Traeg also published early editions of the quartets K387, 421/417*b*, 428/421*b*, 458, 464 and 465.

In 1798 the elder Traeg became an agent for Breitkopf & Härtel*, a fact which led to frequent contacts between him and Constanze*, as emerges from her correspondence with the Leipzig firm.

(Weinmann[5,10])

Trattner, Johann Thomas von (b. Johrmannsdorf, near Güns, Hungary, 11 November 1717; d. Vienna, 31 July 1798). Owner of bookshops and printing works in Vienna (where he lived) and several other prominent cities in the Habsburg empire. In a letter to Hagenauer* on 21 January 1768, Leopold Mozart described Trattner's bookshop as the most important in Vienna. Trattner was ennobled in 1764. Between 1773 and 1777 he built an imposing residence on the Graben, which became known as the 'Trattnerhof'; it was demolished in 1911.

In 1750 Trattner married Maria von Retzenheim (d. 1775), and in 1776, Maria Theresia von Nagel (1758–93), the daughter of the court mathematician Joseph Anton von Nagel. Only two of the twenty-one children born during the two marriages reached adulthood. Maria Theresia von Trattner became one of Mozart's earliest piano pupils after he settled in Vienna in 1781.

From January to September 1784 Mozart and Constanze* rented accommodation at the Trattnerhof, and during their stay there Mozart gave three subscription concerts on 17, 24 and 31 March in a private hall of the building, each time playing a new piano concerto (K449, 450 and 451). The list of subscribers which he sent to his father on 20 March contained no fewer than 176 names.

Trattner was godfather to the last three of Mozart's sons (Carl Thomas*, Johann Thomas Leopold* and Franz Xaver Wolfgang*), and his wife was godmother of Mozart's daughter Theresia*. Mozart dedicated the Piano Sonata K457 and the Fantasia K475 to her.

(Cloeter)

Umlauf, Ignaz

Umlauf, Ignaz (b. Vienna, 1746; d. Meidling, near Vienna, 8 June 1796). Austrian composer. He was a viola player in the Burgtheater orchestra in Vienna from 1772, Kapellmeister of German opera from 1778 to 1783, and thereafter deputy to Salieri* as conductor of Italian opera. His Singspiel *Die Bergknappen* (text by Joseph Weidmann*) opened the new era of German opera on 17 February 1778. Over the next five years the Burgtheater produced several more of his operas, of which the most successful was *Die schöne Schusterin, oder Die pücefarbenen Schuhe* in 1779, to a text by Johann Gottlieb Stephanie*. At the first performance of Mozart's re-orchestrated version of Handel*'s *Messiah* K572 on 6 March 1789, Mozart directed the orchestra, Umlauf the singers.

Mozart was no admirer of Umlauf's music. About one Singspiel (probably *Das Irrlicht, oder Endlich fand er sie*), he wrote to his father on 6 October 1781: 'You should not think that it is good just because it took him a year to write it. Between ourselves, I would have taken it for the work of fourteen or fifteen days.' Regarding *Welches ist die beste Nation?* (13 December 1782), a comedy by Cornelius Hermann von Ayrenhoff (1733–1819) with musical numbers by Umlauf, he wrote on 21 December 1782: 'A wretched text which I was asked to set, but I did not accept . . . The music is moreover so bad that I don't know whether the first prize for wretchedness should be awarded to the poet or the composer.' (Badura-Skoda², Branscombe¹³)

Valesi, Giovanni [real name: Johann Evangelist Walleshauser] (b. Unterhatten-hofen [Hattenhofen], Bavaria, 28 April 1735; d. Munich, 10 January 1816). German tenor and singing teacher; the original Gran sacerdote di Nettuno (*Idomeneo**), and perhaps the first Contino del Belfiore (*La finta giardiniera**).

He was engaged as singer at the court of Prince–Bishop Johann Theodor at Freising, and in 1756 entered the service of Duke Clemens Franz of Bavaria (1722–70) in Munich. The duke sent him to Italy to complete his studies; it was there that he assumed his Italian name. After the duke's death he joined the Munich court Kapelle, of which he remained a member until 1798. He also made guest appearances in Florence, Siena, Dresden, Prague and Berlin. Among his many pupils were Johann Valentin Adamberger* and Carl Maria von Weber. After hearing the singer Margarethe Kaiser in Munich in 1777, Mozart wrote to his father: 'Her teacher is Valesi; and from her singing you can tell that he knows how to sing and also how to teach singing' (letter of 2 October 1777). (Schmid H.)

Vanhal [Vanhall, Wanhal], **Johann Baptist** [Jan Křtitel] (b. Nové Nechanice, Bohemia, 12 May 1739; d. Vienna, 20 August 1813). Prolific Czech composer whose output included orchestral and chamber music, as well as many pieces for the keyboard. He was also a popular teacher; one of his pupils was the future composer, music publisher and piano maker Ignace Joseph Pleyel (1757–1831). Vanhal was already a proficient organist and violinist by the time he arrived *c.*1761 in Vienna, where he studied with Carl Ditters von Dittersdorf. After a two years" stay in Italy and a further spell in Vienna, followed by visits to Hungary and Croatia (partly for the purpose of recuperating from a severe attack of mental illness), he returned *c.*1780 to the Austrian capital. There he lived on income earned from teaching and composing.

Mozart was familiar with some of his music before meeting the man himself: at Augsburg on 19 October 1777 he performed a violin concerto by Vanhal at the Holy Cross monastery. In Vienna, on at least one occasion, he played quartets with Vanhal, Haydn* and Dittersdorf (*see* STORACE). Vanhal's reputation as a composer stood high in his day. For her concert in Vienna on 19 August 1791, the armonica player Marianne Kirchgässner* announced performances of both Mozart's Adagio and Rondo K617 and Vanhal's new Variations on the duet 'Nel cor non più mi sento' from Paisiello*'s opera *La molinara*.

(Postolka[4])

Varesco, Giovanni Battista (probably baptized Trento, 26 November 1735; d. Salzburg, 29 August 1805). Court chaplain in Salzburg from 1766; librettist of *Idomeneo** and *L'oca del Cairo**. While he readily made the textual changes requested by Mozart for *Idomeneo*, he became dissatisfied with the fee he had agreed to. 'It suddenly struck me that Herr Varesco may have conceived the ungodly Italian idea that we had secured more favourable terms and were keeping the extra money,' Leopold Mozart wrote, on 4 January 1781, to Wolfgang who was then in Munich. He went on to speculate that Varesco might have formed that suspicion because he was half-Italian – which, he added, was even worse than being pure Italian. Or perhaps Varesco was judging them by his own character: 'It probably occurred to him that there might be other persons of the same type as himself.' In another letter, on 22 January, Leopold referred to him as a 'grasping, avaricious fool'.

The correspondence between Mozart and his father about *Idomeneo* shows clearly that Mozart, though considerably younger than Varesco, was the dominant partner in their artistic collaboration. That Mozart deliberately assumed that superior position is evident from his letter of 21 June 1783 concerning the story which Varesco had proposed for a new opera (*L'oca del Cairo*): 'I quite like the plot . . . But I consider it very insulting that Herr Varesco should express doubts about the likely success of the opera. I can assure him that his text will not please unless the music is good, for music is the most important factor in any opera. Therefore, if the opera is to be a success and he hopes to be rewarded accordingly, he must alter and recast the libretto as much and as frequently as I wish, and not follow his own ideas, for he has not the slightest knowledge or experience of the theatre.'

Varesco also wrote the libretto for Michael Haydn*'s opera *Andromeda e Perseo* (1787).

(Kramer)

Villeneuve, Luisa. Italian soprano; the original Dorabella (*Così fan tutte**). She was engaged in Vienna in 1789, having made her reputation at the Teatro San Moisè in Venice in 1787 and 1788, notably in Pietro Alessandro Guglielmi's operas *La cameriera di spirito* and *Le nozze disturbate* and in Martín y Soler*'s *Una cosa rara* and *L'arbore di Diana*. Her Viennese début as Amor in the latter opera, on 27 June 1789, was a triumph. The critic of the *Wiener Zeitung* wrote: 'Her charming appearance, her refined, expressive acting and her beautiful, stylish singing received the applause they merited.' Mozart composed three arias for her in 1789, the first to be sung in Domenico Cimarosa's *I due baroni di Rocca Azzurra* ('Alma grande e nobil core' K578), the others in Martín y Soler's *Il burbero di buon cuore* ('Chi sa, chi sa, qual sia' K582, and 'Vado, ma dove? oh Dei!' K583). These tailor-made vehicles for displaying Villeneuve's vocal accomplishments constitute a tribute to an exceptionally gifted singer, as does the music which Mozart wrote for Dorabella.

Several scholars (among them R. Angermüller, J. H. Eibl and O. Michtner) believe that she may have been a sister of Adriana Gabrieli*, who created Fiordiligi. If she was, then Da Ponte*'s description, in the libretto to *Così fan tutte*, of Dorabella and Fiordiligi as two sisters from Ferrara must have been a private joke. The two sopranos also appeared together in Guglielmi's *La pastorella nobile* on 24 May 1790. Villeneuve furthermore sang Donna Giovannina in Weigl*'s *La caffettiera bizzarra* on 15 September 1790. In his diary on 11 February 1791, Zinzendorf* mentioned the rumour that Leopold II* was in love with her. She appears to have left Vienna in 1791. In 1798 she sang Rosina in Anfossi*'s *Gli artigiani* in Rome.

(Angermüller[15], Eibl in *Mozart: Briefe*, Michtner)

Vitásek [Witassek, Wittassek, Wittaschek], **Jan (Matyáš Nepomuk) August** [Johann Matthias] (b. Hořín, near Mělník, 22 February 1770; d. Prague, 7 December 1839). Bohemian composer, pianist and teacher. He studied with Franz Xaver Duschek (*see* DUSCHEK, JOSEPHA) and through the Duscheks met Mozart, of whose music he became a notable interpreter. He played one of Mozart's piano concertos (perhaps K595) at a concert in Prague on 26 April 1791, and also performed at the Mozart memorial concert there on 13 June 1792. On 7 February 1794, again in Prague, he played the D minor Concerto K466 in Constanze*'s presence. She was herself a participant at yet another Mozart concert there on 15 November 1797 (*see also* CAMPI), at which Vitásek appeared as soloist in a 'grand and powerful concerto' by Mozart. For this latter occasion, he furthermore composed the music for a 'German scena' written by August Gottlieb Meissner (*see* MARIA LUISA), which, together with a chorus from *La clemenza di Tito**, was designed to celebrate the Peace of Campo Formio signed by Austria and France the previous month. Vitásek's other compositions included numerous sacred works, many songs and a melodrama, *David, oder Die Befreiung Israels*, which was produced in Prague in 1810.

From 1814 until his death Vitásek was choirmaster at St Vitus's Cathedral in Prague. In 1824 he was offered, but refused, the post of choirmaster at St Stephen's Cathedral in Vienna. In 1837 he was made an honorary member of the Gesellschaft der Musikfreunde in Vienna.

(Postolka[1], Simpson)

Vogler, Georg Joseph [Abbé Vogler] (b. Pleichach, near Würzburg, 15 June 1749; d. Darmstadt, 6 May 1814). German composer, organist, theorist and teacher. After studying theology and law, he became almoner at Karl Theodor*'s court at Mannheim in 1771, and soon afterwards court chaplain. He subsequently went to Italy for two years to study music at Bologna (with Padre Martini*), Padua, Venice and Rome. On his return to Mannheim in 1775 he was appointed vice-Kapellmeister. In 1776 he founded the 'Mannheim Tonschule', where he put into practice the musical theories which he expounded in *Tonwissenschaft und Tonsetz-kunst* (published that same year) and other writings. He did not accompany the court to Munich in 1778, but in 1784 he was named Kapellmeister there. From

1786 until 1797 he held a similar position in Stockholm. In 1807 he was appointed Kapellmeister and councillor for ecclesiastical affairs in Darmstadt at the court of Grand Duke Louis I of Hesse-Darmstadt (1753–1830).

Mozart met him shortly after arriving at Mannheim in 1777. 'Herr vice-Kapellmeister Vogler . . . is a wretched musical jester,' he wrote to his father on 4 November 1777. 'He is a very conceited but quite incompetent man.' Mozart was equally scathing about Vogler's theoretical studies: 'His book [*Tonwissenschaft . . .*] teaches one arithmetic rather than composition' (13 November). Nor was Mozart impressed by Vogler's performance on the organ: 'An unintelligible jumble . . . I would sooner watch him than listen to him' (18 December). And he was particularly incensed by Vogler's disparagement of the 'greatest masters', especially Johann Christian Bach*: 'I felt like grabbing him by the hair, but pretended not to have heard, said nothing and walked away' (13 November). In addition to church and instrumental music, Vogler wrote nine operas, which were generally unsuccessful. 'The music pleased me very little, for it gave the impression of having been composed by Herr Vogler in a paroxism of high fever,' Leopold Mozart reported to Nannerl* on 13 February 1787, after hearing *Castore e Polluce* in Munich.

In view of the small regard in which Mozart held Vogler, it is rather ironic that his son Franz Xaver Wolfgang* should later have received instruction in composition from him. It is still more ironic that the Munich opera company should have taken to replacing the final scene of *Don Giovanni** with the furies' chorus from the aforementioned *Castore e Polluce* (not until 1839 was the original ending restored). (Grave M. H., Reckziegel, Zenger)

Waldstätten, Martha Elisabeth, Baroness, *née* [?]von Schäffer (baptized Vienna, 5 January 1744; d. Klosterneuburg, near Vienna, 11 February 1811). She married Baron Hugo Joseph Dominik Waldstätten (1737–1800) on 3 August 1762, but was living apart from him in the Leopoldstadt district of Vienna when Mozart made her acquaintance in 1781. In April 1783 she bought a house at Klosterneuburg, where she had moved a few months earlier. Later her financial situation deteriorated and she was obliged to sell the house in 1803; she died in poverty. She had three sons: Dominik Joseph (b. 1765), Philipp Joseph (b. 1769), and Karl Borromäus (b. 1773).

The baroness was a generous friend to Mozart and Constanze*. In 1781 Mozart celebrated his name day, 31 October, at her house. Constanze stayed with her for a month that autumn, for a briefer period the following spring, and again shortly before her marriage. On the wedding-day, 4 August 1782, the baroness offered the newlyweds a supper which Mozart, in a letter to his father on 7 August, described as 'more princely than baronial'. She moreover corresponded with Leopold and tried to set his mind at rest about Constanze's suitability as a wife for Wolfgang. 'I am under a great obligation to the baroness . . . I should very much like to give her some pleasure,' Mozart wrote to his father on 31 August. Leopold obligingly dispatched four calves' (or ox) tongues, a Salzburg speciality. Later that same year, at Mozart's request, the baroness offered free board and lodging to his pupil Josepha Auernhammer*, who had lost her father a few months previously.

On 15 February 1783 Mozart appealed to her to pay a debt he owed and thereby help him 'not to lose my honour and my good name'. It may be assumed that she complied with this request also, for on 22 March he wrote expressing his profound gratitude for all her acts of kindness and friendship, and asked her to accept a box for his grand concert at the Burgtheater the next day. In 1784 she was among the subscribers to his Trattnerhof concerts (*see* TRATTNER); she was herself an excellent pianist and is believed to have taken lessons with Mozart. On 19 April 1785 he and Constanze, together with Leopold, who was on an extended visit to Vienna, dined with her at Klosterneuburg. 'I am eager to meet this *lady of my heart*, since even unseen, I have already become the *man of her heart*,' Leopold informed Nannerl* on 16 April, presumably citing an expression used by the baroness in one of her letters.

Mozart's own letters contained some references to her rather free lifestyle. After reproaching Constanze, in his letter of 29 April 1782, for permitting a man to measure her calves during a game of forfeits, he wrote: 'If it is true that the baroness allowed this to be done to her, that is a very different matter, for she is an older woman who cannot possibly attract any more – and, in any case, she is flirtatious by nature. I hope, dearest friend, that, even if you should not wish to become my wife, you will never lead a life like hers.' In a letter on 8 January 1783, in which Mozart warned his father not to join in discussions concerning the possible engagement by the baroness of the Salzburg court trumpeter Ignaz Fink (presumably as a music teacher), he again hinted at her promiscuity: 'Fink is quite unsuitable from her, for she wants someone for herself and not for her children – and then you must also understand that the words *herself – for herself* have rather a special meaning in this context. She has already had several persons of that kind in her house, but the arrangement never lasted very long . . . As a result, her reputation is none too good. She is weak. But I shall say no more, and the little I have said is for you only, for I have received very many kindnesses from her, and it is therefore my duty to defend her as far as possible, or at any rate to say nothing.'
(Briellmann, Schuler[13])

Walsegg-Stuppach, Franz, Count (b. 1763; d. Schloss Stuppach, near Wiener Neustadt, 11 November 1827). Wealthy estate-owner, passionately interested in music and the theatre. Every Tuesday and Thursday he arranged private chamber-music concerts at his house, at which he played the cello or flute; on Sundays there were theatricals. He also, through third parties, used to commission quartets which he then copied and passed off as his own works.

When his wife Anna (*née* von Flammberg) died on 14 February 1791, he ordered a memorial from the sculptor Johann Martin Fischer and, at the same time, commissioned – again through an intermediary (who did not disclose the count's name) – a Requiem from Mozart. The arrangements were probably made either by a clerk of his Viennese lawyer Johann Sortschan or by his business manager Franz Anton Leitgeb.

Eventually, some time after Mozart's death, Constanze* supplied a manuscript copy of the completed Requiem K626 (*see* EYBLER, and SÜSSMAYR) to Walsegg-Stuppach. He directed a performance of it at the Neukloster, a Cistercian monastery at Wiener Neustadt, on 14 December 1793, using a score which bore the title 'Requiem composto del Conte Walsegg'. Nevertheless David Humphreys, in *The Mozart Compendium*, characterizes Walsegg-Schuppach as 'a harmless crank rather than the villainous plagiarist depicted by 19th-century biographers of Mozart', and concludes that 'there is no reason to believe that he seriously intended to pass off

Mozart's Requiem as his own composition'. The Requiem had already received a public performance in Vienna on 2 January 1793 (*see* SWIETEN). Later Walsegg-Stuppach arranged it for string quintet.

(Biba, Deutsch[11], *Mozart Compendium*)

Walter, (Gabriel) Anton (b. Neuhausen an der Fildern, Swabia, 5 February 1752; d. Vienna, 11 April 1826). Prominent Viennese piano and organ manufacturer; son of Georg Walter (1713–1800), a joiner and organist. Little is known about Anton Walter's early life and career. On 27 January 1780, in Vienna, he married Anna Elisabeth Reisinger (d. 1818), the widow of Franz Schöffstoss. In 1796 Schönfeld, in his *Jahrbuch der Tonkunst von Wien und Prag*, called Walter and Streicher (*see* STEIN), the two most innovative piano makers in Vienna: 'All the rest copy either the one or the other; Walter especially has many imitators, since several makers were trained by him.' Schönfeld particularly recommended Walter's instruments to the virtuoso player (while he praised the Streicher piano especially for the pure, even and delicate nature of its tone). Beethoven* was among the musicians who used Walter's instruments. In the early 1800s the firm's name was changed to 'Walter und Sohn' – the 'son' referring presumably to Walter's stepson Georg Christoph Joseph Schöffstoss (b. 1767), for Walter had no sons of his own.

Mozart owned one of Walter's instruments, which he valued greatly and used in his concerts. 'Since I have been here,' Leopold Mozart wrote to Nannerl* from Vienna on 12 March 1785 (he had arrived on 11 February), 'your brother's fortepiano has been transported at least twelve times to the theatre or to some other house . . . Every Friday it is transported to the Mehlgrube, and it has also been taken to Count Zichy's and Prince Kaunitz's.' (In addition to various other engagements, Mozart was giving six weekly concerts at the Mehlgrube casino, starting on 11 February.) Constanze* tried unsuccessfully to sell this piano in 1793. In 1810 she sent it to her son Carl Thomas Mozart* in Milan. 'If you love it only half as much as I have done, you will never part with it,' she wrote on 7 May 1810. He did part with it, however, in 1856, when he presented it to the Mozarteum in Salzburg on the occasion of the centenary celebrations of his father's birth. The piano was restored in 1936–7 by the Nuremberg firm 'Pianohaus Wilhelm Rück' (but the special pedalboard attached by Mozart had been lost). The instrument stands today in the Mozart Museum at No. 9 Getreidegasse in Salzburg.

(Franz, Meisel/Belt[2], Rück, Schönfeld)

Weber [later Lange], **(Maria) Aloisia** [Aloysia] **Louisa Antonia** (b. Zell im Wiesental, *c*.1760; d. Salzburg, 8 June 1839). German soprano; daughter of Fridolin Weber* and Caecilia Weber*. The original Madame Herz (*Der Schauspieldirektor**), and Donna Anna in the first Viennese production of *Don Giovanni**.

When Mozart met Aloisia at Mannheim in late 1777, she was already an accomplished singer, well liked by the Elector Palatine Karl Theodor*. She also received some acting lessons from Theobald Hilarius Marchand (*see* MARCHAND). 'She sings most excellently,' Mozart wrote to his father on 17 January 1778, 'and has a beautiful, pure voice. All she lacks is dramatic force; once she acquires that, she could sing *prima donna* roles in any theatre.' In a note on 7 February he added that Aloisia's greatest merit was her 'superb cantabile singing'. At the end of January

Mozart and Aloisia, accompanied by Fridolin Weber, travelled to Kirchheim-bolanden to perform before Princess Caroline of Nassau-Weilburg (1743–87). On this occasion Aloisia sang two arias from Mozart's *Lucio Silla** and played the piano, for she was also a competent pianist (at a concert at Christian Cannabich*'s on 12 March 1778, she took the second part in the Triple Concerto κ242, and in December 1800 she played a sonata by Ignace Joseph Pleyel at a concert in Amsterdam).

Mozart coached Aloisia in several arias – and, at the same time, fell in love with her. Writing to his father on 4 February, he claimed that, under his tuition, she had made spectacular progress with her singing in a very short time; he was accordingly proposing to travel to Italy with her, her father and her sister Josepha, in order to establish her there as a leading operatic diva. Nothing came of this plan, however, Leopold having reacted to it 'with amazement and horror' in his letter of 11–12 February and forbidden the proposed journey.

From Paris Mozart wrote a long letter to Fridolin Weber on 29 July 1778, in which he discussed Aloisia's career prospects and suggested stratagems for inducing the elector to offer her an appointment. He also tried to get her an engagement at the Concert Spirituel for the coming winter, but without success (*see* LEGROS). However, later that summer Aloisia, whose singing had made an impression on Count Seeau*, was offered a well-paid post at Munich, as was her father, and the Webers moved there with the elector's court (*see* KARL THEODOR). Their new proximity to Salzburg was used by Leopold Mozart as a fresh argument in urging Wolfgang to return promptly to his duties in Archbishop Colloredo's service. He moreover assured Wolfgang that he was 'not in the least opposed' to his love for Aloisia: 'I was not against it when her father was poor,' he wrote on 23 November 1778, 'so why should I be so now, *when she can make your happiness* – even if you cannot make hers.' But when Wolfgang stayed with the Webers in Munich (25 December 1778 – mid-January 1779) on his return journey to Salzburg, he was rejected by Aloisia. 'Today I can do nothing but weep . . . My heart is too full of grief,' he wrote to his father on 29 December, without, however, revealing the cause of his unhappiness. The reasons for the rejection are not known. Perhaps Leopold had been justified in warning Wolfgang, in his letter of 23 November, that Fridolin Weber's future attitude might be affected by his change of fortune: 'He flattered you when he needed you – perhaps now he will not even admit that you ever showed or taught her anything. People who were poor are usually mighty proud when their fortunes improve.' That may also have been Aloisia's case.

In the autumn of 1779 the Webers moved to Vienna, where Aloisia had been given a contract with the German opera company, probably on the recommendation of Count Adam Franz Hartig (1724–83), the Austrian ambassador in Munich. She made a successful début on 9 September as Hännchen in *Das Rosenfest von Salency*, a Singspiel based on *La rosière de Salency* by François-André Philidor and others. Over the next thirteen years she appeared in both the German and Italian repertoires; her performances covered a wide range, from soubrettes to young lovers to highly dramatic roles. Her voice, though not considered very strong, was praised for its range and for its clarity, accuracy and affecting quality. In his *Jahrbuch der Tonkunst von Wien und Prag*, Schönfeld expressed great admiration for her brilliant technique, for the purity of her trills 'from the softest *piano* to the loudest *forte* and back to a dying piano'. Michael Kelly* wrote of her in his *Reminiscences*: 'She had a greater extent of high notes than any other singer I ever heard.' Her other roles at the Burgtheater included Zemire in André-Ernest-Modeste Grétry's *Zemire und Azor* [*Zémire et Azor*] (13 October 1779), Claudia in Beecke*'s *Claudine von Villa Bella* (13 June 1780), Rezia in Gluck*'s *Die Pilgrime von Mekka* (26 July 1780), Elena Belfiore in Domenico Cimarosa's *Il falegname* (25 July 1783), and Olivetta in Sarti*'s *Le gelosie villane* (17 October 1783). From October 1785 until February 1789 she appeared with the German opera company.

By the time Mozart arrived in Vienna in March 1781, Aloisia was married to the actor Joseph Lange*. The wedding had taken place on 31 October 1780; Aloisia was to bear her husband six children. 'I truly loved her,' Mozart wrote to his father on 16 May 1781, 'and I feel that I am still not indifferent to her; fortunately for me, her husband is a jealous fool who does not let her out of his sight, so that I have few opportunities of seeing her.' It is true that in a letter to Leopold on 15 December 1781 he accused her of being 'a false, malicious woman and a coquette', but he appears to have been influenced against Aloisia by her own mother at that time, and, in any case, wished to convince his father of Constanze*'s moral superiority over her sisters. After their marriage the Mozarts maintained friendly relations with the Langes, and Mozart collaborated with Aloisia professionally on various occasions.

Apart from the music in *Der Schauspieldirektor*, Mozart wrote the following arias for her: *Alcandro, lo confesso . . . Non so d'onde viene* K294, in 1778 (*see* BACH); *Popoli di Tessaglia . . . Io non chiedo, eterni Dei* K316/300b, which he presented to her on 9 January 1779 in Munich ('I have written it solely for her and [it] fits her like a tailor-made dress,' he had assured his father on 3 December 1778); *Nehmt meinen Dank, ihr holden Gönner* K383, in 1782; *Mia speranza adorata . . . Ah, non sai qual pena sia* K416, 'Vorrei spiegarvi, oh Dio' K418, 'No, che non sei capace' K419, all in 1783; and the revised version of *Ah se in ciel, benigne stelle* K538, in 1788.

In addition to taking the aforementioned roles in *Der Schauspieldirektor* and *Don Giovanni*, Aloisia replaced Cavalieri* as Konstanze (*Die Entführung**) in Vienna, and she sang the same role in Hamburg and perhaps also in Berlin in 1789. She furthermore took part in the first performance of Mozart's re-orchestrated version of Handel*'s *Messiah* K572 on 6 March 1789, and probably also in the first performance of his arrangements of *Alexander's Feast* K591 and the *Ode for St Cecilia's Day* K592 in 1790. At two concert performances in Vienna of *La clemenza di Tito**, on 29 December 1794 and 31 March 1795, she sang Sesto.

In 1795 she separated from her husband, and subsequently undertook a concert tour with Constanze through Germany. In 1797 she sang in Hamburg, in 1798 and 1800–01 in Amsterdam, in 1801 in Paris, in 1802 in Frankfurt. From 1813 to 1819 she lived in Zurich, where she was in great demand as a singing teacher. She subsequently resided in Vienna until 1831. Mary Novello (*see* NOVELLO) met her there in 1829 and thought her 'a very pleasant woman but broken by misfortune – she is parted from her husband who allows her so little that she is obliged to give lessons which at her age she finds a great hardship'. Aloisia claimed that 'Mozart always loved her until the day of his death, which to speak candidly she fears had occasioned a slight jealousy on the part of her sister [i.e. Constanze]'.

Since the annual allowance which Lange had made her ceased at his death on 17 September 1831, she applied for and was granted the small government pension due to former members of the court theatre. That same year she moved to Salzburg, where her sisters Constanze and Sophie Haibel* were living. She died in great poverty. (*See also* TAUX.)

(Eibl[1], Kelly, Michtner, Novello, Schönfeld, Schuler[7])

Weber, (Maria) Caecilia, *née* Stamm (b. Mannheim, 1727; d. Vienna, 22 August 1793). Mozart's mother-in-law. Daughter of Johann Otto Stamm, a senior official in the Elector Palatine's service, and of his wife Sophie Elisabeth, *née* Wimmer. She married Fridolin Weber* at Freiburg on 4 September 1756. (For information on the life of the Webers and their contacts with Mozart prior to 1781, see WEBER, ALOISIA and WEBER, FRIDOLIN.)

When Mozart arrived in Vienna in March 1781, Caecilia Weber was a widow living with her two youngest daughters, and taking in lodgers to make ends meet. In early May Mozart, having been ordered to leave the House of the Teutonic Order (*see* COLLOREDO), gladly accepted her offer of a room. 'Believe me, old Madame Weber is a most obliging woman,' he wrote on 16 May to his father, who at once suspected her motives and repeatedly urged Wolfgang to find different lodgings. In Leopold's eyes – as indeed in the opinion of many modern writers – 'old Madame Weber' was an unprincipled, if not downright immoral, woman scheming to secure a husband for Constanze*. Mozart refused to see her in that light, even after Constanze's guardian Thorwart* had forced him to give a written undertaking either to marry Constanze within three years or pay her compensation: 'Madame Weber is no longer her own mistress and is obliged to leave particularly matters of this kind entirely to the guardian . . .' he explained to his father on 16 January 1782. 'Certainly Herr von Thorwart was at fault – but not so grievously that he and Madame Weber deserve to be clapped in irons and made to sweep the streets, with signs bearing the words "Seducers of youth" hung around their necks . . . Even if what you write were true, namely that to catch me she threw her house open to me, gave me a free run of it, put all possible opportunities in my way, etc., that would still be excessive punishment. But I need hardly tell you that you are mistaken.'

There is, however, evidence in Mozart's letters that Caecilia Weber became increasingly impatient to see the marriage concluded, and that her attitude was causing friction between Constanze and herself. 'My reason for not wishing to wait much longer is not just on my own account, but above all on Constanze's,' Mozart wrote to his father on 23 January 1782. 'I must rescue her as soon as possible.' They had no intention of falling in with her mother's wish that they should live in her apartment after the wedding, he informed Leopold a week later, adding: 'On the contrary, Constanze plans to visit her mother as rarely as possible, and I shall do my best to ensure that she does not do so at all.' To Nannerl* he wrote on 13 February: 'Our pleasure at seeing each other is largely spoiled by her mother's bitter tirades . . . hence my desire to free and rescue her as soon as possible.' More explicit still is his letter of 27 July, in which he besought his father to give his consent without delay: 'Most people think we are already married. This incenses her mother, and the poor girl and myself are being tormented to death.' On 31 August, four weeks after the marriage, Mozart wrote to his father: 'I don't know how you could ever have imagined that my highly esteemed mother-in-law might come to live with us. I did not marry my bride so quickly in order to lead a life of unpleasantness and disputes, but to enjoy peace and happiness. The only way to achieve this was to get away from her mother. We have visited her twice since our wedding. On the second occasion the arguing and bickering started all over again, and my poor wife began to cry. I quickly put an end to the quarrel by saying that it was time for us to leave. Since then we have not been back, nor do we intend to go except on her mother's or sisters' birthdays or name days.'

Very little is known about Mozart's and Constanze's relations with her mother over the next nine years, other than that, following the birth of their first child, he wrote to his father on 18 June 1783: 'My mother-in-law, by her present kindness, makes up for all the unhappiness she inflicted on her daughter before her marriage.' In describing the final period of Mozart's life, Sophie Haibel* recalled, in her letter to Constanze and Nissen* of 7 April 1825, that he had become increasingly fond of his mother-in-law and she of him, and that he had frequently visted her and Sophie at their lodgings in the suburb of Wieden, each time bringing coffee or some other small gift to please her. On 13 October 1791 (perhaps also already on 9 October) Mozart took his mother-in-law to a performance of *Die Zauberflöte**.
(Blümml)

Weber [later Mozart, then Nissen], **(Maria) Constanze (Caecilia Josepha Johanna Aloisia)** (b. Zell im Wiesental, 5 January 1762; d. Salzburg, 6 March 1842). Soprano; wife of Mozart, and later of Georg Nikolaus Nissen*. Daughter of Fridolin Weber* and Caecilia Weber*.

When Mozart first knew her at Mannheim in 1777–8, she was about sixteen. At that time he had eyes (and ears) only for her sister Aloisia Weber*, and he did not mention Constanze in his letters. It was not until he became Caecilia Weber's lodger in Vienna in May 1781 – by which time Aloisia was married – that he was attracted to Constanze and, propelled towards an early wedding by her mother and her guardian, Johann von Thorwart*, he married her on 4 August 1782 at St Stephen's Cathedral. The match does not appear to have pleased his father greatly. He did not make Constanze's acquaintance until summer 1783, when she and Wolfgang arrived in Salzburg on a three months' visit. While there, she sang one of the soprano parts in a performance of Wolfgang's (uncompleted) Mass in C minor K427/417a at St Peter's Abbey on 26 October. In 1785 Leopold stayed with Wolfgang and Constanze in Vienna for some ten weeks (11 February – 25 April).

Constanze bore Mozart six children: Raimund Leopold*, Carl Thomas*, Johann Thomas Leopold*, Theresia Constanzia Adelheid Friederike Maria Anna*, Anna Maria*, and Franz Xaver Wolfgang*; only Carl Thomas and Franz Xaver reached adulthood. Everything suggests that Mozart loved Constanze and was happy with her. Michael Kelly*, who knew them quite well, referred to her in his *Reminiscences* as 'a German lady of whom [Mozart] was passionately fond'. Mozart's letters, both to his father and to Constanze herself, certainly bear this out. Attention has been drawn to two letters, one written on 29 April 1782, i.e. before their marriage (*see* WALDSTÄTTEN), the other in August 1789, in which he reproved her for behaving without due discretion; but the mere fact that she preserved these letters surely indicates that the 'indiscretions' were of a trivial nature.

The following passages from letters addressed by Mozart to Constanze in the summer of 1791 when she was staying at Baden are typical in their affectionate tone:

Weber, Fridolin

'At five o'clock tomorrow morning we shall drive out in our three carriages, so between nine and ten I expect to feel in your arms all the joy which a man who loves his wife as I do is capable of feeling' (7 June); 'You can give me no greater pleasure than by being merry and in good spirits, for if I *know for certain* that *you* lack for nothing, then all my troubles are a joy and delight for me. The most wretched and difficult situation in which I could possibly find myself becomes of little importance if I know that you *are well* and *in good spirits*' (6 July); 'The time, the happy time of our reunion is drawing ever nearer' (9 July).

Following Mozart's death, Constanze petitioned Leopold II* on 11 December 1791 for a pension. His successor, Francis II, awarded her on 13 March 1792 an annual sum of some 266 gulden, starting that year. Over the next decade, she succeeded in improving the dire financial situation in which Mozart had left her. She arranged performances of his works (including several concert performances of *La clemenza di Tito**), and undertook a concert tour in Germany in 1795–6, together with her sister Aloisia Lange and the Viennese pianist and composer Anton Eberl (who, in 1791, had written a cantata *Bey Mozarts Grabe*). At her request, the Abbé Maximilian Stadler* examined Mozart's manuscripts, with the assistance of the Danish diplomat Georg Nikolaus Nissen*; the latter was living at the same address as Constanze in Vienna by September 1798, although they did not marry until 26 June 1809 in Pressburg [Bratislava]. She subsequently sold many of these manuscripts to Johann Anton André* and also corresponded with the Leipzig music publishers Breitkopf & Härtel*. She was increasingly helped in her business affairs by Nissen. From 1810 to 1821 he and Constanze lived in Copenhagen, but after his retirement they settled in Salzburg where he worked on his biography of Mozart. After his death, she arranged for its completion by J. H. Feuerstein (*see* NISSEN).

Mary Novello (*see* NOVELLO) wrote in her diary after meeting Constanze in 1829: 'She speaks French fluently though with a German accent, in Italian she thinks better . . . She is indeed completely a well bred Lady, and though no remains of beauty appear except in her eyes . . . yet she keeps her figure and a certain air, well, for a woman of her age.' The Novellos called on Constanze once more in April 1838 while on their way to Italy. 'We found her still looking cheerful and well, although she must be nearly eighty,' Mary Novello recorded in her diary. In fact, Constanze was then seventy-six years old. She died four years later, six months before Mozart's statue was unveiled in Salzburg, close to the house where she had resided (*see* SCHWANTHALER).

(Kelly, Landon², Novello)

Weber, (Franz) Fridolin (b. ?Zell im Wiesental, 1733; d. Vienna, 23 October 1779). Son of Fridolin Weber (1691–1754), who is believed to have been a singer, violinist and organist, and of Maria Eva Weber, *née* Schlar (1698–1776); his younger brother Franz Anton (1734–1812), a professional musician, was the father of the composer Carl Maria von Weber.

From 1750 to 1752 Fridolin Weber studied law at Freiburg University. Between 1754 and 1763 he was employed as a government official at Zell im Wiesental. On 4 September 1756, at Freiburg, he married Caecilia Stamm (*see* WEBER, CAECILIA). Later he settled in Mannheim, his wife's native city, where he earned his living as a bass, *souffleur* and music copyist at the court theatre. When Mozart made the

Webers' acquaintance in Mannheim in late 1777, they had four daughters (Josepha*, Aloisia*, Constanze*, Sophie*) and a son, Johann Nepomuk (1760–?80); two other sons died in infancy.

Weber and Aloisia are first mentioned in Mozart's correspondence on 17 January 1778. From 23 January to 2 February he travelled with them, first to Kirchheimbolanden, where he and Aloisia performed before Princess Caroline of Nassau-Weilburg, and then to Worms to visit Weber's brother-in-law, Father Dagobert Joseph Benedikt Stamm, who was dean at the cathedral. 'When I travel with [Weber], it is as if I was travelling with you,' Mozart wrote to his father on 4 February. 'That is why I like him so much – because, appearance apart, he is just like you, with the same character and way of thinking.' Since Mozart was then seeking – as it turned out, unsuccessfully – Leopold's approval for a trip to Italy with Aloisia and Weber, he was probably exaggerating in thus portraying the latter as a suitable moral substitute for his father. But he seems to have been genuinely fond of Weber, and not simply pretending because he had fallen in love with Aloisia; certainly his only extant letter to Weber, sent from Paris on 29 July 1778, is an affectionate one: it is addressed to 'Monsieur mon très cher et plus cher ami'. The Webers, for their part, were at that time still highly appreciative of the interest which Mozart took in Aloisia's career. 'They thanked me again and again, and said they only wished that they were in a position to show their gratitude,' he recalled in his letter to his father of 24 March 1778, describing his last visit to the family on the eve of his departure for Paris. 'When I left, they all wept.'

The Webers' life, which had been beset by poverty and debts, took a decisive turn for the better later that year, when both Aloisia and her father were offered good contracts in Munich. The family moved there with the Mannheim court (see KARL THEODOR). In the autumn of 1779 they left Munich for Vienna, where Aloisia had accepted an engagement with the German opera company. Shortly after their arrival Fridolin Weber died.

(For further details concerning the Webers and their contacts with Mozart, see the separate entries for WEBER, CAECILIA and the four daughters.)

Weber [later Hofer, then Mayer], (Maria) Josepha (b. c.1759, Zell im Wiesental; d. Vienna, 29 December 1819). German soprano; the original Queen of Night (*Die Zauberflöte**). Daughter of Fridolin Weber* and Caecilia Weber*. On 15 December 1781, in a letter to his father (in which he sought to show Constanze*'s superiority over her sisters), Mozart described Josepha as 'a lazy, coarse and false woman, as cunning as a fox'. On 21 July 1788 she married his friend, the violinist Franz de Paula Hofer*.

Josepha studied singing with the composer and Kapellmeister Vincenzo Righini (1756–1812) in Vienna. In 1784 Mozart tried (unsuccessfully) to obtain an engagement for her in Munich (see MARCHAND). On 24 January 1789 she appeared at the Freihaus-Theater in *Die eingebildeten Philosophen*, a German version of Paisiello*'s *I filosofi immaginari*. She stayed with the company after it had been taken over by Schikaneder* in the spring of that year. In September 1789 Mozart wrote the aria 'Schon lacht der holde Frühling' K580 for her to sing in a German version (by G. F. W. Grossmann) of Paisiello's *Il barbiere di Siviglia*; however, the proposed performance does not appear to have taken place (*Der Barbier von Sevilla* was not given at the Freihaus-Theater until 1796).

Weber, Sophie

Josepha remained a member of Schikaneder's company until 1805, first at the Freihaus-Theater and, from June 1801, at the Theater an der Wien. During this period she sang several other Mozart roles, in addition to her numerous appearances as the Queen of Night: Donna Laura in *Don Juan*, Christian Heinrich Spiess's German version of *Don Giovanni** (5 November 1792); the Countess in *Die Hochzeit des Figaro*, in Karl Ludwig Gieseke**'s translation of *Le nozze di Figaro** (28 December 1792); Leonore in *Die Schule der Liebe, oder So machen sie's alle!*, Gieseke's German version of *Così fan tutte** (14 August 1794); Konstanze in *Die Entführung** (6 September 1794); and Madame Herz in *Der Schauspieldirektor** (5 August 1797). She also appeared as the Queen of Night at the première of Peter von Winter's *Das Labyrinth, oder Der Kampf mit den Elementen* (see SCHIKANEDER) on 12 June 1798, and she sang the role in thirty-four more performances of the opera that year.

Following Hofer's death (14 June 1796), she married, on 23 December 1797, the actor and singer Friedrich Sebastian Mayer (1773–1835), who was likewise a member of the Freihaus-Theater company; he had appeared there as Sarastro (*Die Zauberflöte*) since 1793, and as Pasha Selim (*Die Entführung*) since 1794. On 8 September 1798 they sang Servilia and Publius in a concert performance of *La clemenza di Tito**, which Constanze put on at the Freihaus-Theater. They repeated these roles at a further performance on 25 March 1799, again at the Freihaus-Theater. At the première of *Fidelio*, conducted by Beethoven* at the Theater an der Wien on 20 November 1805, Mayer sang Pizarro.

Josepha (b. 29 August 1790), a daughter from Josepha Weber's marriage to Franz de Paula Hofer, was herself later engaged at the Theater an der Wien (after her marriage to Karl Hönig in 1813, she adopted the stage-name 'Hofer-Hönig'). She was also a pianist; at the aforementioned performance of *La clemenza di Tito* on 25 March 1799 she played a concerto by Franz Anton Hoffmeister* between the two acts of the opera.

(Blümml)

Weber [later Haibel], **Sophie** (b. ?1763; d. Salzburg, 26 October 1846). Daughter of Fridolin Weber* and Caecilia Weber*. She was the only one of Constanze*'s sisters present at her wedding to Mozart. According to J. H. Eybl, Sophie was engaged at the Burgtheater for the 1780–81 season and made her début as Röschen in the rustic comedy *Der Bettler* by Johann Christian Bock (1750–85).

On 7 January 1807, at Djakovar [Dakovo] in Slavonia, she married Jakob Haibel (1762–1826), who had been a comic actor, tenor and composer with Schikaneder*'s company at the Freihaus-Theater in Vienna. His most successful work was the Singspiel *Der Tiroler Wastel* (text by Schikaneder) which, between 1796 and 1801, received no fewer than 118 performances at the Freihaus-Theater alone. After the death of his first wife Katharina (*c*.1768–1806) he accepted the post of choirmaster of Djakovar Cathedral. He died at Djakovar on 27 [?24 or ?25] March 1826. Shortly afterwards Sophie joined the recently widowed Constanze in Salzburg, and the two sisters lived together until Constanze's death in 1742. (*See also* TAUX.)

On 7 April 1825 Sophie sent a long letter to Nissen* and Constanze which dealt mainly with Mozart's last illness and death. Her recollections, evidently written in

response to a request from Nissen, who was preparing a biography of Mozart, constitute the most detailed extant account of Mozart's final hours. In August 1829 Sophie told Vincent Novello* that only she, Constanze and Dr Closset* had been present at Mozart's death, and that she had held him in her arms as he died.
(Eibl in *Mozart: Briefe*, Novello)

Weidmann, Joseph (b. Vienna, 24 August 1742; d. Vienna, 16 September 1810). Actor, singer and librettist; he played Puf (or perhaps Herz) at the première of *Der Schauspieldirektor**.

Weidmann started out as a dancer at Brünn [Brno] in 1757 before turning to acting, and then performed with various companies in Linz, Salzburg (1764), Prague (1765), Linz again (1766–71) and Graz (1772). In 1773 he was engaged at the Burgtheater, Vienna, where he made his début as Chevalier Arnold in *Pamela* (a German version by Friedrich Wilhelm Weiskern* of Goldoni's *Pamela fanciulla*). He was to remain a member of the company for thirty-seven years. During that time, he became one of the most admired of Viennese actors. He played a wide range of characters, but excelled particularly in comic parts, especially those written in Viennese dialect; he also appeared in small singing roles. One of his greatest successes was as Maler Schwindel in Gluck*'s *Die Pilgrime von Mekka*. In addition, he wrote Singspiel librettos, notably *Die Bergknappen*, which, with music by Umlauf*, was the first work performed by the newly established German opera company, on 17 February 1778. His brother Paul (1746–1810) was the author of a number of tragedies and comedies; some of the latter contained roles tailor-made for Joseph Weidmann's talents.

Joseph's son Franz Karl Weidmann (?1787–1867) became a successful playwright.
(Fränkel, Michtner, Zechmeister)

Weigl, Joseph (b. Eisenstadt, 28 March 1766; d. Vienna, 3 February 1846). Austrian composer and Kapellmeister. His father, the cellist Joseph (Franz) Weigl (1740–1820), and his mother, the soprano (Anna Maria) Josepha Weigl, *née* Scheffstoss, were employed at the Esterházy court at Eisenstadt and Eszterháza until 1769, when they were offered engagements in Vienna: Joseph became principal cellist at the Kärntnertor-Theater, while his wife was given a contract at the Burgtheater. While at Eisenstadt, she had sung at the premières of Joseph Haydn*'s operas *Acide* II XXVIII:1 and *La canterina* II XXVIII:2. In Vienna she appeared in the title role in the 1770 production of Gluck*'s *Alceste*.

Joseph Weigl Jr., who had Haydn for his godfather, studied law, but soon switched to a career in music. His acquaintance with the president of the Education and Censorship Commission, Baron van Swieten*, led to his participation in the regular Sunday concerts at the latter's apartment. 'No one can imagine such delight . . . ' he later wrote in his autobiography. 'To hear Mozart play the most difficult scores with his own incomparable skill, and at the same sing and correct the mistakes of the others, could only fill one with the greatest admiration.'

The first of Weigl's more than thirty operas, *Die unnütze Vorsicht, oder Die betrogene Arglist* (written for a marionette theatre), was produced at the Burgtheater in 1783; he was to achieve his greatest success with the Singspiel *Die Schweizerfamilie* in

1809. He also composed music for several ballets (*Pigmalione, Alonso e Cora, Alcina*), as well as numerous cantatas; in August 1791, at Eszterháza, he conducted his new cantata *Venere ed Adone* (*see* CLEMENZA DI TITO, LA). In addition, he composed several sacred works.

Weigl was introduced into the court opera orchestra by his teacher Salieri* in 1785. He became deputy Kapellmeister at the court theatre in 1790 and Kapellmeister in 1792. In 1804 he was appointed director of music for both German and Italian opera. In his memoirs Weigl claimed to have accompanied 'to Mozart's satisfaction' at all rehearsals of *Le nozze di Figaro** and of the Viennese production of *Don Giovanni**; he may also have directed rehearsals of *Così fan tutte**. He took over the conducting of *Figaro* from Mozart after the first two (or three) performances.

In 1802 Weigl married Elisabeth Bertier, a maidservant at the court, by whom he had three children.

(Angermüller[9])

Weiser, Ignaz Anton von (b. Salzburg, 1 March 1701; d. Salzburg, 26 December 1785). Owner of a flourishing textile store in Salzburg; ennobled in 1747. He was a member of the Salzburg city council from 1749, and mayor from 1772 until 1775, when he resigned following a dispute with Archbishop Colloredo* over financial matters.

Weiser was a half-brother of Johann Lorenz Hagenauer*'s wife. His own wife Martha Theresia, *née* Brentano, was a native of Augsburg, like Leopold Mozart. His contacts with the latter went back at least to 1741; it was perhaps Weiser who arranged for the newlywed Mozarts to rent an apartment in Hagenauer's house in the Getreidegasse in 1747. Through the marriage of his daughter Maria Domenica Columbia to the Prague pharmacist Adalbert Hambacher, he was the grandfather of the singer Josepha Duschek*. It was during a visit to Salzburg in August 1777 that the Duscheks made the acquaintance of the Mozart family. In 1787 Leopold Mozart gave music lessons to Maria Anna, a daughter of Weiser's son Franz Xaver Andreas Athanasius Weiser (1739–1817).

Weiser was the author of several minor works, notably the text of Leopold's cantatas *Christus begraben* (1741) and *Christus verurteilt* (1743); the libretto for the sacred Singspiel *Die Schuldigkeit des ersten Gebots**; and a German verse paraphrase of a poem composed in Wolfgang's honour, partly in Latin and partly in Italian, by Antonio Maria Meschini at Verona in January 1770 ('Amadeo Mozart dulcissimo puero et elegantissimo lyristae . . .').

Weiskern, Friedrich Wilhelm (b. Saxony, 1710; d. Vienna, 29 December 1768). Actor and translator. Son of a Swabian cavalry officer. He arrived in Vienna in 1734 and began his acting career by playing minor character parts, but he gradually expanded his repertoire and eventually became a great favourite with audiences; he was particularly successful in improvised comedy. In 1764 he translated, together with J. H. F. Müller*, the libretto of *Les amours de Bastien et Bastienne* (*see* BASTIEN UND BASTIENNE).

(Zechmeister)

Wendling, Dorothea, *née* Spurni (b. Stuttgart, 21 March 1736; d. Munich, 20

August 1811). German soprano; the original Ilia (*Idomeneo**). Daughter of the horn
player Franz Spurni and the lutenist Maria Dorothea Spurni. She was appointed a
court singer at Mannheim in 1752, and that same year married the flautist Johann
Baptist Wendling*. She moved to Munich some time after Karl Theodor* became
Elector of Bavaria. In later years she devoted herself entirely to teaching; her pupils
included her daughter Elisabeth Augusta ['Gustl'] Wendling* and her niece
Dorothea (*see* WENDLING, ELISABETH AUGUSTA ['LISL.']). The poet and novelist
Christoph Martin Wieland (1733–1813) wrote to Sophie von La Roche in 1777:
'Her manner of singing surpasses anything I have ever heard, even from the famous
[Gertrud] Mara. This alone is true singing – the language of the soul and the heart.'
Mozart also wrote for her the scena *Basta, vincesti . . . Ah, non lasciarmi, no* K486a/
295a in 1778.
(Würtz[5])

Wendling, Elisabeth Augusta ['Gustl'] (b. Mannheim, 4 October 1752; d.
Munich, 18 February 1794). German soprano. Daughter of the flautist Johann
Baptist Wendling* and the soprano Dorothea Wendling*. She studied singing with
her mother, and by 1769 was performing in public at Mannheim. 'The daughter,
who was at one time the mistress of the Elector [Karl Theodor*], plays the piano
very nicely,' Mozart wrote to his father from Mannheim on 8 November 1777.
'Then I played myself . . . They were all so pleased that I had to kiss the ladies. This
was no hardship in the daughter's case, for she is quite attractive.' Mozart's mother*
informed Leopold on 20 November 1777 that Elisabeth was 'very beautiful' and that
'the Bach in England' [i.e. Johann Christian Bach*] had wanted to marry her.
Mozart set two poems to music for her: 'Oiseaux, si tous les ans' by Antoine Ferrand
K307/284d and 'Dans un bois solitaire' by Antoine Houdar de La Motte K308/
295b.
    Later she sang in Munich, where her début on 13 November 1784 as Julie in
Georg Benda's *Romeo und Julie* was a spectacular success. In October 1785 Leopold
reported to Nannerl* that she had become the mistress of Count Seeau*.
(Würtz[8])

Wendling, Elisabeth Augusta ['Lisl'], *née* Sarselli (b. Mannheim, 20 February
1746; d. Munich, 10 January 1786). German soprano; the original Elettra
(*Idomeneo**). Daughter of the tenor Pietro Sarselli, who was a member of the
Mannheim court opera from 1745 until 1767, and of his wife Carolina, *née*
Volvasori, who also sang there from 1747 to 1752. She herself joined the company in
1761. In 1764 she married the violinist Franz Anton Wendling (1729–86), who had
been playing in the Mannheim orchestra since 1755. (He was a brother of the
flautist Johann Baptist Wendling*.) Mozart heard her sing in Ignaz Jakob
Holzbauer*'s opera *Günther von Schwarzburg* on 5 November 1777, in a role which,
he wrote to his father on 14 November, was 'not right for her voice'. The following
year she and her husband moved with the court to Munich (*see* KARL THEODOR).
Her last appearance there was probably as Zelmira in Alessio Prati's *Armida
abbandonata* in 1785.
    A. Einstein conjectured that Mozart had written the scena *Ma che vi fece, o stelle, la
povera Dircea . . . Sperai vicino il lido* K368 for her in Munich in 1780–81, after

completing *Idomeneo*. However, more recently, W. Plath has ascribed its composition to the years 1779–80, in Salzburg.

Lisl's daughter Dorothea (1767–1839) studied singing with Dorothea Wendling*, and was appointed *virtuosa da camera* in Munich in June 1788. She later married Johann Melchior Güthe (1753–1812), a physician.
(Einstein, Plath[1], Würtz[6,7])

Wendling, Johann Baptist (b. Rappoltsweiler, Alsace, 17 June 1723; d. Munich, 27 June 1797). German flautist and composer. From 1747 to 1750 he played in the Zweibrücken court orchestra. In 1751 he joined the court orchestra in Mannheim, where he also taught the Elector Karl Theodor*. In 1778 he moved with the court to Munich.

He was a highly accomplished performer. 'I had the pleasure of hearing, in addition to several good singers, an admirable flautist, Herr Wendling,' Leopold Mozart wrote to Hagenauer* from Schwetzingen on 19 July 1763. Wendling's reputation transcended the confines of the elector's court. On 6 April 1772 he took part in the first performance of Johann Christian Bach*'s cantata *Endimione* at the King's Theatre, London; he also gave concerts in Vienna, Prague and Paris. He himself composed several concertos and much chamber music, all featuring the flute.

Wendling's wife Dorothea* (the original Ilia in *Idomeneo*) and his daughter Elisabeth Augusta [Gustl]* were well-known sopranos. His brother Franz Anton (1729–86) was a violinist with the Mannheim and, from 1778, the Munich orchestra. Franz Anton's own wife Elisabeth Augusta [Lisl]* (the original Elettra) and his daughter Dorothea were also successful singers.

When Mozart was seven he met the Wendlings briefly in July 1763 at Schwetzingen, the elector palatine's summer residence. He came to know the family much better during his stay at Mannheim in 1777–8, when he was regularly invited to their midday meal. Wendling moreover proposed that he and Mozart, together with the oboist Friedrich Ramm* and the ballet-master Etienne Lauchéry (1732–1820), should travel to Paris during Lent 1778; there, he assured Mozart, he would find ample opportunities for his talents. Mozart's original enthusiasm for this journey eventually waned, as did his warm feelings for the Wendlings: 'My mother* and I have discussed the matter,' he wrote to his father on 4 February 1778, 'and we are agreed that we do not like the life the Wendlings lead. He is a thoroughly honest and very decent fellow, but he has no religion whatsoever, and neither has the rest of the family . . . Ramm is a good enough fellow, but he is a libertine . . . I am horrified at the mere thought of being, if only during the journey, in the company of people whose way of thinking is so fundamentally different from my own and that of all honest persons.' Although Mozart's mother attributed his changed attitude mainly to the influence of his new friends, the Webers (*see* WEBER, FRIDOLIN), she genuinely deplored the fact that Wendling's wife and daughter 'do not go to church from one end of the year to the other, never go to confession or hear mass', and she confided to Leopold, in her letter of 22 February, that 'I prayed every day that God might prevent this journey'. In the end, Wendling and Ramm left on 15 February, and Mozart and his mother followed on 14 March.

In Paris Wendling lived up to their belief in his innate goodness: 'Herr Wendling

made a great reputation for [Wolfgang] before we even arrived here,' Mozart's mother wrote to Leopold on 5 April, 'and he has now introduced him to his friends. He really is full of kindness towards his fellow men.' While in Paris, Mozart composed the Sinfonia Concertante KAnh.9/297B for Wendling, Punto*, Ramm and Ritter* (see LEGROS). Mozart last met Wendling and his wife in Frankfurt in the autumn of 1790.
(Terry, Würtz[9])

Wetzlar von Plankenstern, Raimund, Baron (b. 1752; d. Grünberg, 29 September 1810). Son of the wealthy merchant and banker Karl Abraham Wetzlar von Plankenstern (1715–[?16]–99), a native of Offenbach am Main who converted from Judaism to Catholicism in 1777 and was later ennobled.

Baron Raimund Wetzlar was married to Maria Theresia, *née* Calmer [Balmer] de Piquenay (d. Vienna, 20 or 21 April 1793). From December 1782 until late February 1783 he was Mozart's and Constanze*'s landlord at the 'Little Herberstein House' (then owned by Count Joseph Herberstein) on the Hohe Brücke in Vienna. Not only did he not charge the Mozarts any rent, but when he needed the rooms for another person, he even paid their removal expenses to temporary lodgings on the Kohlmarkt, as well as their rent there. Understandably, Mozart referred to him, in letters to his father on 21 May and 18 June 1783, as an 'honest' and a 'good and true' friend. Wetzlar became, at his own request, godfather to Mozart's first child, whose first name was accordingly Raimund (the second, Leopold, was of course chosen in honour of his grandfather). At the christening at the Am Hof church, Philipp Martin stood proxy for the baron.

Both Baron Wetzlar and his father were among the subscribers to Mozart's Trattnerhof concerts in March 1784 (see TRATTNER), as was his sister Baroness Regina Josepha Aichelburg (1757–1813). According to Da Ponte*'s memoirs, he first met Mozart at Baron Wetzlar's. In 1798 Wetzlar's summer villa, near the Meidling Gate, was to be the scene of several piano contests between Beethoven* and the Austrian pianist and composer Joseph Wölfl (1773–1812), whom Wetzlar greatly admired. According to Schönfeld, Wetzlar was himself a fine guitarist.
(Da Ponte, Schönfeld)

Widl, Rufinus (b. Frauenwörth Island in the Chiemsee, 26 September 1731; d. Obing, near Seeon, 12 March 1798). Author of the text of *Apollo et Hyacinthus**, the 'interludium' which Mozart set to music in 1767. A Benedictine of Seeon Abbey, he taught philosophy at Freising before becoming a teacher at the Gymnasium in Salzburg in 1763. In 1770 he was appointed prior of Seeon Abbey. At the time of his death he was parish priest at Obing.

Willmann, (Maximiliana Valentina) Walburga (b. Bonn, 18 May 1769; d. Mainz, 27 June 1835). Pianist; said to have been a pupil of Mozart. She was a member of a notable family of musicians and singers. Her father, (Johann) Ignaz Willmann (1739–1815), a competent performer on the flute, violin and cello, entered the Elector of Cologne's service at Bonn in 1767, and later held appointments at Brünn [Brno], Kassel (where, from 1805 until 1808, he was director and conductor of the court theatre) and elsewhere. Another daughter,

Winter, Felix

(Johanna) Magdalena (1771–1801), a singer, was engaged at the court theatre in Vienna in 1795. She reportedly received, and rejected, a proposal of marriage from Beethoven*; in 1796 she married Anton(io) Galvani, a merchant from Trieste. One of Willmann's sons, Max(imilian Friedrich Ludwig) (1767–1813), became a cello virtuoso. He played in the orchestra of Prince Thurn und Taxis at Regensburg until 1798 and later with Schikaneder*'s company in Vienna.

On 16 March 1784 Walburga, Magdalena and Max played at a concert in Vienna. They performed again at the Kärntnertor-Theater in that city on 7 March 1787, when Walburga played a piano concerto by Mozart (perhaps K503). Subsequently she was engaged as *virtuosa di camera* at the court theatre in Bonn. On 28 September 1797, in Vienna, she married Franz Xaver Huber (1755–1814), later the librettist of Beethoven's oratorio *Christus am Ölberge* op. 85. From 1800 until 1804 she undertook several concert tours.

Willmann's first wife Maria Elisabeth having died in 1789, Ignaz Willmann married the soprano Marianne de Tribolet (1768–1813) in 1793. In March 1795 she appeared as Konstanze in *Die Entführung** at the Freihaus-Theater, Vienna, and on 12 June 1798 as Pamina in Peter von Winter's *Das Labyrinth, oder Der Kampf mit den Elementen* (*see* SCHIKANEDER); from 1805 to 1812 she sang in Kassel. Their daughter Caroline Willmann (1796–*c*.1860) was an excellent soprano who sang in Pest, Vienna, and several cities in Germany.

(Pisarowitz[1,3,8])

Winter, Felix (Cajetan) (b. Salzburg, 30 May 1722; d. Salzburg, late October or early November 1772). Bass; according to the libretto of *La finta semplice**, the original Simone. He was a chorister at Salzburg Cathedral from 1744 until 1753, and a court singer from May 1753 until his death. During a two-years' stay in Italy from November 1755, he sang with success in Rome and Naples. His voice possessed a considerable compass which extended well into the tenor range.

(Angermüller[11])

Winter, Sebastian (b. Donaueschingen, 1743; d. Messkirch, Baden-Württemberg, 11 April 1815). He accompanied the Mozarts as their general servant and hairdresser on their journey from Salzburg to Paris in 1763. There he left them on 3 March 1764 to enter the service of Prince Joseph Wenzel Fürstenberg (1728–83) at Donaueschingen. Leopold Mozart provided him with a warm letter of recommendation. No doubt the Mozarts met him once more during their stay at Donaueschingen in October 1766. In 1769 Winter married Therese Renn.

In 1784 Leopold corresponded with Winter, who was then valet to the new ruler, Prince Joseph Maria Benedikt Fürstenberg. The latter, who maintained his own court orchestra, purchased through Winter copies of the three piano concertos K413/387*a*, 414/385*p* and 415/387*b*. In forwarding the scores, Leopold tried to interest the prince also in six piano sonatas by Wolfgang. In 1786 the latter was himself in correspondence with Winter whom he addressed as 'Dearest friend' and, in one letter (30 September), as 'companion of my youth'. Winter bought copies of several compositions on behalf of his master, but nothing came of Mozart's offer to write regularly a desired number of pieces for the prince, against a fixed annual remuneration.

(Wiedemann)

Zinzendorf und Pottendorf, Johann Karl, Count (b. Dresden, 1 January 1739; d. Vienna, 5 January 1813). Son of Count Friedrich Christian Zinzendorf and his second wife, Sophie, *née* Countess Gallenberg; nephew of Count Nikolaus Ludwig Zinzendorf (1700–60), the German religious and social reformer who played a pivotal role in the re-establishment of the Moravian Church.

Soon after arriving in Vienna in 1761, Zinzendorf was appointed a councillor at the treasury. During the next fourteen years he travelled in Europe on official business, and in the course of these journeys he met many prominent persons, among them Rousseau and Voltaire in France, Hume in Scotland, and Linnaeus in Sweden. He subsequently became governor of Trieste (1776–82), president of the court audit office (from 1782), and prime minister (1808–09). He had converted from Pietism (a movement in the Lutheran Church) to Catholicism in 1764.

The fifty-seven volumes of his diaries, written in French, contain numerous comments on contemporary events, as well as many interesting observations on theatrical and operatic performances. There are several entries relating to Mozart's first visit to Vienna in 1762. On 9 October he wrote: 'In the evening, at 8 o'clock, I called for [Count] Lamberg and we went together to [Count] Col[l]alto's where [Marianna] Bianchi sang and a little boy, who is reportedly only five and a half years old, played the harpsichord.' And on 17 October: 'Then on to [Count] Thurn's [?Thun's] where the small child from Salzburg and his sister played the harpsichord. The poor little fellow plays marvellously, he is an amusing, lively and delightful child, his sister's playing is masterly, and he applauded her. Mlle de Gudenus, who plays the harpsichord well, gave him a kiss, and he wiped his face . . .'

Zinzendorf's opinions on some of the singers associated with Mozart's operas are quoted in the relevant articles (e.g. *see* STORACE). His remarks about the operas themselves were far from uniformly enthusiastic. In an entry on 30 July 1782, he described *Die Entführung** as 'an opera of which the music is pilfered from various others'. On 1 May 1786, after attending the première of *Le nozze di Figaro**, he wrote: 'The opera bored me'; but after listening to a performance of it in German on 2 January 1799, he wrote: 'Beautiful music by Mozart'. As for *Don Giovanni**, he observed on 7 May 1788, after hearing the Viennese première, that 'Mozart's music is pleasant and very varied'; yet on 23 June 1788 he complained that he had been 'very bored' by that evening's performance. He liked *Così fan tutte**, though: 'Mozart's music is charming and the subject quite amusing,' he wrote after attending the first performance on 26 January 1790. On the other hand, he found *La clemenza di Tito**, the première of which he attended in Prague, a 'most tedious spectacle'. About *Die Zauberflöte** he wrote on 6 November 1791: 'The music and the stage-designs are pretty, the rest an incredible farce.'

(Deutsch[8], Wurzbach, Zinzendorf)

Masonic Lodges

'**Zur neugekrönten Hoffnung**' ['New-Crowned Hope'] **Masonic Lodge.** Joseph II*'s decree of 11 December 1785 ordering a reduction in the number of lodges led, in Vienna, to the dissolution of the 'Zur Beständigkeit' ['Constancy'] and 'Zum heiligen Joseph' ['Saint Joseph'] Lodges, and to the consolidation of the other six lodges in two new ones: thus the 'Zur wahren Eintracht' ['True Concord'], 'Zum Palmbaum' ['Palm Tree'] and 'Zu den drei Adlern' ['Three Eagles'] Lodges combined to form the new 'Zur Wahrheit' ['Truth'] Lodge, whose members chose Ignaz von Born* as their Master, while the 'Zur gekrönten Hoffnung' ['Crowned Hope'], 'Zur Wohltätigkeit'* and 'Zur den drei Feuern' ['Three Fires'] Lodges fused into the new 'Zur neugekrönten Hoffnung' Lodge, whose first Master was Baron Gebler*. Mozart, formerly in the 'Zur Wohltätigkeit' Lodge, accordingly became a member of the 'Zur neugekrönten Hoffnung' Lodge; the songs 'Zerfliesset heut', geliebte Brüder' K483 and 'Ihr, unsre neuen Leiter' K484 were presumably composed to mark its opening. For the inauguration of the lodge's new temple on 18 November 1791 Mozart composed the cantata K623.

At the end of 1793, faced with increasing hostility from certain obscurantist circles and with Emperor Francis II's deep mistrust of 'secret societies', the two remaining lodges voluntarily ceased their activities.

(Landon², Schuler¹²)

'**Zur Wohltätigkeit**' ['Beneficence'] **Masonic Lodge.** Founded in early 1783 by some members of the 'Zur gekrönten Hoffnung' ['Crowned Hope'] and 'Zum heiligen Joseph' ['Saint Joseph'] Lodges; Baron Otto Heinrich Gemmingen-Hornberg* was elected its first Master. Within a year the membership exceeded thirty, and it continued to increase. As a result of Joseph II*'s decree of 11 December 1785 ordering a reduction in the number of lodges, the lodge became part of the new 'Zur neugekrönten Hoffnung'* Lodge.

Mozart was admitted to the lodge as an Entered Apprentice on 14 December 1784; he was passed as Fellow Craft Mason (Journeyman) on 7 January 1785; later (there is no record of the precise date) he was raised to Master Mason. (*See also* MOZART, LEOPOLD.)

(Schuler¹¹)

Mozart's Operas

Apollo et Hyacinthus (K38). Intermezzo in three acts, written so as to be interspersed with the five acts of the Latin play *Clementia Croesi*. The text of both the intermezzo and the play was by Rufinus Widl*. The work was first performed in the Great Hall of Salzburg University on 13 May 1767 as a traditional end-of-term theatrical production. The singers were students or choristers:

Oebalus (tenor):	Mathias Franz de Paula Stadler*
Melia (soprano):	Felix Fuchs
Hyacinthus (soprano):	Christian Enzinger
Apollo (alto):	Johann Ernst
Zephyrus (alto):	Joseph Vonderthon
Two Priests of Apollo (?basses):	Joseph Anton Bründl*, Jakob Moser

The above title did not appear in the libretto of the play and intermezzo which was published in Salzburg in 1767; it was inserted by Nannerl* in Leopold Mozart's manuscript catalogue of Wolfgang's early works when she sent it to Breitkopf & Härtel* in 1799. Leopold had described the intermezzo simply as 'Music to a Latin play for the University of Salzburg, for five voices'. (*NMA* II/5/1)

Ascanio in Alba (K111). *Festa teatrale* in two parts. Text by Giuseppe Parini*. First performed at the Teatro Regio Ducal, Milan, on 17 October 1771, with the following cast:

Venere (soprano):	Geltrude Falchini
Ascanio (mezzo-soprano):	Giovanni Manzuoli*
Silvia (soprano):	Antonia Maria Girelli*
Aceste (tenor):	Giuseppe Luigi Tibaldi*
Fauno (soprano):	Adamo Solzi

On 18 March 1771 Leopold Mozart wrote to his wife* from Verona: 'Yesterday I received a letter from Milan, announcing one from Vienna which I am to receive to Salzburg, and which will fill you with amazement and bring our son everlasting honour.' The opera *Ascanio in Alba*, commissioned by Maria Theresa*, formed part of the festivities celebrating the marriage of Archduke Ferdinand* to Maria Beatrice Ricciarda d'Este on 15 October 1771. Giuseppe Parini has left a general account of these festivities (see FERDINAND).

In a letter to his wife on 19 October 1771, Leopold claimed that *Ascanio in Alba* had completely outshone the other festival opera, Hasse*'s *Il Ruggiero, ovvero L'eroica gratitudine*. In a further letter on 26 October he related that at the third performance on 24 October the archducal couple had called for two arias to be repeated (*see* GIRELLI, MANZUOLI), and had expressed their admiration for the composer by applauding and shouting 'Bravissimo Maestro'. The second

performance had taken place on 19 October; there were to be two more performances, on 27 and 28 October.
(Dahms, *NMA* II/5/5)

Bastien und Bastienne (K50/46b). Singspiel in one act. Text by Friedrich Wilhelm Weiskern*, Johann Heinrich Friedrich Müller*, and Johann Andreas Schachtner*, after *Les Amours de Bastien et Bastienne* (1753) by Charles Simon Favart (1710–92), Marie-Justine-Benoîte Favart (1727–72) and Harny de Guerville. This *opéra comique*, a parody of Jean-Jacques Rousseau's *Le devin du village* (1752), was repeatedly performed at the Burgtheater during the 1750s and 1760s. The French libretto was eventually translated into German, probably at Count Durazzo*'s suggestion, by Weiskern and Müller (the latter contributed Nos 11–13); their version was published in Vienna in 1764. Subsequently the text was revised and augmented by Schachtner, and it was this later version which was set to music by Mozart. The characters in the Singspiel are as follows:

> Bastienne (soprano)
> Bastien (tenor)
> Colas (bass)

Nissen* states in his biography of Mozart that *Bastien und Bastienne* was first performed at Dr Anton Mesmer*'s Viennese residence in 1768. The first documented performance is that presented by the Gesellschaft der Opernfreunde at the Architektenhaus in Berlin on 2 October 1890.
(*NMA* II/5/3)

Clemenza di Tito, La (K621). *Opera seria* in two acts. Text by Metastasio*, revised by Caterino Mazzolà*. Metastasio's text had been set by at least fourteen composers before Mozart, beginning with Antonio Caldara in 1734 and including Hasse* (1735), Gluck* (1752), Nicolò Jommelli (1753), Holzbauer* (1757) and Sarti* (1771). Mazzolà shortened the original text by about one third.

On 8 July 1791, in Prague, Domenico Guardasoni* signed a contract with the Bohemian Estates, the governing body of Bohemia, for the production of a new opera, to be performed on the occasion of Emperor Leopold II*'s coronation as King of Bohemia in September of that year. In July, while on a visit to Vienna, he offered the commission to Salieri*, who declined it. Salieri later stated that he had been obliged to turn down the invitation because of the additional duties he had assumed at the Vienna opera in order to allow Joseph Weigl* time to compose his cantata *Venere et Adone* for Eszterháza (where it was performed in August). It was apparently only after Salieri's refusal that Guardasoni commissioned Mozart to write *La clemenza di Tito*.

The new opera was produced at the National Theatre in Prague on 6 September 1791. Both Leopold II and Empress Maria Luisa* were present. For the occasion, Mozart and Constanze* had travelled to Prague, accompanied by Franz Xaver Süssmayr*. The performance was directed by Mozart, and his friend the clarinettist Anton Stadler* played in the orchestra. The cast was as follows:

Tito Vespasiano (tenor):	Antonio Baglioni*
Vitellia (soprano):	Maria Marchetti-Fantozzi*
Servilia (soprano):	Signora Antonini
Sesto (soprano):	Domenico Bedini* (?Carolina Perini)
Annio (soprano):	Carolina Perini (?Domenico Bedini)
Publio (bass):	Gaetano Campi*

In his biography of Mozart, Otto Jahn (*see* BREITKOPF & HÄRTEL) stated that at the première the part of Sesto was taken by Carolina Perini and that of Annio by Bedini. However, J. A. Westrup and C. Raeburn, in separate articles published in 1958 and 1959, argued strongly that Sesto must have been sung by the castrato Bedini and Annio by Perini. This was accepted by H. C. Robbins Landon in his book *1791: Mozart's Last Year* (1988). On the other hand, F. Giegling, in his edition of the opera (*NMA*, 1970), and R. Angermüller in *Vom Kaiser zum Sklaven* (1989) adhere to Jahn's cast list.

The opera had a mixed reception. Zinzendorf* considered it a 'most tedious spectacle', while the empress reportedly expressed her displeasure much more forcefully (*see* MARIA LUISA); but Leopold II was, according to Zinzendorf, delighted with Maria Marchetti's performance. *La clemenza di Tito* was first heard in Vienna in a concert performance at the Kärntnertor-Theater on 29 December 1794, when Aloisia Lange* sang Sesto. It was produced in London on 27 March 1806, the first of Mozart's operas to be performed there.

Thirteen numbers from *La clemenza di Tito*, sung to a new text by Cäsar Max Weigel, provided the bulk of the score for the opera *König Garibald*, which was performed in Munich on 15 and 20 February 1824 to mark the silver jubilee of Maximilian IV Joseph's accession to the Electorate of Bavaria on 16 February 1799 (he became King of Bavaria on 1 January 1806). The vice-Kapellmeister of the Munich court orchestra, Joseph Hartmann Stuntz (1793–1859), composed an introduction and a finale to the opera. The plot was based on an old legend describing the courtship by the Lombard King Authari of Theolinde, daughter of Duke Garibald – who, in the opera, became 'König Garibald I der Bojuarier' (i.e. of the Baiuwarii, the ancestors of the Bavarians).

(Angermüller[15,] Giegling, Landon[2], *NMA* II/5/20, Raeburn[2], Scharnagl, Westrup)

Così fan tutte, o sia La scuola degli amanti [*All Women are Like That, or The School for Lovers*] (K588). *Dramma giocoso* in two acts. Libretto by Lorenzo da Ponte*. First produced at the Burgtheater, Vienna, on 26 January 1790, with the following cast:

Fiordiligi (soprano):	Adriana Gabrieli*
Dorabella (soprano):	Luisa Villeneuve*
Ferrando (tenor):	Vincenzo Calvesi*
Guglielmo (baritone):	Francesco Benucci*
Don Alfonso (bass):	Francesco Bussani*
Despina (soprano):	Dorotea Bussani*

Don Giovanni

Ten performances were given in Vienna in Mozart's lifetime, all of them between January and August 1790.

Two early German versions of *Così fan tutte* were K. L. Gieseke*'s *Die Schule der Liebe, oder So machen sie's alle!* (produced at the Freihaus-Theater, Vienna, on 14 August 1794) and C. F. Bretzner's free adaptation *Weibertreue, oder Die Mädchen sind von Flandern* (published in Leipzig, also in 1794). Bretzner, who had accused Mozart of misusing his play *Belmonte und Constanze* in *Die Entführung**, was delighted with *Così fan tutte*, which he called, in the introduction to his Singspiel, 'this masterpiece by the immortal Mozart'.
(*NMA* II/5/18)

Don Giovanni [full title: *Il dissoluto punito, o sia Il Don Giovanni* (*The Libertine Punished, or Don Giovanni*)] (K527). *Dramma giocoso* in two acts. Libretto by Lorenzo da Ponte*, after *Don Giovanni Tenorio, o sia Il convitato di pietra* by Giovanni Bertati (1735–*c.*1815); the latter text, set to music by Giuseppe Gazzaniga (1743–1818), had been performed at the Teatro San Moisè, Venice, on 5 February 1787. Mozart's opera was produced at the National Theatre in Prague on 29 October 1787, with the following cast:

Don Giovanni (baritone):	Luigi Bassi*
Commendatore (bass):	Giuseppe Lolli*
Donna Anna (soprano):	Teresa Saporiti*
Don Ottavio (tenor):	Antonio Baglioni*
Donna Elvira (soprano):	Caterina Micelli
Leporello (bass):	Felice Ponziani*
Masetto (bass):	Giuseppe Lolli
Zerlina (soprano):	Caterina Bondini*

Mozart conducted the first few performances, Johann Joseph Strobach* the subsequent ones.

The première, originally planned for 14 October, was to celebrate the marriage of Archduchess Maria Theresia (1767–1827), a daughter of Archduke Leopold [later Leopold II*], to Prince Anton Clemens of Saxony (1755–1836) [King of Saxony from 1827]. The actual wedding took the form of two ceremonies, the first in Florence on 8 September, with Archduke Ferdinand* standing proxy, the second at Dresden on 18 October, when both parties were present. The Archduchess came to Prague for the première accompanied by her brother, Archduke Franz. However, since *Don Giovanni* was not ready in time, *Le nozze di Figaro** was given instead on 14 October, under Mozart's direction; the new opera was not presented until 29 October, after Maria Theresia had left Prague. (In Vienna, the marriage festivities included the gala première on 1 October of Martín y Soler*'s new opera, *L'arbore di Diana.*)

The first Viennese performance of *Don Giovanni* took place at the Burgtheater on 7 May 1788, with the following singers:

Don Giovanni:	Francesco Albertarelli*
Commendatore:	Francesco Bussani*
Donna Anna:	Aloisia Lange*
Don Ottavio:	Francesco Morella*
Donna Elvira:	Catarina Cavalieri*
Leporello:	Francesco Benucci*
Masetto:	Francesco Bussani
Zerlina:	Luisa Laschi-Mombelli*

The Viennese *Don Giovanni* differed in certain significant respects from the Prague version: Don Ottavio's aria 'Il mio tesoro intanto' was omitted, and Mozart wrote a new number, 'Dalla sua pace' K540a, for Morella; he also added the duet 'Per queste tue manine' K540b for Zerlina and Leporello, and the scena 'In quali eccessi, o Nume . . . Mi tradì quell'alma ingrata' K540c for Donna Elvira.

There were fourteen more performances at the Burgtheater in 1788, after which the opera was not heard again in Vienna in Mozart's lifetime. After the seventh performance Laschi-Mombelli, who was pregnant, was replaced by Therese Teyber*. At the last performance, on 15 December 1788, Joseph II*, who had been away from Vienna during most of that year leading his army in a campaign against the Turks, heard the opera for the first time. His absence had, however, not prevented him from writing to Count Rosenberg-Orsini* on 16 May that 'Mozart's music is much too difficult for the singers'. (Some scenes from the opera may have been performed at court before he left for the front on 29 February, or he must have been basing his judgment on reports from Vienna.) Zinzendorf*, in his diary on 12 May, recorded the remark made by an aristocratic lady that the music was 'learned, but little suited to the voice'. Da Ponte, in his memoirs, reported Joseph II as observing: 'The opera is divine, perhaps even more beautiful than *Figaro*, but it is not food for the teeth of my Viennese', and Mozart as commenting, on being told of the statement: 'Let us give them time to chew it.'

By the middle of the following century the exceptional qualities of *Don Giovanni* were evidently fully appreciated in Vienna, for on 25 May 1869 the new opera house on the Ringstrasse was inaugurated with a performance of the work (in German). And it was the second opera to be presented during the festivities marking the reopening of the same building, following its restoration after the Second World War: Beethoven*'s *Fidelio* was performed on 5 November 1955, *Don Giovanni* the next evening.

(Da Ponte, Deutsch[8], *NMA* II/5/17, Payer)

Entführung aus dem Serail, Die [*The Escape from the Seraglio*] (K384). Singspiel in three acts. Libretto by Johann Gottlieb Stephanie*, after *Belmonte und Constanze, oder Die Entführung aus dem Serail* by Christoph Friedrich Bretzner (1748–1807). The latter text, with music by Johann André (*see* ANDRE, JOHANN ANTON), was produced at the Doebbelin Theatre in Berlin on 25 May 1781 and published in Leipzig that same year. Turkish subjects had been treated several times before then, most recently in the Singspiel *Adelheit von Veltheim* by Gustav Friedrich Wilhelm Grossmann, which, set to music by Christian Gottlob Neefe (1748–98), had its première in Frankfurt am Main on 23 September 1780. Mozart's opera was first performed at the Burgtheater, Vienna, on 16 July 1782, with the following cast:

Konstanze (soprano):	Catarina Cavalieri*
Blonde (soprano):	Therese Teyber*
Belmonte (tenor):	Johann Valentin Adamberger*
Pedrillo (tenor):	Johann Ernst Dauer*
Osmin (bass):	Ludwig Fischer*
Pasha Selim (speaking role):	Dominik Jautz*

Mozart initially intended making the Pasha a singing role for the tenor Joseph Walter, who had been at the Burgtheater since 1780 (he should not be confused with the singer Johann Ignaz Walter). But when Walter's contract was not renewed in 1782, Mozart turned the role into a speaking part for Jautz.

The opera was given eleven more times at the Burgtheater in 1782, and received thirty more performances at the court theatres between 1783 and 1788. *Die Entführung* had considerable success outside Vienna as well. It also drew a public protest from Bretzner: 'A certain individual in Vienna, named *Mozart*, has had the audacity to misuse my drama *Belmonte und Constanze* for an opera text . . .' The same Bretzner later became a great admirer of Mozart (*see* COSÌ FAN TUTTE).

It was with *Die Entführung* that Mozart first conquered Prague, a city which was to play a very important role in his musical career (*see* NOZZE DI FIGARO, LE, DON GIOVANNI and CLEMENZA DI TITO, LA). 'I can testify to the enthusiasm which the performance of this opera [in late 1782] evoked both among connoisseurs of music and the general public,' Niemetschek* recalled in his biography of Mozart. 'It was as if what had been heard and known until then was not really music at all.' (Angermüller[3], Favier, *NMA* II/5/12, Rech[2])

Finta giardiniera, La [*The Pretended Girl Gardener*] (K196). *Dramma giocoso* in three acts. First performed at the Salvator-Theater, Munich, on 13 January 1775, with Rosa Manservisi* in the principal role of Sandrina; the rest of the cast is not known with certainty (*see* CONSOLI, ROSSI and VALESI). The libretto was formerly thought to have been the work of Raniero de Calzabigi (1714–95), with revisions by Marco Coltellini*, but Mozart is now believed to have used a libretto published anonymously in Rome in December 1773; the author was probably Giuseppe Petrosellini*. It had been set by Pasquale Anfossi*, whose opera was produced at the Teatro delle dame in Rome in December 1773 or January 1774. The characters are as follows:

> Don Anchise (tenor)
>
> Sandrina (soprano)
>
> Count Belfiore (tenor)
>
> Arminda (soprano)
>
> Ramiro (male soprano)
>
> Serpetta (soprano)
>
> Roberto (bass)

A German version of Mozart's opera was presented by Johann Böhm*'s theatrical company at Augsburg on [?]1 May 1780 under the title *Die verstellte Gärtnerin*. This translation, which used to be attributed to Johann Andreas Schachtner*, may in fact have been prepared by the actor and singer Hans [Johann] Franz Joseph Stierle (b. 1741; d. after 1800), a member of Böhm's company. On the other hand, the different German version copied by Mozart into his manuscript score probably was by Schachtner.
(Angermüller², *NMA* II/5/8)

Finta semplice, La [*The Pretended Simpleton-Girl*] (K51/46a). *Opera buffa* in three acts. Libretto by Marco Coltellini*, after the play of the same title by Carlo Goldoni (1707–93), which was itself inspired by Destouches's French comedy *La fausse Agnès, ou Le poète campagnard* (1736). Goldoni's text had been set to music by Salvatore Perillo, whose opera was performed in Venice in 1764.

In 1768 Wolfgang was asked by Joseph II*, probably when the Mozarts were received at court on 19 January, whether he would like to write an opera (according to Leopold Mozart's letter to Hagenauer* of 30 January – 3 February 1768). He thereupon composed *La finta semplice*. However, despite Leopold's strenuous efforts, culminating in an appeal to the emperor himself, the opera, although apparently finished, was not produced in Vienna that year. Leopold was furious and alleged intrigues by various individuals, foremost Giuseppe Affligio* (*see also* GLUCK).

It has been repeatedly stated that the *La finta semplice* was first performed at Archbishop Schrattenbach*'s palace in Salzburg on 1 May 1769, but this supposition is not supported by any contemporary document. That a performance did take place at Salzburg that year or, at any rate, that one was planned is, however, confirmed by the publication there in 1769 of the libretto, whose title page reads: *La finta semplice. Dramma giocoso per musica, da rappresentarsi in corte, per ordine di S.A. Reverendissima Monsignor Sigismondo arcivescovo e prencipe di Salisburgo . . . .* Mozart is named as the composer, and the cast-list indicates that the following singers appeared (or were to appear):

Rosina (soprano):	Maria Magdalena Lipp*
Don Cassandro (bass):	Joseph Hornung*
Don Polidoro (tenor):	Franz Anton Spitzeder*
Giacinta (soprano):	Maria Anna Braunhofer*
Ninetta (soprano):	Maria Anna Fesemayr*
Fracasso (tenor):	Joseph Nikolaus Meissner*
Simone (bass):	Felix Winter*

In the Viennese production planned by Leopold Mozart in 1768, these roles were to have been sung by Clementina Baglioni*, Francesco Caratoli*, Gioacchino Garibaldi*, Teresa Eberardi*, Antonia Bernasconi*, Filippo Laschi*, and Domenico Poggi*.
(*NMA* II/5/2)

Idomeneo, re di Creta [*Idomeneus, King of Crete*] (K366). *Dramma per musica* in

Lucio Silla

three acts. Text by Giovanni Battista Varesco*, after Antoine Danchet's libretto for the opera *Idoménée* by André Campra (1660–1744) which had been produced in Paris in 1712. Mozart's opera was first performed at the court theatre [later Cuvilliés-Theater], Munich, on 29 January 1781, with the following cast:

Idomeneo (tenor):	Anton Raaff*
Idamante (soprano):	Vincenzo dal Prato*
Arbace (tenor):	Domenico de' Panzachi*
Ilia (soprano):	Dorothea Wendling*
Elettra (soprano):	Elisabeth Wendling*
Gran Sacerdote (tenor):	Giovanni Valesi*

A first version of the libretto, together with a German translation by J. A. Schachtner*, appeared in Munich in early 1781, followed shortly afterwards by the publication of Varesco's revised Italian text.

The opera was first heard in Vienna in an amateur performance conducted by Mozart at the palace of Prince Johann Adam Auersperg (1721–95) on 13 March 1786. Situated on the Glacis, beyond the Hofburg, the building contained a private theatre which was used for plays and concerts, and, from 1781, also for operas. Idomeneo was sung by Giuseppe Antonio Bridi*, Idamante by Baron Pulini*, Ilia by Anna von Pufendorf*, and Elettra by Countess Hortensia Hatzfeld*. For this occasion Mozart substantially revised his score, in order to adapt the role of Idamante, conceived for a castrato, to the tenor voice. For this purpose he changed Idamante's part in ensembles, and substituted a new love duet for Ilia and Idamante, 'Spiegarti non poss'io' K489, for the original one in Act III. He furthermore replaced the opening scene of Act II, which consisted of recitative dialogue between Arbace and Idomeneo followed by Arbace's aria 'Se il tuo dol', by a new aria for Idamante, 'Non temer, amato bene' K490, preceded by recitative dialogue between Ilia and Idamante; as accompaniment for the aria he wrote a solo violin obbligato for Count Hatzfeld*.

In 1802 the Abbé Maximilian Stadler* drew on *Idomeneo* to arrange incidental music for the tragedy *Coriolan* by Heinrich Joseph von Collin (1771–1811; Beethoven*'s overture to the play was not written until 1807). The first stage performance in Vienna of Mozart's opera took place at the Kärntnertor-Theater on 13 May 1806, in a fairly free German translation by Georg Friedrich Treitschke (1776–1842).

(Dietrich, Höslinger, *NMA* II/5/11)

Lucio Silla (K135). *Dramma per musica* in three acts. Text by Giovanni de Gamerra*, probably revised by Metastasio*. First performed at the Teatro Regio Ducal, Milan, on 26 December 1772, with the following cast:

Lucio Silla (tenor):	Bassano Morgnoni
Giunia (soprano):	Anna de Amicis*
Cecilio (soprano):	Venanzio Rauzzini*
Lucio Cinna (soprano):	Felicità Suardi

Celia (soprano):	Daniella Mienci
Aufidio (tenor):	Giuseppe Onofrio

(*NMA*, II/5/7)

Mitridate, re di Ponto [*Mithridates, King of Pontus*] (κ87/74a). *Opera seria* in three acts. Text by Vittorio Amedeo Cigna-Santi*, after Racine's tragedy *Mithridate* (1673) which had already been translated into Italian by Giuseppe Parini*. The opera was produced at the Teatro Regio Ducal, Milan, on 26 December 1770, with the following cast:

Mitridate (tenor):	Guglielmo d'Ettore*
Aspasia (soprano):	Antonia Bernasconi*
Sifare (soprano):	Pietro Benedetti
Farnace (alto):	Giuseppe Cicognani
Ismene (soprano):	Anna Francesca Varese
Marzio (tenor):	Gaspare Bassano
Arbate (soprano):	Pietro Muschietti

Mozart conducted the first three performances. *Mitridate* was a great success. 'The theatre has been completely filled for the six performances which have taken place so far,' Leopold Mozart wrote to Padre Martini* on 2 January 1771, 'and each evening two arias have had to be repeated, and most of the others have been warmly applauded.' Cigna-Santi's libretto had previously been set by Quirino Gasparini (1721–78) in 1767.
(NMA II/5/4)

Nozze di Figaro, Le [*The Marriage of Figaro*] (κ492). *Opera buffa* in four acts. Libretto by Lorenzo da Ponte*, after the French comedy *La folle journée, ou Le mariage de Figaro* by Pierre-Augustin Caron de Beaumarchais (1732–99), which was produced at the Comédie-Française, Paris, on 27 April 1784. This play formed part of a trilogy, being preceded by *Le barbier de Séville, ou La précaution inutile* (23 February 1775 and followed by *L'autre Tartuffe, ou La mère coupable* (6 June 1792). A German translation of *Le mariage de Figaro* was prepared by Johann Rautenstrauch (1746–1801) for Kumpf and Schikaneder*, who planned to present the play at the Kärntnertor-Theater, Vienna, on 3 February 1785 (*see* SCHIKANEDER). The performance was, however, forbidden by the authorities, although they permitted the publication of the text that same year. Other German versions soon appeared. Da Ponte's libretto was published in Vienna in 1786, both in the original Italian and in German.

Michael Kelly* recalled in his *Reminiscences* that at the first rehearsal with full orchestra Mozart received an ovation after Figaro's Act I aria 'Non più andrai, farfallone amoroso': 'The whole of the performers on the stage, and those in the orchestra, as if actuated by one feeling of delight, vociferated Bravo! Bravo! Maestro. Viva, viva, grande Mozart.' The première took place at the Burgtheater, Vienna, on 1 May 1786, with the following cast:

Oca del Cairo, L'

Figaro (bass):	Francesco Benucci*
Susanna (soprano):	Nancy Storace*
Dr Bartolo (bass):	Francesco Bussani*
Marcellina (soprano):	Maria Mandini*
Cherubino (soprano):	Dorotea Bussani*
Count Almaviva (baritone):	Stefano Mandini*
Don Basilio (tenor):	Michael Kelly
Countess Almaviva (soprano):	Luisa Laschi*
Antonio (bass):	Francesco Bussani
Barbarina (soprano):	Anna Gottlieb*
Don Curzio (tenor):	Michael Kelly

The first two (or three) performances were conducted by Mozart himself, subsequent ones by Weigl*. At the second performance, on 3 May, five numbers were encored; at the third, on 8 May, seven had to be repeated, the Susanna–Cherubino duettino 'Aprite, presto aprite, è la Susanna' even twice. This prompted Joseph II* to decree that henceforth, 'in order not to extend unduly the length of operatic performances', no number for more than a single voice was to be repeated. Altogether, Le nozze di Figaro was performed four times at the Burgtheater in May 1786, then at Schloss Laxenburg in June, and thereafter only five more times in Vienna that year, once each in July, August, September, November, and December; it was then not heard again there until August 1789 when it reappeared in a somewhat revised form (see GABRIELI).

The opera had a far greater success in Prague, where Mozart was especially revered. It was produced by Bondini*'s company in late 1786, under the direction of Johann Joseph Strobach*, with Felice Ponziani* as Figaro, Caterina Bondini* as Susanna, and Luigi Bassi* as the Count. 'No piece . . . has ever caused such a sensation here as the Italian opera *The Marriage of Figaro*', the *Prager Oberpostamts-zeitung* reported on 12 December. Mozart was invited to Prague and travelled there with Constanze*. 'No one talks about anything but Figaro here,' he wrote to Gottfried von Jacquin* on 15 January 1787. 'Nothing is played, piped, sung or whistled but Figaro. Nobody wants to hear any opera other than Figaro. Always Figaro, and nothing but Figaro! It is certainly a great honour for me.' The extraordinary success which *Le Nozze di Figaro* enjoyed in Prague led directly to the commission for *Don Giovanni**.

The apartment which Mozart occupied in Vienna in what is now called the 'Figaro-Haus' (Domgasse 5 / Schulerstrasse 8, close to St Stephen's Cathedral) from October 1784 until April 1787 and where he composed this opera, is now a museum. Leopold Mozart stayed in the apartment during his visit to Wolfgang and Constanze in 1785.
(Boese, Kelly, *NMA* II/5/16)

Oca del Cairo, L' [*The Cairo Goose*] (**K422**). *Drama giocoso per musica*. Text by Giovanni Battista Varesco*. In December 1782 Count Rosenberg-Orsini* suggested that Mozart should compose an Italian opera for the Italian ensemble about to be established in Vienna. Mozart's search for a suitable text eventually led him back to Varesco, the librettist of *Idomeneo**. The characters are as follows:

Don Pippo (bass)
Donna Pantea (?)
Celidora (soprano)
Biondello (tenor)
Calandrino (tenor)
Lavina (soprano)
Chichibio (bass)
Auretta (soprano).

The music of only six numbers is known: two arias, two duets, a quartet, and the first finale. Mozart appears to have abandoned the project in December 1783 or early 1784.
(*NMA* II/5/13, Tyson)

Re pastore, Il [*The Shepherd King*] (K208). Serenata in two acts. Text by Metastasio*. First performed at Archbishop Colloredo*'s palace in Salzburg on 23 April 1775, on the occasion of a visit by Archduke Maximilian Franz*. The characters are as follows:

Alessandro (tenor)
Aminta (soprano)
Elisa (soprano)
Tamiri (soprano)
Agenore (tenor)

The principal role of the 'shepherd king' Aminta was sung by the castrato Tommaso Consoli*, a member of the Munich opera company who may have created the part of Ramiro at the recent première (13 January) of Mozart's *La finta giardiniera**. The remaining parts were no doubt taken by singers of the Salzburg court ensemble. Thus the two tenor roles (Alessandro, Agenore) are likely to have been taken by Franz Anton Spitzeder* and Felix Hofstätter (*c.*1744–1814), the soprano roles (Elisa, Tamiri) by Maria Anna Fesemayr*, Maria Anna Braunhofer*, or Maria Magdalena Lipp*.

Metastasio's libretto had first been set by Giuseppe Bonno* (1751), and subsequently by several other composers before Mozart, among them Sarti* (1752), Hasse* (1755), Gluck* (1756), Niccolò Piccinni (1760) and Pietro Alessandro Guglielmi (1767). Consoli had himself, in 1774, sung Elisa in Munich in an abbreviated two-act version of Guglielmi's (originally five-act) opera. It was the text of this shortened version, published in Munich in 1774, which Mozart used for his 'seranata'.
(Hortschansky, *NMA* II/5/9)

Schauspieldirektor, Der [*The Impresario*] (K486). *Komödie mit Musik* in one act.

Schuldigkeit des ersten Gebots, Die

Libretto by Johann Gottlieb Stephanie*. First performed in the Orangery at Schönbrunn Palace, Vienna, on 7 February 1786. Two different casts have been proposed by Mozart scholars for the première: the one given by Otto Jahn in his biography of Mozart (*see* BREITKOPF & HÄRTEL) and widely adopted by later writers (recently, by O. Michtner and R. Angermüller) appears in brackets below; the other one was put forward by C. Raeburn in 1955 and has been accepted by, among others, G. Croll in his edition of the work (*NMA*, 1958) and A. Holden in *The Mozart Compendium* (1990).

Frank (speaking part):	Johann Gottlieb Stephanie
Eiler (speaking part):	Johann Franz Hieronymus Brockmann*
Puf (bass, but largely a speaking part):	Joseph Weidmann*
	(Joseph Lange*)
Herz (speaking part):	Joseph Lange (Joseph Weidmann)
Madame Pfeil (speaking part):	Maria Anna Stephanie*
	(Johanna Sacco*)
Madame Krone (speaking part):	Johanna Sacco
	(Maria Anna Adamberger*)
Madame Vogelsang (speaking part):	Maria Anna Adamberger
	(Maria Anna Stephanie)
Monsieur Vogelsang (tenor):	Johann Valentin Adamberger*
Madame Herz (soprano):	Aloisia Lange*
Mademoiselle Silberklang (soprano):	Catarina Cavalieri*

Der Schauspieldirektor formed the first part of a double-bill offered by Joseph II* to the Governors-General of the Netherlands, Duke Albert Kasimir of Sachsen-Teschen (1738–1822) and his wife, the emperor's sister Marie Christine (1742–98). It was followed by Salieri*'s 'divertimento teatrale' *Prima la musica, poi le parole*, composed on a text by Giambattista Casti and sung by Stefano Mandini*, Francesco Benucci*, Celeste Coltellini* and Nancy Storace*. *Der Schauspieldirektor* was subsequently presented at the Kärntnertor-Theater on 11, 18 and 25 February 1786, after which it was not heard in Vienna again until 5 August 1797, when it was performed by Schikaneder*'s company at the Freihaus-Theater.
(Angermüller[15], Michtner, *NMA* II/5/15, Raeburn[1])

Schuldigkeit des ersten Gebots, Die [*The Obligation of the First Commandment*] (K35). Sacred Singspiel in three parts: the first composed by Mozart, the second by Michael Haydn*, the third by Anton Cajetan Adlgasser*. Text by Ignaz Anton von Weiser*, inspired by Mark XII, v.30: 'And thou shalt love the Lord thy God with all thy heart, and with all thy soul, and with all thy mind, and with all thy strength.' The three different parts were performed in the Knights' Hall of the archbishop's palace in Salzburg on successive Thursdays, beginning with Mozart's on 12 March 1767. The characters and their interpreters, according to the libretto printed in Salzburg that same year, were as follows (the first character does not appear in Part I):

Ein lauer und hinnach eifriger Christ (tenor):	Joseph Meissner*
[A lukewarm, later zealous Christian]	
Der Christen-Geist (tenor):	Franz Anton Spitzeder*
[Christianity]	
Der Welt-Geist (soprano):	Maria Anna Fesemayr*
[Worldliness]	
Die göttliche Barmherzigkeit (soprano):	Maria Magdalena Lipp*
[Divine Mercy]	
Die göttliche Gerechtigkeit (soprano):	Maria Anna Braunhofer*
[Divine Justice]	

During her visit to Vienna in 1969, Queen Elizabeth II presented to the Republic of Austria a splendid facsimile, made specially for the occasion, of the autograph score of *Die Schuldigkeit*. This score, which was bought by Prince Albert, Queen Victoria's husband, from Johann Anton André* in 1841, has been in the Royal Library at Windsor Castle since 1863.
(Köchel, *NMA* I/4/1, Weinmann[13])

Semiramis (κAnh.11/315e). Duodrama. Mozart so greatly admired Georg Benda*'s 'duodramas' that he decided, while in Mannheim in November 1778, to compose one himself, based on Gemmingen-Hornberg*'s melodrama *Semiramis*. The project was not completed, and the fragment is lost. (For Mozart's own definition of this genre, *see* BENDA; cf. ZAIDE.)

Sogno di Scipione, Il [*Scipio's Dream*] (κ126). *Azione teatrale.* Text by Metastasio*. Probably composed between April and August 1771, as a contribution to the celebrations planned for the fiftieth anniversary, on 10 January 1772, of Archbishop's Schrattenbach*'s ordination. Following Schrattenbach's death on 16 December 1771, Mozart dedicated the work to his successor Colloredo*. Contrary to earlier suppositions, it is now thought unlikely that the work was staged in Colloredo's honour in May 1772; however, the possibility of an unstaged performance has not been entirely ruled out. The characters are as follows:

> Scipione (tenor)
> La Costanza (soprano)
> La Fortuna (soprano)
> Publio (tenor)
> Emilio (tenor)

Metastasio's prime source was Cicero's *Somnium Scipionis*, in Book VI of his *De Republica*. The Scipio in question is Scipio Aemilianus Africanus Numantinus (185[?4]–129 BC).
(*NMA* II/5/6)

Sposo deluso, Lo, ossia La rivalità di tre donne per un solo amante [*The Deluded Bridegroom, or The Rivalry of Three Women for one Lover*] (κ430/424a). *Opera*

Zaide

buffa in two acts. Librettist unknown; the text is based on that of Domenico Cimarosa's *Le donne rivali*, first produced in Rome in 1780.

The work, which is believed to date from 1783–4, is incomplete. Only the overture and four numbers from Act I have survived in manuscript, largely in the form of sketches: a quartet for Bettina, Don Asdrubale, Pulcherio and Bocconio; an aria for Eugenia; an aria for Pulcherio; and a trio for Eugenio, Don Asdrubale and Bocconio. Mozart indicated that he had the following singers in mind for the different roles:

Bocconio (bass):	Francesco Benucci*
Eugenia (soprano):	Nancy Storace*
Don Asdrubale (tenor):	Stefano Mandini*
Bettina (soprano):	Catarina Cavalieri*
Pulcherio (tenor or high baritone):	Francesco Bussani*
Gervasio (tenor):	Signor Pugnetti
Metilde (soprano):	Therese Teyber*

(Campana, *NMA* II/5/14, Tyson)

Zaide (κ344/336*b*). Singspiel in two acts. Text probably by Johann Andreas Schachtner*, after *Das Serail, oder Die unvermuthete Zusammenkunft in der Sclaverey zwischen Vater, Tochter und Sohn* (text by Franz Joseph Sebastiani [?1722–72], music by Joseph Friebert [1724–99]). The libretto of the latter Singspiel was published at Bozen [Bolzano] in 1779.

Mozart worked on the opera in 1779–80, but left it incomplete, although most of the music was written down. It was published by Johann Anton André* in Offenbach in 1838, under the title *Zaide* (no title appears in the manuscript). Since Mozart had not left an overture, André printed one of his own composition; he also added a final chorus. The subject of *Zaide* is very close to that of *Die Entführung**. The score contains two 'duodrama' numbers: Gomatz in Act I and Soliman in Act II recite certain lines to musical accompaniment (for Mozart's own definition of this genre, *see* BENDA; cf. SEMIRAMIS). The characters in the opera are as follows:

> Zaide (soprano)
> Gomatz (tenor)
> Allazim (bass)
> Sultan Soliman (tenor)
> Osmin (bass)
> Zaram (speaking role)
> Four Slaves (tenors)

The first known performance took place at Frankfurt am Main, on 27 January 1866. The overture played on that occasion was that of *Die Entführung*.
(Neumann, *NMA* II/5/10)

Zauberflöte, Die [*The Magic Flute*] (κ620). Singspiel in two acts. Libretto by

Emanuel Schikaneder*. First performed at the Freihaus-Theater, Vienna, on 30 September 1791, with the following cast:

Sarastro (bass):	Franz Xaver Gerl*
Tamino (tenor):	Benedikt Schack*
Speaker (bass):	Herr Winter
Queen of Night (soprano):	Josepha Hofer*
Pamina (soprano):	Anna Gottlieb*
Papageno (bass):	Emanuel Schikaneder
Papagena (soprano):	Barbara Gerl*
Monastatos (tenor):	Johann Joseph Nouseul*
Three Priests:	Urban Schikaneder (*see* SCHIKANEDER) (bass), Johann Michael Kistler (tenor), Christian Hieronymus Moll (speaking part)
Three Ladies (sopranos):	Frl. Klöpfer, Frl. Hofmann, Elisabeth Schack (*see* SCHACK)
Three slaves (speaking parts):	Karl Ludwig Giesecke*, Wilhelm Frasel, Johann Nikolaus Starke
First Boy:	Anna Schikaneder (*see* SCHIKANEDER)

The first two performances (30 September and 1 October) were conducted by Mozart, later ones by the company's Kapellmeister, Johann Baptist Henneberg*. In October 1791 alone the opera was given some twenty times. Zinzendorf* mentioned in his diary on 6 November that there had been a 'huge audience' that evening. Schikaneder announced the hundredth performance on 23 November 1792, the 200th on 22 October 1795, and the 300th on 1 January 1798, but in his study *Das Freihaus-Theater auf der Wieden* (1937) O. E. Deutsch points out that the first two of these performances were in reality only the 83rd and 135th. The opera was first given outside Vienna in Prague on 25 October 1792.

(Deutsch[1,8], *NMA* II/5/19, Schuler[14])

The Viennese Theatres
of Mozart's Time

The two Viennese theatres most frequently mentioned in this book are the Kärntnertor-Theater and the Burgtheater. A few observations on their history, particularly in the eighteenth century, may therefore be useful (on the Freihaus-Theater and the Theater an der Wien, see the article on SCHIKANEDER).

The Kärntnertor-Theater – known originally as 'Das Theater nächst dem Kärntnertor' ['The Theatre beside the Carinthian Gate'] – stood approximately on the site of today's Hotel Sacher, just behind the modern Opera House, and was intended by the City of Vienna to be the first permanent local theatre for German-speaking actors. Nevertheless, when it opened on 30 December 1710, it was occupied by an Italian troupe; however, they soon ran into financial difficulties and were replaced within a few months by a company under the direction of the Austrian actor Joseph Anton Stranitzky (1676–1726), who developed a highly successful type of extemporized popular comedy, in which he himself played the clown 'Hanswurst'. This genre was to constitute the most characteristic dramatic fare at the Kärntnertor-Theater over the next fifty years, first under Stranitzky and subsequently under the comic actors Gottfried Prehauser (1699–1769) und Johann Joseph Felix von Kurz (1717–83). Already by the 1730s, however, the frequent coarseness and verbal obscenities of extemporized vernacular comedy were being condemned in Austria and particularly in Germany, where Johann Christoph Gottsched (1700–66) led the attack. In Vienna Philipp Hafner (1735–64) was to transform traditional extemporized farce into a non-improvised, more refined comical genre. Extemporized farce was officially banned in 1770 (see GEBLER).

In addition to popular farce, the Kärntnertor-Theater increasingly offered German drama, as well as translations from French authors (notably Corneille, Racine, Marivaux) and occasionally of English plays, such as Thomas Otway's *Venice Preserv'd*. In November 1761 the original Kärntnertor-Theater burnt down. The new building, which opened on 9 July 1763, became predominantly a literary theatre. On 16 January 1773 it presented the first Viennese performance of Shakespeare's *Hamlet*, in a rather free adaptation of Christoph Martin Wieland's German translation (see HEUFELD).

Long before then, however, a new theatre had opened in Vienna which was destined to surpass the Kärntnertor-Theater in fame; in particular, it was to play a significant role in the history of opera, as well as in Mozart's career. In 1741 the entrepreneur Franz Joseph Selliers was authorized by Empress Maria Theresa to convert the 'Hofballhaus', at his own expense, into a theatre suitable for the production of operas and plays; this building, on the Michaeler-Platz, had previously been used by the court for real tennis (it was connected to the palace by a private passage). Thus was born 'Das Theater nächst der Burg' ['The Theatre beside the Palace'], which would be more commonly known as the 'Burgtheater'.

The first opera presented there, on 3 [?5] February 1742, in the presence of Empress Maria Theresa, is generally believed to have been *Ambleto* by Giuseppe

The Viennese Theatres of Mozart's Time

Carcani (1703–79). Productions of Italian opera became increasingly important under the impresario Baron Rocco dello Presti (1747–52), who engaged several leading Italian singers. In 1752, to please the aristocracy, a resident French theatrical company was established at the Burgtheater; it was not dissolved until 1772. In his turn, Count Durazzo, who was Superintendent of Spectacles from 1754 until 1764, concentrated on promoting French *opéra comique* and Italian *opera seria*. With his encouragement, Gluck was able to put his own ideas on operatic reform into practice, starting with *Orfeo ed Euridice* which was produced on 5 October 1762 (*Alceste* followed on 16 December 1767 and *Paride ed Elena* on 30 November 1770). After the departure of the French actors at the end of 1772, permission was given for thrice-weekly performances of Italian opera. In December 1774 it was decided to present *opéra comique* once a week at the Burgtheater and on two further evenings at the Kärntnertor-Theater.

For most of the period before 1776, the administration of the Burgtheater and Kärntnertor-Theater was in the hands of a series of lessees (*see also* AFFLIGIO). In 1776, however, the Burgtheater was placed under the direct control of the court. Joseph II then decided to dismiss the Italian singers, dancers and musicians, and to bestow on the 'Theatre beside the Palace' the status of 'Deutsches Nationaltheater' ['German National Theatre']; the title of 'k.k. National-Hofschauspieler' ['Imperial and Royal National Court Actor'] was conferred on the German actors who had been performing at the Kärntnertor-Theater and were to transfer to the Burgtheater, and their salaries would henceforth be paid by the court. The Burgtheater thus became the officially designated and subsidized centre for drama and opera in German, with a formally appointed company of actors and singers; the year 1776 has, accordingly, been traditionally regarded as the date for the foundation of the modern Burgtheater. Count Rosenberg-Orsini was given overall responsibility for the court theatres, a position he retained until 1791.

Unlike the Burgtheater, the Kärntnertor-Theater was to be leased to outside troupes for any kind of theatrical entertainment, in German or another language. Furthermore, permission was also granted for the presentation of such entertainment at suburban locations. The proclamation of this general licence ('allgemeine Spektatelfreiheit') opened the way for the establishment, during the 1780s, of a number of theatres outside the inner city: the Theater in der Leopoldstadt was founded in 1781, the Freihaus-Theater auf der Wieden in 1787, and the Theater in der Josefstadt in 1788. It was at these new theatres that popular comedy was henceforth to flourish.

In the autumn of 1776 Joseph II sent one of Vienna's most prominent actors, Johann Heinrich Friedrich Müller, on an extensive tour of theatres in Germany; as a result, the Burgtheater company was strengthened by the engagement of a number of excellent actors and singers. Between 1778 and 1783 attention at the Burgtheater focused on the development of the Singspiel (i.e. comic opera in German); the repertoire included both new works and adaptations of French *opéra comique* and Italian *opera buffa*. During the seasons 1778–81 the Burgtheater gave each month eight or nine performances of Singspiels, which usually shared the programme with a play. Spoken drama was, in fact, habitually presented on each of the six evenings when the theatre was open during the week (it remained closed on Fridays).

Mozart's *Die Entführung aus dem Serail* (1782) has remained the most celebrated

198

product of this period. It was also among the last Singspiels to be produced at the Burgtheater at this time, for the 1783–84 season saw the triumphant return of Italian opera, presented by a group of splendid singers, most of them newly recruited from Italy. The stars of this company were Francesco Benucci and Nancy Storace, who, in 1786, would create the roles of Figaro and Susanna in *Le nozze di Figaro*. German opera, meanwhile, moved to the Kärntnertor-Theater (*Die Entführung* was given there on several occasions), and it also flourished in the suburban theatres founded during the 1780s. Mozart's *Die Zauberflöte* had its première at the Freihaus-Theater.

The two court theatres not only provided regular performances of drama and opera; they were also frequently used for concerts. Thus Mozart's very first public appearance in Vienna was at a concert at the Kärntnertor-Theater on 3 April 1781. He subsequently performed on a number of occasions at the Burgtheater, and his cantata *Davidde penitente* had its first two performances there on 13 and 15 March 1785. In 1810 the functions of the two court theatres were formally separated: drama now became the sole province of the Burgtheater, while opera was exclusively assigned to the Kärntnertor-Theater.

Both theatres were replaced in the second half of the nineteenth century by more modern buildings sited on the Ringstrasse. The new Opera House was inaugurated on 25 May 1869 with Mozart's *Don Giovanni*; even so, the Kärntnertor-Theater did not close until 17 April 1870, following a final performance of Rossini's *Guillaume Tell*. The old Burgtheater presented its last play, Goethe's *Iphigenie auf Tauris*, on 12 October 1888. Two days later the new Burgtheater opened with Grillparzer's *Esther* and Schiller's *Wallensteins Lager*. In the twentieth century the two new theatres were severely damaged during the Second World War and had to be extensively rebuilt. Both reopened in 1955: the Burgtheater on 15 October with Grillparzer's tragedy *König Ottokars Glück und Ende*, and the Opera House on 5 November with Beethoven's *Fidelio*, which was followed the next day by a performance of *Don Giovanni*.

Bibliography and Abbreviations

Abert	Abert, A. A., 'Hasse', in *MGG*
AcM	*Acta Musicologica* (Basle)
Acta Moz	*Acta Mozartiana* (Kassel 1954/5, Wiesbaden 1956–65, Regensburg 1966–8, Augsburg from 1969)
ADB	*Allgemeine Deutsche Biographie* (56 vols, Munich, 1875–1912; reprinted Berlin, 1967–71)
Affligio	Affligio, G., *Vita di Giuseppe Affligio/Lebensgeschichte des Giuseppe Affligio.* Aus dem Nachlass von B. Paumgartner herausgegeben von G. Croll und H. Wagner (Kassel, 1977)
Aigner	Aigner, T., 'Wenn Mozart mit aller Kunst des Lipp fugierte', *WF*, xlv (1978), pp. 3–10
Allorto	Al[lorto], R., 'Parini', in *ES*
ALBK	*Allgemeines Lexikon der Bildenden Künstler von der Antike bis zur Gegenwart*, begründet von U. Thieme und F. Becker (37 vols, Leipzig 1907–50); reprinted Leipzig, 1970–71)
AMZ	*Allgemeine Musikalische Zeitung* (Leipzig)
Angermüller[1]	Angermüller, R., 'Die Errichtung des Salzburger Mozart-Denkmals', *ÖMZ*, xxvi (1971), Heft 8, pp. 429–34
Angermüller[2]	——, 'Wer war der Librettist von *La finta giardiniera?*' *MJb 1976/77*, pp. 1–8
Angermüller[3]	——, '*Les époux esclaves ou Bastien et Bastienne à Alger*: Zur Stoffgeschichte der *Entführung aus dem Serail*' *MJb 1978/79*, pp. 70–88
Angermüller[4]	——, 'Bonno', in *New Grove*
Angermüller[5]	——, 'Da Ponte', in *New Grove*
Angermüller[6]	——, 'Mozart, Franz Xaver Wolfgang', in *New Grove*
Angermüller[7]	——, 'Paradis', in *New Grove*
Angermüller[8]	——, 'Salieri', in *New Grove*
Angermüller[9]	——, 'Weigl, Joseph (ii)', in *New Grove*
Angermüller[10]	——, 'Der Tanzmeistersaal in Mozarts Wohnhaus, Salzburg, Makartplatz 8', *MM*, xxix (1981), Heft 3/4, pp. 1–13
Angermüller[11]	——, 'Die vorgesehenen Sänger für die Wiener (1768) und Salzburger (1769) Erstaufführungen von Mozarts *La finta semplice*', *WF*, l (1983), pp. 3–17
Angermüller[12]	——, 'Testament, Kodizill, Nachtrag und Sperrelation der Freifrau Maria Anna von Berchtold zu Sonnenburg, geb. Mozart (1751–1829)', *MJb 1986*, pp. 97–132
Angermüller[13]	——, 'Friedrich Schlichtegrolls Nekrolog auf Ignaz von Born', *MM*, xxxv (1987), pp. 42–55
Angermüller[14]	——, 'Die Autographensammlung des Alois Taux', *MM*, xxxvii (1989), pp. 177–85
Angermüller[15]	——, *Vom Kaiser zum Sklaven: Personen in Mozarts Opern. Mit bibliographischen Notizen über die Mozart-Sänger der Uraufführungen und Mozarts Librettisten* (Munich, Salzburg, 1989)

Bibliography and Abbreviations

Angermüller[16]	——, *Das Salzburger Mozart-Denkmal. Eine Dokumentation (bis 1845) zur 150-Jahre-Enthüllungsfeier. Mit einem kunsthistorischen Beitrag von A. Hahnl* (Salzburg, 1992)
Antolini	Antolini, B. M., 'De Amicis', in *DBI*
Antonicek	Antonicek, T., 'Auernhammer', in *MGG*
Apollonio	A[pollonio], M., 'Metastasio', in *ES*
Arneth	Arneth, A. von, *Graf Philipp Cobenzl und seine Memoiren* (Vienna, 1885)
Autexier	Autexier, P. A., 'Wann wurde die Maurerische Trauermusik uraufgeführt?', *MJb 1984/85*, pp. 6–8
Badura-Skoda[1]	Badura-Skoda, E., 'Salomon', in *MGG*
Badura-Skoda[2]	——, 'Umlauf', in *MGG*
Badura-Skoda[3]	——, and Badura-Skoda, P., 'Zur Echtheit von Mozarts Sarti-Variationen kv.460', *MJb 1959*, pp. 127–39
Badura-Skoda/ Herrmann	——, and Herrmann, H., 'Eybler', in *New Grove*
Baldwin/Wilson	Baldwin, O., and Wilson, T., 'Davies, Cecilia', in *New Grove*
Baser	Baser, F., 'Mozarts Freund Sickingen, durch neue Enthüllungen gebrandmarkt', *MM*, xxix (1981), pp. 20–23
Beechey	Beechey, G., 'Linley, Thomas', in *New Grove*
Biba	Biba, O., '"Par Monsieur François Comte de Walsegg"', *MM*, xxix (1981). Heft 3/4, pp. 34–40
Blümml	Blümml, E. K., *Aus Mozarts Freundes- und Familienkreis* (Vienna, Prague, Leipzig, 1923)
Boese	Boese, H., 'Die Mozart-Wohnung im Figaro-Haus', *WF*, xlv (1978), pp. 5–7
Branscombe[1]	Branscombe, P., 'Böhm, Johann', in *New Grove*
Branscombe[2]	——, 'Bondini, Pasquale', in *New Grove*
Branscombe[3]	——, 'Henneberg, Johann Baptist', in *New Grove*
Branscombe[4]	——, 'Marchand, Theobald Hilarius', in *New Grove*
Branscombe[5]	——, 'Schack', in *New Grove*
Branscombe[6]	——, 'Schikaneder, Emanuel', in *New Grove*
Branscombe[7]	——, 'Stephanie, Gottlieb', in *New Grove*
Branscombe[8]	——, 'Teyber, Anton', in *New Grove*
Branscombe[9]	——, 'Teyber, Elisabeth', in *New Grove*
Branscombe[10]	——, 'Teyber, Franz', in *New Grove*
Branscombe[11]	——, 'Teyber, Matthäus', in *New Grove*
Branscombe[12]	——, 'Teyber, Therese', in *New Grove*
Branscombe[13]	——, 'Umlauf, Ignaz', in *New Grove*
Braubach	Braubach, M., *Maria Theresias jüngster Sohn: Max Franz. letzter Kurfürst von Köln und Fürstbischof von Münster* (Vienna, Munich, 1961)
Braunbehrens	Braunbehrens, V., *Salieri: Ein Musiker im Schatten Mozarts* (Munich, 1989)
Brauneis	Brauneis, W., '"... wegen schuldigen 1435 f 32 xr": Neuer Archivfund zur Finanzmisere Mozarts im November 1791', *MM*, xxxix (1991), pp. 159–63
Breitinger[1]	Breitinger, F., 'Jungfer Tanzmeister Mitzerl und Joli Sallerl, zwei angebliche Liebchen Mozarts', *NMJb*, i (1941), pp. 39–48
Breitinger[2]	——, 'Mozarts Taufpate Kaufmann Gottlieb Pergmayr', *SV*, 28 March and 17 April 1964

Bibliography and Abbreviations

Briellmann   Briellmann, A., '"Hochschätzbareste Gnädige Frau Baronin!":
                    Ein bisher unveröffentlicher Brief Mozarts aus der Paul Sacher
                    Stiftung, Basel', *MJb 1987/88*, pp. 233–48
Brockhaus   *Brockhaus Enzyklopädie* (25 vols, Wiesbaden, 1966–81)
Brofsky[1]   Brofsky, H., 'Martini, Giovanni Battista', in *New Grove*
Brofsky[2]   ——, 'Tibaldi, Guiseppe', in *New Grove*
Brook et al.   Brook, B. S., Campbell, D., and Cohn, M. H., 'Gossec', in *New
                    Grove*
Burney[1]   Burney, C., 'Mozart', in A. Rees, *The Cyclopaedia; or Universal
                    Dictionary of Arts, Sciences, and Literature* (39 vols, London,
                    c.1805–19)
Burney[2]   ——, *A General History of Music From the Earliest Ages to the Present
                    Period (1789)* (2 vols, New York, 1935)
Burney[3]   ——, *Music, Men, and Manners in France and Italy, 1770. Being the
                    Journal Written by Charles Burney, Mus.D., during a Tour through
                    those Countries* . . . Transcribed from the original manuscript in
                    the British Museum . . . and edited with an Introduction by H.
                    E. Poole (London, 1969)
Burney[4]   ——, *The Present State of Music in France and Italy. A Facsimile of the*
                    [2nd, corrected] *1773 London Edition* (New York, 1969)
Burney[5]   ——, *The Present State of Music in Germany, the Netherlands and
                    United Provinces. A Facsimile of the* [2nd corrected] *1775 London
                    Edition* (London, 1969)
Campana   Campana, A., 'Il libretto de *Lo sposo deluso*', *MJb 1989/90*, pp. 73–
                    87
Casanova   Casanova, *Mémoires*. Texte présenté et annoté par R. Abirached
                    (3 vols, Paris, 1958–60)
Cloeter   Cloeter, H., *Johann Thomas Trattner: Ein Grossunternehmer im
                    Theresianischen Wien* (Graz, Cologne, 1952)
Cranmer   Cranmer, M., 'Streicher', in *New Grove*
Croll[1]   Croll, G., 'Eine zweite, fast vergessene Selbstbiographie von Abbé
                    Stadler', *MJb 1964*, pp. 172–84
Croll[2]   ——, '"Die Antretterischen" und die Mozarts. Die "Final-
                    Musik" (κv185/176a [*sic*]) und die "Andretterin Musik"',
                    ÖMZ, xxxiii (1978), pp. 497–511
Croll[3]   ——, 'Johann Michael Haydn in seinen Beziehungen zu Leopold
                    und Wolfgang Amadeus Mozart', *MJb 1987/88*, pp. 97–106
Croll[4]   ——, 'Girelli', in *New Grove*
Croll[5]   ——, 'Salzburg', in *New Grove*
Croll/Vössing   ——, and Vössing, K., *Johann Michael Haydn: Sein Leben, sein
                    Schaffen, seine Zeit* (Vienna, 1987)
Cruciani   Cruciani, A., 'Consoli, Tommaso', in *DBI*
Dahms   Dahms, S., 'Mozarts festa teatrale *Ascanio in Alba*', *ÖMZ*, xxxi
                    (1976), Heft 1, pp. 15–24
Da Ponte   Da Ponte, L., *Memorie e altri scritti*, a cura di C. Pagnini (Milan,
                    1971)
DBI   *Dizionario Biografico degli Italiani* (Rome, 1960–)
Dean   Dean, W., 'Durazzo', in *New Grove*
DEUMM   *Dizionario Enciclopedico Universale della Musica e dei Musicisti.
                    Diretto da A. Basso. Le biografie* (8 vols, Turin, 1985–8)

Bibliography and Abbreviations

Deutsch[1]	Deutsch, O. E., *Das Freihaus-Theater auf der Wieden, zur Feier seiner Eröffnung vor 150 Jahren (14. Oktober 1787)* (Vienna, 1937)
Deutsch[2]	——, 'Count Deym and his Mechanical Organs', *ML*, xxix (1948), pp. 140–45
Deutsch[3]	——, 'Der rätselhafte Gieseke', *Mf*, v (1952), pp. 152–60
Deutsch[4]	——, 'Die Mesmers und die Mozarts', *MJb 1954*, pp. 54–64
Deutsch[5]	——, 'Aus Schiedenhofens Tagebuch', *MJb 1957*, pp. 15–24
Deutsch[6]	——, 'Das Fräulein von Auernhammer', *MJb 1958*, pp. 12–17
Deutsch[7]	——, 'Dr. Med. Anton Schmith: Ein vergessener Freund Mozarts', *MJb 1960/61*, pp. 22–8
Deutsch[8]	——, 'Mozart in Zinzendorfs Tagebüchern', *SMZ*, cii (1962), pp. 211–18
Deutsch[9]	——, 'Sartis Streitschrift gegen Mozart', *MJb 1962–63*, pp. 7–13
Deutsch[10]	——, 'Schichtegroll und Konstanze', *MM*, xi (1963), Heft 1/2, pp. 3–4
Deutsch[11]	——, 'Zur Geschichte von Mozarts Requiem', *ÖMZ*, xix (1964), pp. 49–60
DiChiera[1]	DiChiera, D., 'Mysliveček', in *MGG*
DiChiera[2]	——, 'Mysliveček', in *New Grove*
DiChiera/Libby	——, and Libby, D., 'Sarti', in *New Grove*
Dies	Dies, A. C., *Biographische Nachrichten von Joseph Haydn* (Vienna, 1810)
Dietrich	Dietrich, M., '"Wiener Fassungen" des *Idomeneo*', *MJb 1973/4*, pp. 56–76
Dittersdorf	Dittersdorf, K. von, *Lebensbeschreibung, seinem Sohne in die Feder diktiert.* Neu herausgegeben von B. Loets (Leipzig, 1940)
DNB	*Dictionary of National Biography* (63 vols, London, 1885–1900; 3 Supplements, 1901)
Drake	Drake, J. D., 'Benda, Georg', in *New Grove*
Edwards	Edwards, O., 'Fisher, John Abraham', in *New Grove*
Eibl[1]	Eibl, J. H., 'Wer hat das Engagement Aloisia Webers an die Wiener Oper vermittelt?', *MJb 1962/63*, pp. 111–14
Eibl[2]	——, 'Ein "ächter Bruder": Mozart und Michael Puchberg', *Acta Moz*, xxvi (1979), Heft 1, pp. 41–6
Eibl[3]	——, '". . . una porcheria tedesca"? Zur Uraufführung von Mozarts *La clemenza di Tito*', *ÖMZ*, xxxi (1976), pp. 329–34
Eibl[4]	——, 'Bemerkungen zu dem Artikel "Die Grazer Ausgabe von Schlichtegrolls *Mozarts Leben* (1794) und ihr 'Verleger' Joseph Georg Hubeck" von Otfried Hafner', *MM*, xxvii (1979), Heft 3/4, pp. 25–6. Followed by a note by Otfried Hafner, p. 26. [*See* 'Hafner[2]' below]
Eibl/Senn	*Mozarts Bäsle-Briefe.* Herausgegeben und kommentiert von J. H. Eibl und W. Senn (Kassel, Munich, 1978)
Einstein	Einstein, A., *Mozart: His Character, His Work* (New York, 1945). German version: *Mozart: Sein Charakter, sein Werk* (Stockholm, 1947)
Eisen	Eisen, C., *New Mozart Documents: A Supplement to O. E. Deutsch's Documentary Biography* [*see* '*Mozart: Dokumente*' below] (London, 1991)
ES	*Enciclopedia dello Spettacolo* (11 vols, Rome, 1954–68)

Esch	Esch, C., 'Michele Mortellari, Johann Christian Bach und Wolfgang Amadé Mozart: Eine neu aufgefundene Fassung der Arie "Io ti lascio" KV 621a (= Anh.245) und die verschollene Szene für Tenducci (Paris 1778) KV 315b (= Anh.3)', *MM*, xxxix (1991), pp. 133–58
Favier	*Vie de W. A. Mozart par Franz Xaver Niemetschek, précédée du Nécrologe de Schlichtegroll*. Présentation, traduction et notes par G. Favier (Saint-Etienne, 1976)
Fellerer	Fellerer, K. G., 'Mozart und Händel', *MJb 1953*, pp. 47–55
Fellmann	Fellmann, H. G., *Die Böhmsche Theatertruppe und ihre Zeit: Ein Beitrag zur deutschen Theatergeschichte des 18. Jahrhunderts* (Leipzig, 1928)
Fétis	Fétis, F. J., *Biographie universelle des musiciens et bibliographie générale de la musique* (2nd edn, 8 vols, Paris, 1868–70). *Supplément et complément* (2 vols, Paris, 1878–81)
Fischer¹	Fischer, K. von, 'Sind die Klaviervariationen über Sartis "Come un' agnello" von Mozart?', *MJb 1958*, pp. 18–29
Fischer²	——, 'Sind die Klaviervariationen KV.460 von Mozart? Eine Replik', *MJb 1959*, pp. 140–45
Fischer K. A.	Fischer, K. A., 'Johann Andreas Stein, der Augsburger Orgel- und Klavierbauer', *ZHVS*, l (1932/3), pp. 149–77
Fiske¹	Fiske, R., 'Storace, Nancy', in *New Grove*
Fiske²	——, 'Storace, Stephen', in *New Grove*
Fiske³	——, 'Tenducci', in *New Grove*
Fitzlyon	Fitzlyon, A., *The Libertine Librettist: A Biography of Mozart's Librettist Lorenzo da Ponte* (London, 1955)
Forbes	Forbes, E., 'Prince Karl von Lichnowsky', in *New Grove*
Förster	Förster, 'Brockmann', in *ADB*
Fränkel	Fränkel, L., 'Weidmann, Joseph', in *ADB*
Franz	Franz, G. von, 'Mozarts Klavierbauer Anton Walter', *NMJb*, i (1941), pp. 211–17
Freeman¹	Freeman, R. N., 'Albrechtsberger', in *New Grove*
Freeman²	——, 'Stadler, Maximilian', in *New Grove*
Freiberger	Freiberger, H., *Anton Raaff (1714–1797): Sein Leben und Wirken, als Beitrag zur Musikgeschichte des 18. Jahrhunderts* (Cologne, 1929)
GDEU	*Grande Dizionario Enciclopedico Utet* (19 vols, Turin, 1966–73)
Gebler/Nicolai	*Aus dem Josephinischen Wien: Geblers und Nicolais Briefwechsel während der Jahre 1771–1786*. Herausgegeben und erläutert von R. M. Werner (Berlin, 1888)
Geiringer	Geiringer, K. and I., 'Stephen und Nancy Storace in Wien', *ÖMZ*, xxxiv (1979), Heft 1, pp. 18–25
Gen	*Genealogie* (Neustadt-an-der-Aisch)
Giegling	Giegling, F., '*La clemenza di Tito*: Metastasio, Mazzolà, Mozart', *ÖMZ*, xxxi (1976), pp. 321–9
Goethals	Goethals, F.-V., *Dictionnaire généalogique et héraldique des familles nobles du Royaume de Belgique* (4 vols, Brussels, 1849–52)
Goldinger	Goldinger, W., 'Archival-genealogische Notizen zum Mozart-Jahr', *Neues Augsburger Mozartbuch* [*ZHVS*, lxii–lxiii], 1962, pp. 77–96
Göthel	Göthel, F., 'Stein Familie', in *MGG*
Grasberger	Grasberger, F., 'Weigl', in *MGG*

Bibliography and Abbreviations

Grave	Grave, F. K., 'Holzbauer', in *New Grove*
Grave M. H.	Grave, M. H., 'Vogler, Georg Joseph', in *New Grove*
Grossegger	Grossegger, E., *Freimaurerei und Theater 1770–1800: Freimaurer-dramen an den k.k. privilegierten Theatern in Wien* (Vienna, 1981)
Gugitz	Gugitz, G., 'Von W. A. Mozarts kuriosen Schülerinnen', *ÖMZ*, xi (1956), pp. 261–9
Haas¹	Haas, R., 'Durazzo', in *MGG*
Haas²	——, 'Eberlin', in *MGG*
Haas³	——, 'Eybler', in *MGG*
Haas⁴	——, 'Abt Stadlers vergessene Selbstbiographie', *MJb 1957*, pp. 78–84
Hadden	Hadden, J. C., *George Thomson, the Friend of Burns: His Life and Correspondence* (London, 1898)
Hafner¹	Hafner, O., 'Franz Deyerkauf, Initiator des ältesten Mozart-Denkmals der Welt', *MM*, xxiv (1976), Heft 1/2, pp. 7–16
Hafner²	——, 'Die Grazer Ausgabe von Schlichtegrolls *Mozarts Leben* (1794) und ihr "Verleger" Joseph Georg Hubeck', *MM*, xxvii (1979), Heft 1/2, pp. 18–21, and Heft 3/4, p. 26. [See also 'Eibl⁴' above]
Hamann¹	Hamann, H. W., 'Mozarts dramatischer Entwurf *Der Salzburger Lump in Wien*', *AcM*, xxxiv (1962), pp. 195–201
Hamann²	——, 'Mozarts Schülerkreis: Versuch einer chronologischen Ordnung', *MJb 1962/63*, pp. 115–39
Hansell¹	Hansell, K. K., 'De Amicis', in *New Grove*
Hansell²	——, 'Manzuoli', in *New Grove*
Hansell³	——, 'Noverre', in *New Grove*
Hansell⁴	——, 'Rauzzini', in *New Grove*
Hansell S.¹	Hansell, S., 'Baglioni, Antonio', in *New Grove*
Hansell S.²	——, 'Baglioni, Francesco', in *New Grove*
Hansell S.³	——, 'Hasse, Johann Adolf', in *New Grove*
Hausner	Hausner, H. H., 'Bemerkungen zu Schlichtegrolls Mozart-Biographie', *MM*, xxvi (1978), Heft 3/4, pp. 21–4
Häussermann	Häussermann, E., *Das Wiener Burgtheater* (Vienna, 1975)
Heartz¹	Heartz, D., 'Raaff', in *New Grove*
Heartz²	——, 'Leutgeb and the 1762 Horn Concertos of Joseph and Johann Michael Haydn', *MJb 1987/88*, pp. 59–68
Hedler	Hedler, G., 'Mozarts bester Freund, August Clemens Graf Hatzfeld', *Acta Moz*, x (1963), Heft 1, pp. 10–14
Heigel	Heigel, 'Karl Theodor', in *ADB*
Hellmann	Hellmann-Stojan, H., 'Stadler, Maximilian', in *MGG*
Herrmann	Herrmann, W., 'Therese Pierron und das Haus F3,5', in *Das Mannheimer Mozart-Buch*, herausgegeben [von] R. Würtz (Wilhelmshaven 1977), pp. 49–58
Hess	Hess, E., 'Stadler, Anton', in *MGG*
Hitzig	Hitzig, W., 'Die Briefe Franz Xaver Niemetscheks und der Marianne Mozart an Breitkopf & Härtel', *Der Bär (Jahrbuch von Breitkopf & Härtel)*, 1928, pp. 101–16
Hoffmann	Hoffmann-Erbrecht, L., 'Hässler', in *MGG*
Höft	Höft, B., ' "wie das andante, so ist sie": Mannheimerinnen um Mozart', in *176 Tage W. A. Mozart in Mannheim*, herausgegeben von K. von Welck und L. Homering . . . (Mannheim, 1991), pp. 28–41

Honolka	Honolka, K., *Papageno: Emanuel Schikaneder, der grosse Theatermann der Mozart-Zeit* (Salzburg, Vienna, 1984). English version: *Papageno: Emanuel Schikaneder, Man of the Theater in Mozart's Time*, trans. by J. M. Wilde; general ed. R. G. Pauly (Portland, Oregon, 1990)
Hortschansky	Hortschansky, K., '*Il re pastore*: Zur Rezeption eines Librettos in der Mozart-Zeit', *MJb 1978/79*, pp. 61–70
Höslinger	Höslinger, C., 'Die ersten Aufführungen des *Idomeneo* in Wien: 1786, 1806', *MJb 1986*, pp. 25–8
Hüffer	Hüffer, 'Cobenzl, Johann Philipp', in *ADB*
Hughes	Hughes, R., 'Novello, Vincent', in *New Grove*
Hummel[1]	Hummel, W., *Nannerl, Wolfgang Amadeus Mozarts Schwester* (Zurich, Leipzig, Vienna, 1952)
Hummel[2]	——, *W. A. Mozarts Söhne* (Kassel, 1956)
Hurwitz	Hurwitz, J., 'Franz Xaver Wolfgang Mozart: Freemason', *MM*, xxxvi (1988), pp. 99–104
Iesuè[1]	Iesuè, A., 'Ceccarelli', in *DBI*
Iesuè[2]	——, 'Coltellini, Celeste', in *DBI*
JHGGA	*Jahrbuch der Heraldisch-Genealogischen Gesellschaft Adler* (Vienna)
JVGSW	*Jahrbuch des Vereines für Geschichte der Stadt Wien* (Vienna)
Kahl	Kahl, W., 'Hummel', in *MGG*
Kelly	Kelly, M., *Reminiscences*. Edited with an Introduction by R. Fiske (London, 1975)
King[1]	King, A. H., 'Kelly, Michael', in *New Grove*
King[2]	——, 'Köchel', in *New Grove*
Klein	Klein, H., 'Unbekannte Mozartiana von 1766/67', *MJb 1957*, pp. 168–85
Köchel	Köchel, L. Ritter von, *Chronologisch-thematisches Verzeichnis sämtlicher Tonwerke Wolfgang Amadé Mozarts* (6. Auflage, bearbeitet von F. Giegling, A. Weinmann, G. Sievers, Wiesbaden, 1964)
Komma[1]	Komma, K. M., 'Cannabich, Familie', in *MGG*
Komma[2]	——, 'Fränzl', in *MGG*
Komorzynski[1]	Komorzynski, E., 'Sänger und Orchester des Freihaustheaters', *MJb 1951*, pp. 138–50
Komorzynski[2]	——, 'Mozart und Marie Therese Paradis', *MJb 1952*, pp. 110–16
Komorzynski[3]	——, 'Johann Baptist Henneberg, Schikaneders Kapellmeister (1768–1822)', *MJb 1955*, pp. 243–5
Komorzynski[4]	——, 'Wo Johann Michael Puchberg begraben wurde', *WF*, xliii (1976), pp. 26–30
Kramer	Kramer, K., 'Giovanni Battista Varesco: Versuch einer Biographie', *Acta Moz*, xxvii (1980), Heft 1, pp. 2–15
Kraus	Kraus, H., 'W. A. Mozart und die Familie Jacquin', *ZfMw*, xv (1932–3), Heft 4, pp. 155–68
Kreutz	Kreutz, W., 'Mozart und die Freimaurer der Kurpfalz', in *176 Tage W. A. Mozart in Mannheim*, herausgegeben von K. von Welck und L. Homering . . . (Mannheim, 1991), pp. 76–83
Krieg	Krieg, W., 'Um Mozarts Totenmaske: Ein Beitrag zur Mozartikonographie', *NMJb*, iii (1943), pp. 118–43
Kuhe	Kuhe, W., *My Musical Recollections* (London, 1896)
Kutsch/Riemens	Kutsch, K. J., and Riemens, L., *Grosses Sängerlexikon* (2 vols, Bern, 1987)

Bibliography and Abbreviations

Landon[1]	Landon, H. C. Robbins, *Haydn: Chronicle and Works* (5 vols, London, 1976–80)
Landon[2]	——, *1791: Mozart's Last Year* (London, 1988)
Landon[3]	——, *Mozart: The Golden Years* (London, 1989)
Layer[1]	Layer, A., 'Beecke', in *New Grove*
Layer[2]	——, 'Demmler', in *New Grove*
Layer[3]	——, 'Graf, Friedrich Hartmann', in *New Grove*
LDG	*Lexikon der deutschen Geschichte. Personen, Ereignisse, Insitutionen, von der Zeitwende bis zum Ausgang des 2. Weltkrieges.* Herausgegeben von G. Taddey (Stuttgart, 1983)
Lepsius	Lepsius, B., 'Karl Heinrich Joseph Reichsgraf v. Sickingen', in *ADB*
Lequin	Lequin, F., 'Mozarts "... rarer Mann"', *MM*, xxix (1981), Heft 1/2, pp. 3–19
Lesure	Lesure, F., 'Heina', in *New Grove*
Libby	Libby, D., 'Coltellini, Marco', in *New Grove*
Lindner	Lindner, D., *Ignaz von Born, Meister der Wahren Eintracht: Wiener Freimaurerei im 18. Jahrhundert* (Vienna, 1986)
London Stage	*The London Stage, 1660–1800: A Calendar of Plays, Entertainments & Afterpieces, together with Casts, Box-Receipts and Contemporary Comment . . .* , Part 4: *1747–1776*. Ed. with a Critical Introduction by G. W. Stone, Jnr (3 vols, Carbondale, Illinois, 1962); Part 5: *1776–1800*. Ed. with a Critical Introduction by C. B. Hogan (3 vols, Carbondale, 1968)
Loreto	Loreto Tozzi, A. M., 'Coltellini, Marco', in *DBI*
Lynham	Lynham, D., *The Chevalier Noverre, Father of Modern Ballet: A Biography* (London, 1950)
Macdonell	M[acdonell], G. P., 'Barrington, Daines', in *DNB*
Marocco	Marocco, G., 'Cigna Santi', in *DBI*
Martin	Martin, F., *Salzburgs Fürsten in der Barockzeit* (4th, revised edn, Salzburg, 1982)
Meisel/Belt[1]	Meisel, M., and Belt, P. R., 'Stein, Johann Andreas', in *New Grove*
Meisel/Belt[2]	——, and Belt, P. R., 'Walter, Anton', in *New Grove*
Meloncelli[1]	Meloncelli, R., 'Baglioni', in *DBI*
Meloncelli[2]	——, 'Bernasconi, Antonia', in *DBI*
Meyer	Meyer, F. L. W., *Friedrich Ludwig Schröder: Beitrag zur Kunde des Menschen und des Künstlers* (Hamburg, 1823)
Mf	*Die Musikforschung* (Kassel)
MGG	*Die Musik in Geschichte und Gegenwart: Allgemeine Enzyklopädie der Musik.* Herausgegeben von F. Blume (14 vols, Kassel, 1949–68). Supplement (2 vols., Kassel, 1973–9). *Register* (Kassel, 1986)
Michtner	Michtner, O., *Das alte Burgtheater als Opernbühne, von der Einführung des deutschen Singspiels (1778) bis zum Tod Kaiser Leopolds II. (1792)* (Vienna, 1970)
MJb	*Mozart-Jahrbuch* (Leipzig, since 1950 Salzburg)
ML	*Music and Letters* (London)
MM	*Mitteilungen der Internationalen Stiftung Mozarteum* (Salzburg)
Mondolfi	Mon[dolfi], A., 'Petrosellini', in *ES*
Morley-Pegge Fitzpatrick	Morley-Pegge, R., and Fitzpatrick, H., 'Punto', in *New Grove*

Moroda	Moroda, F. D. de, 'Rodolphe', in *New Grove*
Mount-Edgcumbe	Mount-Edgcumbe, Earl of, *Musical Reminiscences of the Earl of Mount Edgcumbe. Containing an Account of the Italian Opera in England from 1773 to 1834*, 4th edn (London, 1834; reprinted New York, 1973)
Mozart: Bibliothek	Konrad, U., and Staehelin, M., *allzeit ein buch: Die Bibliothek Wolfgang Amadeus Mozarts.* Ausstellungskataloge der Herzog August Bibliothek, No. 66 (Wolfenbüttel, 1991)
Mozart: Briefe	*Mozart: Briefe und Aufzeichnungen. Gesamtausgabe.* Gesammelt . . . von W. A. Bauer und O. E. Deutsch (4 vols, Kassel, 1962–3). *Kommentar*, auf Grund der Vorarbeiten von W. A. Bauer und O. E. Deutsch erläutert von J. H. Eibl (2 vols [Vols V–VI], Kassel, 1971). *Register* [Vol. VII], zusammengestellt von J. H. Eibl (Kassel, 1975). Further notes in: J. H. Eibl, 'Mozart: Briefe und Aufzeichnungen. Gesamtausgabe. Weiterer Nachtrag (1) zum Kommentar', *MJb 1976/77*, pp. 289–302, and 'Mozart: Briefe . . . Nachtrag (2) zum Kommentar', *MJb 1980/83*, pp. 318–52
Mozart Compendium	*The Mozart Compendium: A Guide to Mozart's Life and Music.* Ed. H. C. Robbins Landon (London, 1990)
Mozart: Dokumente	*Mozart: Die Dokumente seines Lebens.* Gesammelt und erläutert von O. E. Deutsch (*NMA* X/34, Kassel, 1961). Vol. II: *Addenda und Corrigenda*, zusammengestellt von J. H. Eibl (Kassel, 1978). English version: *Mozart: A Documentary Biography.* Trans. E. Blom, P. Branscombe and J. Noble (London, 1965; 2nd edn, 1966; 3rd edn, 1990). [*See also* 'Eisen' above']
Mozart in Italia	*Mozart in Italia: I viaggi*, a cura di G. Barblan; *Le lettere*, a cura di A. della Corte (Milan, 1956)
MR	*The Music Review* (Cambridge)
Müller	Müller, J. H. F., *Abschied von der k.k. Hof- und National-Schaubühne, mit einer kurzen Biographie seines Lebens und einer gedrängten Geschichte des hiesigen Hoftheaters* (Vienna, 1802)
Müller von Asow	Müller von Asow, E. H., 'Meuricoffre-Coltellini: Ein Ehepaar aus Mozarts Bekanntenkreis', *WF*, xxvi (1958), Heft 1, pp. 1–9
Münster[1]	Münster, R., 'Marchand', in *MGG*
Münster[2]	——, 'Nissens *Biographie W. A. Mozarts*: Zu ihrer Entstehungsgeschichte', *Acta Moz*, ix (1962), Heft 1, pp. 2–14
Münster[3]	——, 'Unbekannte Schattenrisse von Schauspielern, Sängern und Musikern aus Mozarts Freundes- und Bekanntenkreis', in *Das Mannheimer Mozart-Buch*, herausgegeben [von] R. Würtz (Wilhelmshaven, 1977), pp. 137–61
Münster[4]	——, 'Bernasconi, Antonia', in *New Grove*
Mus	*Musica* (Kassel, Basle)
Neumann	Neumann, F.-H., 'Zur Vorgeschichte der *Zaide*', *MJb 1962/63*, pp. 216–47
New Grove	*The New Grove Dictionary of Music and Musicians.* Ed. S. Sadie (20 vols, London, 1980)
NMA	*Wolfgang Amadeus Mozart: Neue Ausgabe sämtlicher Werke* [*Neue Mozart-Ausgabe*] (105 vols, Kassel, 1955–91)
NMJb	*Neues Mozart-Jahrbuch* (Regensburg)
Nohl	Nohl, L., *Mozart* (Leipzig, 1863; 2nd, enlarged edn [*Mozarts Leben*], Leipig, 1877)

Bibliography and Abbreviations

Norris   Norris, G., 'Hässler, Johann Wilhelm', in *New Grove*

Novello   *A Mozart Pilgrimage: Being the Travel Diaries of Vincent & Mary Novello in the Year 1829.* Transcribed and compiled by Nerina Medici di Marginano; ed. Rosemary Hughes (London, 1955)

ÖBL   *Österreichisches Bibliographisches Lexicon 1851–1950.* Herausgegeben ... unter der Leitung von L. Santifaller (Vienna, 1957–)

Oldman[1]   Oldman, C. B., 'Dr. Burney and Mozart', *MJb 1962/63*, pp. 75–81

Oldman[2]   ——, 'Dr. Burney and Mozart: Addenda and Corrigenda', *MJb 1964*, pp. 109–10

Oldman[3]   ——, 'Charles Burney and Louis de Visme', *MR*, xxvii (1966), pp. 93–7

Olleson[1]   Olleson, E., 'Swieten', in *MGG*

Olleson[2]   ——, 'Swieten', in *New Grove*

ÖMZ   *Österreichische Musikzeitschrift* (Vienna)

Orel[1]   Orel, A., 'Freystädtler', in *MGG*

Orel[2]   ——, 'Mozart auf Goethes Bühne', *MJb 1953*, pp. 85–94

Orel[3]   ——, 'Gräfin Wilhelmine Thun (Mäzenatentum in Wiens klassischer Zeit)', *MJb 1954*, pp. 89–101

Orel[4]   ——, 'Sarastro ... Hr. Gerl, Ein altes Weib ... Mad. Gerl', *MJb 1955*, pp. 66–89

Orel[5]   ——, 'Neue Gerliana', *MJb 1957*, pp. 212–22

Parke   Parke, W. T., *Musical Memoirs, Comprising an Account of the General State of Music in England, from the First Commemoration of Handel, in 1784, to the Year 1830. Interspersed with Numerous Anecdotes, Musical, Histrionic, &c.*, (2 vols, London, 1830; reprinted in 1 vol, New York, 1970)

Pauly[1]   Pauly, R. G., 'Adlgasser', in *New Grove*

Pauly[2]   ——, 'Eberlin, Johann Ernst', in *New Grove*

Pauly/Sherman   ——, and Sherman, C. H., 'Haydn, Michael', in *New Grove*

Payer   Payer von Thurn, R., *Joseph II. als Theaterdirektor: Ungedruckte Briefe und Aktenstücke aus den Kinderjahren des Burgtheaters.* Gesammelt und erläutert von R. Payer von Thurn (Vienna, Leipzig, 1920).

Pfannhauser   Pfannhauser, K., 'Teyber', in *MGG*

Pichler   Pichler, K., *Denkwürdigkeiten aus meinem Leben.* Mit einer Einleitung und zahlreichen Anmerkungen nach dem Erstdruck und der Urschrift neu herausgegeben von E. K. Blümml (2 vols, Munich, 1914)

Pisarowitz[1]   Pisarowitz, K. M., 'Willmann, Ignaz', in *MGG*

Pisarowitz[2]   ——, 'Der k.k. Kammerdiener Strack', *MM*, ix (1960), Heft 1/2, pp. 5–6

Pisarowitz[3]   ——, 'Die Willmanns', *MM*, xv (1967), pp. 7–12

Pisarowitz[4]   ——, 'Zum Bizentenar einer Blinden: Marianne Kirchgässner (1769–1808)', *Acta Moz*, xvi (1969), Heft 3/4, pp. 72–5

Pisarowitz[5]   ——, 'Mozarts Schnorrer Leutgeb: Dessen Primärbiographie', *MM*, xviii (1970), Heft 3/4, pp. 21–6.

Pisarowitz[6]   ——, '"Müasst ma nix in übel aufnehma ...": Beitragsversuche zu einer Gebrüder-Stadler-Biographie', *MM*, xix (1971), Heft 1/2, pp. 29–33

Pisarowitz[7]   ——, 'Der Bär, den man uns aufband: Differenzierungen ewig Verwechselter', *Acta Moz*, xx (1973), Heft 1, pp. 62–8

Pisarowitz[8]	——, 'Willmann', in *New Grove*
Piscitelli	Piscitelli Gonnelli, G., 'Bussani', in *DBI*
Plath[1]	Plath, W., 'Beiträge zur Mozart-Autographie II: Schriftchronologie 1770–1780', *MJb 1976/77*, pp. 131–73
Plath[2]	——, 'André, Johann Anton', in *New Grove*
Plath[3]	——, 'Mozart, Leopold', in *New Grove*
Platinga	Platinga, L., *Clementi: His Life and Music* (London, 1977)
Platinga/Tyson	——, and Tyson, A., 'Clementi, Muzio', in *New Grove*
Plesske	Plesske, H.-M., 'Breitkopf & Härtel', in *New Grove*
Pohl	Pohl, C. F., *Joseph Haydn* (3 vols, Leipzig, 1875–1927)
Pollak	Pollak, F., 'Tilgner', in *ADB*
Postolka[1]	Postolka, M., 'Vitásek', in *MGG*
Postolka[2]	——, 'Dušek, Josefa', in *New Grove*
Postolka[3]	——, 'Kozeluch', in *New Grove*
Postolka[4]	——, 'Vanhal', in *New Grove*
Preihs	Preihs, C., 'Mozarts Beziehungen zu den Familien von Thun-Hohenstein', *NMJb*, iii (1943), pp. 63–86
Prod'homme	Prod'homme, J.-G, 'Deux collaborateurs italiens de Gluck, II: Giuseppe d'Affligio', *RMI*, xxiii (1916), pp. 201–18
Raaff	'Skizze zu Raaffs, des Sängers, Legensgeschichte', *AMZ*, 10 and 17 October 1810
Raeburn[1]	Raeburn, C., 'An Evening at Schönbrunn', *MR*, xvi (1955), pp. 94–110
Raeburn[2]	——, 'Mozarts Opern in Prag', *Mus*, xiii (1959), pp. 158–63
Raeburn[3]	——, 'Bassi, Luigi', in *New Grove*
Raeburn[4]	——, 'Benucci', in *New Grove*
Raeburn[5]	——, 'Cavalieri, Catarina', in *New Grove*
Raeburn[6]	——, 'Gottlieb', in *New Grove*
Raeburn[7]	——, 'Laschi', in *New Grove*
Raeburn[8]	——, 'Mandini, Stefano', in *New Grove*
Raeburn[9]	——, 'Saporiti', in *New Grove*
Rainer	Rainer, W., 'F. A. Spitzeder als Klavierlehrer am Kapellhaus', *MJb 1964*, pp. 138–41
Rau	Rau, U., 'Beer', in *MGG*
Rech[1]	Rech, G., 'Das Mozart-Wohnhaus', *MJb 1951*, pp. 131–7
Rech[2]	——, 'Bretzner contra Mozart', *MJb 1968/70*, pp. 186–205
Reckziegel	Reckziegel, W., 'Vogler, Georg Joseph', in *MGG*
Repertorium	*Repertorium der diplomatischen Vertreter aller Länder*, Vol III: *1764–1815*. Herausgegeben ... von O. F. Winter (Graz, Cologne, 1965)
Rieger	Rieger, E., *Nannerl Mozart: Leben einer Künstlerin im 18. Jahrhundert* (Frankfurt am Main, 1990)
RMI	*Rivista Musicale Italiana* (Turin, then Milan)
Robinson	Robinson, B., 'Doles', in *New Grove*
Robinson M. F.[1]	Robinson, M. F., 'Anfossi', in *New Grove*
Robinson M. F.[2]	——, 'Metastasio', in *New Grove*
Robinson M. F.[3]	——, 'Paisiello', in *New Grove*
Rolandi	Ro[landi], U., 'Cigna-Santi', in *ES*
Rosenberg	Rosenberg, A., *"Die Zauberflöte": Geschichte und Deutung von Mozarts Oper* (Munich, 1964)

Bibliography and Abbreviations

Rück   Rück, U., 'Mozarts Hammerflügel erbaute Anton Walter, Wien: Technische Studien, Vergleiche und Beweise', *MJb 1955*, pp. 246–61

Rushton   Rushton, J., 'Legros', in *New Grove*

Sabel   Sabel, H., 'Maximilian Stadler und Wolfgang Amadeus Mozart', *NMJb*, iii (1943), pp. 102–12

Sachs   Sachs, J., 'Hummel, Johann Nepomuk', in *New Grove*

Sarti   'Sarti-Variationen, KV 460', *MJb 1971/72*, p. 55

Scarabello   Scarabello, G., 'Da Ponte', in *DBI*

Scharnagl   Scharnagl, A., '*König Garibald*, Oper in zwei Aufzügen. Gedichtet von Cäsar Max Heigel, Musik von Mozart', *MJb 1980/83*, pp. 113–18

Scharnagl/Haase   ——, and Haase, H., 'Graf', in *MGG*

Schenk   Schenk, E., *Wolfgang Amadeus Mozart: Eine Biographie* (Vienna, Zurich, 1955; 2nd edn [*Mozart: Sein Leben, seine Welt*], Vienna, Munich, 1975). English version: *Mozart and his Times*, ed. and trans. R. and C. Winston (New York, 1959)

Schmid[1]   Schmid, E. F., 'Artaria', in *MGG*

Schmid[2]   ——, 'Beecke', in *MGG*

Schmid[3]   ——, 'Mozart, Leopold', in *MGG*

Schmid[4]   ——, 'Der Mozartfreund Joseph Bullinger', *MJb 1952*, pp. 17–23

Schmid[5]   ——, 'Gottfried van Swieten als Komponist', *MJb 1953*, pp. 15–31

Schmid[6]   ——, 'August Clemens Graf Hatzfeld', *MJb 1954*, pp. 14–33

Schmid H.   Schmid, H., 'Valesi, Giovanni', in *New Grove*

Schmieder[1]   Schmieder, W., 'Breitkopf', in *MGG*

Schmieder[2]   ——, 'Breitkopf & Härtel', in *MGG*

Schneider   Schneider, C., *Geschichte der Musik in Salzburg von der ältesten Zeit bis zur Gegenwart* (Salzburg, 1935)

Schönfeld   Schönfeld, J. F. von, *Jahrbuch der Tonkunst von Wien und Prag* (Vienna, 1796)

Schuler[1]   Schuler, H., 'Zur Familiengeschichte des Johann Joseph Lange', *MM*, xxii (1974), pp. 29–37

Schuler[2]   ——, 'Der "hochfürstlich salzburgische Hof- und Feldtrompeter" Johann Andreas Schachtner: Ein Beitrag zu seiner Familiengeschichte', *Acta Moz*, xxiv (1977), Heft 1, pp. 10–13

Schuler[3]   ——, 'Der Hoftenorist Franz Anton Spitzeder, Freund der Familie Mozart: Zu seiner Biographie und Familiengeschichte', *JHGGA*, 3rd series, ix (1974/8), pp. 27–35

Schuler[4]   ——, 'Münchener Künstlerfamilien aus dem Mozartschen Freundeskreis', *Gen*, xxviii (1979), Heft 2, pp. 435–49

Schuler[5]   ——, 'Die Salzburger Familie Gilowsky von Urazowa und ihre Beziehungen zu den Mozarts', *WF*, xlvi (1979), pp. 27–35

Schuler[6]   ——, 'Die Salzburger Familien Antretter, Kolb und Ränftl. Mit Bemerkungen zu Mozarts "Finalmusik" (KV 185/167a)', *Gen*, xxviii (1979), Heft 5, pp. 529–47

Schuler[7]   ——, 'Miszellen zu Aloysia Lange geb. Weber', *Acta Moz*, xxviii (1981), Heft 1, pp. 32–5

Schuler[8]   ——, 'Mozart und das hochgräfliche Haus Lodron: Eine genealogische Quellenstudie', *MM*, xxxi (1983), pp. 1–17

Schuler[9]   ——, 'Die Herren und Grafen von Arco und ihre Beziehungen zu den Mozarts. Anmerkungen zu Mozart-Briefen', *MM*, xxxii (1984), pp. 19–34

Schuler[10]	——, 'Fürsterzbischof Hieronymus von Colloredo: Herkunft und Ahnenerbe', *MM*, xxxiv, (1986), pp. 1–30
Schuler[11]	——, ' "Mozart von der Wohlthätigkeit": Die Mitglieder der gerechten und vollkommenen St.-Johannis-Freimaurer-Loge "Zur Wohltätigkeit" im Orient von Wien', *MM*, xxxvi (1988), pp. 1–56
Schuler[12]	——, 'Die Mozart-Loge "Zur neugekrönten Hoffnung" im Orient von Wien', *MM*, xxxvii (1989), pp. 1–44
Schuler[13]	——, 'Mozarts Akademien im Trattnersaal 1784. Ein Kommentar zum Mozart-Brief: Wien, 20. März 1784', *MM*, xxxviii (1990), pp. 1–47
Schuler[14]	——, 'Das *Zauberflöten*-Ensemble des Jahres 1791: Biographische Miszellen', *MM*, xxxix (1991), pp. 95–124
Schuler[15]	——, 'Mozarts "Maurerische Trauermusik" KV477/479a. Eine Dokumentation', *MM*, xl (1992), pp. 46–70
Schurig	Schurig, A., *Wolfgang Amadeus Mozart: Sein Leben und sein Werk* (Leipzig, 1913; 2nd edn, 1923)
Senn[1]	Senn, W., 'Mozart, Schüler und Bekannte – in einem Wiener Musikbericht von 1808', *MJb 1976/77*, pp. 281–8
Senn[2]	——, 'Barbara Ployer, Mozarts Klavierschülerin', *ÖMZ*, xxxiii (1978), Heft 1, pp. 18–28
Simpson	Simpson, A., 'Vitásek', in *New Grove*
SMZ	*Schweizerische Musikzeitung* (Berne, Zurich)
Sonnenfels	Sonnenfels, J. von, *Briefe über die Wienerische Schaubühne.* Herausgegeben von H. Haider-Pregler (Graz, 1988)
Spatzenegger	Spatzenegger, H. 'Neue Dokumente zur Entstehung des Mozart-Denkmals in Salzburg', *MJb 1980/83*, pp. 147–66
Steptoe	Steptoe, A., 'Mozart, Mesmer and *Così fan tutte*', *ML*, lxvii (1986), pp. 248–55
Stiefel[1]	Stiefel, E., 'Baglioni', in *MGG*
Stiefel[2]	——, 'Rudolph', in *MGG*
Stolzenburg	Stolzenburg, A., 'Eine wenig bekannte Mozart-Gedenkstätte im Bridischen Garten in Rovereto (Trient)', *Acta Moz*, xxvii (1990), Heft 1, pp. 3–10
SV	*Salzburger Volksblatt* (Salzburg)
Temperley	Temperley, N., 'Attwood', in *New Grove*
Terry	Terry, C. S., *John Christian Bach* (2nd edn, London, 1967; reprinted Westport, Connecticut, 1980)
Tyson	Tyson, A., 'Proposed New Dates for Many Works and Fragments Written by Mozart from March 1781 to December 1791', in *Mozart Studies*, ed. C. Eisen (Oxford, 1991), pp. 213–26
Ullrich[1]	Ullrich, H., 'Paradi(e)s, Maria Theresia von', in *MGG*
Ullrich[2]	——, 'Die blinde Glasharmonikavirtuosin Marianne Kirchgässner und Wien: Eine Künstlerin der empfindsamen Zeit', *JVGSW*, xxi–xxii (1965–6), pp. 255–91
Unverricht	Unverricht, H., 'Salomon, Johann Peter', in *New Grove*
Valentin[1]	Valentin, E., 'Das Testament der Constanze Mozart-Nissen, mit biographischen Notizen über Constanze und Georg Nikolaus Nissen', *NMJb*, ii (1942), pp. 128–75
Valentin[2]	——, 'Mozarts "Weinwirt Albert": Skizzen zu einem Porträt', in *Festschrift Karl Gustav Fellerer zum sechzigsten Geburtstag . . .* (Regensburg, 1962), pp. 549–57

Bibliography and Abbreviations

Valentin³	——, *'Madame Mutter': Anna Maria Walburga Mozart (1720–1778)* (Augsburg, 1991)
Vigée-Lebrun	Vigée-Lebrun, L.-E., *Souvenirs* (2 vols, Paris, 1835)
Volek	Volek, T., 'Guardasoni', in *New Grove*
Wandruszka	Wandruszka, A., *Leopold II, Erzherzog von Österreich, Grossherzog von Toskana, König von Ungarn und Böhmen, Römischer Kaiser* (2 vols, Vienna, Munich, 1963–5)
Wangermée	Wangermée, R., 'Gossec', in *MGG*
Warburton/Derr	Warburton, E., and Derr, E. S., 'Bach, Johann Christian', in *New Grove*
Wegele	Wegele, L., *Der Lebenslauf der Marianne Thekla Mozart* (Augsburg, 1967)
Weinmann¹	Weinmann, A., 'Hoffmeister', in *MGG*
Weinmann²	——, *Vollständiges Verlagsverzeichnis Artaria & Comp.* (Vienna, 1952)
Weinmann³	——, *Kataloge Anton Huberty (Wien) und Christoph Torricella* (Vienna, 1962)
Weinmann⁴	——, *Die Wiener Verlagswerke von Franz Anton Hoffmeister* (Vienna, 1964)
Weinmann⁵	——, *Verlagsverzeichnis Johann Traeg (und Sohn).* (2nd, enlarged and revised edn, Vienna, 1973)
Weinmann⁶	——, 'Artaria', in *New Grove*
Weinmann⁷	——, 'Hoffmeister, Franz Anton', in *New Grove*
Weinmann⁸	——, 'Lausch', in *New Grove*
Weinmann⁹	——, 'Torricella', in *New Grove*
Weinmann¹⁰	——, 'Traeg', in *New Grove*
Weinmann¹¹	——, 'Eine Italienerin aus Währing', *WF*, xlviii (1981), p. 22
Weinmann¹²	——, 'Eine Italienerin aus Währing: Notwendige Korrektur', *WF*, xlix (1982), p. 35–6
Weinmann¹³	——, 'Ein Mozart-Faksimile als Staatsgeschenk', *WF*, l (1983), pp. 18–19
Weinstock	Weinstock, H., *Rossini: A Biography* (New York, 1968)
Weiss	Weiss, W., 'Das Weiterleben der *Zauberflöte* bei Goethe', *MJb 1980/83*, pp. 227–37
Werner	Werner, A. J., 'Seine Ärzte, seine Krankheiten, sein Tod', in *Wolfgang Amadeus: Summa summarum. Das Phänomen Mozart: Leben, Werk, Wirkung*, herausgegeben von P. Csobádi (Vienna, 1990), pp. 101–18
Wessely¹	Wessely, O., 'Koželuch', in *MGG*
Wessely²	——, 'Süssmayr', in *MGG*
Wessely³	——, 'Martín y Soler', in *New Grove*
Wessely⁴	——, 'Süssmayr', in *New Grove*
Weston¹	Weston, P., *Clarinet Virtuosi of the Past* (London, 1971)
Weston²	——, 'Beer, Joseph', in *New Grove*
Weston³	——, 'Stadler, Anton', in *New Grove*
Westrup	Westrup, J. A., 'Two First Performances: Monteverdi's *Orfeo* and Mozart's *La clemenza di Tito*', *ML*, xxxix (1958), pp. 327–35
WF	*Wiener Figaro* (Vienna)
Wiedemann	Wiedemann, H.-R., 'Ein "Figaro" als Förderer Mozartscher Schöpfungen', in *Festschrift Albi Rosenthal*, herausgegeben von Rudolf Elvers (Tutzing, 1984), pp. 291–4.

White	White, C., 'Strinasacchi', in *New Grove*
Wirth[1]	Wirth, H., 'André', in *MGG*
Wirth[2]	——, 'Benda', in *MGG*
Wlassack	Wlassack, E., *Chronik des k.k. Hof-Burgtheaters* (Vienna, 1876)
Wolff	Wolff, C., 'The Composition and Completion of Mozart's Requiem, 1791–1792', in *Mozart Studies*, ed. C. Eisen (Oxford, 1991), pp. 61–81
Würtz[1]	Würtz, R., '"... ein sehr solider Geiger": Mozart und Ignaz Fränkl', *Acta Moz*, xvi (1969), Heft 3/4, pp. 65–72
Würtz[2]	——, 'Cannabich, Christian' in *New Grove*
Würtz[3]	——, 'Fischer, Ludwig', in *New Grove*
Würtz[4]	——, 'Fränzl, Ignaz', in *New Grove*
Würtz[5]	——, 'Wendling, Dorothea (i)', in *New Grove*
Würtz[6]	——, 'Wendling, Dorothea (ii)', in *New Grove*
Würtz[7]	——, 'Wendling, Elisabeth Augusta (i)', in *New Grove*
Würtz[8]	——, 'Wendling, Elisabeth Augusta (ii)', in *New Grove*
Würtz[9]	——, 'Wendling, Johann Baptist', in *New Grove*
Würtz/Alexander	——, and Alexander, P. M., 'Danzi, Franz', in *New Grove*
Wurzbach	Wurzbach, C. von, *Biographisches Lexikon des Kaiserthums Oesterreich, enthaltend die Lebensskizzen der denkwürdigen Personen, welche 1750 bis 1850 im Kaiserstaate und in seinen Kronländern gelebt haben* (60 vols, Vienna, 1856–91)
Zanetti[1]	Z[anetti], E., 'Baglioni', in *ES*
Zanetti[2]	——, 'Coltellini, Celeste', in *ES*
Zanetti[3]	——, 'Coltellini, Marco', in *ES*
Zapperi[1]	Zapperi, A., 'Bassi, Luigi', in *DBI*
Zapperi[2]	——, 'Benucci', in *DBI*
Zapperi[3]	——, 'Bondini', in *DBI*
Zechmeister	Zechmeister, G., *Die Wiener Theater nächst der Burg und nächst dem Kärntnerthor von 1747 bis 1776* (Vienna, 1971)
Zellweker	Zellweker, E., *Das Urbild des Sarastro: Ignaz v. Born* (Vienna, 1953)
Zenger	Zenger, M., *Geschichte der Münchener Oper*. Nachgelassenes Werk herausgegeben von T. Kroyer (Munich, 1923)
ZfMw	*Zeitschrift für Musikwissenschaft* (Leipzig)
ZHVS	*Zeitschrift des Historischen Vereins für Schwaben [und Neuburg]* (Augsburg)
Zimmerschmied	Zimmerschmied, D., 'Mozartiana aus dem Nachlass von J. N. Hummel', *MJb 1964*, pp. 142–50
Zinzendorf	*Wien von Maria Theresia bis zur Franzosenszeit: Aus den Tagebüchern des Grafen Karl von Zinzendorf*. Ausgewählt, aus dem Französischen übersetzt, eingeleitet und kommentiert von H. Wagner (Vienna, 1972)

Index of Mozart's Works, by Köchel Number*

* The numbers cited are normally those of the first and, where different, of the sixth editions of the Köchel catalogue. (For some notes on these and other editions, *see* KÖCHEL..)

Index of Mozart's Works

Index of Mozart's Works

Index of Mozart's Works

Index of Mozart's Works

Index of Mozart's Works

Index of Persons and Operas

Index of Persons and Operas

Index of Persons and Operas

Index of Persons and Operas

Index of Persons and Operas

Index of Persons and Operas

Index of Persons and Operas

Index of Persons and Operas

Index of Persons and Operas